Vindic

Gou

A unique daily devotional that defends God against false accusations made against Him

By Troy J. Edwards

Vindicating God

A unique daily devotional that defends God against false accusations made against Him

Troy J. Edwards

Copyright © 2015 by Troy J. Edwards

Cover design by the artistically creative team of Teri Mayumi Edwards and Takako Edwards

Published by **Vindicating God Ministries**

Introduction

Over the centuries there have been many attacks on the God and Father of our Lord Jesus Christ. However, God's character has never been more maligned than it has been in this century. Atheists, agnostics, Satan worshippers, and pretentious politicians have blasphemed the God worshipped by true Christians and have accused Him and His people of all sorts of malicious acts.

Many of these critics have cherry-picked through the Bible, misquoted the Word of God, and have misrepresented God to others. Those who do not take the time to know God intimately and study His Word for themselves become easy prey to these denigrators. Even churches and pastors have fallen for the deception promoted by God's enemies. They have become embarrassed by the Bible and many of them deny the truth that it is God's written revelation to man. Denying the Bible has led to acceptance of practices that this book forbids and teachings about God that are blasphemous.

Many of our theologians have not been helpful either. On the contrary they have exacerbated the problem. Erroneous predestination theology has made God to look like a puppet master who manipulates all of the events in the world for an egotistical glory that we are not allowed to comprehend or question. From this false teaching God is said to be the inflictor of sickness, the creator of disaster, and the chooser of who goes to heaven or hell after death. According to them, freedom of choice is irrelevant. They claim that if you accept Jesus as your Savior then it is only because *God chose you. You had no choice in the matter*. If you rejected Him this too is *God's choice* and not yours. He supposedly created you for the express purpose of sending you to hell.

Naturally men rebel at such presentations of God's character. This ideology has created many of the enemies of God and the church that we have today. Yet, the predestinarian groups are not alone in misrepresenting God. There are the extreme Fundamentalists who hold up signs saying, "God hates fags." This is a "fundamentalism" devoid of love that forgets that God loves the sinner while hating the sin (John 3:16). This type of preaching has also denigrated God's character and made Him to appear austere and unloving. Few desire to know a God who is this hateful.

If this were not enough, some of our theologians present a God who is quite stingy. He works no miracles today and rarely, if ever, answers prayer. If they believe that God does work miracles, even that is rare. His healing power for our bodies is only for a select few so we should not expect Him to remove pain. He is said to have sent such trials to build us up and make us stronger. This too has served to make many atheists and agnostics from some who were once believers. When one has prayed, their child dies and then they are "comforted" with the idea that God took the child (or the child's father, etc.) for His own personal reasons, many shun such a cruel deity.

Finally, there are sincere worshippers of Christ who love Him dearly but are quite ignorant of how to deal with difficult passages in the Bible that might be used by God's enemies to paint a false picture of Him. Many remain confused as to how to deal with passages that seem to go against what they know by their experience is a loving God. I believe that these daily devotions can assist believers in this endeavor. When one meditates daily on the truth of God's character then they will not be easily swayed by those who speak against it. They will see that there are better ways to understand the passages often presented by those who choose to denigrate God's character.

Not everyone can read a more than 200 page book committed to defending God's character, but most can read a daily devotion or meditation. I would encourage you to read these devotions with an open Bible and a pen. Let God speak to you. If you read these devotions and you begin to see that God is a loving God and you even come to like Him more, then I have fulfilled my purpose in writing them. Blessings to you dear reader.

Do all Things Happen for a Reason?

*"Did you notice my servant Job?" the Lord asked. "There is no one on earth as faithful and good as he is. He worships me and is careful not to do anything evil. You persuaded me to let you attack him **for no reason at all**, but Job is still as faithful as ever."* (Job 2:3; Good News Translation)

A friend is diagnosed with cancer, several teenagers are killed in a car accident on their way to college, a child is killed by a stray bullet in a drive by shooting, a man breaks into an apartment and brutally rapes a woman, a child is molested and killed by a pedophile, a great marriage is ending in divorce due to infidelity, a company goes bankrupt and the sole provider of the home loses his job....

The list can go on. Bad things happen to so many people. There is more negative than positive in this world. When these things happen we feel that we need something to say that brings comfort. One of many phrases chosen by our comforters (both Christian and non-Christian) is, "Well, all things happen for a reason".

The statement usually means that God caused, planned or purposefully allowed someone to suffer a misfortune for an undetermined reason. One may not discover the reason in this life, but in the "sweet-by-and-by" all things will be made clear.

Job suffered a number of misfortunes: his children, his property, and the loss of his health. The first two chapters in Job reveal that Satan was the agent of destruction. Many claim that God had a divine secret plan for all of this and that Satan was merely doing God's bidding. However, God says that there was no good reason for any of this to happen to Job. God did not design these satanic attacks. Satan, by falsely accusing God and Job, provoked and instigated the whole thing. There was no divine plan.

God has been blamed for Satan's work even when it was clear that Satan was the culprit. We blame God by saying that He had a reason for *allowing it*. But God says that there was no particular reason for Job to suffer as he did. He places the whole plan for Job's ruin on Satan.

Let us stop looking for some mystical good in evil situations. Satan's work is what it is and is to be *resisted*, not embraced (James 4:7). Let us stop blaming God by assigning divine reasons for things that God says are completely Satan's doing and not His.

Do all Things Work Together for Good?

And we know that all things work together for good to them that love God, to them who are the called according to his purpose. (Rom. 8:28; King James Version)

During tragic events we hear statements such as "God is in control," or "all things happen for a reason." Romans 8:28 is referenced in support. Children are on drugs? Husband was killed by a stray bullet? An unsaved family member dies and goes to hell? Somehow, "All things work together for good." I have found this to be a terrible application of this verse. Yet, the KJV and other translations render it in a way that leads us to believe that all the above has been ordained by God for our good.

The James Moffat Translation renders the passage differently: *"We know also that those who love God, those who have been called in terms of his purpose,* **have his aid and interest in everything."** Romans 8:28 is teaching us that God comes to supply His *aid* and *interest* in everything. However, He is "a gentleman" and does not force His aid upon us. He requires our *cooperation*. In his commentary on Romans, C. H. Dodd comments on the Moffat translation:

> ....the familiar translation is not an admissible rendering of the Greek. Paul did not write: 'All things work together for good to them that love God.' The literal translation is: 'With those who love God, He' (or, according to the other reading, 'God') 'co-operates in all respects for good.' Dr. Moffat has paraphrased this somewhat freely, but with fidelity to the meaning.[1]

It is sad that the devil has used this passage to deceive many Christians into believing that sickness, poverty, tragedy, sin, etc. are from the hand of God. He has deceived many into believing that to "grin and bear these things" and to "thank God for them" is living in victory. A passage that should strengthen confidence in God's aid has been used to cause Christians to proclaim a counterfeit victory with a "bend over and take it" theology.

The victory does not come from calling good evil and evil good or in calling a blessing what God has clearly stated is a curse (Isa. 5:20; Deut. 30:15, 19). The victory comes from appropriating the help of God in resisting all of the evil that comes into our lives.

---

[1]Dodd, C. H. **The Epistle of Paul to the Romans** (New York: Harper and Brothers Publishers,), pp. 137, 138

January 3

Giving Thanks <u>IN</u> All Things

Rejoice evermore. Pray without ceasing. ***In*** *every thing give thanks: for this is the will of God in Christ Jesus concerning you. Quench not the Spirit* (1 Thess. 5:16-19)

We are taught in some passages of Scripture that we are to thank God in *everything*. Some have understood these Scriptures to insinuate that God is the force behind all that happens to us. Certainly the Bible teaches that God's people are to have "an attitude of gratitude." This attitude should be demonstrated in *all* circumstances, no matter what we are going through. However does this mean that God is behind the circumstances?

If we apply this passage in the way that we have been traditionally taught then should we thank God every time someone commits adultery? Should we thank God when we or someone else commits some other horrible sin that is not pleasing to God? God forbid!!! Nonetheless, taking the traditional interpretation to its logical conclusion would lead us down this path. Acts of sin are not in line with God's will and we are not to thank God *for* them. Neither should we thank God *for* other evils that may occur in our lives.

If we are to give thanks *for* everything, then why didn't Jesus practice this in the middle of a storm He went through (Mark 4:35-41)? Why didn't He simply thank the father for the storm instead of rebuking it? When we read Acts 5:40-42 we see that the apostles did not thank God for the persecution itself, but rejoiced that they were counted worthy to suffer for the cause of Christ.

We do not thank God *for* EVERYTHING as if He were the one bringing evil upon us. God has works (John 14:10-12) and Satan also has works (1 John 3:8) and the Bible clearly distinguishes between the two. We must not thank God *for* the devil's works. Nevertheless, to be thankful to God even *in the midst of trials* (not *because* of the trials) is a powerful weapon against the devil (1 Cor. 15:57). God is able to change any circumstance brought by the devil as we trust Him (Ps. 91:15-16; Rom. 8:28).

Christians should always maintain a grateful demeanor and not grumble, moan, and complain when they are faced with trials. While God's people are to praise God in all circumstances, we should not attribute Satan's works to God. We are never to feel obligated to thank God *for* whatever happens. Thank Him *in* whatever happens but not *for* whatever happens. This is what Paul is teaching here.

There is no Darkness in God at All

*This then is the message which we have heard of him, and declare unto you, that God is light, and **in him is no darkness at all**.* (1 John 1:5)

The message that Jesus came to declare to us is that God is light— He is completely good, pure, holy, flawless, and without a trace of evil. God is so much light that He cannot even produce a shadow (James 1:17).

Why did Jesus have to bring this message to the world? There has been too much misinformation about God that prevails even in this present time. In the Bible as well as in many other cultures, light is almost always equated with all that is good and darkness is almost always synonymous with evil (Job 30:26; Isa. 5:20; John 3:19-20). Even more, darkness is symbolic of Satan and his kingdom of death, destruction and deprivation (Luke 22:53; Acts 26:18; Eph. 6:10-12; Col. 1:12-14).

There is much evil and darkness in our world and God is constantly getting the blame for it. A child is brutally murdered and at his funeral some well-meaning minister says, "God took this little child home. He needed another flower up in Heaven." A drunk driver kills a single mother and her three babies end up in foster care. Yet some will say that "her number came up. It was just her time to go". Does this paint a positive picture of a deity who is nothing but pure good? Can a pure and good God be at fault for making children into orphans and bringing grief to parents for the selfish reason of needing yet *another flower*?

Satan not only steals, kills, and destroys (John 8:44; 10:10) but he has deceived the majority of the human race into believing that God is the one behind it all. Jesus had to come to earth to set the record straight. He demonstrated to men that God is nothing like that which He has been falsely accused of being. Instead of killing, Jesus saved lives; instead of sending sickness, Jesus healed; instead of sending evil spirits, Jesus casted them out; instead of sending natural disasters, Jesus rebuked them.

Jesus' message to the world is that God is not evil. There is no darkness in Him. He is not the source of our problems but the solution to them. He can be trusted. Embrace Him and connect with Him through Christ our Savior.

January 5

God is the Father of "Lights" and not of "Evils"

"Every good gift and every perfect gift is from above, and cometh down from the Father of lights, with whom is no variableness, neither shadow of turning" (James 1:17)

James calls God the "Father of lights". In John 8:44 Satan is called the father of liars and murderers. You can only "father" or produce what is in you (Matt. 7:16-20). God is only able to produce light (good) and Satan is only able to produce darkness (evil).

Another translation of James 1:17 says, *"Every good gift, every perfect gift, comes from above. These gifts come down from the Father, the creator of the heavenly lights, in whose character there is no change at all"* (Complete English Bible). There simply is no change in God's character. He cannot go from being good to bad nor can He produce evil from His goodness.

One must be careful not to confuse God with the works of darkness. God is not the father of murdering and lying. He is the "Father of Lights". James says, *"Every **good** gift and every perfect gift is from above, and cometh down from the Father of lights."* The fact that James connects God as "the Father of Lights" to the truth that only *good* gifts come down from Him is no coincidence. God is only the source of good and not of evil. He cannot produce evil (Matt. 7:14-16).

Therefore sickness, for example, is not from above. In Deuteronomy 28:61 we read, *"also every sickness and every stroke which is not written in the book of this law; Jehovah doth cause them to **go up upon thee** till thou art destroyed"* (Young's Literal Translation). God "inflicts" sickness only by allowing Satan to do it (1 Cor. 5:5). He only allows this when we remove ourselves from His protection and go into Satan's territory through sin. Nonetheless, sickness and other darkness comes from *below* and *not from above*. The only way for light to produce darkness is to withdraw.

If we are to enter into genuine relationships with God, we must know that He is not the One behind the miseries in life because He is only good. Since we are "children of the light" then let us, like Jesus, declare to a world blinded by Satan the truth about our Heavenly Father who is nothing but pure good (Luke 16:8; John 12:36; Eph. 5:8; 1 Thess. 5:5).

January 6

Is God the Creator of Good *and* Evil? (Part One)

I form the light, and create darkness: **I make peace, and create evil***: I the LORD do all these things.* (Isa. 45:7)

Based on this passage some have declared that God is the creator of all darkness and evil. Did God actually create evil as He did the earth, the heavens, angels, animals, and humans? Can evil even be considered a *created* thing? Such an idea contradicts other Scriptures concerning the nature and character of God. For example, we are told that God is "Light" (1 John 1:5). If there is no darkness in God then how could He have created it? Jesus said only that which is *in* a person is what comes *out* of Him (Matt. 15:18-20; 12:35).

Other passages teach that God is a *God of peace*, who only desires peace, and not evil (1 Cor. 14:33; Jer. 29:11). If God is the author of peace and only wants to give peace rather than evil, how could He be the creator of evil? The Bible also makes it implicitly clear that God hates evil and that He has absolutely nothing to do with it (Psalm 5:4; Prov. 8:13; Jer. 44:4-5; Prov. 6:16-19; Zech. 8:17; Deut. 28:31; Hab. 1:13; Job 34:10-12). If God hates evil then why would He create it? This would appear to be an extreme contradiction.

To solve what *appears to be* an apparent contradiction, based on the above, some commentators say that God is not the creator of *moral evil*, i.e. sin, but that He is the One who directs *calamities and disasters* in His providence. Certainly God is not the author of *moral* evil (1 John 2:16; James 1:13; Eccl. 7:29) and theologians are correct in stating that the "evil" in Isa. 45:7 is not the *evil of sin* but of its *punishments*.[2] From this theologians attempt to vindicate God by saying that He is the creator of the disasters, troubles, woe, and hardships which are the *punishments* for evil.

However, I do not find this to be very helpful. **It still makes God responsible for certain types of horrendous evils that harm and destroy**, which contrasts with a number of statements by Jesus concerning Himself (John 10:10; Luke 9:51-56). Can one still trust God if He is not the author of moral evil but is still the author of "natural evil?" We will delve further into this tomorrow.

---

[2] Other translations render Isa. 45:7 as God *"creating calamity"* (New American Standard Bible), *"create disaster"* (New International Version), *"preparing evil"* (Young's literal Translation), *"I cause troubles"* (New Century Version), *"sending troubles"* (Bible in Basic English), *"I create woe"* (The Complete Jewish Bible), *"create hardship"* (Peshitta - Lamsa Translation).

January 7

Is God the Creator of Good and Evil? (Part Two)

I form the light, and create darkness: ***I make peace, and create evil:*** *I the LORD do all these things.* (Isa. 45:7)

Yesterday we learned that some theologians believe that Isaiah 45:7 teaches us that God is the creator of "natural evil" (as judgment). While it is a step away from making God the author of *moral* evil, further examination of this passage vindicates God from authoring *any* evil.

God is the source of only good (Psa. 85:12; 86:5; 106:1; 107:1; 118:1, 29; 135:3; 136:1). He is not the source of evil *or its results.* Evil produces evil (Matt. 7:15-20). The fruit of evil is death and destruction (Ps. 7:14-16; 34:15-21; Prov. 1:31; 22:8; Gal. 6:7-8; Hosea 8:7; 10:13; Jer. 12:13). God is not the giver of evil fruit, but Satan is (John 8:44; 10:10).

In the context of Isa. 45:7, the Lord was at war with Babylon and He was letting them know that as a part of His judgment upon them He would *allow* calamity or trouble to come their way. The calamities are the result of judgment upon nations like Babylon that oppose God (Isa. 45:24) and who will reap what they have sown (Ps. 7:14-16; Gal. 6:5-6).

So why does God say that He is the creator of darkness and evil in Isa. 45:7? This is resolved as we learn the *language of the Bible.* To understand the problem of evil we must understand the Hebrew language and its "permissive idioms". The language in Isa. 45:7 must be viewed as "permissive" rather than "causative". Dr. Walter C. Kaiser writes:

> "Even though much of the physical evil often comes through the hands of wicked men and women, ultimately God permits it. Thus, the Hebrew way of speaking, which ignores secondary causation in a way Western thought would never do, whatever God permits may be directly attributed to him, often without noting that secondary and sinful parties were the immediate causes of the disaster.... It is God who must allow (and that is the proper term) these calamities to come.[3]

Evil is the result of people removing themselves from God's protection, thus receiving the consequences of their choices in a morally ordered universe. God's responsibility as far as evil is concerned is only to the extent that He created laws of sowing and reaping.

---

[3] Kaiser Jr., Walter C. **Hard Sayings of the Bible** (Downers Grove, IL: Intervarsity Press, 1996), p. 306

January 8

Is God the Creator of Good and Evil? (Part Three)

*I form the light, and create darkness: **I make peace, and create evil**: I the LORD do all these things.* (Isa. 45:7)

Yesterday we learned that Isa. 45:7 must be understood from a "permissive" rather than a "causative" sense. Some passages make this point clear. Deuteronomy 28:15-28, for example, uses the typical punitive language for disobedience and it ascribes to God the tragedies that would fall upon Israel such as *"I will destroy thee.... I will smite thee....I will send enemies.... I will send pestilence... etc."*

However, these are simply Hebrew idioms which ascribe to God as doing the thing which He only permitted. Interpreting Scripture with Scripture, we see that God is not the author of the disasters (evils) that came upon Babylon. He *permits* these disasters due to their sin.

> *"And the Lord said unto Moses, Behold, thou shalt sleep with thy fathers; and this people will rise up, and go a whoring after the gods of the strangers of the land, whither they go to be among them, **and will forsake me, and break my covenant** which I have made with them. Then my anger shall be kindled against them in that day, **and I will forsake them, and I will hide my face from them**, and they shall be devoured, **and many evils and troubles shall befall them**; so that they will say in that day, **Are not these evils come upon us, because our God is not among us?** And **I will surely hide my face** in that day for all the evils which they shall have wrought, in that they are turned unto other gods."* (Deut. 31:16-18).

The word "evils" in the passage above is the Hebrew word "ra"; the same word used in Isa. 45:7. Interpreting Scripture with Scripture we see that evil comes when the Lord is *absent*. This is the proper understanding of the phrase "I create evil".

Examining Isa. 45:7 in light of the above, we see that God is light (1 John 1:9; James 1:17) and creates darkness when He withdraws and darkness prevails. God offers men His light in spite of their rebellion (Isa. 50:10; John 8:12; 12:46; 1 Pet. 2:9) but men reject it because they hate it (John 1:5-11; 3:19-20). Therefore, Isa. 45:7 is *permissive* in that God is *allowing* men the consequences of their choices. God is *not* the author of *physical* or *moral* evil. Evil comes when the source of good that protects from evil is forsaken. This is *permission* and not *causation*.

January 9

Does God Give us Bad Things in Answer to Prayer

If a son shall ask bread of any of you that is a father, will he give him a stone? or if he ask a fish, will he for a fish give him a serpent? Or if he shall ask an egg, will he offer him a scorpion? (Luke 11:11-12)

"Don't ask God for patience because He will send you trials." "I asked God for a brand new car but he gave me a second hand Volkswagen in order to humble me." "I prayed for my uncle's healing but the Lord took him home. I guess it was just his time to go." "I asked God for a healthy baby but He gave me a mentally deformed child to help me learn to be compassionate." "I asked God to use me in ministry. He allowed me to have a crippling accident so that I can minister to disabled people."

What a reputation God has been given for answering prayer by giving us things that hurt us. Certainly we rationalize it to make the bad that God supposedly gives to appear as if it were something good—a blessing in disguise, but deep down inside we know that these things lead us to expect very little that is positive. Many people hear these types of testimonies and do not want to pray. They think that God might slap them with the very opposite of what they have asked for.

As far as I am concerned, this has been a sneaky deception of Satan to hinder prayer in the body of Christ. Why pray if God will only make things worse in order to humble you, teach you a lesson, or punish you for bothering Him in the first place? Only a masochist will attempt to ask anything from this kind of God.

This is why Jesus came to show us a different picture of our Heavenly Father. God is not looking to harm people. He wants to help us, bless us, and deliver us from the plans of Satan for our lives. He will not give rocks for bread, snakes for fish, or scorpions for eggs. When people approached Jesus for healing, He did not kill them or inflict further sickness upon them. He healed them. Jesus and the Father are ONE. He does not do evil in answer to requests for good. When you pray, trust God to only give you good things. Reject and stand against all satanic substitutes.

January 10

God does for us what He Expects us to do for Others

If ye then, being evil, know how to give good gifts unto your children, how much more shall your Father which is in heaven give good things to them that ask him? ***Therefore*** *all things whatsoever ye would that men should do to you, do ye even so to them: for this is the law and the prophets* (Matt. 7:11-12)

I have often heard Bible teachers say, "whenever you see a 'therefore' in the Bible, you need to read further to find out what it is 'there for.'" This is definitely sound advice as a "therefore" is a conjunction that connects two thoughts together.

In this case, Jesus is saying that God only dispenses good things to men when He is asked. He does not give us anything dangerous or harmful in response to our requests. He is a God full of love and compassion and only wants our good. Jesus then tells His listeners (and readers) to follow the Father's example and do the same kind of good to others as you would expect from them.

Here is another good reason to reject many of the traditional ideas about God that have been fed to us through the centuries: these ideas about God make it appear as if God is violating His own law of love. Jesus is telling us in His "therefore" to follow God's example in how He dispenses good things to those that ask Him. If we followed some of the false ideas about God then we would be giving people cancer, making them to have accidents, placing them in temptation situations, and other things that the Father is accused of doing in answer to prayer.

We know that to do such things to other human beings goes against the very ideals that are inherent in love. To kill someone's child and leave a mother grieving because we needed a little flower in our garden or to have a young girl raped so that she can learn to minister to rape victims would land us in the psycho ward. People would not look at our actions as acts of love but as demented behavior in which we deserved to be locked up for.

Yet, this is the very picture that many present concerning God: that He would do things to us that we, nor He, would not expect us to want done to us by others nor would the majority of sane people want to do to anyone else. If we would not do such horrible things to each other nor would we want them done to us then let us stop believing that God would do them.

January 11

Who's Fault is it that Our Prayers are Unsuccessful?

Then came the disciples to Jesus apart, and said, Why could not we cast him out? And Jesus said unto them, Because of your unbelief.... (Matt. 17:19-20a)

We pray and pray for someone's healing and they remain sick. In some cases they even die. We pray for someone's deliverance and they remain in bondage to the evil spirit tormenting them or to the sinful habit destroying them. We pray with people for jobs, money, homes, cars, and many other essential needs and the person prayed for is in no better state.

Some comfort themselves with the idea that the one being prayed for has no faith. Others simply believe that there must be some unknown sin in their lives blocking the answer. Then there are those who simply sum it up to the will and sovereignty of God. After all, if it were God's will, the prayer would be answered.

In many cases the first two answers may be correct, but one should only accept this if the Holy Spirit has revealed it. Otherwise, we should not assume that such may be the case. The third one is definitely not an option since it is always God's will to heal, deliver, and supply our needs (James 5:14-16; Phil. 4:19).

We must learn to accept responsibility for our lack of answers to prayer rather than blaming others and, even worse, blaming God. God has commissioned us to preach the good news and assist those in need of healing, deliverance and material provision. He would not suddenly withdraw from us His divine power to fulfill His command.

The problem stems with us: our belief about God, His character, the integrity of His promises, and His desire to help. Often, because we do not understand God's heart of compassion for others, we lack it as well and are reluctant to persist in getting a breakthrough for others. Faith is knowing the truth about God and standing on the integrity of His Word. Unbelief is questioning God's character and the veracity of His promises. If we truly get to know God then we can do great things for others. After all, those who know their God shall be strong and do great exploits (Dan. 11:32).

January 12

A Study in Contrasts

"The thief cometh not, but for to steal, and to kill, and to destroy: I am come that they might have life, and that they might have it more abundantly" (John 10:10)

God invited Adam to partake of every tree in the garden. He only forbade Adam from one single tree and this was for his protection. God told Adam that his disobedience would bring death (Gen. 2:17). Sadly, Adam forfeited the life of God and brought the whole world under Satan's reign of death (Rom. 5:12; Heb. 2:14-15).

Jesus came to restore the *life* that Adam forfeited when he yielded to Satan. Jesus is *not* the one who steals, kills, and destroys. He comes in love to restore what the thief stole from mankind. Jesus redeems us from Satan's evil reign of death and destruction by offering us a new birth and translating us into His kingdom (John 3:1-5). He also gives us a better understanding about God that leads to abundant life (John 17:3). Therefore, we can see that Jesus' attitude towards us is the exact opposite of Satan's.

Some argue that the "thief" is a reference to the religious leaders rather than Satan. This is a moot point. The religious leaders certainly took on the nature of Satan (Luke 22:53; John 8:44; 2 Cor. 11:13-15; 1 John 3:7-12). Therefore we rightly refer to the thief as Satan. Some scholars agree:

> "These words ....carry us beyond scribes and Pharisees, beyond all merely human teachers, good or bad, and contrast Jesus Christ with the great adversary of men. When he said, 'All that came before me are thieves and robbers,' he certainly did not refer to Old Testament prophets who spake by his spirit; no[r] did he refer primarily to the scribes and Pharisees, but to Satan, the arch enemy, who first seduced mankind, and to the human teachers in all ages who have been actuated by Satan's spirit. All who sought to enslave and destroy men by alienating them from God and leading them into any form of idolatry, gross or refined, were thieves and robbers. This included the evil one and all his agents."[4]

So John 10:10 is a definite contrast between the mission of God and the mission of Satan. Let us learn not to get the two confused. Accept one and stand your ground against the other based on the blood of Jesus.

---

[4] Gibson, Joseph T. **Jesus Christ: The Unique Revealer of God**, © 1915 by Fleming H. Revell, p. 294

January 13

What actually Destroys People?

My people are being destroyed because they don't know me. Since you priests refuse to know me, I refuse to recognize you as my priests. Since you have forgotten the laws of your God, I will forget to bless your children (Hosea 4:6; New Living Translation)

Certainly the devil comes to kill, steal, and destroy (John 10:10). But how does he manage to do it? One way he is able to do this is by keeping us from knowing the truth about God. Satan has falsely accused God and painted such a distorted picture of Him that He is not recognized as the loving God that the Biblical writers depicted Him. Satan has distorted the Word of God in order to present his false ideas about God.

Because people do not really know God they have accepted the lie and are allowing a multitude of preventable circumstances designed to destroy them. Many accept much of the works of the devil as acts of God because they really do not know God.

Notice that it is not God who destroys people. It is our ignorance and willing rejection of His Word that brings destruction upon us. It was Adam's rejection of God's Word that destroyed him and the same is happening all over the world today. Sadly it is even happening in our churches where the Bible no longer has a preeminent place in the instruction of God's people. Also, many churches that claim to teach the Bible are still telling people that God is the One who, in His sovereignty, brought about the negative life issues that people have to deal with.

When God says, *"I will also reject thee.... seeing thou hast forgotten the law of thy God, I will also forget thy children,"* (KJV) He is not being vindictive here. This is simply the law of reciprocity at work. God does all that He possibly can to reach out to erring mankind but it is He that is rejected when we reject His Word (Psalm 81:10-16; Prov. 1:24-28; Isa. 30:15; 65:2; Jer. 5:3; 32:33; Zech. 7:11; Luke 7:30; 13:34; John 5:39-40).

For God to force His desires on us would make Him a tyrant, thus giving Satan's accusations merit. Therefore God gives us the freedom to choose or reject His ways. Love cannot be forced and neither can the blessings that accrue from that love. If we want to remain willingly ignorant and reject God's Word, God has no choice but to let it happen. Know God, know His Word, and avoid destruction.

January 14

Is God's Will A Mystery?

Having <u>made known unto us</u> the mystery of his will, according to his good pleasure which he hath purposed in himself (Eph. 1:9)

You have heard the saying, "God's ways are mysterious, His wonders to perform." We hear this when something happens to someone, good or bad, that we cannot find a rational explanation for. We believe that God is somehow behind the incident, working through some sort of "secret providence". Is this an idea that can be supported by God's Word?

Paul tells us that the will of God is no mystery to His children. We learn it by reading His Word and the Holy Spirit's illumination or by praying and asking God to reveal His will to us (James 1:5-7; Prov. 3:5, 6).

The Bible tells us, *"Wherefore be ye not unwise, but understanding what the will of the Lord is"* (Eph. 5:17). The Bible tells us that it is unwise not to understand what the will of the Lord is. That is why He provides wisdom. Those who hold to God's will as some type of "mystery" are being unwise according to Paul's teaching. We are to seek God's will before *assuming* that outward circumstances are somehow His will for us.

Calvinists teach a "secret will" of God and a "revealed will." These *two wills* contradict one another (though Calvinists would not put it in those terms). For example, Calvinists acknowledge the revealed will of God is that all men be saved (1 Tim. 2:4; 2 Pet. 3:9), but the secret will of God is that some are predestined for heaven and others to hell. This is all based on some supposed secret decree within the counsels of the Almighty. One anti-Calvinist disagrees:

> "The attempt to delve into the mind of God apart from what he has revealed in the Bible is work of 'dead orthodox' theologians who pass their philosophical speculations and theological implications from one generation to the next."[5]

Let us be cautious in accepting any circumstance that contradicts God's Word as having come to us via some "mysterious providence". Verify all circumstances by the Word of God and resist those in the Name of Jesus that contradict the Word.

---

[5] Vance, Laurence **The Other Side of Calvinism** (Pensacola, FL: Vance Publications, 1991, 1999), pp. 300, 301

January 15

God's "Secret Things" and that which is "Revealed"

The secret things belong unto the LORD our God: but those things which are revealed belong unto us and to our children for ever, that we may do all the words of this law (Deu. 29:29).

Some misinterpret this passage to imply that there is a *secret will* of God that is contrary to or distinct from His *revealed will*. However, the passage simply states that there are some things God has not yet revealed to His people. That which He does reveal is that which belongs to us. Nothing in the passage implies a conflict between a *revealed* and a *secret* will.

The passage teaches that what is revealed is sufficient for us to live by (Deut. 8:3). We are not to live by anything that contradicts God's Word. Those who emphasize a mysterious providence or sovereignty that implies that God is behind negative circumstances that go contrary to His Word are actually in violation of this passage since they are making claims for that which has not been revealed.

The same God who spoke those words to Moses also told Amos, *"Surely the Lord GOD will **do nothing, but he revealeth his secret** unto his servants the prophets"* (Amos 3:7). If God were doing the things that He is often accused of doing secretly without having ever revealed what He was going to do to His prophets first then this would make God a liar. That is **impossible** (Num. 23:19; Psalm 89:33-35; Titus 1:2; Heb. 6:17-19). Therefore, God is not secretly doing things that contradict His Word.

Only that which is revealed belong to us and if we are confronted with any circumstances that contradict that which has been revealed, then we must understand that it is not God's doing, it does NOT belong to us and we are to confront it authoritatively with God's Word.

The passage is to be understood within the full context of Deuteronomy. God gives revelation so that things can go well with us (Deu. 4:40; 6:1-3, 19, 19). God reveals this as the longing of His heart (Deu. 5:29; 30:15, 19). In Deut. 28 and the majority of 29, God states that the majority of negative issues that would come in the lives of His people were not the result of any secret sovereign will but rather the result of disobedience to the revealed will. Embrace the revealed will of God and reject all else.

January 16

Satan Is the Source of Tribulation and Persecution

"...It is like the people who hear God's teaching, but then the devil comes and takes it away from their hearts. So they cannot believe the teaching and be saved ...they don't have deep roots. They believe for a while. But when trouble comes, they give up." (Luke 8:12-13; New Century Version)

Many blame God for bringing trials, tribulations and persecutions their way. God has specifically stated in His word that He is not the source of our troubles (James 1:13). Trials, tribulations, and persecutions are designed to turn us away from God's word. Satan uses these devices to tempt us into giving up on God, believing that His Word will not work on our behalf.

The Holy Spirit has given the body of Christ much revelation in the past years. We have had much teaching and insight into the deep truths of God's Word. He has shown us how to walk in victory in every area of our lives. BUT YOU CANNOT HAVE VICTORY WITHOUT A BATTLE.

Satan knows that once we allow God's Word to become a part of us then we will pose a strong threat to him and his kingdom. When we embrace a significant truth from God's word, he will send his demonic forces after us to take that truth away. If he can send enough negative circumstances to get us off the Word of God, he will do it.

That is why we are encouraged to stand on God's Word even in the midst of trouble. No matter what the circumstances look like, no matter how contrary they are to what the Word of God says about them, continue to stand on the Word. God will see you through: *"Many are the afflictions of the righteous: but the Lord delivereth him out of them all."* (Psalms 34:19).

God has promised to deliver us from the problems that Satan will send our way. He has promised to manifest his blessings in our lives that we are trusting Him for. Trust Him for deliverance. There is no way that we can escape tribulation or persecution, but we can be the *victor* and not the *defeated*.

January 17

God is Love

*Beloved, let us love one another: for love is of God; and every one that loveth is born of God, and knoweth God. He that loveth not knoweth not God; **for God is love.** In this was manifested the love of God toward us, because that God sent his only begotten Son into the world, that we might live through him* (1 John 4:7-8)

A deranged man has finally tracked down his wife. She left him some time ago because of his consistent pattern of physical and emotional abuse. Afraid for her life she has kept herself hidden. But he loves her so much he must find her. Now that he has her he tells her, "I love you too much to let you go. If I can't have you then no one can." He then pulls out a gun and kills her.

Some seem to believe that this is the kind of "love" that God has— one in which He abuses us physically and emotionally and then kills us when we try to get away from Him. Many of our sermons from the pulpit have helped to reinforce this false idea about "love" as it relates to God. Is this what it means for God to be loving?

Notice that God manifests His love toward us by sacrificing Himself. He sent His only Son in the world to die for sinful creatures that were in rebellion against Him (Rom. 5:1-8). God is not looking to hurt us and proves this by His ultimate sacrifice on our behalf. Since God is love then He is unable to do anything that could hurt or harm others: *"**Love worketh no ill to his neighbour***: therefore love is the fulfilling of the law"* (Rom. 13:10).

Within His love God gives us genuine choices. We can accept or reject His love on our behalf. He does this without coercion. However, He does warn us about the alternative, which is slavery to Satan and sin. Nonetheless, God, in His love, begs and pleads with us to choose Him because only through voluntary submission is He able to protect us from the one who actually does desire to do us harm.

God's love is an unselfish love that looks beyond its own desires to see what it can do for others. God's love is an "others-focused" love. This is completely opposite of Satan's distorted substitutes that seeks to gratify its own needs and when it is done with its object, the love is gone (2 Sam. 13:1-20). Wouldn't you rather have the love that looks to heal rather than hurt others? Receive God's love. He permeates love because *He is love.*

January 18

Jesus First Mission: Restore Understanding of God

Jesus came to die for lost humanity. He died the death that we deserved (Isa. 53:4-10; 1 Pet. 2:24). But before going to the cross to pay for our sins, the sinless Son of God had to spend a few years teaching people the truth about the One who sent Him.

Adam lost the eternal life he possessed when he stopped knowing and understanding God. Jesus said, *"And this is life eternal, that they might know thee the only true God, and Jesus Christ, whom thou hast sent"* (John 17:3). When we have placed ourselves under Satan's bondage of death then our understanding of God becomes twisted. From the time of Adam to Jesus, Satan worked continuously to distort the truth about God. Part of the mission of Jesus was to offer men His eternal life which leads to freedom from Satan's wicked reign. But He had to first give us an understanding of God's true nature:

> *We know that whoever is born of God does not sin; but he who has been born of God keeps himself,[e] and the wicked one does not touch him. We know that we are of God, and the whole world lies under the sway of the wicked one. And **we know that the Son of God has come and has given us an understanding, that we may know Him who is true**; and we are in Him who is true, in His Son Jesus Christ. This is the true God and eternal life* (1 John 5:18-20; NKJV)

Notice the contrasts between God and Satan. Satan is described as the *wicked one* or the *evil one*. God is described as the One who is *true*. The word "true" means "the real thing" or "opposite to what is fictitious".

John is telling us that Jesus Himself is God. Jesus perfectly represents to us what God is actually like (John 14:8-11; 2 Cor. 4:4; Heb. 1:1-3). Jesus never hurt anyone but healed and delivered people from satanic oppression (Acts 10:38). Jesus fed the hungry, delivered people from sin, and averted natural disasters.

Jesus never gave sickness, temptation, famine, natural disasters or condemned anyone in wrath and judgment. The Father and the Holy Spirit are just like Jesus. If you want to know what God is like, Jesus has revealed Him. He is exactly like Jesus. *He is Jesus.*

January 19

Exposing Satan's Opposite Malignant Character

The field is the world; the good seed are the children of the kingdom; but the tares are the children of the wicked one; The enemy that sowed them is the devil; the harvest is the end of the world; and the reapers are the angels (Matt. 13:38-39)

In order to reveal the truth about God, Jesus also had to expose the real culprit behind the ills that we suffer in this world. In the gospels Jesus revealed to us that Satan's character is so malignant that two of the many titles ascribed to him are "the evil one" (Mat. 5:37; 6:13; John 17:15; 2) and "the wicked one" (Mat. 13:19, 38). Furthermore, the demonic forces that work for Satan and who are the source of much sickness, disease, sin and tragedy in our world are also called *evil* (Luke 7:21; 8:2). Throughout the gospels Jesus revealed several things about Satan in contrast to God:

- Satan is the evil one who brings temptation to sin. God is the One who delivers from sin (Matt. 4:1-11; 6:13; Luke 4:1-14).
- Satan is the evil one who brings sickness and disease. God is the One who heals (Luke 13:16).
- Satan is a liar and murderer who brings persecution and seeks to kill (John 8:44).
- Satan brings deprivation, death and destruction. God gives His own life for us (John 10:10).
- Satan has a kingdom that subjects people to his demonic torments. God has come to rescue them (Matt. 12:25-29; Luke 11:17-22).
- Satan is the one who attempts to hinder us from our God-given missions (Matt. 16:22-23).
- Satan has a certain amount of power to harm, but God has given us authority over him and his power (Luke 10:17-20).
- God gives His Word because He desires our salvation. Satan steals the Word to keep us from being saved (Luke 8:12).
- Satan desires to sift God's servants as wheat. Jesus prays for us so that our faith will not fail (Luke 22:31).
- Satan enters into people to betray others (Luke 22:3; John 13:27).
- Satan is responsible for natural disasters (Luke 8:22-25; 9:51-56).
- Satan is the "ruler" (prince) of this world, but Jesus has conquered his domain (John 12:31; 14:30; 16:11, 33).

Jesus gives us a clear expose of the enemy. He is the exact opposite of God. While God is loving and good, Satan is mean, hateful and evil. What a contrast.

January 20

The Highest Type of Faith?

Though he slay me, yet will I trust in him: but I will maintain mine own ways before him (Job 13:15).

Some believe that God predestined all events and all are under His control. They believe that all things happen to us for some mysterious good. Those who embrace this deterministic theology usually promote the passage above as an example of "the highest type of faith." For example, Oswald Chambers wrote, "'Though He slay me, yet will I trust Him' - this is the most sublime utterance of faith in the whole of the Bible" (*My Utmost for His Highest*, p. 31).

Yet many scholars would disagree with this translation. One commentary says, "Though he slay me, yet will I trust in him, a rendering which one is most unwilling to surrender. But it must be confessed that it is a translation which it is impossible to defend, for the verb in the latter half of the clause does not mean trust, but rather wait for something or someone" (Gibson, Edgar C. S. *The Book of Job*, p. 66). Numerous Bible translations also reject the KJV rendering. Here is one example out of many: "*Behold, he will slay me; **I have no hope**: Nevertheless I will maintain my ways before him*" (American Standard Version).

Most importantly, this idea contradicts what Jesus says are examples of the highest type of faith. When Jesus spoke of "great faith" it was in relation to a man who had confident expectation that his servant would be healed. Another time it was in relation to a woman who persisted in worship until her daughter was delivered (Matt. 15:22-28). Jesus never spoke of anyone having great faith to be slain by God. On the contrary, any failure to believe God for deliverance from satanic oppression was considered by Jesus to be "little faith" and "unbelief" (Matt. 8:26; 13:58; 17:19-20).

Trust is not submitting to every circumstance as if God was somehow responsible for them and had some divine mysterious purpose for them. Trust is not fatalism, queue sera, sera, or passive. Trust in God is actually accepting His promise as true and acting upon their stated conditions. True trust in God will not wish and hope that God *might* do something; true trust in God is to know exactly what God said He would do and then having a confident assurance that He will do the very thing that He promised. Job was not by any means making a statement of "fatalistic faith." Job was defending himself to his three so-called friends who falsely accused him of sinning and bringing his trials upon himself.

God's Word Is the Only Basis for Trust

VAU. Let thy mercies come also unto me, O LORD, even thy salvation, according to thy word. So shall I have wherewith to answer him that reproacheth me: <u>for I trust in thy word</u> (Psalm 119:41, 42)

We are to put our trust in God's Word. It is the only basis upon which we will know God's actions toward us. Only by His Word can we know what He will do on our behalf in any situation. Sadly, there are a number of popular writers that promote an idea of trust that is inconsistent with Scripture. For example, Jerry Bridges, in a popular book, writes:

> "Confidence in the sovereignty of God in all that affects us is crucial to our trusting Him. If there is a single event in all of the universe that can occur outside of God's sovereign control then we cannot trust Him. His love may be infinite, but if His power is limited and His purposes can be thwarted, we cannot trust Him. However, the Scripture explicitly teaches that God rules as surely on earth as He does in Heaven. He permits, for reasons known only to Himself, people to act contrary to and in defiance of His revealed will, but He never permits them to act contrary to His Sovereign will:"[6]

In other words, what Bridges is saying is that God "sovereignly willed" for people to act contrary to His revealed will. This is ridiculous. Should we *"...do evil, that good may come?"* (Rom. 3:8).

With all due respect, Bridges is <u>wrong</u>. The basis for trusting God is *not* "the sovereignty of God" or "the providence of God," especially as some men define these statements. The basis for trusting God is *the Word of God*. To trust on the basis of "sovereignty" or "providence" has led so many to fatalism rather than a true focused trust in God to intervene on their behalf or to change their negative situation for their betterment.

The Word of God says, *"In whom ye also trusted, after that ye heard the word of truth, the gospel of your salvation: in whom also after that ye believed, ye were sealed with that holy Spirit of promise"* (Eph. 1:13). In another place Paul wrote, *"So then faith cometh by hearing, and hearing by the word of God"* (Rom. 10:17). Trust is based on *information* rather than mysterious sovereign uncertainties. Trust-faith finds it source in the Word of God.

---

[6]Bridges, Jerry **Trusting God Even When Life hurts** (Colorado Springs, CO: Navpress, 1988), p. 44

January 22

Trust is having Knowledge of what God will Do

*What time I am afraid, I will trust in thee. In God I will
praise his word, in God I have put my trust; I will not fear
what flesh can do unto me* (Psalm 56:3, 4)

One cannot have both trust in God and fear of men and circumstances. We possess either one or the other but not both. If we fear men or circumstances it is due to having accepted the words or threats of men. If we trust God then it is due to having accepted His Word as having more weight than that of men.

Fear comes to all of us, however, it is our decision to let it continue with us or to resist it. The Psalmist states that when fear comes he will make a quality decision to trust in God. True trust will be demonstrated by praise in God and His Word to us. Trust will also demonstrate itself through a positive affirmation of faith.

In order to have faith in a person, you must be able to trust what they say. We cannot separate a person from his or her word. Trust is not abstract and simply throwing caution into the air. God has given us a revelation of His will and expects us to know it so that we can have a firm foundation for trusting Him. His Word tells us what He is willing to do on our behalf. Faith or trust is to know what God will *actually* do:

*For **I will** surely deliver thee, and thou shalt not fall by the
sword, but thy life shall be for a prey unto thee: **because
thou hast put thy trust in me**, saith the LORD.* (Jer. 39:18)

*Who delivered us from so great a death, and doth deliver:
in whom **we trust that he will yet deliver us*** (2 Cor. 1:10)

God is a God of integrity who not only cannot lie, but finds it impossible to do so (Titus 1:1, 2; Heb. 6:17, 18). There is no difficulty in believing someone when we believe that he or she could never lie. On the contrary it becomes easier to trust such an individual.

What God says that he will do is the revelation of his will. Every "I will" or "He will" is a revelation of "God's will." Some seem to put trust in a vacuum. Their faith and trust is not targeted. I think too many have mistaken *fatalism* for *faith*. Do not buy into this substitute for faith. Develop faith based on the integrity of God's Word.

January 23

Taste and See how Good God Is

This poor man cried, and the Lord heard him, and saved him out of all his troubles. The angel of the Lord encampeth round about them that fear him, and delivereth them. ***O taste and see that the Lord is good: blessed is the man that trusteth in him.*** *O fear the Lord, ye his saints: for there is no want to them that fear him. The young lions do lack, and suffer hunger: but they that seek the Lord shall not want any good thing* (Psalm 34:6-10).

One definition of "taste" is, "to become acquainted with by experience" (Webster's Dictionary). This idea is brought out in this Psalm when we are told that the man who *trusts* in God is blessed (which means "happy"). The Psalmist is confident that when one tastes and see how good God really is then he or she will have no difficulty trusting Him.

But how do we go about "tasting" God's goodness? We are to "taste and see" that God is good by the wonderful things that He does for us. Notice some of the things in this Psalm that is attributed to God's goodness. The psalmist mentions the angelic protection that God provides to those who fear (reverence and worship) Him. This is a far cry from the false depiction of God we are given by some in which God is behind accidents and every tragic event that comes our way. If that is our experience of God then it is no wonder that some have claimed to have tasted of Him and have been left with a bitter taste in their mouths.

The Psalmist also mentions God's abundant provision to those that suffer lack. This provision comes to those who do not seek the provision itself, but the *Provider* (Matt. 6:33). The reason that so many continue to suffer lack is because they do not seek the Lord. The reason many do not seek the Lord is because they do not trust Him. The reason they do not trust Him is because, rather than tasting for themselves to see how good He is, they have accepted false ideas about God. Many have embraced a distorted definition of God's goodness that appears to be more in line with the acts of Satan than with what we know to be in line with the universal definition of "good".

Get hungry for the truth about God. Taste and see how good He really is. You will be so glad that you did.

January 24

Abundant in Goodness

*And the Lord passed by before him, and proclaimed, The Lord, The Lord God, merciful and gracious, longsuffering, and **abundant in goodness and truth**, Keeping mercy for thousands, **forgiving iniquity and transgression and sin**, and that will by no means clear the guilty; visiting the iniquity of the fathers upon the children, and upon the children's children, unto the third and to the fourth generation* (Ex. 34:6-7)

When Moses asked to see God's glory (Ex. 33:17-23), God gave him a revelation of His character. On the basis of this revelation, Moses was able to successfully intercede for Israel when they sinned and opened themselves up for destruction (Num. 14:17-20). Because of His goodness, God is ready to forgive our iniquities: *"For thou, Lord, **art good, and ready to forgive**; and plenteous in mercy unto all them that call upon thee"* (Psalm 86:5).

Sometimes God is depicted by Bible expositors as having a cruel mean streak in the Old Testament. He is looked upon as harsh, unforgiving and quick to judge at the slightest transgression. It is erroneously implied that Jesus had to come for the express purpose of tempering the Father's desire to bring harsh judgment upon worthless sinners. We are even told by some that Christians should avoid the Old Testament since only the New Testament (specifically the epistles) is applicable.

However, when we look for God's revelations of Himself in the Old Testament we see anything but a cruel and merciless deity. God did not switch personalities from the Old to the New. He was merciful and forgiving under the Old Covenant just as He is in the New Covenant.

Jesus did not die and resurrect in order to change God's character or His attitude toward us. Jesus died in order to legally rescue us from Satan's tyranny, thus providing the Father a legal basis upon which forgiveness can be extended and no one can accuse Him of being unfair to Satan and the fallen angels. Before Jesus, the second member of the Triune Godhead, gave His own life, the animal sacrifices provided a covering which pointed to His redemptive work.

In other words, even in the Old Testament, God provided every possible way to extend His love, mercy, and forgiveness to fallen man. This is an example of abundant goodness. This same God is ever ready to forgive you and love you regardless of what you have done. Embrace His abundant goodness.

January 25

A Good God Redeems us from the Enemy

*O give thanks unto the Lord, **for he is good**: for his mercy endureth for ever. Let the redeemed of the Lord say so, whom he hath **redeemed from the hand of the enemy*** (Psalm 107:1-2)

"All things are under God's control, including the devil. If God has allowed the devil to attack you then He has a reason for it. Even the enemy is under God's control and can do nothing without His permission." For some this type of statement brings a certain amount of comfort. The thought is, "After all, if I have to suffer so much, even if it is Satan that is bringing the assaults, God must have a plan and a greater purpose in it."

However, not everyone is able to take comfort in such sentiments. There are many who have suffered significant hurt and pain at the hand of the enemy. They feel that God has let them down because He did not stop the enemy or rescue them from his attacks. When they are told that God allowed the enemy to do what was done for some unknown reason the natural response is, "Why me Lord? What did I do to deserve this?" This latter group does not see God as a good God if He "sics" the devil on His own children because of some mysterious plan for their lives.

The Bible agrees with their frustration. The Psalmist believed that God is good, not because He sends the enemy against His people, but because *He redeems them from the enemy*. While the Psalmist is more than likely referring to physical enemies in this passage, we New Testament believers know that Satan is the power working behind them (Eph. 6:10-12). The New Testament refers to Satan as "the enemy" (Luke 10:17-20). The name "Satan" itself means "adversary". Therefore the passage above, as confirmed by the New Testament itself, can easily be applied to Satan (Col. 1:12-14).

In the Bible, to "redeem" someone is to buy them back from captivity. God's goodness is shown in how He has redeemed His people from Satan's reign of death, destruction and deprivation. Now one must ask their self why would God, who paid such a heavy price, the blood of His dear Son, use the enemy that He purchased you from to work some mysterious plan by sending him against you? Sometimes religious people need to let common sense prevail over mystical concepts.

The Psalmist says that the proof that God is good is that in His mercy, He bought us from the hand of the enemy and set us free from his oppression. We need not accept the wiles of the devil. We have been redeemed. Let us stand against his attacks.

January 26

A Good God Delivers and Heals

Fools because of their transgression, and because of their iniquities, are afflicted. Their soul abhorreth all manner of meat; and they draw near unto the gates of death. Then they cry unto the Lord in their trouble, and he saveth them out of their distresses. **He sent his word, and healed them, and delivered them from their destructions. Oh that men would praise the Lord for his goodness,** *and for his wonderful works to the children of men!* (Ps. 107:15-21)

Why are people afflicted? While this is certainly not true of all people that are suffering, those that the Psalmist refers to as "fools" are said to have brought upon themselves their own affliction by their sin.

The Psalm does not say that God is the One who brings upon them their punishment; He is not the One afflicting them because of their sin. The Bible is clear that sin has built in consequences that destroy us (Rom. 6:23; James 1:15). Basically, sin contains within itself its own seeds of destruction (Gal. 6:5-6). We live in a morally ordered universe where there are consequences to our actions.

This is also another reason why those being afflicted due to their sin are referred to as "fools". A fool is someone who is deceived. He is ignorant, blinded, or does not seem to care about the outcome of his or her behavior. A fool is one who is carelessly living for the moment. I suppose all of us can claim to have been in this category at one time or another.

God demonstrates His *goodness* in that He delivers and heals people from the results of their foolishness. He does not have to do this. He has the right to let us suffer what we deserve. Yet, inherent in His goodness is the desire to rescue people from the results of their own intentional foolishness.

God is not the *afflicter*. He is the *healer* and *deliverer*. The real afflicter is *sin*. Therefore one should not blame God for the results of the sin. Nor should one be afraid to go to God to receive deliverance and healing. The psalm says that they cried out to God and He delivered and healed. God is so good that He is willing to heal and deliver us from our own foolishness when we repent and cry out to Him. Oh praise the Lord for His goodness. Hallelujah!

January 27

Love and Mercy are Inherent in Goodness

Hear me, O Lord; for thy lovingkindness is good: turn unto me according to the multitude of thy tender mercies (Psalm 69:16)

During a discussion with someone who embraced a particular theological perspective about God that attributes evil as well as good to Him, we were discussing the nature of what is good and evil. I pointed out that certain horrendous evils cannot come from the hands of a good God. His response was something to the effect that, "it all depends on how one defines 'good' as it relates to God. What may be 'good' from our perspective may not always be good from God's perspective."

One can be easily prejudiced by theological systems with their philosophical speculations about what it means for God to be and do good. Nevertheless, we must always look to the Bible, the very inspired Word of God itself, for correct definitions of God's goodness. The psalm above tells us that love and mercy are ingredients of His goodness.

God's Word equates "evil with hatred" and "love with good": *"And they have rewarded me evil for good, and hatred for my love"* (Psalm 109:5). Basically "love and good" are two opposite sides of a coin and so is "evil and hatred". Many of the things that certain Evangelical denominations blame on God would definitely fall under the "evil and hatred" category. Love could not do some of the things God is often accused of doing (Rom. 13:10).

Rather than doing that which is harmful to others, God's goodness, which is manifested by His unselfish love, is always looking for a way to bring benefit to others:

So let me remind you of the Eternal's enduring love, and why we should praise Him. Let me tell you again how the Eternal gives and gives and gives. All God's wonders and goodness are done for Israel's benefit according to His great mercy and compassion (Isa. 63:7; Voice)

God's goodness is manifested by His love and His love is others-focused. God is always looking for the best possible way to benefit and bless people. Our sin shuts us off from His goodness, but His mercy brings us back to it when we repent. Indeed God is "gooder" than we ever imagined.

January 28

God Overrules Free Sinful Actions against Us

*But as for you, ye thought evil against me; but God meant
it unto good, to bring to pass, as it is this day, to save much
people alive* (Gen. 50:20)

As we look at this theme of God's goodness, there are always proof
texts used by those who advocate the idea that God can ordain or cause evil
in order to bring about good. This has too often been the case with the
passage above. Yet, it would appear upon a general reading that they have
solid Biblical support for their assertion. **The Living Bible** gives what I
believe is the real thought behind this passage: *"As far as I am concerned,
God turned into good what you meant for evil, for he brought me to this
high position I have today so that I could save the lives of many people."*

God did not move Joseph's brothers to commit evil acts. The Holy
Spirit reveals that their acts were the result of *envy* which is a product of
Satan (Acts 7:9; James 3:14-16). Thomas Jackson expounds further:

"Are we then to understand that God was a party to the
murderous hostility of Joseph's brethren? To the heartless sale of
their brother? To the sale of him in Egypt by the selfish
Ishmaelites? To the vile accusation of his mistress? Or that God
approved of all these acts, which were connected with Joseph's
advancement? The answer is, Not at all. They were
transgressions of His holy law, and among the "abominable
things that" He "hateth;" and He held the guilty parties
answerable for these their misdoings. Nor were any of these
sinful actions necessary in order to the accomplishment of God's
purposes of mercy in connexion with the famine which then
prevailed. He does not need even the wisdom of men in order to
the fulfilment of His plans; and much less does He need their
sins; for the resources of His wisdom are endless, and His power
is infinite. He overruled for good the envy and malice of Jacob's
sons; and He overruled for good the infamous falsehood of
Joseph's mistress; but He approved of neither, and He needed
neither."[7]

God has given men free will. He neither ordains nor wants sin. But
when people sin against us He will overrule it as He did for Joseph so that
in the end we triumph over the evil that was done to us.

---

[7] Jackson, Thomas **The Providence of God Viewed in the Light of Holy
Scripture** (London: John Mason, 1862), pp. 324, 325.

January 29

Did God Send Joseph to Egypt (Part 1)?

And God sent me before you to preserve you a posterity in the earth, and to save your lives by a great deliverance. So now it was not you that sent me hither, but God: and he hath made me a father to Pharaoh, and lord of all his house, and a ruler throughout all the land of Egypt. (Gen. 45:7-8)

Men in their distorted picture of God have attempted to redefine *good* in order to maintain the Biblical truth about God's goodness while at the same time teaching doctrines in which God does, what appears to the average human, to be evil acts. As we saw yesterday, statements made by Joseph are often proof-texted to support these ideas. This has served to extinguish an aggressive faith that stands against demonic evil and claims God's promises.

However, these passages are indeed recorded in the inspired Word of God and must be addressed if we are to put our full and undying faith in the Bible as we should. So how do we address Joseph's statement, *"So now it was not you that sent me hither, but God"*? One rule of Bible interpretation is to always interpret the Old Testament in light of the New Testament. Stephen, speaking by the Spirit of God, says this about Joseph's brethren:

*And the patriarchs, **moved with envy**, sold Joseph into Egypt: but God was with him, And delivered him out of all his afflictions, and gave him favour and wisdom in the sight of Pharaoh king of Egypt; and he made him governor over Egypt and all his house* (Acts 7:9-10).

Rather than saying that God used the brothers to send Joseph, Stephen says that God was with him despite the actions of his brothers and delivered him. The Holy Spirit speaking through Stephen never says that God made Joseph's brothers sin. Stephen states that God was with Joseph and *overruled* the sinful acts of his brothers.

God is love (1 John 4:8) and love *"envieth not"* (1 Cor. 13:4). "Envyings" are the works of the flesh and not the fruit of the Spirit (Gal. 5:19-21). Satan works through envy (James 3:14-16). God does not make people become envious (Matt. 7:17-18). Is this a Bible contradiction? No. We will continue to examine Gen. 45:7-8 tomorrow for further understanding of its application.

January 30

Did God Send Joseph to Egypt (Part 2)?

And God sent me before you to preserve you a posterity in the earth, and to save your lives by a great deliverance. So now it was not you that sent me hither, but God: and he hath made me a father to Pharaoh, and lord of all his house, and a ruler throughout all the land of Egypt. (Gen. 45:7-8)

Yesterday we learned from the passage above that Joseph told his brothers, *"So now it was not you that sent me hither, but God"*. Many people have embraced a substitute for faith called fatalism due to how they were taught from this passage. However, the New Testament says, *"And the patriarchs, **moved with envy**, sold Joseph into Egypt"* (Acts 7:9a). But are Joseph's statements the inspired Word of God? If so, why do they contradict the New Testament?

Joseph's statements are indeed the inspired Word of God. However, if Westerners do not learn to understand Hebrew idioms, especially the "permissive" idiom so often used by the Hebrews, they will always teach contradictory ideas about God. Richard Twopeny explains:

> "The great point of religion impressed upon the mind of the Israelites was the absolute supremacy of Jehovah in every thing, and his providential interference in every circumstance, which could affect the welfare of their family or people. From whence the transition to that expression was very easy, **which describes those actions of men, as his doing, of which he only overruled the event.** Thus Joseph says to his brethren, Gen. xlv. 8. "So now it was not you, but God, that sent me here:" by which he does not mean to deny that his brothers had sent him thither, for he expressly says so, ver. 5; but to ascribe the whole to his providence, who had so wonderfully made use of their sin to the preservation of their whole family."[8] (Emphasis are mine)

God spoke His Word using the language of the people of that time. Our job as His people in this modern age is to take the time to study His modes of expressions so that we do not misrepresent Him when teaching His Word to others.

---

[8] TwoPeny, Richard **Dissertations on Some parts of the Old and New Testaments, Which have been Supposed Unsuitable to the Divine Attributes** (London: C and J Rivington, 1824), pp. 16, 17

An Act of God?

While he was yet speaking, there came also another, and said, **The fire of God** *is fallen from heaven, and hath burned up the sheep, and the servants, and consumed them; and I only am escaped alone to tell thee* (Job 1:16)

Many of us rightfully chastise the insurance companies that call natural disasters, "an act of God". However, God has long been blamed for acts that He really had nothing to do with. When we read verses 6 to 12 of Job chapter 1, we learn that Satan made false accusations against God and Job. He then challenged God to prove him a liar by allowing him to destroy Job's life. God reluctantly allowed this test in order to remove doubt about His and Job's character from the minds of the watching angels.

The people during Job's time had very little revelation of a being called Satan. Therefore, everything was attributed to God including the work of Satan. God Himself, using the modes of expression of the people of that time takes responsibility for Satan's actions, even though He was not pleased with them (Job 1:11-12; 2:3). As some scholars have noted:

> "Since there is no developed picture of a devil or satan in most of the Old Testament, God takes responsibility for everything, even for evil he might have prevented. God stands above opposing deities; his power is unsurpassable, according to the Hebrew Bible. And in that world of competing deities and rival religions, absolute control was essential. In other words, in order to meet ancient Israelites in terms they could understand in their world, God takes ultimate responsibility."[9]

The Old Testament believers had a good reason for attributing these things to God. They did not have a full revelation concerning the works of the devil that have been given since the time that Jesus manifested in the flesh. However, our Lord Jesus and His inspired writers of the New Testament have given us a fuller understanding of the true personality behind evil, including natural disasters. Therefore, we should stop blaming God, accepting evil, and stand against it by our authority in Christ.

---

[9] Clark, Douglas R.; Brunt, John C. (editors) **Introducing the Bible Volume I: The Old Testament and Intertestamental Literature** (New York: University Press of America, 1997), p. 171

February 1

God's Word Reveals His Character

I will worship toward thy holy temple, and praise thy name
for thy lovingkindness and for thy truth: for thou hast
magnified thy word above all thy name (Psalm 138:2)

Many people do not really understand what God is saying here because in our Western Society we have no true concept that defines what is meant by a person's "name". In most places the word certainly means "name" as we Westerners understand it (like naming a child "William") but, and especially in the case with God, it has far more meaning.[10] God is saying in Psalm 138:2 that He places His Word above *His reputation*. Another way to phrase it is that *His Word reveals His reputation* or the truth concerning *His character and nature*.

The Hebrew word for "name" in this passage is *shem* which means, "reputation, fame, glory" (Studylight.org). The Complete Jewish Bible renders the latter part of the passage, *"....for you have made your word [even] greater than the whole of your reputation."* The Strong's Concordance defines *shem*, "As a mark or memorial of individuality; by implication honor, authority, character" (Strong's #8034). Jeff A. Benner of the Ancient Hebrew Research Center writes:

> "What is God's name? Most will answer with Yahweh or God but we must remember that a name or *shem* in Hebrew is the character of the individual so the correct question should be 'What is God's character?'"[11]

We cannot have any sufficient knowledge of God's reputation— what He is truly like, what are His characteristics, etc. apart from His Word. Satan knows that the best way to cast aspersions upon God's character is to attack His Word. Destroying a person's reputation is as simple as causing people to doubt the truth of what they say. Satan has done this for centuries. Believe what God's Word says about His character and refuse all teachings and theological concepts that contradict it.

---

[10] One Hebrew teacher says, "So it's easy to see why lazy translators will translate SHEM as 'name', even where that translation makes no sense at all." Penton, Glenn The Hebrew Word Shem http://beth-abraham.org/shem.html (Last accessed: May 6, 2014)

[11] Benner, Jeff A. Exodus 20:7, http://www.ancient-hebrew.org/40_exodus1.html (Last accessed: May 6, 2014)

February 2

Distorting God's Word to Destroy His Loving Reputation

And the serpent said unto the woman, Ye shall not surely die: For God doth know that in the day ye eat thereof, then your eyes shall be opened, and ye shall be as gods, knowing good and evil (Gen. 3:4-5)

There is no doubt that the serpent being referred to in this passage is *Satan* (Rev. 12:9; 20:2; 2 Cor. 11:3, 13-15). Here Satan falsely accuses God of being insecure, selfish, and a liar. Satan suggested to Eve that God was holding back from her and Adam for selfish reasons. He brought doubts to her mind concerning God's love, goodness, and integrity.

If we allow anything other than God's Word to reveal who He is then Satan will take advantage of us as he has already done to the majority of the church. Satan attacks the Word, especially as it pertains to God's character and reputation. His successful distortion of the truth concerning God's goodness is exactly what brought the downfall of man from the very beginning.

The twisting of God's character starts with twisting His Word. Before Satan was able to deceive Eve through his character assassination, the first couple had no doubts about God's goodness, love and integrity. After Adam and Eve accepted Satan's attack on God's Word, it became easy to lose trust in God's goodness and love. As S. D. Gordon wrote:

> The first thing he did was to raise a doubt about God's love. "Hath God said you shall not eat of any of the trees? What a hard God He is! Lovely trees! Delicious fruit! It was made to be eaten; it will nourish your body. What a cruel God He is! Can't you eat of this fruit? What an awful God you have got!" That is the suggestion, a doubt about God's love.... Satan begat doubt. It was doubt of God's love that was the first born. Doubt of God's love gave birth to doubt of God Himself.[12]

How sad that Satan successfully feeds so many people the same lie today. People rebel against God primarily because they do not really know Him. Knowing God's Word and rejecting anything that contradicts it will help us to know God Himself.

---

[12] Gordon, Samuel D. **Quiet Talks on The Tempter** (New York: Fleming H. Revell, 1910), p.

February 3

Results of Believing Satan's Character Assassination

"And the Lord God called unto Adam, and said unto him, Where art thou? And he said, I heard thy voice in the garden, and I was afraid, because I was naked; and I hid myself" (Gen. 3:9-10)

Notice what happened to the first couple after they acted on Satan's character assassination: *They became afraid of God.* When God called out to Adam and asked him where he was, God receives the sad, heart-breaking response that we find in the above passage.

Adam and Eve were never afraid of God's voice prior to this event. Before this they enjoyed wonderful fellowship with God. After feeding on Satan's character assassination, they became afraid of Him. Satan painted God as a cruel selfish tyrannical person so when He came into the garden to look for Adam, they thought that He was about to bring the hammer down on them for their disobedience.

Adam lost His love for God and His revelation of God's love for him: *"There is no fear in love; but perfect love casteth out fear: because fear hath torment. He that feareth is not made perfect in love"* (1 John 4:18). When we become afraid of the loving God and run away *from* Him instead of running *to* Him it is because we have believed Satan's twist and perversion of God's Word concerning God's reputation and character rather than what God's Word says about these things. We have a children's song that says, "Jesus loves me this I know, for the Bible tells me so." The Bible is God's written revelation to us today. If we doubt the Bible as God's Word then it becomes easier to doubt anything else about God, including His existence.

Sadly, most of humanity believes in God's existence, but very few believe in His love. His Word has been distorted and His reputation has been maligned. If we are to have the intimate, loving relationship with God that He longs to have with us, we must study His Word and learn the truth about Him. Only through this can we dispel the lies of Satan and the sorrows that we encounter as a result of those lies.

February 4

Knowledge of God Destroys Satan's Works in Our Lives

*(For the weapons of our warfare are not carnal, but mighty through God to the pulling down of strong holds;) Casting down imaginations, and every high thing that exalteth itself against **the knowledge of God**, and bringing into captivity every thought to the obedience of Christ* (2 Cor. 10:4-5)

Adam failed to stand on God's Word and as a result plunged mankind under a dominion of death and tyranny. Adam should have taken the Word of God to refute the lies that came into his mind concerning God's nature. This gives us insight into our own failures as well. How often have we accused God of doing things to us that He had nothing to do with?

A correct understanding of God is the only way to know Him and to see His true character (Jer. 9:24). This understanding can only come as we know what God says about Himself in His Word because He places His Word above His own character and reputation. Therefore the only way to destroy the lying tactics of Satan is to have a true knowledge of God.

The New Life Version renders the latter part of verse 2 Cor. 10:4 as, *"Those things God gives to fight with destroy the strong-places of the devil."* The devil places negative ideas in our minds concerning God. However, as we give God's Word first place in our lives, it will bring healing to us in every area, to include our minds (Prov. 4:20-22).

God's Word will destroy the devil in the sense that it will destroy his lying strongholds over our minds. It will cast down every high thing that Satan brings to us *"that exalteth itself **against** the knowledge of God."* Satan brought a "high thing" to Eve that ran in opposition to the knowledge of God. She and her husband then forsook the Word of God and lost sight of the truth about Him. In Hosea, we see that the knowledge of God comes by the agency of His Word (Hosea 4:6).

Adam lost his knowledge of God. He began to see God as unkind and capricious. Adam no longer valued God's Word to him. This caused a separation between Adam and God and he died spiritually that day. This "spiritual death" came because Adam separated himself from the protective life of God (Gen. 2:17; Isa. 59:1-2; Eph. 2:1-6), thus placing himself under Satan's kingdom of evil, darkness and death (Rom. 5:17; Col. 1:12-14; Heb. 2:14-15; 1 John 5:18-19). When we know God we will know Him as loving and not as someone "out to get us" as Adam began to believe.

February 5

The Death of Little Children is NEVER God's Will

Even so it is not the will of your Father which is in heaven,
that one of these little ones should perish (Matt. 18:14)

They all came to the funeral with sadness. However, the attendees knew that they were there to comfort the grieving family and to honor the memory of the little child who had just passed away. He was killed by a drunk driver whose car careened out of control, smashed through the wooden fence, and ran over the child while he was playing safely in the back yard. He suffered intense pain on his way to the hospital. The doctors worked hard to save his life. He went through several hours of surgery but died on the operating table. He was only 3years old.

After gazing at the little child's body sitting in the coffin, the minister looked up at the crowded church and said, "God loved Bobby very much. He needed another little flower in His heavenly garden so He took Bobby." Many of the attendees were not Christians. Some were so stricken with grief that they did not really listen to anything the minister had to say. Their minds were caught up in their own thoughts.

Some there who were believers in Christ gave a sad amen to the minister's words, affirming their belief in them and taking comfort from them. Many unstable Christians began to question whether this God that they were serving was any better than the devil. Others who were not Christians began to hate God and religion. They wondered what kind of God could be so selfish as to send a drunk driver to kill an innocent little child and bring such terrible grief to parents who attended church three times a week, volunteered at homeless shelters and gave much of their time and resources to helping the poor.

In Matthew 18, Jesus had just admonished the crowd concerning His love for little children. He made several statements that clearly expressed His anger towards anyone that would do anything to harm children. Yet, in our day when someone does something that harms children, be it molestation, murder, or any other kind of abuse, ministers have taught that these things happened in accordance with God's mysterious will. Jesus repudiates such a ridiculous notion when He says that it is not the Father's will that any child should be destroyed. The pain and death of a child is never God's will. He grieves along with the family who lost their child. Let us be careful not to blame God for the results of sinful actions such as drunk driving, stray bullets, abuse, or pedophilia.

February 6

Jesus and the Father have the Same Purpose in Mind

I and my Father are one. Then the Jews took up stones again to stone him. Jesus answered them, Many good works have I shewed you from my Father; for which of those works do ye stone me? (John 10:30-32)

What kind of "works" did Jesus do? He healed the sick, raised the dead, casted out devils, fed the hungry, gave money to the poor, lifted heavy burdens, and presented the good news about a loving Father who was ready to receive sinners and set them free from their sins. Eventually Jesus would do the ultimate work of taking man's sin upon Himself and dying on the cross on our behalf. All of these works Jesus described as "good".

The religious leaders did not deny that Jesus did good works. However, they were ready to stone Him for making Himself equal with God when He said that He and the Father are ONE. The Jewish leaders were so blinded by religious hatred that they failed to see what a wonderful truth Jesus just related to them.

If Jesus and the Father are *one* and Jesus is equal to God, then this means that God is all about doing *good* works and undoing the bad works of the devil (Acts 10:38; 1 John 3:8). By doing these good works and then stating that He and God are one, Jesus was conveying the fact that God Himself desires to heal, to deliver, to set men free from their burdens and to have a renewed and restored relationship with sinful man. By saying that He and the Father are one, Jesus was saying, "God is just like me."

However, the religious leaders hated Jesus because He stepped on their Satan-inspired traditions and doctrines. These traditions and doctrines burdened and oppressed the people. The leaders taught that the sickness and demonism that many of them suffered was the result of either personal sin (even in the womb) or the sins of their parents (see John 9:1-4).

To have a God who, rather than distributing divine retribution for infractions against the Jew's burdensome additions to God's liberating laws (James 1:25), but instead sets men free from the results of sin, was going against all that the Jewish leaders taught in order to hold their grip on the people.

Things have not changed much, if at all, since the time of Jesus. Ministers still present to us a stern deity ready to strike at the slightest infraction. Sometimes this stern deity strikes for arbitrary reasons that are mysterious and meant for His own glory. Does such a deity sound like Jesus to you? If we are given any picture of God that does not look like Jesus then this is a false picture. The Father and Jesus are one and are represented as doing only good works.

February 7

Jesus and the Father are Exactly Alike

If ye had known me, ye should have known my Father also: and from henceforth ye know him, and have seen him (John 14:7)

People seem to have ideas about "God" and Jesus that contradict one another. Some look at God (primarily the Person of the Trinity that Jesus reveals to us as "the Father") as a harsh vindictive deity who is ready to pour out His wrath and judgment at the slightest breach of His law. These same people see Jesus as the One who is kind and forgiving and ready to extend mercy no matter how large our failure may be.

These ideas come from an incorrect understanding of how God is portrayed in the Old Testament. We hope to correct these misunderstandings in this daily devotional as well as in our other teaching materials. Nonetheless, Jesus came to show us that the Father is exactly like Him. He said that to know Him is to know the Father as well.

If we think of Jesus as kind, gentle, merciful, compassionate, self-sacrificing, and willing to forgive even major sins then we certainly have an accurate picture of Jesus but we have just described the Father as well. Jesus said that to know Him is to know the Father. Therefore, everything that Jesus is, the Father is likewise.

There is no need to look at the Father as the wrathful vengeful deity that Jesus came to rescue us from. On the contrary, it was the Father who sent Jesus to rescue us from our sins and the bondage that they put us under. He sent Jesus to rescue us from the consequences of our own rebellion.

The Father sent Jesus because the Father Himself is kind, compassionate, gentle, self-sacrificing, and very forgiving. If the Father was not like Jesus then He would never have sent Jesus in the first place. Jesus would have had to come of His own accord which then would have been independent of the Father. This is something Jesus never could have done. Jesus did only what the Father told Him to do.

Therefore every display of compassion, love, mercy, forgiviness and even the sacrifice that Jesus made to the death was Jesus showing exactly what the Father is like. The Father is just like Jesus. Therefore, to know Jesus is to know the Father.

February 8

Jesus has shown us the Father

Philip saith unto him, Lord, show us the Father, and it sufficeth us. Jesus saith unto him, Have I been so long time with you, and yet hast thou not known me, Philip? he that hath seen me hath seen the Father; and how sayest thou then, Show us the Father? (John 14:8-9)

All of us have experienced the frustration and disappointment of sharing an important truth only to discover that the people that we have been sharing with have difficulty grasping it. One can easily detect the disappointment in our Lord's words in response to Phillip's request to "show us the Father."

Jesus' disappointment with Philip is due to the fact that there was an obvious misconception about the Father. The misconception was that He was totally different than Jesus. For the disciples to have given up their livelihoods and their way of living to travel and minister with Jesus means that they saw something about Him that they did not want to lose. They saw Jesus as someone they were willing to spend the rest of eternity with.

Who wants to spend their life with an uncompassionate tyrant? Who wants to be a mistreated and unloved slave for even a day, let alone an eternity? Yet these disciples were mourning the fact that Jesus was about to be taken from them in order to make the ultimate sacrifice for the redemption of all mankind. They loved being around Him.

However, to be asked to be shown the Father meant that they did not see Him in the same way that they saw Jesus. They obviously did not see the love of the Father though they saw the love of the Son. They did not see the longing of the Father to have them close to Him though they saw it in Jesus. However, Jesus wanted them to understand that the same love that He had for the disciples was the same love that the Father had. Jesus was a mirror reflection of the Father in every detail.

The Father is deeply in love with His creatures. He was making a very big sacrifice by giving up His only begotten Son to die on behalf of a sinful rebellious people. He was sacrificing the best He had—a part of Himself. This is a magnitude of love that is difficult for the selfish carnal mind to comprehend. Therefore, when you need to be shown the Father, just look at the life and acts of Jesus.

February 9

The Father Working through Jesus

Believest thou not that I am in the Father, and the Father in me? the words that I speak unto you I speak not of myself: but the Father that dwelleth in me, he doeth the works. Believe me that I am in the Father, and the Father in me: or else believe me for the very works' sake. (John 14:10-11)

It has been said that if the Father had come to earth as a man instead of Jesus then the history that we read about Jesus in the gospels would have been no different. Jesus did nothing different than what the Father would have done. On the contrary, the Father was doing the works of healing, deliverance, and provision through Jesus. Every act of compassion, every act of mercy, and every act of love was the Father working through Jesus.

When accused of casting out demons by partnering with Satan, Jesus said, *"But if I **with the finger of God** cast out devils, no doubt the kingdom of God is come upon you"* (Luke 11:20). Here we see that it was the Father working through Christ (by the power of the Holy Spirit) to deliver people from Satan's kingdom. Jesus said that God's kingdom—His sovereign reign—was demonstrated through Christ casting out devils.

Peter would later say that Jesus healed all that were oppressed of the devil because "God was with him" (Acts 10:38). The Father Himself , working through Jesus dealt with the sicknesses and bondages that Satan placed on men and women. This is a vitally important truth. God has been blamed for centuries for the devil's work. Some almost seem to think that Jesus came to do battle with God's kingdom rather than Satan's.

Jesus went out of His way to vindicate the Father. All of His miraculous works were done from a sense of intense love and compassion for those who were under Satan's tyranny. His intense love for man was demonstrated by an intense hatred for the evil Satan brought upon man. Whenever the religious leaders, those who gave a picture of a harsh deity that delighted in burdening people, questioned the source of His miracles, Jesus used the opportunity to point out that the Father is the One working through Him.

If people were paying attention and watching Jesus' life as they should have then they would have seen exactly how the Father Himself works. They would have understood the character of the true God because He worked through Jesus. The Father's character is no different than Jesus' because He was the One working through Jesus.

February 10

Satan Blinds People to the Truth about God

*In whom the god of this world hath blinded the minds of
them which believe not, lest the light of the glorious gospel
of Christ, who is the image of God, should shine unto them*
(2 Cor. 4:4)

Other translations can help us to understand what Paul is really
telling us about Jesus: *"Christ is the one who is **exactly like God**"* (Easy to
Read Version); *"They cannot see the light, which is the good news about
our glorious Christ, **who shows what God is like**"* (Contemporary English
Version); *"They cannot see how bright and wonderful Christ is. **He is just
like God himself**"* (World English New Testament).

For the past several days we have said that to see Jesus is to see
God. The Father and Son (and the Holy Spirit) are no different from one
another. All of the kindness, gentleness, caring, and compassion that we
find displayed in Jesus throughout the gospels is a projection of exactly
what God is like. Jesus is just like God because He is God.

This is the truth that Satan has been blinding men to for centuries.
Read the histories of the Roman Catholics and the crusades with all of the
rape, murder, and brutality. You get a picture of someone who is nothing
like Jesus. On the contrary, they were more like the devil. The devil did his
dirty work through this so-called "church" and blamed it on God.

Look at John Calvin's Geneva. Calvin ran his city like a dictator.
People were banished, persecuted, and even executed for opposing him. He
presented a picture of a harsh deity that inflicted accidents, sickness and
pain simply because He was "sovereign" and had the right to do so.

The Roman Catholics and many of the Reformers failed to look to
Jesus to teach their doctrine of God. They looked to mystics and secular
philosophers and drew from them ideas about God. They then took
passages of Scripture out of context in order to claim that their idea of God
was a Biblically accurate one.

Sadly, so many people have eaten the poison fruit of these
teachings and have gotten sick of God. Many of the atheists today rail
against a deity that is nothing like Jesus. Some atheists are quick to
acknowledge what a good man Jesus was (though they question His deity).
They have been blinded by Satan but the fault partially lies with God's own
people. We have failed to show people that God is exactly like Jesus. In our
sharing the gospel we need to give the unsaved this light. Knowing that
God is just like Jesus is the "gospel" or the good news that will work
towards helping them see the truth.

February 11

What does it mean for Jesus to be "The Word of God"?

In the beginning was the Word, and the Word was with God, and the Word was God. The same was in the beginning with God (John 1:1-2)

I have often been perplexed by this passage. I always thought of a "word" as something spoken or written. I have never had any difficulty in understanding the Bible as the Word of God but could not understand how the second person of the Trinity could be the "Word of God." After all, Jesus is a *person*.

I have read some very strange explanations of John 1:1-2. Some of them bordered on teaching that Jesus is a created being or that He was somehow "birthed" through the Father's spoken word, thus giving Him a beginning. To accept these teachings would be to reject Christ's deity, which we refuse to do. Jesus is very much God with no beginning just like the Father.

So what does it mean for Jesus to be "the Word"? When I understood that "Word" also means "message" then I began to understand it more. When I gained further understanding about the fact that Jesus came with the purpose of showing us what the Father is *really* like then the lights came on. Jesus is God's message to the world telling us the kind of person that God truly is. The writer of Hebrews expounds upon this very truth:

*In the past God spoke to our people through the prophets. He spoke to them many times and in many different ways. And now in these last days, **God has spoken to us again through his Son**. He made the whole world through his Son. And he has chosen his Son to have all things. The Son shows the glory of God. **He is a perfect copy of God's nature**, and he holds everything together by his powerful command. The Son made people clean from their sins. Then he sat down at the right side[a] of God, the Great One in heaven* (Heb. 1:1-3; Easy to Read Version)

Because Jesus is just as much God as the Father, and because He and the Father are exactly alike, then Jesus is the perfect message, the precise Word that God wants the world to hear. If you, like many Christians and non-Christians, think that Jesus was a wonderful person, then the message for you as that God is indeed wonderful. He is nothing like what Satan has claimed about Him (2 Cor. 4:4).

February 12

Only Jesus can Show us what the Father is Like

The Word became a man and lived among us. We saw his divine greatness—the greatness that belongs to the only Son of the Father. The Word was full of grace and truth.... No one has ever seen God. **The only Son is the one who has shown us what God is like.** *He is himself God and is very close to the Father* (John 1:14, 18; Easy to Read Version)

Yesterday we learned what it meant for Jesus to be called "the Word of God". We learned that this does not mean that Jesus was birthed by a spoken Word from God as some teach. This would make Jesus a *created* being. This is impossible since Jesus is the Creator of *all* things (John 1:1-3; Eph. 3:9; Col. 1:16-17; Rev. 4:11). "Word" is synonymous with "message". God sent Jesus to us as a message from Himself to show us what He is like.

How did God send this message? He did this by having the second member of the Triune Godhead come to earth as a man. This was the way to make the message more effective. John wrote that no one had ever seen God. He was not speaking from a *physical* standpoint. John was talking about the fact that men did not know what God was truly like. They did not know His character or the fullness of His love for man.

Men had been given many truths concerning God throughout the Old Testament and were given glimpses of His love. However, they had no real idea of what He is really like because they had no living example walking among them. Many of God's best representatives during the Old Testament times had too many flaws that reflected poorly on the One they were supposed to represent. Therefore, men still had not fully seen God through them.

Due to His immense love for man, God sent the One who knew Him best—the One who has been with Him throughout all of eternity. He sent the One who is exactly like Him in every fashion. He sent us someone who could represent Him perfectly.

Take note that Jesus was full of "grace and truth". Another word for "grace" is "loving-kindness". God sent Jesus to show us a God who was full of loving-kindness. This is the truth about Him that has been distorted throughout the centuries by satanic blindness. God wanted us to see that He is not that mean ogre in the sky waiting to destroy at the slightest push, but a God who is gracious, loving, kind, and longing for relationship with man.

February 13

Murderers do not know the Father or Jesus

These things have I spoken unto you, that ye should not be offended. They shall put you out of the synagogues: yea, the time cometh, that whosoever killeth you will think that he doeth God service. And these things will they do unto you, because they have not known the Father, nor me (John 16:1-3)

There is a well-established, but very seldom taught spiritual principle in which we become exactly what we worship (Psalm 115:1-8; 135:15-18; Matt. 5:43-48; Luke 6:35-36; Rom. 12:1-2; 2 Cor. 3:18; Eph. 5:1-2). In other words, we take on the characteristics of the object of our worship.

Have you ever seen those who are obsessed with a particular pop star, famous actress or some other public figure? They begin to talk like them, walk like them, wear their hair like theirs and dress as the object of their worship dresses. They know every lyric to their songs, every line they spoke in a movie, or have memorized the speeches of their favorite public figure and will quote them as many true Christians quote the Bible. They will purchase all products related to the famous object of their affection and buy every magazine that features them. They have become like their idol.

This holds true also for murderers and persecutors. Jesus said that when they persecute and kill God's people they believe that they are actually serving and worshipping God. However, Jesus says that they do this because they do not even know the Father or the Son. This obviously means that they have a distorted concept of God that has nothing to do with what God is really like.

Those who are willing to persecute and kill others in the name of God have not looked at how God is represented through Jesus Christ. They have accepted a warped understanding of what God is like by the false information that Satan has given them. God is not a hater, persecutor, or murderer. God is for peace and saving lives. These are some of the major differences between God and the devil (John 10:10).

Be it Muslims who strap bombs on themselves and kill for Allah or "Christians" who put people to death for "heresy" or for "witchcraft", the character of God is not reflected in them because God is totally unlike them. When we know God and we know Jesus, we will live to help others, even those we may strongly disagree with, rather than persecuting and killing them in the name of God. Killing is a disservice to God.

February 14

To Know Jesus is to know the Father

Then said they unto him, Where is thy Father? Jesus answered, Ye neither know me, nor my Father: if ye had known me, ye should have known my Father also (John 8:19)

The fact that the religious leaders during our Lord's time would ask such a question proved that they did not know God. They had seen Jesus perform miracles that relieved men and women of oppressing sickness and pain. They had seen Jesus offer forgiveness to those burdened by sin's tyranny. Instead of rejoicing and seeing the hand of God in these things, the Pharisees became angry and sought to kill the Lord (John 8:40).

As a matter of fact, these religious zealots accused Jesus of operating by the power of Satan. They claimed that He casted out demons by the authority of the prince of demons (Matt. 9:34; 12:24). They accused Him of being demon possessed when He gave them God's Word (John 7:20; 8:48-49; 10:20). Here are men who had studied the Scriptures and should have known better, but they were willfully blinded by satanically inspired traditions. They preferred their religion rather than the *truth*.

Very little has changed in our own day. Many ministers are telling us that God ceased working miracles after a certain period of time. They claim that this happened either after the last of the original apostles died (because it is falsely alleged that only the original apostles worked miracles) or after the canon of Scripture (the Bible) was complete which meant that God no longer had a need for the use of miracles to reach people. This is known in theological circles as the doctrine of *cessationism*.

The byproduct of this blatant lie is that when God decides to move in miracles of healing, deliverance, prophecy and other supernatural manifestations, those who embrace cessationist ideology accuse these ministers that God is working through of being used by Satan. They claim that those who receive the baptism with the Holy Spirit with tongues as evidence are manifesting a demon. These ministers have gone on a campaign of persecution through their books and radio programs.

Some may disagree with me but I fully believe, based on the Biblical evidence, that those who would say such things really do not know Jesus. Therefore they do not know the Father. To believe that God no longer works in miraculous power to relieve men of satanic burdens, and to persecute those who do believe it of serving the devil is proof that they do not know God. To know Jesus is to know the Father and to know that they are not *persecutors* but *deliverers* from oppression (Acts 10:38).

February 15

The Murderous Spirit of Satan

Ye are of your father the devil, and the lusts of your father
ye will do. He was a murderer from the beginning, and
abode not in the truth, because there is no truth in him.
When he speaketh a lie, he speaketh of his own: for he is a
liar, and the father of it (John 8:44)

Jesus said this to the religious leaders who were anxious to kill Him
for nothing more than jealousy (John 8:40-41). Jesus had upset their
religion which was full of stringent man-made laws that were supposed to
keep the wrath of God at bay. One can see from the attitude of these leaders
that God's command to "love your neighbor as yourself" and "not to
murder" only applied under circumstances that they were free to determine
within their own traditions.

These leaders deceived themselves into believing that they were
serving God. Jesus set the record straight when He told them that they were
really serving the devil. The devil was a *murderer* from the beginning and
these religious leaders had taken on his very characteristics. Jesus was
declaring to them and anyone who would listen that God is nothing like
this.

Even in our day we have men who occupy church pulpits and tell
us that God sends sickness, disease, earthquakes, tsunamis, hurricanes,
typhoons, terrorist attacks, accidents, poverty and a multitude of other
negative things. They, in essence, teach that God is a murderer. I believe
that it was the great Methodist evangelist, John Wesley, who told a
Calvinist preacher, "Your God is my devil."

Jesus has done everything possible to help us distinguish between
the works of God and the devil. Jesus never went around killing and
murdering. He went about saving lives and rescuing people from death.
Jesus never taught His followers to kill in His Name. Instead, He told them
to heal, deliver, and receive protection in His Name (Mark 16:15-20).

If you believe that God is a tyrannical despot bent on the
destruction of others then it is very easy to take on a similar personality.
We become like the object of our worship. That is what happened to the
Pharisees. They were murderers because they saw God as one. However,
they were actually worshipping the "god of this world" (2 Cor. 4:4).

Believe that God is a God of love and you will take on His
character. Believe that He hates and kills and you may not have a problem
doing so either. But remember that when you do, you become like the
"father" you are connected to.

February 16

The Reason for Old Testament "Holy Wars" (Part 1)

The kings came and fought, then fought the kings of Canaan in Taanach by the waters of Megiddo; they took no gain of money. They fought from heaven; **the stars in their courses fought against Sisera** (Judges 5:19-20)

Many people are troubled by the numerous references to war in the Old Testament. Some are most troubled by the fact that God even commanded the Israelites to fight. Atheists use the Old Testament Biblical "holy wars" to paint a false picture of a cruel deity that they can hate and excuse themselves from worshipping. However, many sincere Christians are also troubled by all of the physical violence in the Old Testament. They have a difficult time reconciling this with the picture of God given to us by our Lord and Savior, Jesus the Messiah, in the New Testament.

Many things that trouble God's people can be resolved when they understand that there is an ongoing spiritual battle in the Heavenlies that has spilled over into our world (2 Kings 6:15-17; Eph. 6:10-13). The "stars" that Deborah is singing about is referring to angelic beings both good and evil (Job 38:7; Rev. 1:16, 20; 12:3-4, 7-9).

When the king of Assyria threatened Israel and blasphemed God, King Hezekiah and the prophet Isaiah cried out to God. God sent an angel to deal with the situation (2 Chron. 32:20-22; Isa. 37:33-36). We see from this that a *physical* problem was dealt with through *spiritual* means, which proves that the root of the problem in the first place is spiritual.

During the time in which the Old Testament was written, many things were resolved by physical warfare. However, much of the warfare we find in the Old Testament is symbolic of the ongoing war between satanic forces of evil and God's forces of good. It was Satan who was behind the evil kings in the Old Testament that threatened Israel (Job 1:12, 14, 15; Isa. 14:4-17; Eze. 28:12-19; Luke 4:5-8; John 8:44; 12:31; 14:30; 16:11; 2 Cor. 4:4; 1 John 5:18-19; Rev. 20:1-8).

Satan is the one who deceives nations (Rev. 20:3, 8). It was Satan who often sought to destroy Israel since it was through this nation that the Messiah would come to render him his ultimate defeat and free the rest of the world that is under his control. Even today Satan is behind the Islamic terrorist attacks and wars in the Middle East.

Just like Biblical times, these battles are not simply just a bunch of angry nations that can't get along. Diplomacy will not work against demons. Whether we like it or not, we are involved in this war. We must keep our armor on and use it (Eph. 6:10-18).

February 17

The Reason for Old Testament "Holy Wars" (Part 2)

"They sacrificed unto devils, not to God; to gods whom they knew not, to new gods that came newly up, whom your fathers feared not" (Deut. 32:17)

Moses exposed the fact that the gods of the other nations were satanic beings when he wrote the passage above (see also Lev. 17:7; 2 Chron. 11:15; Psalm 106:35-38; 1 Cor. 10:20-21; Rev. 9:20). The people during this time were not as ignorant of spiritual realities as many of us might be led to believe. Many recent studies concerning historical documents from the Ancient Near East have taught us that the nations during those times strongly believed in a spiritual warfare scenario in which the victory over evil was determined in the spirit realm.

A thorough study of both the Ancient Near East texts and the Bible itself tells us that the kings during these times were commanded by their "god" to go to war against certain nations. They relied heavily upon their deity to help them win these wars. These kings were the human or earthly representation of their nation's deity.

These "gods" instigated wars against Israel and each other because Satan is the true source and originator of violence (Ezekiel 28:14-16; John 8:44). It is Satan that moves men to kill each other and he is the one behind the nations that oppressed Israel during Old Testament times. While God abhors violence He is not a wimpy God that can just let violent beings go about their merry way destroying things. God wars to protect and defend the subjects of His Kingdom. But He does not do this alone. He enlists our help.

When the Israelites served God then they had protection and peace because God kept the forces at bay that Satan controlled. When the Israelites backslid and began to worship the gods of the other nations, not realizing that by doing this that they were worshipping Satan and fallen angels, God allowed them to have their way (2 Chron. 16:8-9; Psalm 81:10-16).

While most of us do not engage in the type of fighting that Israel had to do, we must learn from the Old Testament how warfare in the spirit realm is conducted. I am sure that this will not resolve all of our troubled tensions with Old Testament holy war, but it will lessen these tensions by a great degree if we begin to see that these were not only physical wars but a "spill over" from the cosmic warfare taking place in the heavenly realms between God's forces and those of Satan.

February 18

Why did God Command the Destruction of Nations?

They did not destroy the nations, concerning whom the LORD commanded them: But were mingled among the heathen, and learned their works. And they served their idols: which were a snare unto them. ***Yea, they sacrificed their sons and their daughters unto devils,*** *And shed innocent blood, even the blood of their sons and of their daughters, whom they sacrificed unto the idols of Canaan: and the land was polluted with blood. Thus were they defiled with their own works, and went a whoring with their own inventions.* (Psalm 106:34-39)

Many atheists and others opposed to Christianity often cite Old Testament "holy wars" as an example of why they could never serve the God of the Bible. They feel that God often sent Israel on missions to kill, plunder, and destroy for no valid or justifiable reason. Sadly, God's commands to invade and destroy nations have even perplexed genuine Christians, thus moving them to reject the Old Testament as being a relevant document for God's people today.

Very few atheists are willing to take the time to understand the true reasons behind God's actions in the Old Testament. But for the born again Christian, it is the wrong attitude to reject any portion of God's Word. The New Testament itself teaches us that the Old Testament is for doctrine, correction, and encouragement (2 Tim. 3:16; 1 Cor. 10:6; Rom. 15:4)

Several questions are answered in this psalm concerning why God commanded these nations to be destroyed. One of them has to do with the unseen spiritual warfare that we are all involved in. These nations were serving the devil without repentance and spreading their demonic religion to other nations. Their religion caused such depravity that innocent people were killed, including some of the very children of these worshippers of demons.

God had given them centuries to repent (Gen. 15:13-16). Yet they chose to continue in the worship of demons and to destroy the lives of others. God could not allow these nations to continue and completely pollute the earth. This would make Him unjust. Therefore He made Israel His instrument of judgment. Sadly, Israel failed to fully obey and became defiled by the very sin they were supposed to rid the land from.

Today, God may be calling you to rid yourself of some sin in your life before it takes you over, thus destroying your life and your family. Seek God's help in removing sin from your life before Satan is able to hold you in complete bondage to whatever it is.

February 19

God's Mercy Extended to the Nations

And he said unto Abram, Know of a surety that thy seed shall be a stranger in a land that is not theirs, and shall serve them; and they shall afflict them four hundred years; And also that nation, whom they shall serve, will I judge: and afterward shall they come out with great substance. And thou shalt go to thy fathers in peace; thou shalt be buried in a good old age. But in the fourth generation they shall come hither again: for the iniquity of the Amorites is not yet full (Gen. 15:13-16)

When God told Him His plans concerning Sodom and Gomorrah, a despondent Abraham, concerned about his nephew Lot, responded:

That be far from thee to do after this manner, to slay the righteous with the wicked: and that the righteous should be as the wicked, that be far from thee: Shall not the Judge of all the earth do right? (Gen. 18:25)

God is indeed the judge of all the earth and He will do right. Abraham's problem was not that God would destroy the wicked, but that the righteous would unfairly suffer as well. Today when modern Westerners read about the Israelite conquest of the surrounding nations and the fact that this was all commanded by God, they seem to believe that God was a bloodthirsty tyrant who did wrong by a bunch of nations minding their own business. This simply is not the case. God was not about to destroy a nation full of righteous people.

The surrounding nations were exceedingly wicked. However, the judge of all the earth extended mercy—*four hundred years* of mercy! But sooner or later the wickedness would become full and affect other parts of the earth. This was Satan's plan for world domination.

God extended mercy in order to give them a chance to come into the true knowledge of God. They had Abraham, Melchizedek, and others who proclaimed the true God to them. There was no reason to remain steeped in satanic worship and all of the selfish destruction of their fellow men that came with it. If God did not eventually judge their wickedness then the judge of all the earth would have done wrong.

God is indeed a judge, but a very merciful One. He gave these nations more than enough time to repent. They got worse. God was left with no choice but to judge them. Israel would be His instrument.

February 20

Satanically Influenced Nations

Ye shall therefore keep my statutes and my judgments, and shall not commit any of these abominations; neither any of your own nation, nor any stranger that sojourneth among you: (For all these abominations have the men of the land done, which were before you, and the land is defiled;) (Lev. 18:26-27)

Read through Leviticus 18 and take note of the sins being committed by the nations that God was going to dispossess. It was not only the blatant worship of false gods that posed a problem but the horrendous acts that they led to. There were sexual perversions such as incest, bestiality, and homosexuality. People in our generation have made these perversions acceptable practices for the majority of the world and therefore look upon God as being too stringent in condemning them. However, these practices lead to outbreaks of all kinds of diseases and other epidemics.

Even more, there was the devaluation of human dignity and human life. Children were sacrificed in torturous ways in order to appease their local deities. Even those in our day who don't seem to have any difficulty with the legal slaughter of innocent unborn children might balk at roasting an infant alive in a fire. Nonetheless, if these nations were to continue to exist it would only be a matter of a few centuries that these acts could bring destruction to all of mankind. This is exactly what Satan has been planning in His war against God and humanity.

Sadly people don't get it and reject these Old Testament truths and the necessity for these "holy wars." Modern day people have been desensitized to the horror of sin and its results. Liberal ideology proclaims the false idea that what one person does for pleasure has no effect on others or on society as a whole. This has impacted how we view God's standards and His methods for dealing with them. Furthermore, pacifist ideas have crept into much of our thinking about God in which we could never see Him using violent means for handling a situation (due to false interpretations of Jesus' explanations of God's laws).

However, God tells the Israelites that the very land was defiled due to these sins. Like any plague, if God were to allow it to spread it could only mean the destruction of the earth as a whole. It was incumbent upon God as the judge of all the earth to deal with the spread of sin in the world.

However, there is a practical lesson for us as well. Are we allowing sin to dwell in our hearts? If we are we must deal with it and ask God to remove it before it completely defiles us and we are destroyed by it.

February 21

God's Original Nonviolent Plan for the Heathen Nations

I will send my fear before thee, and will destroy all the people to whom thou shalt come, and I will make all thine enemies turn their backs unto thee. And I will send hornets before thee, which shall drive out the Hivite, the Canaanite, and the Hittite, from before thee (Exodus 23:27-28)

While we do not accept extreme pacifist ideas, we should recognize that God is a warrior by necessity and not by desire. God is at war because Satan and his followers have declared war on God and mankind. God is at war on our behalf. Though God is not a "pacifist," He does abhor violence and killing. He does all that He is able to do to prevent it. A statement that God once made to King David tells us that He does not like His reputation associated with blatant bloodshed (1 Kings 5:3; 1 Chron. 28:2-3).

In His initial plan concerning the Israelites possessing the land, God appeared to have introduced a method by which there would have been no fighting or bloodshed on Israel's part. He would have simply sent fear and hornets to drive the inhabitants out of the land and allow Israel to take possession (Joshua 2:9-11; 6:1).

Man's actions have a tendency to change God's plans and methods. For example, God never originally wanted to send spies into the land of Canaan. He wanted the people to trust His Word. But the Israelites asked for it to be done (Deut. 1:22-25), so God gave in to their request and commanded that it be done (Num. 13:1-3).

The sad results of this particular act changed another one of God's plans. Ten of the twelve spies came back with an evil report (a report of unbelief that contradicted God's promises). The people believed it, cried all night, and then threatened to kill Aaron and Moses. Whereas God was going to send them into the land immediately, He now changed the plan to wait forty years for the first generation of unbelieving Israelites to die off.

So what brought the change to where God commanded *Israel* to fight instead of Him sending hornets to drive away the inhabitants of the land? Scripture never seems to say. Whatever the reason for the change of plans, the evidence from the passages cited above would indicate that it probably had something to do with Israel's behavior.

As Christians, we should remember that the weapons of our warfare are not carnal, but mighty through God for dealing with spiritual enemies (2 Cor. 10:4-5; Eph. 6:10-18). God's preferred way for us to solve our problems is to let Him fight for us.

February 22

Did God order the Slaughter of Women and Children? (Part 1)

*But of the cities of these people, which the Lord thy God doth give thee for an inheritance, thou shalt **save alive nothing that breatheth** ....That they teach you not to do after all their abominations, which they have done unto their gods; so should ye sin against the Lord your God* (Deut. 20:16, 18).

One of the most difficult things to understand is God's command to kill women and children during war (Deuteronomy 2:34; 3:6; Joshua 6:21; 8:25; 1 Sam. 15:3). Some explanations such as "God is sovereign so He can do as He pleases," or "God's standard of holiness is higher than ours" may be true but they do not solve the problem.

A sovereign God who also claims to be love would not have such a difficult command recorded in the Bible without a reasonable explanation. God does not dismiss sincere seekers with an attitude that says, "I am the boss so I do whatever I want. How dare you question me?"

Keep in mind that these nations were completely demonized. The demonic infection effected every single being and object to include men, women, children, beast, and property. Jesus had not yet come and defeated Satan so the Israelite could not engage in deliverance ministry. Failure to utterly destroy everything associated with these nations and their demons would open a door for Satan to bring the same infection to Israel, which is proven to be true time and time again throughout their nation's history.

Israel had no defense against demonic power at that time apart from destroying the people and objects in which the demons dwelt. Sadly, this not only included adult men and women, but beasts, babies and inanimate objects as well (Joshua 7:1-26).

After Jesus conquered Satan in the wilderness He returned in the power of the Spirit and brought deliverance to the captives held by Satan's power (Matt. 4:23-24; Luke 4:1-18). Rather than having to command the slaughter of Canaanite children, Jesus was able to *legally* deliver them from the demonic forces that manifested through them (Matt. 15:21-28).

God's people have been commissioned to bring supernatural healing and deliverance to those who have been bound by the false gods of heathen nations (Mark 16:15-20). God's people in the Old Testament only had one option to stay free from demonic principalities which was to slaughter its hosts. Today, because of Christ's work through His death, burial and resurrection, we have the authority to deal with the demons themselves (Luke 10:17-20).

February 23

Did God order the Slaughter of Women and Children? (Part 2)

Now go and smite Amalek, and utterly destroy all that they have, and spare them not; but slay both man and woman, infant and suckling, ox and sheep, camel and ass (1 Sam. 15:3)

We may have difficulty understanding this from our modern day western minds, but the killing of the women and children along with everything else was an act of practical wisdom on God's part. If Israel had left the children alive they would have been orphans. Without parents around to care for them they would have died slower and more painfully agonizing deaths. This was much more cruel than slaughtering them.

To avoid leaving the infants as uncared for orphans or placing future enemies within their own households, Israel would have to leave the mothers alive if they kept the children alive. The mothers would still have taught them to worship the gods of their nations and the children would have grown up manifesting the same demonic practices. Eventually they would have infected Israel.

If the Israelites had taken the children and raised them, sooner or later the children would have found out their true heritage. They would have learned how the Israelite family that adopted them were the ones who killed their parents and destroyed their country. They would have sought vengeance. Vengeance would have led to them reforming their nation and reviving its demonic practices.

We must realize that those babies have a tendency to grow up and become a problem. For example, nearly forty years after Saul failed to "utterly destroy" the Amalekites as God had commanded Him in the passage above, one of those children contributed to his death:

And David said unto the young man that told him, Whence art thou? And he answered, I am the son of a stranger, an Amalekite. And David said unto him, How wast thou not afraid to stretch forth thine hand to destroy the Lord's anointed? (2 Samuel 1:13-14)

I believe that this offers a reasonable and Biblical explanation for why God had to command this slaughter. Today there is no need to do such a thing because we can bring healing and deliverance to those in demonized cultures as we share with them the gospel of Jesus Christ.

February 24

An Accurate Description of God

Love suffers long and is kind; love does not envy; love does not parade itself, is not puffed up; does not behave rudely, does not seek its own, is not provoked, thinks no evil; does not rejoice in iniquity, but rejoices in the truth; bears all things, believes all things, hopes all things, endures all things (1 Cor. 13:4-7; New King James Version)

Since John said that "God is love" (1 John 4:16) then we can say on good authority that the description of love in the passage above describes God fully. God is everything that love is. God is patient and kind. God is not proud, rude, and selfish and He is not easily angered. He does not dwell on evil nor does He take any joy in anyone's sin or the consequences that result from it.

This is the exact opposite of some pictures that are given to us about God from both past and present day theologians. Some portray God as ready to punish and destroy with the first offense. We have been made to believe that God is very rude and shows little kindness. He seems to have no time for our thoughts and won't even listen. As a matter of fact He may slam the door right in front of us because He can't stand the sight of us.

The "rude" God that we are sometimes told about does not care anything about what we want but will force His arbitrary will upon us. He will save the elect and they have no say so in the matter. He will punish and destroy those He has sovereignly decreed will be reprobate and He has not given them a choice as to whether or not they even want to be reprobate. He will force His will on us through accidents, sickness, hardships and other matters. Even more, some theological traditions present God as very proud. He forces His will on us for His own glory and is not concerned about those He considers to be insignificant worms.

Thankfully, this is a false deity built from philosophical pontifications rather than the One described by John and Paul. The God of the Bible is more concerned about others than He is about Himself. He is patient and is willing to suffer for years until we straighten ourselves out. He is kind and self-sacrificing. The God described in Scripture loves the sight of us and really cares about what we want. He is willing to listen intently and keeps an open door policy.

The God of the Bible is a God of love. He is deeply in love with humanity. He is the God described by Paul. He is the God that most of us really want.

February 25

What "Kind" of God do You Serve?

But love ye your enemies, and do good, and lend, hoping for nothing again; and your reward shall be great, and ye shall be the children of the Highest: <u>for he is kind</u> unto the unthankful and to the evil. (Luke 6:35)

The majority of Christians do not have a problem with God being "kind". They believe that He is kind to those who *deserve* His kindness. We expect Him to be kind to those who serve Him, those who worship Him, those who go out of their way for others, and those who give of their resources for the cause of Christ. Yet look at who Jesus says that God is kind to: God is kind to the *unthankful* and the *evil*.

God is kind to the very people that are far from deserving it. This is the kind of God that we have—one of overwhelming love and kindness who desires the salvation of all. This is the kind of God that has been hidden from us, though hidden in plain sight since Jesus has revealed Him. This is also the kind of God that we are not only to stand in awe of and admire, but to emulate.

God does not have one standard for Himself and another for His people. He actually tells us to model ourselves after Him. So why do we meet so many *mean* "Christians"? The Bible teaches us that the image of God we most hold on to is the one that we become (2 Cor. 3:18). Many church-goers have an image of a cruel, vengeful God who predestines people to hell, is the cause of accidents, inflicts people with sickness and disaster, withholds answers to prayer and has no real desire to supply our needs. Hence, they become and act just like the picture of the one that they worship. That is why they also treat others unkindly. The true God is very loving and kind to EVERYONE!

The reason why much of the church has not had the impact on the world of lost sinners that it should have is because we have believed in a God more interested in the judgment and destruction of sinners than He is in saving them. Rest assured that God is going to judge, but this is only by necessity and not by desire. God would prefer to win them over by His love. Kindness is His love in action. If God's people began to imitate Him instead of looking for ways to get back at our enemies then we might make a greater impact for Him. Therefore, let us learn His character and become more like Him. Let's be kind even to those who hate us regardless of who they are.

Act like God

Watch what God does, and then you do it, like children who learn proper behavior from their parents. Mostly what God does is love you. Keep company with him and learn a life of love. Observe how Christ loved us. His love was not cautious but extravagant. **He didn't love in order to get something from us but to give everything of himself to us. Love like that** (Eph. 5:1-2; the Message Bible)

There is an old saying that "birds of a feather flock together". There really is much truth to this saying because the people you spend the most time with are the ones whose behavior you will begin to imitate. The Bible itself teaches this from the negative aspect when it says, *"Don't let anyone fool you. 'Bad companions make a good person bad'"* (1 Cor. 15:33; New International Reader's Version. See also Psalm 1:1-3). Those who you spend the most time with are those whose behavior you will imitate.

This is one of the reasons that God wants us to spend as much time in His presence as we can. This is the reason God wants us to learn the truth about Him and to disregard all false pictures of Him. While God longs for personal intimacy with His children, this longing is not only to meet His desire for our companionship, but also that we will learn what He is like and begin to act like Him.

God not only explains to us what love is but He provides us with the ultimate object lesson. He shows us from His own willingness to give up His life for selfish vile creatures that were willing to kill their God rather than embrace Him. God's kind of love puts others ahead of Himself. He is completely focused on others to the point of dying on their behalf. There really is no greater love than this (John 15:13).

There is another old proverb that says that, "the apple does not fall far from the tree." As God's own children we should be acting like our Daddy. Sadly, many Christians have been given a distorted picture of our Heavenly Father and this is what we have reflected and shown to the world. Most do not seem to want the kind of Father we have offered.

When we have the right image of our God—one of unselfish love willing to give up His very life for selfish humans—then we will imitate it and the world will have a truer picture of what He is like. So let us learn what our God is like and then reflect that same behavior.

February 27

A Love like no Other

For when we were yet without strength, in due time Christ died for the ungodly. For scarcely for a righteous man will one die: yet peradventure for a good man some would even dare to die. But God commendeth his love toward us, in that, while we were yet sinners, Christ died for us (Rom. 5:6-8)

How can you measure a love like this? God did not die for people who "deserved it". He died for the least deserving, which is pretty much all of us.

This is definitely the difference between Jesus and the deities of the different world religions and cults. Every religion and cult makes their adherents work towards some type of favor from their deity. The majority of them focus on a fear factor to ensure compliance. None of the deities of these religions would ever lovingly sacrifice themselves for the good of mankind. On the contrary, if men offend these "gods" then they will quickly inflict divine retribution. Such are the systems set up by Satan and his fallen angels in order to appease man's basic need for God.

Christians who are called into missions and to reach people of other nations, cultures, and religions need to major on this point. Why would anyone want our God if He acts no different than theirs? If their god continues to burden them because of their sins and expresses constant hatred of them for their shortcomings than what good is telling them about our God if they will get more of the same?

The good news is that the God that we know in Jesus Christ loves flawed humanity so much that He was willing to die for us to prove that love. Instead of looking for how to destroy a people that offended Him, He instead looked for a way to give the ultimate expression of love which is to die for unrighteous people so that they can become right with Him.

No man can really understand that kind of love until they have come to know this Lover-God. If He had sacrificed Himself for people that loved Him and treated Him well then it would be easy to understand. But to die for the very ones who disobeyed Him, who cursed Him, who spat in His face and disregarded His laws and showed Him all types of disrespect? Now that is a love unfathomable. No sin-filled man can understand this because sin is the product of selfishness. However, when we come to know the righteous God who died for sinners, we come into a revelation of unmatched unselfish love.

February 28

For God so Loved the World

For God so loved the world, that he gave his only begotten
Son, that whosoever believeth in him should not perish, but
have everlasting life. For God sent not his Son into the
world to condemn the world; but that the world through
him might be saved (John 3:16-17)

This has to be the most familiar and often quoted passage in the Bible. Saints and sinners alike can quote this passage without blinking an eye. What is so amazing about this fact is that even though the majority of the Western world knows this passage like the back of their hands, they still have a wrong concept of God.

Why do so many people believe that the Father and Jesus have two distinct personalities? It is as if the Father is judgmental and ready to condemn sinners and the Son says, "No Father! I will go and die in their stead! Do to me what you really want to do to them!" I am sure that it saddens the heart of the whole Triune Godhead that so many people think of the Father this way.

The Holy Spirit seemed to push John to show how the Father's love was fully involved in the redemptive work of Jesus. Certainly Jesus was willing to die on man's behalf, but it was not to appease a judgmental God who gets His kicks from throwing sinners into hell. On the contrary, it was a joint decision of love between all three members of the Godhead.

Which is easier to do: sacrifice your own life or give up someone that you love dearly as a sacrifice to deliver a rebellious people who are in bondage to Satan's tyranny? For me it would be easier to die myself on behalf of others than to deliver any of my own children. This was not an easy thing for the Father to do. Yet the Holy Spirit speaking through John says that He so loved us that He gave us Jesus.

Jesus so loved us that He was willing to lay down His life for us. But the Father so loved us that He was willing to give up someone who was more dear to Him than anything He had ever created – EXCEPT YOU AND I! Jesus was and still is so precious to the Father. Yet, He saw us as so valuable and so precious that He was willing to allow His Son to sacrifice Himself.

This word "world" includes every single human inhabitant that ever lived on planet earth. God does not have a "selective love." He loved everyone and proved it by the sacrifice of our precious Savior.

February 29

God wants Relationship with Us

In other words, God was using Christ to restore his relationship with humanity. He didn't hold people's faults against them, and he has given us this message of restored relationships to tell others (2 Cor. 5:19; God's Word Translation)

Jesus did not come only to save sinners from an eternal hell. Certainly this is a major aspect of redemption. We should be thankful that because of Christ we will not have to spend eternity in such a horrible place. However, salvation from hell and the lake of fire is not limited to this aspect of Christ's redemptive work.

Hell is simply the product of a broken relationship with God. God never once intended for any human being to go to that horrible place. Hell is basically a place where spirts go who have no relationship with God. Satan and his angels rebelled against God and severed all ties with Him so this place was prepared for them (Matt. 25:41). It was simply an accommodation for those who did not want to be in God's presence.

However, when God created man He created us for the specific purpose of having relationship. He wanted to be a Father of a very large family that He could love on and they would love Him and one another. His plans were thwarted when Adam and Eve broke relationship with Him. They accepted Satan's character assassination of God and acted upon his suggestion to join him in rebellion against Him.

Since then men have avoided relationship with God in order to indulge lusts and pleasures. Due to the bondage of sin that we fell under we have had no idea how we could have a relationship with Him. As a matter of fact, we weren't even sure that He wanted it. God was in Christ showing us that He desires relationship and how we can have it with Him.

This shows us that God was just as much for our redemption as Jesus was. Redemption was not simply a matter of Jesus trying to appease an angry God on our behalf. It was God working through His Son because He longed for relationship with us.

Islam, Buddhism, Hinduism nor even the pseudo-Christian cults offer anything of this sort from their systems of religion. They may offer cold philosophy and a works-based salvation, but none of them will present to you a God who is longing for relationship with you. Only Christ does that. If you don't know Him, He longs for you to. Just tell Him you want to have a relationship. He's been waiting for you to ask.

March 1

Distinguishing God's Work from Satan's

*And many of them said, He hath a devil, and is mad; why
hear ye him? Others said, These are not the words of him
that hath a devil. Can a devil open the eyes of the blind?*
(John 10:20-21)

People who are blinded by hatred and prejudice will not use logic
or common sense. Only a moment ago Jesus had healed a man who had
been born blind. Those during Jesus' time who were familiar with the
activities of demons knew that they were evil and never extended mercy to
anyone. Certainly demons did not go around opening blind eyes.

Sadly, Jesus, after giving a man sight, was accused of being demon
possessed. Jesus went around undoing Satan's works against mankind and
while doing so was accused of having a demon Himself. Instead of praising
God for His wonderful works among men, some during Jesus' time
attributed it to satanic forces.

Thanks be to God that there were some rational voices in the
crowd. Some could not conceive of a demon possessed man going around
healing the blind. They knew that Satan's power was limited and that only
God could do such great things. We know today that Satan would not even
heal a blind man without requiring something of him. Jesus did it from a
pure unselfish motive of love.

It is vitally important to distinguish between the works of God and
the works of Satan. Too many, even in our day, have the two confused.
Ascetics and Calvinist theologians have, for centuries, attributed blindness
and other sicknesses to God. They have told us that God has given people
these types of handicaps for His glory. After all, everything that happens is
supposedly His will for us in their theological system.

Cessationist theologians, those who do not believe that God does
miracles today, have attributed all modern day supernatural works of
healing, deliverance and other miracles that set men and women free as
coming from Satan. It is such an ignorance of God's Word when we
attribute what the normal mind knows is good to Satan and attribute what
we know is bad to God (Matt. 7:7-11).

When we study our Bibles, especially the miracles of healing, we
learn that only God has healed and asked for nothing in return. When we
read about sickness, the majority of it is seen to be the results of sin or
willful neglect. It is never once stated in the Bible that sickness and demon
possession is a blessing from God. Therefore, learning to distinguish
between the works of God and those of Satan can be a matter of life and
death as well as health and sickness.

March 2

God's Works are Good and Satan's are Oppressive

How God anointed Jesus of Nazareth with the Holy Ghost and with power: who went about doing good, and healing all that were oppressed of the devil; for God was with him (Acts 10:38)

A clear distinction between the works of God and Satan is that God's works are good and Satan's are oppressive. In this passage we are given a clear definition of what God Himself says is good. We can take it on the authority of Scripture that healing is considered by God to be something that is good.

We can also take it on the authority of God's Word that sickness is a work from Satan and God sees it as something oppressive. To oppress someone is to heavily burden them with the intent to crush them. This is what Satan was doing to mankind by inflicting sickness, disease and pain.

In light of this Scripture it is perplexing that so many theologians have taught and some continue to teach that God inflicts sickness in order to mature us, to teach us, and other "blessings". Sadly, God is being blamed for Satan's work despite the plain teaching of God's Word that Satan is the oppressor and uses sickness as his tool.

.Nowhere in Scripture do we ever read that God was behind the acts of Satan in oppressing people. Instead, God the Father was with God the Son who was healing people by the power of God the Spirit. When Jesus came to earth He did not once inflict anyone with sickness nor did He leave anyone sick who came to Him for healing. Since Jesus perfectly represents the type of person that God truly is (John 14:8-11; 2 Cor. 4:4; Heb. 1:1-3) then we can see that everything He did was according to what God willed for mankind.

Therefore, if we are going to introduce God to those who are sick and hurting they must come to understand that He is not the One oppressing them. On the contrary, people must begin to understand that God is intent on delivering them from the oppressor and His sickness. God wants to give good gifts to those that ask Him and healing is good (Matt. 7:11).

We must remove the satanic blinders that have distorted the true meaning of what is good and what is evil. Anything connected to Satan has nothing beneficial about it. Christians must stop trying to find good in what God has said is oppression. We are to look only for what God describes as good. Healing is good. It is a work of God. Ask Him to do it for you.

March 3

Satan Places People into Bondage but God Releases them

The Lord then answered him, and said, Thou hypocrite, doth not each one of you on the sabbath loose his ox or his ass from the stall, and lead him away to watering? And ought not this woman, being a daughter of Abraham, whom Satan hath bound, lo, these eighteen years, be loosed from this bond on the sabbath day? (Luke 13:15-16)

Jesus once told the Pharisees, *"The sabbath was made for man, and not man for the Sabbath"* (Mark 2:27). God did not make man as a slave to the Sabbath or any law. The Pharisees did not understand the purpose of God's laws and most especially the Sabbath. God never created the Sabbath and other laws in order to prove His superiority over man. Every single law that God created was for man's benefit, to include the Sabbath.

The Sabbath was made for man to rest his body and reflect on his Creator. It was an opportunity for God to express His love for His creation. Sadly, Satan knows how to twist God's laws, make them appear arbitrary and then use the law of *liberty* (James 1:25) to keep people in bondage.

How we view God's laws determines how we view God Himself. If we see His laws as stern requirements that are to be strictly abided by for no other reason than He said so, we will see God as a cold dictator. However, if we see that a loving God gave us laws for our benefit and protection then we will see Him for the loving God that He is.

This woman that Jesus healed was in bondage to Satan's tyranny of sickness. Sadly, the Pharisees saw God as a stern cold dictator and became just like the deity that they worshipped. Therefore, instead of rejoicing that a woman was healed, they became critical of the healing because their god does not want his laws imposed upon no matter what. The type of god that they worshipped would rather have a woman suffer under bondage than to dare break a law (as it was falsely interpreted by them).

God is more concerned about people and their needs than He is about man-made rules, laws, and programs. Sometimes we may have a program in our churches and Christian meetings and want to stick strictly to the schedule. God may want to "disturb" our "regularly scheduled program" in order to heal or deliver people that are in bondage. If we are annoyed with God doing something different than what our set agenda is, perhaps we need to question the purpose for why we are doing these things.

Since Jesus has come to set people free from satanic bondage then this must be our agenda as well. Everything that we do must have the same purpose in mind or we need to stop doing it.

March 4

God's Sovereignty versus Satan's Usurpation

And if Satan cast out Satan, he is divided against himself; how shall then his kingdom stand? And if I by Beelzebub cast out devils, by whom do your children cast them out? therefore they shall be your judges. But if I cast out devils by the Spirit of God, then the kingdom of God is come unto you (Matt. 12:26-28)

One dictionary defines "kingdom" as "the domain over which the spiritual sovereignty of God or Christ extends, whether in heaven or on earth."[13] This definition along with Jesus' words above helps us to understand a very important truth about God's sovereignty which is that *not everything that happens is God's will or under God's control.* God is not controlling the actions of the devil. His kingdom (His sovereign government) is actually at war with Satan's kingdom (his usurped government). Jesus' teaching goes against many of the modern ideas concerning what it means for God to be sovereign.

Jesus had just casted a devil from a man that kept him blind and mute. In our day there are some who advocate a strict idea about God's sovereignty in which everything happens is due to a divine decree that was made by Him. In their view, when we encounter someone today who is handicapped in any way (blind, deaf, unable to speak, walk, etc.) their belief is that God willed this upon those suffering these maladies.

Yet Jesus tells us that such is not the case. Jesus says that Satan has a kingdom too. While God's kingdom is greater and possesses much more power, and while Satan certainly is not God's equal, God recognizes that Satan has a kingdom and it is opposed to His.

God's sovereignty is a loving one in which He is at war against a usurper. He is not the One who makes people blind, deaf, dumb, and crippled in any other way. God is the One who is seeking to spread His sovereign reign that brings healing and deliverance from these inflictions that Satan brings upon man. The sign of God's sovereign reign is not in sickness and disease, but in its deliverance from these things. We must learn to recognize the true sovereignty of God. Where people are being delivered from sickness, disease and oppression, which is where God is demonstrating His sovereignty.

---

[13] kingdom. Dictionary.com. Collins English Dictionary - Complete & Unabridged 10th Edition. HarperCollins Publishers. http://dictionary.reference.com/browse/kingdom (accessed: November 04, 2014).

March 5

Does God Make Handicapped People?

And the LORD said unto him, Who hath made man's mouth? or who maketh the dumb, or deaf, or the seeing, or the blind? have not I the LORD? (Exodus 4:11)

Atheists point to this passage to prove that the God of the Bible is unworthy of worship. Christians who teach divine determinism use this passage to prove that handicaps are God's will. Both groups suffer from the inability to follow simple Biblical rules of interpretation.

The New Testament reveals that evil spirits cause dumbness and blindness: *"Then was brought unto him one possessed with a devil, blind, and dumb: and he healed him, insomuch that the blind and dumb both spake and saw"* (Matt. 12:22). From the ministry of Jesus we learn that Satan and evil spirits are responsible for men becoming handicapped. Does that mean that Exodus is wrong? Didn't God Himself make the statement?

God often took responsibility for the devil's work during Old Testament times (Job 2:3-6). But apart from understanding Hebrew idioms we may unintentionally malign God and falsely accuse Him of doing the devil's work. Some scholars have looked at the background of the Hebrew culture and have helped us to understand God's use of such expressions:

> It is possible that some references to direct divine involvement in events may reflect a view of divine pancausality that was popular in the ancient Near East. In the deterministic idiom of the culture, actions that were simply permitted by God, mediated through agents, or accomplished through the laws of nature, can be attributed directly to God.... In the context of such a worldview, it is possible and perhaps likely that references to Yahweh closing wombs (1 Sam. 1:6), creating handicapped babies (Exod. 4:11), giving Saul's wives to David (2 Sam. 12:8), and the like, are an accommodation to the mindset of the culture ....his involvement may be more indirect than the language of the text suggests. The situations described may reflect His permissive will, rather than his ideal or his moral will.[14]

In the Old Testament God is often said to do the thing which He merely allowed or permitted. This background truth helps us to read the Old Testament in a different light and see a God of only goodness rather than One who arbitrarily inflicts people with sickness and handicaps.

---

[14] Howard, David M.; Grisante, Michael A. **Giving the Sense: Understanding and Using Old Testament Historical Texts** (Grand Rapids, MI: Kregel Publications, 2003), p. 58

March 6

Sickness must be REBUKED and not EMBRACED

And he arose out of the synagogue, and entered into Simon's house. And Simon's wife's mother was taken with a great fever; and they besought him for her. And he stood over her, and **rebuked the fever;** *and it left her: and immediately she arose and ministered unto them* (Luke 4:38, 39)

Take note that Jesus *rebuked* Peter's mother-in-law's fever. He did not tell her that it was a blessing sent from God. He did not tell her that it was a test that she was going through that she needed to pass with patience. He did not say with a mighty preacher's voice that "Gawd es en control. Let Him work out His will in you." He did not even pray for her to be healed. Jesus aggressively went after the fever itself and rebuked it.

To rebuke someone, or in this case, *some thing*, is to issue a stern reprimand. It is to inform the person or thing that you disapprove of its present activity. Biblically speaking, it is commanding it to cease from its current works and to depart from one's presence. Jesus had to have been angry with this fever to have rebuked it.

Now, if sickness is sent by God then this would mean that Jesus was fighting against the Father's works. This would mean that the Godhead is divided. That is impossible since Jesus made it clear that He and the Father are ONE (John 10:30; 17:11, 21). Whatever attitude the Son had towards this sickness, the Father was feeling it likewise. Therefore, the fever could by no means be the work of God.

Too often our ministers pray over the sick with no expectation of results. The reason being is that many of them believe that to pray for the removal of sickness is to go against the will of God for the sick one. You can hear it when they make such statements in their prayers like, "if it be thy will, please heal so-and-so, otherwise, give them the strength to pass this test" or some other similar unbiblical platitude.

If we, like Jesus, begin to see sickness, not as an agent of God's blessing, but rather, as an enemy invader that God hates, then we will begin to follow our Lord's example and take the same aggressive action that He took concerning Peter's mother.

God's people have been given authority over sickness and disease (Luke 10:17-20). Do not embrace it as a friend. Be like Jesus and rebuke it as an enemy who dares to trespass.

March 7

Healed of Evil Spirits

*And it came to pass afterward, that he went throughout every city and village, preaching and shewing the glad tidings of the kingdom of God: and the twelve were with him, And certain women, **which had been healed of evil spirits and infirmities**, Mary called Magdalene, out of whom went seven devils* (Luke 8:1-2)

In today's passage we continue to explore the origins and nature of sickness and disease. This passage is one of the clearest concerning sickness and God's attitude towards it. God approves of sickness just as much as He approves of demonic activity—which is to say that *He does not approve of it.*

We see from this passage that sickness is more often than not the work of spirits that are under Satan's control (Matt. 12:26-28; Luke 13:11-16). Furthermore, these spirits are described as being "evil". And finally, they are connected to the infirmities that many suffer from. We can deduce from this that sickness has its origins with Satan and rebellious fallen spirits and because they are evil then sickness is evil.

Note that the women in the passage were *healed* of evil spirits and infirmities. This means that every healing that Jesus and the apostles wrought through Jesus was not only an attack on Satan's kingdom, but also a conquering of it. Healing is simply freeing someone from captivity to something evil that is destroying them. Jesus came to conquer Satan and evil spirits.

God is all for man's deliverance. He is heartbroken over being constantly blamed for things that His Word reveals are the results of evil spirits. God is not evil, He does not utilize evil spirits, and wants no credit for their work upon man. On the contrary, He wants men and women free from these spirits.

God's people must come to know the truth about God and stop believing the lies that attribute these things to Him. God has sent us to a lost and dying world and how we present Him is important. Even more, our beliefs about Him determine how we react to evils suck as sickness. Since we are told that they are the work of demons then we must take the same attitude towards sickness as we would do with sin: recognize its source and resist it with authority in Jesus' Name.

Cured from Demons

> *And in that same hour **he cured many of their infirmities
> and plagues, and of evil spirits**; and unto many that were
> blind he gave sight. Then Jesus answering said unto them,
> Go your way, and tell John what things ye have seen and
> heard; how that the blind see, the lame walk, the lepers are
> cleansed, the deaf hear, the dead are raised, to the poor the
> gospel is preached* (Luke 7:21-22)

This passage is similar to the one that we studied yesterday. Luke
writes that Jesus *"**cured** many of their infirmities and plagues, and of evil
spirits"*. Note that Jesus did not merely remove germs from people, restore
limbs, vocal functions and sight. Jesus actually went to the very source of
the problem which was *spiritual* in nature. The passage says that He *cured*
people from evil spirits.

According to the Strong's dictionary, the word "evil" in the
original Greek means among several things, "hurtful, that is, evil
....figuratively calamitous; also (passively) ill, that is, diseased." The evil
that these spirits do is connected to what is hurtful, calamitous, ill, and
diseased". This is a fitting description of their work and cannot be
connected to a God of love. This is a demonstration of pure satanic hatred
towards man.

Furthermore, the word "plagues" used in this passage according to
Strong's dictionary means, "a *whip* (literally the Roman flagellum for
criminals; figuratively a disease): - plague, scourging." From this we can
see that the primary work of these evil spirits is to torment men (Matt. 4:24;
8:5-7). Again, this proves that sickness does not come from the hands of a
loving God and there is no benefit to being sick.

Strong also says that the word "cured" in this passage means, "to
wait upon menially, that is, (figuratively) to adore (God), or (specifically)
to relieve (of disease)." Jesus said, *"....just as the Son of Man did not come
to be served, but to serve, and to give His life a ransom for many"* (Matt.
20:28; NKJV). Part of the service Jesus came to render to man was
deliverance from evil spirits and their diseases. He adores us so much that
He would come to do this even now. Satan on the other hand hates us and
his only desire is to torment and eventually destroy us. Praise be to God
that we have been given authority over Satan's evil tormenting spirits.

March 9

God's Kingdom Connected to Healing and not Sickness

Then he called his twelve disciples together, and gave them power and authority over all devils, and to cure diseases. And he sent them to preach the kingdom of God, and to heal the sick (Luke 9:1-2)

The Jewish leaders had a limited perspective on what it meant for the Messiah to come. They were under Roman oppression. They wanted to conquer these enemies using physical military might and take back their nation. They were looking for a Messiah who would be a military leader that would defeat all of their enemies militarily.

If only they could have looked beyond the physical veil as Jesus did and see who the real enemy was. If only they could see that it was Satan who needed to be conquered more than the Romans. After all, it was Satan who influenced behind the Roman monarchy.

Sadly, their limited perspective did not allow them to see the real need around them. Here were people all around them in bondage to sickness, demonized, poor, distraught, bound by sin, and without hope. More than a military victory over some physical enemies, these people needed to first see that God was not the angry tyrant that they pictured Him to be. A military victory, far from helping them to understand the truth about God, would have done little more than strengthen the idea that God is a divine dictator who abuses His omnipotent power to get His own way.

Before man can see God's kingdom in physical manifestation they need to see what He is all about. The goal of God's kingdom was to always set men and women free from the kingdom of darkness in every shape and form. This included freedom from the satanic kingdom's work of sickness and disease. So Jesus, rather than arming His disciples with horses, swords, and armor to destroy Roman soldiers, instead armed them with something much more: kingdom authority against sickness and disease.

Jesus' intention was to show that God's kingdom was a kingdom that would free men and women from spiritual bondages and physical ailments. Divine healing is the kingdom agenda and shows that God's kingdom means freedom from every satanic work. After all, what good is it to win a military victory while Satan is able to continually inflict you relentlessly? Kingdom authority to heal sickness and cast out devils shows us that God loves mankind much more than to merely replace one physical oppressive monarchy with another.

March 10

Sickness is Torment

*And when Jesus was entered into Capernaum, there came unto him a centurion, beseeching him, And saying, Lord, my servant lieth at home sick of the palsy, **grievously tormented**. And Jesus saith unto him, I will come and heal him* (Matt. 8:5-7)

One dictionary defines "torment" as "….the infliction of torture by means of such an instrument or the torture so inflicted."[15] Sadly, those who blame God for sickness see Him as a tormentor. Of course people will not outright accuse Him of being one. They often describe God's supposed inflicting of sickness as "an act of love".

We will find statement such as "God placed that on you because *He loves you* and needed to teach you a lesson," "God inflicted you to purify you because He loves you," or "God knew that if He did not afflict you this way then you might go astray and sin against Him. He loves you." Yet, the inspired Scriptures do not describe sickness as an act of *love* but as an act of *torment*.

The majority of Christians I know are against torture. Most of us find it to be a vile and reprehensible act against another human being. Yet, we are quick to imply that a loving God would use such methods to teach lessons, purify us, and keep us from going astray.

Does such an act of torment truly express the love of God? John would disagree. He writes, *"There is no fear in love; but perfect love casteth out fear: because fear hath **torment**. He that feareth is not made perfect in love"* (1 John 4:18). There is no fear or torment in God's love. Therefore, sickness cannot be God's will and He is not the inflictor. John says that *torment* is the opposite from God's perfect love.

Jesus demonstrates the perfect love of God when He told the centurion, *"I will come and heal him."* How do so many "Bible teachers" get it so wrong? Jesus, who demonstrated God's will by all of His actions, presented God as the healer from torment rather than the giver of torment. God is the *healer* and not the *tormentor*. If the centurion saw Jesus as the tormentor he would never have requested His help. We need to see God through this centurion's eyes if we are to have the same great faith that Jesus commended Him for (v. 10). Great faith is built upon knowledge of God's true loving character.

---

[15] torment. Dictionary.com. Dictionary.com Unabridged. Random House, Inc. http://dictionary.reference.com/browse/torment (accessed: November 06, 2014).

March 11

The Source of Sickness and its Torment

*And his fame went throughout all Syria: and they brought unto him all sick people that were taken with **divers diseases and torments**, and those which were possessed with devils, and those which were lunatick, and those that had the palsy; and he healed them* (Matt. 4:24)

We learn yesterday that torment is "the infliction of torture." We also learned yesterday and we see it again in today's passage that torment is connected to sickness. Finally we learned yesterday that torment is something outside of God's perfect love so God cannot be the One bringing sickness with its torments. On the contrary, Jesus reveals the Father as the Healer from torment. The Father is willing to free us from it upon our asking as He did for the centurion's servant.

In today's passage we see that sickness is not only connected to torment but it is connected to demons. Jesus never discriminated in His ministry of healing since He saw that every negative thing that attached itself to man came from the devil. Jesus' desire was to free men from the tormentors and their torment.

Yet we know that in so many places in Scripture, especially in the Old Testament, God is said to be the One who inflicts sickness. Those who doubt the divine inspiration of Scripture often point to these so-called "contradictions" as proof for this false assertion. However, as we have stated in previous devotions, a simple rule of Bible interpretation is to remember the Hebrew's permissive idioms. In other words God is said to do the thing which He merely allowed or permitted.

In Matthew 18 Jesus teaches us the danger of being unforgiving towards others. The one man in His parable who failed to forgive a small debt after God had forgiven him much was actually delivered to the tormentors: *"And his lord was wroth, and **delivered him to the tormentors**, till he should pay all that was due unto him"* (Matt. 18:34).

When we sin against God and refuse to submit to His will He is left with no other choice but to reluctantly "give us up" and turn us over to Satan and his tormentors (Psalm 81:11-16; Hosea 11:8; Rom. 1:24-28; 1 Cor. 5:1-5). This includes unforgiveness as well as other sins. Stepping outside of God's will means being delivered *to* the tormentors. However, when we submit to God He will keep His hand of protection on us and deliver us *from* the tormentors.

March 12

Christ's Redemptive Work and Demons and Sickness

When the even was come, they brought unto him many that were possessed with devils: and he cast out the spirits with his word, and healed all that were sick: That it might be fulfilled which was spoken by Esaias the prophet, saying, Himself took our infirmities, and bare our sicknesses (Matt. 8:16-17)

For over a century now there has been quite a bit of controversy over what has been referred to as "healing in the atonement" or "healing in the redemptive work of Christ". If healing is one of the benefits of Christ's death, burial, and resurrection then, naturally, one is just as guaranteed to receive healing if they believe it as they would salvation from sin.

Sadly, many in the body of Christ have difficulty with this truth. Some of it is due to their experiences of seeing others who claimed to believe it but died from sickness. Others have simply seen good Christians die horrible deaths from sickness and have felt that if anyone *should* have been healed, it should have been *that* person.

One of the things that keep so many from receiving all of the benefits of Christ's redemptive work is the failure to remember what we have actually been redeemed from. If we simply believe that Christ's work of redemption was meant only to appease God's wrath and keep Him from destroying all of us, we will see no other benefit in it other than to make it into Heaven when we die.

On the other hand, if we see it as the Father rescuing us from Satan's kingdom of darkness, death, and destruction, which the Bible teaches, then we will begin to take a different perspective on healing in the atonement (Eph. 2:1-6; Col. 1:12-14; 2:15-16; Heb. 2:14-15). In His redemptive work Jesus also came to destroy the works of the devil (1 John 3:8). In Matt. 8:16-17 we find that sickness is connected to the work of demons, who are ruled by Satan. Matthew, quoting Isaiah, says that it is through Christ's redemption that He was able to heal from sickness and cast out demons.

Healing and deliverance is Christ's way of destroying the works of Satan and setting us free from them. Christ came to earth on a rescue mission. Part of that rescue mission meant giving up His life for us. The other part was rising again and ascending to Heaven in order to be sure that His will is carried out. Sickness is the work of demons, but the work of Christ in His redemption is to set us free from them. Let us claim the benefits.

March 13

Suffering according to the Will of God

Wherefore let them that suffer <u>according to the will of God</u> commit the keeping of their souls to him in well doing, as unto a faithful Creator (1 Pet. 4:19).

Peter tells us that we are to suffer according to God's will. Many read this as if it were saying "it is God's will that you suffer." Those who embrace deterministic theology add further that all that we suffer— sickness, disease, tragedy, heartbreak, persecution, etc.—is God's will for us. Is that what this passage is saying?

"According to the will of God" does not mean that God is the One who is sending the suffering that we experience and that it is His will. It means that when we do suffer we must suffer the way or manner that God wants us to suffer. Another word for "will" in this passage is "desire" or "pleasure". What Peter is saying in this passage is that we should suffer with the type of attitude that pleases God or one that He desires.

In verse 13 Peter says, *"But rejoice, inasmuch as ye are partakers of Christ's sufferings; that, when his glory shall be revealed, ye may be glad also with exceeding joy."* This is speaking about one's *attitude* in suffering. Rejoicing in the midst of trials and suffering is the will of God and not the suffering itself.

The rejoicing is not a masochistic attitude in which we are to pretend to enjoy the trials we face, but because there is an expected end that God has for us. If we rejoice in the midst of our suffering rather than complain and blame Him for it, we will experience our future happiness when the Lord's glory is revealed. Jesus elaborated even further:

Blessed are they which are persecuted for righteousness' sake: for theirs is the kingdom of heaven. Blessed are ye, when men shall revile you, and persecute you, and shall say all manner of evil against you falsely, for my sake. Rejoice, and be exceeding glad: for great is your reward in heaven: for so persecuted they the prophets which were before you. (Matt. 5:10-12)

So again, we are not told that suffering is God's will. Suffering *according* to the will of God means rejoicing in the midst of the suffering. He wants to bless us both now and in eternity but we will block that if we do not have the proper attitude. Are you suffering? Rejoice. God has great things planned for you both now and later.

March 14

Is all Suffering the will of God?

If ye be reproached for the name of Christ, happy are ye; for the spirit of glory and of God resteth upon you: on their part he is evil spoken of, but on your part he is glorified. **But let none of you suffer as a murderer, or as a thief, or as an evildoer, or as a busybody in other men's matters.** *Yet if any man suffer as a Christian, let him not be ashamed; but let him glorify God on this behalf* (1 Pet. 4:14-16)

Many people tell us that God's hand can be seen in all of the events of life. We often attempt to comfort people in their suffering with these words. While I am strongly opposed to the idea that any suffering is instituted by God, I especially need to caution Christians about crediting God for suffering that is the result of our wrong choices.

Peter says that some suffering is the result of being a murderer, a thief, and a busybody. He then tells people not to suffer as a result of this. This means that we have a choice in whether or not we suffer due to our adherence to or failure to follow such advice.

I have read where a major sports star who was quite adulterous contracted AIDS. He claimed that God gave him this disease. However, this is completely wrong thinking unless we were to say that God so controlled this man's behavior that he made him commit the acts that led to the disease. If we cannot say that God made him commit the acts (although, sadly, some theologians would say such blasphemy) then we have no right to blame God for the disease. We will have to conclude that this was the result of wrong personal choices.

The fact that Peter mentions that "busybodies" will suffer as a result of their wrong choices is more relevant to Christians since we have so many gossipers in the church. These "correctors of others' behavior" want to know everyone's business and believe that it is their divine calling to straighten out other people's homes, children, and ministries. When they suffer the reactions of those who do not see them as the spiritual paragons that they purport to be, they claim that they are being persecuted for Christ's sake. In reality, they are suffering for being a busybody.

If you commit murder then you will suffer the consequences. If you steal then you will pay the penalty. If you act as a busybody rather than minding your own business then you will be talked about and persecuted. But no one who makes these choices should dare say that God is the One taking them through such suffering.

March 15

Are We Called to Suffer Sickness and Disease?

If you are __reviled__ for the name of Christ, you are blessed, because the Spirit of glory and of God rests on you. (1 Pet. 4:14)

Many claim that Peter and other New Testament writers teach that it is God's will for us to suffer sickness and disease. Yet, nowhere in Scripture is this taught. Peter certainly does not teach this. Such teaching is the result of taking Scripture out of context to promote a *false* doctrine of suffering.

A closer examination of the passage tells us that the suffering God calls us to endure is to be reviled by men because our testimony for Jesus. We are not to retaliate when we are reviled for His sake but to continue to pray and love those doing the reviling. The word "reviled" means to "denounce" or "insult". You can expect to be denounced, insulted, reproached, and ridiculed for your testimony. In this kind of suffering are we to glorify God. Peter goes on to say, *"...but if anyone suffers as a Christian, he is not to be ashamed, but is to glorify God in this name."* (1 Pet. 4:16)

Peter teaches us that the fiery trials that we are expected to glory in and that brings glory to God has nothing to do with sickness and disease, but in dealing with persecution at the hands of men. Jesus also makes this abundantly clear:

> *Blessed are they which are **persecuted** for righteousness' sake: for theirs is the kingdom of heaven. Blessed are ye, when **men shall revile you, and persecute you**, and shall say all manner of evil against you falsely, for my sake. Rejoice, and be exceeding glad: for great is your reward in heaven: for so persecuted they the prophets which were before you* (Matt. 5:10-12)

Notice that Jesus does not say that one is blessed when they are sick and suffering from a particular disease. Jesus specifically teaches that the blessing comes from being reviled by men for His Name's sake. It is when men speak falsely about us and persecute us that we are to rejoice. We are not to rejoice over sickness but to take God's promises and stand against it in Jesus' Name.

March 16

The Distinction between Sickness and Persecution (Part 1)

Is anyone among you suffering? Let him pray. Is anyone cheerful? Let him sing psalms. Is anyone among you sick? Let him call for the elders of the church, and let them pray over him, anointing him with oil in the name of the Lord. And the prayer of faith <u>will</u> save the sick, and the Lord <u>will</u> raise him up. And if he has committed sins, he <u>will</u> be forgiven (James 5:13-15; NKJV)

James gives us two sets of instructions: one for the *afflicted* and one for the *sick*. James is careful to distinguish affliction from sickness and gives different instructions for both. Affliction, as James uses it within the context of the letter, is in relation to persecution. In verse 10 James says, *"Take, my brethren, the prophets, who have spoken in the name of the Lord, for an example of suffering affliction, and of patience."* This lines up with what Jesus said, *"....for so persecuted they the prophets which were before you"* (Matt. 5:12b).

Prayer for ourselves and our persecutors is to be offered when we are suffering in this manner. However, there is a different and more detailed instruction for those who are sick. The sick person is to expect God's immediate supernatural intervention in the healing of their body. Notice that James uses the word "will" in the above passage. Anytime God says "I will" or the Bible says concerning God that "He will" we can know beyond a shadow of a doubt this "I will" or "He will" is a revelation of "His Will." This means that healing is guaranteed and, unlike "affliction" (persecution), it is not to be endured. Andrew Murray writes:

> "The Lord spoke to the disciples of divers sufferings which they should have to bear, but when He speaks of sickness, it is always as of an evil caused by sin and Satan, and from which we should be delivered. Very solemnly He declared that every disciple of His would have to bear his cross (Matthew 16:24), but He never taught one sick person to resign himself to be sick. Everywhere Jesus healed the sick, everywhere He dealt with healing as one of the graces belonging to the kingdom of heaven."[16]

While affliction-persecution is to be endured, sickness is not to be tolerated but relief from it is to be sought from God immediately.

---

[16] Murray, Andrew **Divine Healing** (Springdale, PA: Whitaker House, 1982), p.9

March 17

The Distinction between Sickness and Persecution (Part 2)

*And he sent, and beheaded John in the prison. And his head was brought in a charger, and given to the damsel: and she brought it to her mother. And his disciples came, and took up the body, and buried it, and went and told Jesus. When Jesus heard of it, he departed thence by ship into a desert place apart: and when the people had heard thereof, they followed him on foot out of the cities. And Jesus went forth, and saw a great multitude, and was moved with compassion toward them, and **he healed their sick.*** (Matt. 14:10-14)

In the case of John the Baptist, Jesus distinguishes between suffering persecution and suffering sickness and disease. Jesus did not stop John's persecution and subsequent death as the result of persecution. Yet He was quick to heal the sick. From this we learn that persecution is to be endured without retaliation to our persecutors. In some cases one may become a martyr for the cause of Christ, but sickness in our bodies is never to be tolerated.

John the Baptist died as the result of the persecution of men. He did not die of sickness and disease for the kingdom. Jesus knew that Satan was behind John's execution so He attacked Satan where it hurt him most which was the healing of sick bodies (Luke 13:16; Acts 10:38). Satan is behind both persecution and sickness. In the former he uses ungodly men that Jesus still loves and still wants to save. In the latter he uses demons and the germs inherent in a fallen world which we must take authority over.

While Christians are to expect suffering at the hands of evil ungodly men, and that they are to rejoice in it, they are not to accept the type of suffering that God did not say was His will. This would include sickness and disease. When we are sick, we are to take God's promises to heal and stand on them.

The suffering that God calls us to suffer is not sickness but to endure the persecution for the preaching of the gospel and living a Christ-like life. Enduring sickness is not suffering for the Lord. Suffering because of our own sin and foolishness should not be blamed on God's sovereignty nor should God be blamed for sickness. Those who teach that men must suffer sickness for the cause of Christ have no Biblical foundation for this teaching.

March 18

The Holy Spirit Loves You

....that will never disappoint us. All of this happens because God has given us the Holy Spirit, who fills our hearts with his love (Romans 5:5; Contemporary English Version)

There are some groups that claim to be Christian but they deny the Triunity of God. Many of these groups deny the deity of Christ and just about all of them deny that the Holy Spirit is an actual person. They see Him only as mere power or influence. What an insult against the third member of the Triune Godhead who has come to live with man and guide him.

The Bible, especially the New Testament, attributes personality to the Holy Spirit. He can be communed with, grieved, hurt, and resisted. He has a mind and He guides. However, one of the most important things about Him is that He *loves*. He could not shed God's love abroad in our hearts (KJV) if He Himself did not love us. I like something that Theodore H. Epp wrote:

> ....the Holy Spirit has the capacity to love. He not only influences us to love, but He also loves us ....Neither is there any question about the Holy Spirit's love for us. He patiently seeks us out when we are in sin and away from God. He regenerates us and begins to transform us into the image of God's Son. If the Father had not loved the world, if the Son had not loved us and died for us, if the Holy Spirit had not loved us, convicted us, and transformed us, where would we be spiritually today? Our salvation depends as much on the love of the Holy Spirit as it does on the love of the Father and of the Son.[17]

If we want to sense the presence of the Holy Spirit with us as we live for Christ, we must not only recognize Him as a person but we must also recognize that He loves us. How can someone as holy as He is live with us and in us while we still do things that break His heart if He did not have such an overwhelming love for us? The Holy Spirit really loves us and is looking out for us. Commune with Him today and thank Him.

---

[17] Epp, Theodore H. **The Other Comforter: Practical Studies on the Holy Spirit** (Lincoln, NE: Back to the Bible, 1966), p. 14

March 19

The Holy Spirit is Just like Jesus

*....and I will ask the Father, and he will give you another comforting Counselor **like me**, the Spirit of Truth, to be with you forever* (John 14:16; Complete Jewish Bible)

In some of our devotions we have emphasized the important truth that the Father and Jesus are exactly alike in personality and mission. All of the love we find in Jesus and all of the acts of kindness and compassion that we see in Him are also in the Father.

Another important truth that is not always expounded upon is the fact that the Holy Spirit is also exactly like Jesus. This is vitally important to know because it is the third member of the Triune Godhead whose presence is always with us and who lives in us. That is why Jesus sought to comfort His disciples by assuring them that He would not leave them comfortless, or like orphans, but would send them *another* Counselor. Again Theodore H. Epp writes:

> The word "another" had a rich message for the disciples. The Greek language, in which the New Testament was written, has two words that are translated "other" or "another." One means "one of the same kind," and the other means "one of another kind." When Jesus said that He was going to send "another comforter," He meant that He was going to send a Comforter of the same kind, a Comforter like Himself.[18]

The Holy Spirit is exactly like Jesus. It was the Holy Spirit who sent Jesus *"to heal the brokenhearted, to preach deliverance to the captives, and recovering of sight to the blind, to set at liberty them that are bruised"* (Luke 4:18). It was through His power that Jesus healed those oppressed by the devil and delivered those in bondage to Satan's minions (Acts 10:38; Matt. 12:28).

This same Holy Spirit is with us and in us. He is walking alongside of us to empower us, protect us, and to keep us from stumbling and falling. He loves us just as the Father and Jesus loves us and desires to have fellowship with us. He does not want us to be afraid of Him but to look at Him in the same way we see Jesus; someone who is full of compassion and is concerned about us in every way.

---

[18] Epp, Theodore H. **The Other Comforter: Practical Studies on the Holy Spirit** (Lincoln, NE: Back to the Bible, 1966), p. 8

March 20

The Holy Spirit is not a Spirit of Bondage

For ye have not received the spirit of bondage again to fear; but ye have received the Spirit of adoption, whereby we cry, Abba, Father (Rom. 8:16)

The word "bondage" conjures up images of being tied down with a rope or chain and unable to have any real freedom of movement. It may also remind us of movies where we saw slaves who were mistreated but could not run and felt the need to endure seemingly hopeless situations. Either way, being in bondage, from a physical standpoint, is not a good situation to be in.

However, there is also spiritual and psychological bondage. Sometimes leaders can establish overbearing laws and rules that are difficult to adhere to. The audience that Paul is addressing felt pressured by the Law of Moses which seemed to require so much in order for people to obtain salvation. Because it was easy to fail to meet all of the requirements of the law, people felt especially burdened. Add all of the stringent Pharisaical ideas and you definitely can keep people tied up spiritually and psychologically. Remind the people of the consequences accrued from breaking the law and people become hopeless.

The Holy Spirit who represents God's mind and ways to us on the earth, reminds us that He is not here to put us in this kind of bondage. On the contrary we are told, *"For the law of the Spirit of life in Christ Jesus hath made me free from the law of sin and death"* (Rom. 8:2). Breaking the law brought natural consequences but the Holy Spirit, rather than coming to put us in bondage to numerous stringent requirements, came to set us free from them.

Now, *the Holy Spirit did not come to set us free to be lawless.* On the contrary, He came to help us establish an intimate relationship with our Heavenly Father, one in which we cry "Abba." The word "Abba" is an intimate term by which we recognize God, not by a prestigious title called "Father" (as some of the Roman Catholic priests) but we see Him as a loving parent who longs to hear His children and be with them. The Holy Spirit is with us to make such an intimate experience as real as possible while we are on the earth.

This sets us free from the fear of the consequences of a broken law. When we have the Spirit of adoption that makes intimacy with the Father a real experience, who would want to sin anyway? In His presence, the power of sin is broken. Let's stop trying to "keep the law" and start living in intimacy with our Father through the precious Holy Spirit.

March 21

Blasphemy against the Holy Spirit

Wherefore I say unto you, All manner of sin and blasphemy shall be forgiven unto men: but the blasphemy against the Holy Ghost shall not be forgiven unto men. And whosoever speaketh a word against the Son of man, it shall be forgiven him: but whosoever speaketh against the Holy Ghost, it shall not be forgiven him, neither in this world, neither in the world to come. (Matt. 12:31-32)

The Holy Spirit had just worked through Jesus to set a man free from satanic bondage (Matt. 12:22-28). The Pharisees, who in their pride, always afraid that Jesus was stealing their thunder, attributed the work of the Holy Spirit to Satan. They did not do this out of ignorance or blindness but with full knowledge (John 10:41).

Blasphemy is to constantly reject the truth about God and to speak evil about Him (Ps. 74:18; Isa. 52:5; Rom. 2:24; Rev. 13:1, 6; 16:9, 11, 21.) When one has constantly twisted the truth about God because it does not fit their personal agenda or ambitions, and then speak in a way that influences others away from this truth, this person is already hardened and are following the influence of Satan himself (Dan. 7:25; Rev. 13:5).

Sadly, so many in our day come very close to this or have already done this. They do the same as the Pharisees when they give Satan credit for God's work. A revival breaks out in a certain region with thousands of souls getting saved and their critics say that this is the work of Satan. A minister holds a divine healing meeting and numerous people are miraculously healed and someone accuses him of using hypnosis. The Holy Spirit reveals a future event to His people through one of His servants and he is accused by established Evangelical leaders of being a false prophet or a fortune teller. The list can go on.

It is blasphemy to believe that the Holy Spirit has anything but love for mankind and that He would intentionally perform in ways that is deceptive. It is blasphemy to believe that the Holy Spirit is unwilling to manifest His power on behalf of fallen broken men. It is blasphemy to believe that anything good that happens to mankind such as a healing, deliverance, new birth, Holy Spirit infilling, or the like is automatically a sign of the devil.

Satan is not looking to help man. He is wicked and will blaspheme the Holy Spirit in order to get others to resist Him and stay in bondage to their sins. Those of us who know Him know that He is good and He works to influence men and set them free (Isa. 10:27; Luke 4:18; Acts 10:38).

March 22

Is Speaking in Tongues of the Devil?

And they were all filled with the Holy Ghost, and began to speak with other tongues, as the Spirit gave them utterance (Acts 2:4)

There are groups who believe that all miracles ceased some time after the apostles died. Naturally the ability to speak in other tongues would have gone out as well. Therefore, any manifestation of tongues among Pentecostal and Charismatic groups is considered by *cessationists* to be either psycho-babble or a demonic manifestation.

There are also other groups who would never deny that God does miracles today but they too are skeptical of Pentecostal and Charismatic experiences of tongues. Some of them claim to have casted demons out of people who manifested tongues. Testimonies and statements of this nature have made people afraid to seek God for this gift.

While we do not dismiss the fact that Satan will often "ape" God's work, we must be careful not to cause one to distrust the Holy Spirit. Jesus said, *"And these signs shall follow them that believe; In my name shall they cast out devils; they shall speak with new tongues"* (Mark 16:17). Jesus said that His signs include authority over demons *and* speaking in tongues. Some groups believe in neither and other groups believe strongly in the deliverance ministry while casting aspersions on speaking in tongues. Yet Jesus said that both are available.

If both have been made available to the believer then there is no need to be afraid of getting a demon when you ask God for the filling of the Spirit with the evidence of tongues. Jesus said, *"Or if he shall ask an egg, will he offer him a scorpion? If ye then, being evil, know how to give good gifts unto your children: how much more shall your heavenly Father give the Holy Spirit to them that ask him?"* (Luke 11:12-13)

God will protect the sincere seeker from receiving a demonic manifestation when He has asked for a promised gift. When we ask for the infilling of the Holy Spirit then, as Luke states in Acts 2:4, it is He who gives us the utterance to speak in tongues. He will not force us to do it. We will speak in tongues as an act of our free-will. But it is the Holy Spirit who provides the supernatural ability to do it. Therefore, if you have not received this precious gift from God, ask Him for it. It's a demon-free gift.

March 23

Hurting the Holy Spirit

And grieve not the holy Spirit of God, whereby ye are sealed unto the day of redemption (Eph. 4:30)

In our tough manly world we sometimes prize the fact that we are not easily hurt or offended by people's insults and actions toward us. Such bravado brings us admiration from more sensitive people who wish that they could be as tough as we are. They wish that they could put on the stoicism that hides the pain that they are actually feeling as they see the tougher people do.

However, when we study deeply what it means to grieve the Holy Spirit we discover that He is a very sensitive person who can be hurt just as much, if not more, than the most sensitive person we may know. Yet, the fact that He continues to put up with us demonstrates a remarkable amount of toughness that comes as the result of His love. This gives a new meaning to the phrase "tough love". It is love that takes pain from those He loves.

Unlike most sensitive humans, though, the Holy Spirit is not offended for selfish reasons. He is grieved by how we often mistreat each other or fail to act like Him in our responses to one another. In the following verses we read:

Let all bitterness, and wrath, and anger, and clamour, and evil speaking, be put away from you, with all malice: And be ye kind one to another, tenderhearted, forgiving one another, even as God for Christ's sake hath forgiven you. (Eph. 4:31-32)

It is our failure to take on the same characteristics as Christ that truly grieves Him. When we choose to be bitter towards other people and hold grudges rather than forgiving them, we are literally ignoring the Spirit of Love who indwells us. We are telling Him that His ways are irrelevant and that we will handle relationships in a more devilish way—the way of the fallen nature from which we were redeemed.

God the Holy Spirit is a tenderhearted person. He is kind and very forgiving. He wants us to see this about Him and take on these same attributes. Everything that He is, He wants us to be and He empowers us to be that way. He never becomes bitter toward us nor does He speak evil of us. He loves us. He wants us to love Him and one another. Let us stop grieving Him and begin loving our brothers and sisters in Christ as well as all those we meet with on a daily basis.

March 24

The Law of the Holy Spirit

For all the law is fulfilled in one word, even in this; Thou shalt love thy neighbour as thyself. But if ye bite and devour one another, take heed that ye be not consumed one of another. This I say then, Walk in the Spirit, and ye shall not fulfil the lust of the flesh (Gal. 5:14-16)

God is not unjust to ask us to do something that He has not given us the ability or resources to accomplish. When we read the above passage we see that the law of God is summed up in the command to love. For some that brings a sigh of relief since they only have to deal with one commandment instead of ten. However, we discovered that when we follow this commandment then there is no need for the other nine. Loving God and our neighbors prevents us from ever breaking the other nine (Rom. 13:9-10).

For others, the love command is probably the most difficult one. Maybe they are not interested in committing adultery nor are they interested in their neighbor's property. But to have to love others who they feel are unlovable? Now that is one of the most difficult commandments for them. Furthermore, their hatred can be justified by how they *believe* (based on faulty interpretations of Scripture) that God gets vengeance upon His enemies. Some wrongly believe and teach that God hates His enemies.

We must always remember that God does not have a double-standard. He does not have one law for us and another for Himself. The way that some people portray God when they speak about His sovereignty, His wrath, or His judgment, we would be led to believe that He was devoid of the love that He commands us to walk in. However, this could not be true based on what we read in verse 16.

We are told that when we walk in the Spirit we will not fulfill the lusts of the flesh. The lust of the flesh is not only sexual sins but it also includes *"hatred, variance, emulations, wrath, strife, seditions, heresies, envyings, murders"* (verses 20-21). These are not *in God* but *in our flesh.* So when we walk in the Spirit we will not fulfill these lusts.

The Holy Spirit cannot enable us to walk in what He is lacking nor can He keep us from walking in that which is in Him. If He has hatred for His enemies as some claim then He could not enable us to walk in love towards them. Therefore, when we walk in the law of the Spirit we become like Him, like Christ, and like the Father. God does not act in fleshly ways towards others. Walking in the Spirit helps us to be as loving as God is.

March 25

The Spirit can be Resisted

Ye stiffnecked and uncircumcised in heart and ears, ye do always resist the Holy Ghost: as your fathers did, so do ye. (Acts 7:51)

"Everything that happens has been ordained by God. He is omnipotent. No one can resist His will." Many who advocate Calvinistic doctrines believe that "might makes right". While teaching the truth that God is indeed all-powerful, they apply this truth incorrectly when they teach that everything occurs, to include evil acts such as accidents, rapes, murders, etc. are the result of His will being done. After all (they say), no one can oppose an omnipotent God.

Possibly the worse application of this teaching is the idea that some are preselected to be saved and others are preselected for hell based solely on a decree from God. If God wants a person saved then nothing can oppose His will. Therefore, those who never receive Christ were preselected to be damned in the first place. Universalists have taken this a step further to teach that eventually all will be saved, including Satan Himself. God's will must always be done because no one can resist it.

God is the most powerful person in the universe but this does not mean that God relates to His creatures on sheer power. The Holy Spirit has been the One who often manifested God's power in the Old and New Testaments but we find from this passage that He can be resisted. Does that mean that those who resist Him are more powerful than Him? No. It only means that He respects the free choices of His creatures.

It is God's will for all to be saved and He is not willing that any should perish (1 Tim. 2:1-6; 2 Pet. 3:9; John 3:16). It is God's will for all men to live free from sickness, pain, and anything that harms them. Why is it that God's will is not fulfilled in many lives? Contrary to Calvinism, people are able to resist God's will for their individual lives (Psalm 81:11; Proverbs 1:24-30; Isa. 30:15; Isa. 65:12; Isa. 66:3, 4; Jer. 19:5; Jer. 32:35; Mat. 23:37; Luke 7:30; John 5:40; Acts 7:51; Rom. 10:21; Heb. 10:29).

This explains why there is so much evil in the world and why God cannot, as of yet, put a stop to it. God respects the free actions of His creatures, even if they use that freedom to oppose His will and hurt others. One day God will set things completely right. However, He will not force His will on those who do not want it. So the Holy Spirit can be resisted because He respects our freedom.

March 26

The Spirit can be Quenched

Quench not the Spirit. Despise not prophesyings. Prove all things; hold fast that which is good (1 Thess. 5:19-21)

"Our churches are dry, we need a move of God's Spirit." "God does not work miracles today." "We will not have that kind of strange behavior in this church. You will stick with the program here." "Why is church so long? Do they always have to have pray for healings? Why is it that everyone is speaking in tongues? I feel uncomfortable here." "Our denomination does not believe in that 'Holy Ghost' stuff. You need to take that somewhere else."

The Holy Spirit longs to manifest Himself in our churches and individual lives. He longs to remove the dryness and bring revival. However, if we have learned anything in the past couple of days, we have learned that though He is powerful, He does not force His will on us. He does not operate in sheer power but in love. Therefore He can be *quenched.*

The word "quench" as used in this passage is the exact same Greek word used in Matthew 25 concerning the foolish virgins who did not bring enough oil for their lamps. We read, *"And the foolish said unto the wise, Give us of your oil; for our lamps are **gone out**"* (v. 8). This means that the fire had been quenched in their lamps. The oil almost always represents the Holy Spirit in Scripture. These foolish virgins allowed Him to be quenched in their own lives. When Jesus came for His church, these foolish virgins were left behind due to their own neglect.

As powerful as the Holy Spirit is, His love for us and His willingness to allow us freedom to accept or reject Him means that we have the power to quench Him. However, when we do this we should cease to wonder why we have dryness in our lives, our churches, and in our ministries. We need to stop blaming God and accusing Him of not caring or coming through for us. He has made numerous promises to do so many things for us but we continue to quench Him.

On the other hand, if we are willing to acknowledge that the fault is ours, ask Him to forgive us, repent, and begin to allow Him to have His way in our lives and churches, we will begin to see a manifestation of His power in miracles, healings, deliverances and salvation. We will see that God is more than willing to do great things through those who are open to His move and who have right motives. When He does move, don't quench Him through complaining, sin, and unbelief. Embrace Him and let Him take over. It always works out better when the Holy Spirit is allowed to take charge.

March 27

Punishment for Insulting the Spirit of Grace (Part 1)

*Of how much sorer **punishment**, suppose ye, shall he be thought worthy, who hath trodden under foot the Son of God, and hath counted the blood of the covenant, wherewith he was sanctified, an unholy thing, and hath done despite unto the Spirit of grace?* (Heb. 10:29)

There seems to be a contrast between the words "punishment" and "grace". Hebrews says that there is a punishment for rejecting what the blood of Jesus has done and insulting the Spirit of *grace*. But isn't grace to be received freely? Why must one feel threatened with punishment if all that God has done was through grace?

This appears to contradict what John tells us about God's love: *"There is no fear in love: but perfect love casteth out fear, **because fear hath punishment**; and he that feareth is not made perfect in love."* (1 John 4:18; American Standard Version). It may help us more when we look at a passage in the 12th chapter of Hebrews:

*Follow peace with all men, and holiness, without which no man shall see the Lord: Looking diligently **lest any man fail of the grace of God**; lest any root of bitterness springing up trouble you, and thereby many be defiled* (Heb. 12:14-15)

When we interpret Scripture with Scripture we come to a better understanding of God's methods and His mode of bringing about punishment. We see from the above passage that it is possible for us to fail, or fall short of God's grace. God's mode of punishment is to allow the circumstances in one's life that His grace would have protected them from to take place (James 4:6-7; 1 Pet. 5:5-9).

Paul said, *"I do not **frustrate** the grace of God"* (Gal. 2:21a) This means that grace can be frustrated, or rather, as the Strong's dictionary defines the word, grace can be "set aside, disesteemed, neutralized, violated, cast off, despised, disannulled, brought to nought," and "rejected."

To "despise" means "to treat contemptuously" and "to insult with malice, hatred, or spite." Basically, when one does this they are pushing the Spirit of grace away from them. Therefore, God is not issuing threats in order to force compliance through fear. He is simply warning of the natural and spiritual consequences that come from forsaking Christ and despising His grace.

Punishment for Insulting the Spirit of Grace (Part 2)

*Of how much sorer **punishment**, suppose ye, shall he be thought worthy, who hath trodden under foot the Son of God, and hath counted the blood of the covenant, wherewith he was sanctified, an unholy thing, and hath done despite unto the Spirit of grace?* (Heb. 10:29)

Yesterday we saw how this passage can make God appear to be vindictive. However, we learned from further study that it is not so much that God is seeking "payback" for offending Him. The passage is actually teaching that when people reject His grace He is left with no choice but to allow them to suffer that which grace had freed them from.

This describes God's method of what we understand to be punishment. It is important that we understand the method by which God is said to punish if we are to understand the truth concerning His loving character. Many people read statements like the one in Heb. 10:29 and think that God directly energizes events that bring punishment upon people. An often stated but little recognized principle of Scripture is the fact that when we push God away, we lose His protection.

For example we read statements in Scripture such as *"The Lord is with you, while ye be with him; and if ye seek him, he will be found of you; but if ye forsake him, he will forsake you"* (2 Chron. 15:2b) and *"because ye have forsaken the Lord, he hath also forsaken you"* (2 Chron. 24:20b; see also 12:5). In Jeremiah punishment is directly connected to God's forsaking, or rather, removing His presence and protection:

*And when this people, or the prophet, or a priest, shall ask thee, saying, What is the burden of the Lord? thou shalt then say unto them, What burden? **I will even forsake you**, saith the Lord. And as for the prophet, and the priest, and the people, that shall say, The burden of the Lord, **I will even punish that man** and his house* (Jeremiah 23:33-34)

Remember that all of this comes about because the people have first forsaken God. The curses in Deut. 28 are the results of the people forsaking God, pushing Him away, and He in turn forsaking them and leaving them to suffer the consequences of their rebellion (Deut. 31:16-17; see also Psalm 81:10-16). When we reject the Blood of Jesus and the Spirit of grace we reject all the benefits that accrue from it.

March 29

Is God Vindictive? (Part 1)

*For we know him that hath said, Vengeance belongeth unto
me, I will recompense, saith the Lord. And again, The Lord
shall judge his people* (Heb. 10:30)

Yesterday we saw that God punishes those who trodden the blood
of Jesus underfoot and insults the Spirit of grace. Seeing that God offers
grace but punishes people who insult His Spirit who distributes and makes
His grace known presents some difficulty. After all, if grace is forced, can it
be grace? Yet, we learned that when we understand God's method of
punishment then we get a better understanding of this alleged contradiction.
For those who reject God's grace He merely allows them to suffer the
consequences that His grace would have protected them from.

However, in the very next verse we are told that God Himself takes
vengeance. Does this contradict what we have said about the previous
verse? Furthermore, does this go contrary to God's admonition not to seek
vengeance on others? Let's look at a passage in Romans that will help us:

*Dearly beloved, avenge not yourselves, but rather give
place unto wrath: for it is written, Vengeance is mine; I
will repay, saith the Lord. Therefore if thine enemy hunger,
feed him; if he thirst, give him drink: for in so doing thou
shalt heap coals of fire on his head* (Rom. 12:19-20)

Many of us have read this as though God is saying, "Don't take
vengeance. I'll get'em back for you." I used to tell people that God can
get'em better than you can. But is that what we are really being taught in
this passage?

Notice the phrase, *"but rather give place unto wrath."* In the first
chapter of Romans, Paul tells us that God's wrath is revealed in how God
allows unrepentant people to suffer the consequences of their own rebellion
(Rom. 1:18, 24-28). This is a truth that is prevalent throughout Scripture
(Deut. 31:17-18; 1 Kings 14:15-16; 2 Kings 17:17-20; 2 Chron. 29:6-8;
Ezra 5:12; Psalm 5:10-12; 9:15-16; Isa 54:8; 57:17; Jer. 33:5; Eze. 22:30-
31). Remember that God is said to be the doer of that which He merely
allowed to happen or did not prevent from happening. So God's vengeance
is to allow the natural consequences of sin to take place (Gal. 6:5-7).

March 30

Is God Vindictive? (Part 2)

For we know him that hath said, Vengeance belongeth unto
me, I will recompense, saith the Lord. And again, The Lord
shall judge his people (Heb. 10:30)

Yesterday we saw that God's "vengeance" is to allow the
unrepentant sinner to suffer the consequences of their rebellion. Further
study of Heb. 10:30 makes this clearer. The writer of Hebrews is citing a
passage from Deuteronomy 32 (in a nuanced form). In the KJV there is
very little difference between Moses' rendering and the writer of the letter
to the Hebrews. However, some other English translations render the
Moses' version differently. Let's look at two literal translations:

....for the day of vengeance and repayment, for the season
when their foot shall slip? *For the day of their calamity is*
near, and impending doom hurries upon them. For Yahweh
shall adjudicate His people and show Himself merciful
over His servants when He sees that the power of their
hand has departed and has become nil for both the
restrained and the ones set free (Deut. 32:35-36;
Concordant Literal Translation)

Unto the days of vengeance and requital: Unto the time
their foot shall totter? ***For, near, is the day of their fate,***
And their destiny speedeth on. *For Yahweh will vindicate*
his people, And upon his servants, will have compassion,—
When he seeth that strength is exhausted, And there is no
one shut up or at large (Rotherham Emphasized Bible)

When we read verse 35 in the literal translations it is speaking
about the working out of God's wrath. Basically, God is telling His people
to step back and let the consequences of sin take its place. Don't interfere
with the sowing and reaping process by trying to take vengeance yourself.
Their sin will destroy them far more than what we can do.

Furthermore, God's part in the whole process is rendered
differently in these literal translations. Instead of a seemingly selfish
vengeance for personal honor, God is looking to vindicate His people.
Instead of judging in order to render a punitive sentence, God is seeking to
show loving compassion. If we accept these literal renderings then God's
character is viewed differently and we will be able to emulate His love even
to the worse of our enemies.

March 31

Can We Love God and be Afraid of Him?

It is a fearful thing to fall into the hands of the living God
(Heb. 10:31)

A difficulty we find in today's passage is the statement, *"It is a fearful thing to fall into the hands of the living God"* This appears to contradict what John tells us about God's love when he writes: *"... fear hath punishment; and he that feareth is not made perfect in love."* (1 John 4:18; American Standard Version). If God wants us afraid of Him then does this mean that He does not want us to be perfected in love? In an earlier chapter of Hebrews we get a little more help in understanding this:

> *Take heed, brethren, lest there be in any of you an evil heart of unbelief, in **departing from the living God**. But exhort one another daily, while it is called To day; lest any of you be hardened through the deceitfulness of sin* (Heb. 3:12-13)

Hebrews is addressing Jewish converts to Christ who were being severely persecuted for their faith. The persecution was so severe that they were tempted to go back into Judaism. If they did this then they would be trodding underfoot the blood of Christ and insulting the Spirit of grace. They would have been counting the great sacrifice of Christ as worthless.

It would have been similar to the Israelites during the time of Moses and their constant desire to return to the slavery of Egypt. After demonstrating so much unbelief in the promises of God, He allowed them to die in the wilderness. It was not that God had abandoned them but they continually abandoned God.

Israel fell into the hands of the living God by losing the best that God had for them when they departed from Him. The Jewish Christians needed to see that they were making the exact same mistake. If they persisted in sin's deceit then they would lose God, go back into Satan's dominion, and be destroyed. The Hebrews writer, speaking in the idiomatic language that the Jews would understand, was stating that God would take responsibility for the destruction that they brought on themselves.

Therefore, stay with God, don't depart from His light and go back into the dominion of darkness, death and destruction (Heb. 2:14-15). *That* is to be feared. Appreciate what Christ has done for you and the grace that the Holy Spirit has bestowed on you.

April 1

What it means to "Fear" God

Thou shalt fear the LORD thy God, and serve him, and shalt swear by his name. Ye shall not go after other gods, of the gods of the people which are round about you (Deut. 6:13-14)

I was always taught that to "fear" God did not mean to be afraid of Him but to reverence Him. I always believed this until I read a book one day that stated that the word "fear" in relation to God actually did mean "to be afraid".

While I dare not argue against the research of scholars who are far more educated than I am, this just did not seem to reconcile with the truth about a loving God who desired intimate relationship. Fear (being afraid of someone) and loving intimacy are polar opposites. Fear makes one an unwilling slave. This is something that Satan utilizes since he desires no relationship (Heb. 2:14-15). When we see how Jesus interpreted Moses' Spirit-inspired admonition to Israel we begin to understand that the *fear of the Lord* is different from satanic-inspired fear:

Then saith Jesus unto him, Get thee hence, Satan: for it is written, **Thou shalt worship the Lord thy God,** *and him only shalt thou serve* (Matt. 4:10)

In the context of Moses' own statement, we learn that there was (and still is) the temptation to go after false gods and worship them. Some do not mind worshipping the true God as long as they can add some of the false sensual gods into the mix as well. Moses was admonishing the Israelites to stay away from the worship of false idols and to love and reverence only Yahweh. The "fear-factor" comes in to play when we worship anyone other than the true God. When we worship other "gods" we place ourselves in bondage to them.

Satan literally promised Jesus the world for only one act of worship. If the arrogance of asking his Creator to worship His creature was not enough, the fact that he would attempt to deceive Jesus into becoming his slave demonstrates the level of Satan's malignancy.

Unlike Satan, God is not looking for *slaves*, but for *children* who worship Him in loving reverence. Fearing God is not to be afraid of Him, but to offer Him loving adoration. So fear the Lord. That is the only "fear" God wants us to have.

April 2

God has to "Seek" Worshippers

But the hour cometh, and now is, when the true worshippers shall worship the Father in spirit and in truth: **for the Father <u>seeketh</u> such to worship him**. *God is a Spirit: and they that worship him must worship him in spirit and in truth* (John 4:23, 24).

Isn't it amazing that the all-knowing, all-powerful omniscient Creator of the universe actually has to *seek*, or rather *look*, for someone who would worship Him? Do not be deceived into believing that the Almighty, all knowing God always finds that which He is looking for. In one of his laments to the Prophet Ezekiel, he says, *"And* **I <u>sought</u> for a man** *among them, that should make up the hedge, and stand in the gap before me for the land, that I should not destroy it:* **but I found none.**" (Eze. 22:30).

How sad that God sought for someone who would pray for the nation of Israel, but could not find that person. God very much wants to withhold judgment and destruction. He will seek as hard as He can until He finds that person. This is unlike our enemy who seeks people for the express purpose of destroying them: *"Be sober, be vigilant; because your adversary the devil, as a roaring lion, walketh about,* **seeking whom he may devour**" (1 Pet. 5:8).

God seeks men in order to keep them from being destroyed (see Jer. 25:6) while Satan seeks men in order to destroy them. What a contrast! Therefore, we should not believe that God's seeking of men and women of a particular character to worship Him is a selfish seeking on God's part. Unlike the adversary, God is seeking *only our good*.

The sad part is that God will sometimes seek and does not find. Man's will is free to choose and God does not violate this free choice. He does not want robots. That is why He finds it necessary to *seek*.

The plain and clear statements of Scripture are that God is seeking for people of a certain character for specific purposes. The Bible is clear that God is seeking people who will love Him, worship Him, and get to know Him intimately. The sad part of this plain clear language is that God does not always get what He wants, or what He is seeking. Perhaps you and I can change that. We are created to worship and we *will* worship someone. We will either worship Satan and the world (which seeks our destruction) or the loving Heavenly Father who seeks only our good. Let's choose to worship God and give Him what He is looking for.

April 3

Is God's Desire for Worship Ego Driven?

*But we all, with open face beholding as in a glass the glory
of the Lord, are changed into the same image from glory to
glory, even as by the Spirit of the Lord* (2 Cor. 3:18)

According to Strong's dictionary, this word "beholding" means "to mirror oneself" and "to see reflected". We are changed into God's likeness by beholding who He truly is. David taught this same truth in the psalms when he wrote, *"As for me, I will behold thy face in righteousness: I shall be satisfied, when I awake, with thy likeness"* (Psalm 17:15). To worship God is to behold Him and be changed into His likeness (Psalm 27:4).

God is the highest person in the entire universe. There is no one greater than Him. To worship Him is to come up to His level. On the other hand, when we worship anything lower than God, we come down to the level of this object and become debased (Rom. 1:23-28; Acts 7:42, 43). Sin is centered around the worship of things lower than God that in the long run debase and destroy us.

God knows that He is the greatest and highest in the universe and desires man to excel to great heights as well. God knows that for man, who was created in His image and likeness, to worship anyone or anything else is to go far lower than His created potential. An example of this debasement is found in Jeroboam's introduction of idolatry to Israel:

*Whereupon the king took counsel, and made two calves of
gold, and said unto them, It is too much for you to go up to
Jerusalem:* **behold thy gods**, *O Israel, which brought thee
up out of the land of Egypt* (1 Kings 12:28)

It is easy to tell that Satan is behind this since Jeroboam does the exact same thing that Israel was condemned for in the wilderness (Ex. 32:4-8). This was part of the "beholding" that they did (Psalm 106:19-21) which made Israel become exactly like the images that they worshipped (Hosea 4:16-17). Concerning those who make idols, David said, *"They that make them are like unto them; so is every one that trusteth in them"* (Psalm 115:8).

Therefore, God's desire for our worship is not *ego driven*. It is *love driven*. He knows very well that we become what we worship because worship is *beholding*. If we worship Him then we behold Him and become like Him. If we worship anything lower than Him we become debased. He loves us and wants the best for us. He is the best that we can have.

April 4

The Glory of God

*And he said, I beseech thee, **shew me thy glory**. And he said, I will make all my goodness pass before thee, and **I will proclaim the name of the LORD before thee;** and will be gracious to whom I will be gracious, and will shew mercy on whom I will shew mercy* (Ex. 33:18-19)

Yesterday we learned that we worship by beholding and it is through beholding that we are changed into the same likeness as God. Paul also tells us in 2 Cor. 3:18 that we *"are changed into the same image from glory to glory."* What is the "glory" that is being spoken of here?

Some tend to think of God's glory as a brilliant bright light and there is certainly some truth to that. However, that is a very limited understanding of the *glory* of God. God and Moses help us to understand the full meaning of God's glory in their conversation in Exodus 33. When Moses asks God to show him His glory, the Lord begins to talk about His goodness, which consists of His graciousness and mercy. He then states that He will answer Moses' request by proclaiming His *Name* before him.

When God speaks about proclaiming His "name" in order to show His glory, He is not using this in the common way that we might understand it in our Western society. In the west, a "name" is often merely a label slapped on us by our parents that may or may not mean much. For God, *His name declared His character and ability*. Therefore, God's glory represents what is true about God. It was this revelation of God that caused Moses to worship Him:

*And the LORD passed by before him, and proclaimed, The LORD, The LORD God, merciful and gracious, longsuffering, and abundant in goodness and truth, Keeping mercy for thousands, forgiving iniquity and transgression and sin, and that will by no means clear the guilty; visiting the iniquity of the fathers upon the children, and upon the children's children, unto the third and to the fourth generation. **And Moses made haste, and bowed his head toward the earth, and worshipped** (Ex. 34:6-8)*

We are to center our worship around God's loving character of goodness. When we know who we worship then we become just like the One we are worshipping. There is no one more deserving of our worship than God because all that is good emanates from Him.

April 5

God's Unselfish Anger towards Idol Worship

And they left all the commandments of the LORD their God, and made them molten images, even two calves, and made a grove, and worshipped all the host of heaven, and served Baal. And **they caused their sons and their daughters to pass through the fire***, and used divination and enchantments, and sold themselves to do evil in the sight of the LORD, to provoke him to anger.* (2 Kings 17:16-17)

Why does God hate idolatry? Is it because He is competing for the affections of men? Is He competitive like we see with sports stars, movie stars, corporate and political leaders, and others who fight for the adulation of the crowds? Is He so insecure that He simply cannot share in privilege of receiving worship from the worthless peasants? That may be the way that Satan has presented God but that certainly is not the truth.

Numerous Bible passages such as the one we are studying today shows us why God becomes angry with idolatry. The majority of them emphasize how the idolators would sacrifice their own children in intensely painful ways to their false deity. This type of murderous worship demonstrates how man can become debased when they worship anyone or anything other than their loving Creator. Idolatry devalues human life and makes it worthless. This is seen in verse 15 of this same passage:

They rejected his regulations and the covenant he had made with their ancestors, along with the warnings he had given them. **They followed worthless images so that they too became worthless***. And they imitated the neighboring nations that the Lord had forbidden them to imitate* (2 Kings 17:15; Common English Bible)

It is no different in our present day Western society where sexual pleasure is worshipped. This leads to the murder of unborn children (abortion), kidnapping of young women and children to be sold as sex slaves, homosexuality, pedophilia, and some very vile pornography. It has led to the spread of diseases, many of them deadly diseases such as AIDS. It has led to one parent and no parent homes. This destructive idolatry has led to the breakup of marriages and families and in so many cases has led to death. Therefore God's anger with idolators is not from a selfish motive but from the damage that is done to the people He loves as a result of idolatry.

April 6

The War of God over Worship

Again, the devil taketh him up into an exceeding high mountain, and sheweth him all the kingdoms of the world, and the glory of them; And saith unto him, All these things will I give thee, if thou wilt fall down and worship me. (Matt. 4:8-9)

Satan and God are locked in a battle over your worship. It is not a physical battle. If the battle was a matter of power the war would have been over before it ever started because God could easily crush Satan from a power standpoint. The struggle for your worship is more of a political battle—an *information* war.

Satan believes that He is more worthy of our worship than God. He pulls out every deceptive trick in his book to make God appear to be unworthy of our worship. God, on the other hand, knows that to worship Satan is to travel on the road to self-destruction. He loves us and is proclaiming the truth about Himself and the devil in order to dissuade us from worshipping him. He knows that when we worship the true God, it opens an avenue for Him to bestow His riches upon us.

Satan is a created being whose goal is to be like the uncreated God. In Isaiah 14, a chapter which most Christians, myself included, believe is a depiction of Satan's original fall, records him as saying, *"I will ascend above the heights of the clouds; I will be like the most High"* (v. 14). Satan has started a futile war against God because He wants to be like God.

Satan's war against God is for the worship of God's creatures. But unlike God, who has placed high standards on the type of worship that He will receive, Satan will take it any way that he can get it. Satan knows that if most men knew exactly who they were worshiping when they worshiped him then they would never do it. Therefore, he must use cunning and deception to receive worship. God wants worship in *truth* but Satan is willing to receive it through deception, control and manipulation.

God is so deeply concerned about mankind that He demands our worship in order to protect us from the malignant intentions of Satan for his worshippers. Anyone who has to manipulate others into giving him worship does not deserve it. This person will eventually kill you. On the other hand, the One who tells you the truth and sacrifices Himself to save you is more than worthy of our worship. Let us worship Him. He's worthy.

April 7

Worship based on Deception

*And **the great dragon was cast out, that old serpent, called the Devil, and Satan**, which deceiveth the whole world: he was cast out into the earth, and his angels were cast out with him* (Rev. 12:9)

John points out that Satan, also referred to as "the dragon," deceives the whole world. It is based on these deceptions that, *"....they **worshipped the dragon** which gave power unto the beast: and they worshipped the beast, saying, Who is like unto the beast? who is able to make war with him?"* (Rev. 13:4)

This is totally different from God who says that, *"they that worship him must worship him in spirit and in truth"* (John 4:24). What is the deception that Satan is using to gain worship from man and what is the truth that God wants us to have in order to offer Him acceptable worship? It all centers on the truth about God.

Satan continually slanders God and deceives the world concerning Him. He has made God appear to be a big powerful judgmental intolerant unloving bully. Satan has deceived the world into believing that God is the One who brings about evil on this earth. He is said by Satan to be the creator of accidents, sickness, and natural disasters. Satan has told the world it is God who manipulates circumstances to ensure that crimes are committed and lives are taken. He is made to appear to be at fault for all of the wars and jihads being suffered today. God is said to cause famines that create poverty and starvation in third world countries.

Satan then presents a number of sinful pleasures by which he can receive our worship. When we think of God as the monster Satan makes Him out to be, it is easier to just go with sensual worldly pleasures that ease the pain.

However, God is constantly trying to counter these satanic lies and present the truth concerning Himself to the world. He has given His very life and blood to prove that He is nothing like the way that Satan has made Him out to be. He is kind, loving and gracious. He is making every possible effort through the church to help the world know the truth so that He can be worshipped in spirit and in truth.

Satan is so desperate for worship that he will use every lie and deception to get it. God, on the other hand, loves us so much that He will only receive our worship based on solid truth. Know the truth about God, worship Him centered on that, and we will avoid worshipping a lie (Rom. 1:24-25).

April 8

Idolatry: The Worship of Demons

What say I then? that the idol is any thing, or that which is offered in sacrifice to idols is any thing? But I say, that the things which the Gentiles sacrifice, they sacrifice to devils, and not to God: and I would not that ye should have fellowship with devils. Ye cannot drink the cup of the Lord, and the cup of devils: ye cannot be partakers of the Lord's table, and of the table of devils. (1 Cor. 10:19-21)

Many would be shocked to learn that idol worship is demonic deception, but Scriptures teach us this very truth. Paul's last statement sounds very close to our Lord's words concerning money: *"Ye cannot serve God and mammon"* (Matt. 6:24). The worship of idols is not limited to worshipping statues made by hand or any other type of heathen ritual. Money, family, career, television, sex, drugs, and a multitude of things that are placed ahead of God is idolatrous and is a sacrifice to demons. Idol worship has demonism behind it (2 Chron. 11:14-16).

Some Christians watch TV shows that grieve the Holy Spirit, but they put their favorite show ahead of what God wants for them. Some Christians fail to control their eating habits and sin through food. Speaking of some infiltrators in the church, Paul said, *"Whose end is destruction,* **whose God is their belly**, *and whose glory is in their shame, who mind earthly things"* (Phil. 3:19).

Others unwittingly put family before God in spite of the Word of the Lord: *"If any man come to me, and hate not his father, and mother, and wife, and children, and brethren, and sisters, yea, and his own life also, he cannot be my disciple"* (Luke 14:26). While we should be careful that we never neglect family for the sake of "ministry" as so many have been guilty of in the past (which served only to drive their family away from Christ), we should be very careful about allowing any family member's desires, opinions, actions, etc. to take precedence over obedience to Christ.

Anything that comes before God, that takes priority over obedience to God, is an idol and an object of our worship. Satan and demons have used what are otherwise legitimate things in our lives to deceive us into worshipping demons. Anything that we make an idol and that takes us away from God is engaging in satanic worship. One need not go to a Satanist church to worship Satan. One only needs to make God anything but first in their lives. On the other hand, when we endeavor to put God first and ahead of anything in our lives, we are engaging in acts of worship.

April 9

Idolatry makes us Forget God

They provoked him to jealousy with strange gods, with abominations provoked they him to anger. They sacrificed unto devils, not to God; to gods whom they knew not, to new gods that came newly up, whom your fathers feared not. Of the Rock that begat thee thou art unmindful, and hast forgotten God that formed thee (Deut. 32:16-18)

When we commit idolatry, we are forgetting about God. We are forgetting who He is, what He has done, and all of His wonderful plans for our future (Jer. 29:11). Satan is the ruler of the demons so any worship rendered to a demon is rendered to him (Matt. 12:23-26; 25:41). Satan is a deceiver and will never tell his worshippers the high cost they will pay in worshipping him and his demons.

Unlike Satan God does not demand our worship for egotistical selfish purposes. Cruel demons demanded that their worshippers put their children through torturous and painful sacrifices (Psalm 106:36-38). This shows us how much they hate those who worship them.

God is the only true God who actually loves His worshippers. False deities, the devil and demons themselves, hate their worshippers with a passion. They will not do anything for anyone that will not come at some personal detrimental cost to them. Actually, they know that any worship of them will incur God's wrath (Rev. 9:20).

On the other hand, God cares about His worshippers and will work on their behalf. He knows that Satan means them no good and thus His reason for forbidding the worship of idols and the demons behind them (Lev. 17:7). The purpose of worship is to exalt the true God because He loves us. We worship to acknowledge and honor His moral perfections, His wonderful majesty, and His great power.

Worship is exalting the Lord based on the understanding of His holiness. Moses and the Israelites received a revelation of God's holiness when he delivered them from the Egyptians: *"Who is like unto thee, O LORD, among the gods? who is like thee, glorious in holiness, fearful in praises, doing wonders?"* (Ex. 15:11). They discovered that none of the false gods compared to the true God based on this specific attribute.

However, we also worship God because He truly loves and cares about His worshippers. He does not want them destroyed by the devil. Worshipping God enables us to always remember Him and keep Him first place in our lives. When we worship Him we know that we are covered by Him and guaranteed His protection and victory.

April 10

Idol Worship is Bondage

*And they served their idols: **which were a snare unto
them**. Yea, they sacrificed their sons and their daughters
unto devils, And shed innocent blood, even the blood of
their sons and of their daughters, whom they sacrificed
unto the idols of Canaan: and the land was polluted with
blood* (Psalm 106:36-38)

Worship consists of giving God first place in our lives. Nothing is
to come before God (Psalm 73:25). Anything that comes before God and
that we desire more than Him has become an object of our worship whether
we realize this or not.

This is the sin of idolatry. Webster's defines idolatry as "Excessive
attachment or veneration for anything; respect or love which borders on
adoration." When God first gave the above commandment to Moses the
pagan nations surrounding Israel worshipped statues made with their own
hands and referred to them as "gods." Even in our day many non-Christian
religions practice this method of idol worship.

While pagan practices exist today even among civilized people,
Christians must understand that even they can fall into the sin of idolatry.
Whenever we are excessively devoted to anything other than God and His
Word we are committing this egregious sin. One need not have a statue in
order to be an idolater. Sadly, any type of idolatry will put us in bondage to
Satan.

Worshipping Satan and demons will snare you. It will trap you and
place you into bondage. God is about freedom and liberty while Satan and
demons are about entrapment and harsh slavery. Yet, when we choose to
worship the true and living God, He delivers us from the enemy's snare:

*HE WHO dwells in the secret place of the Most High shall
remain stable and fixed under the shadow of the Almighty
[Whose power no foe can withstand]. I will say of the Lord,
He is my Refuge and my Fortress, my God; on Him I lean
and rely, and in Him I [confidently] trust! For [then] **He
will deliver you from the snare of the fowler** and from the
deadly pestilence.* (Psalm 91:1-3; The Amplified Bible)

When we worship God for who He is and what He does, we have a
continual reminder of His promises. We place ourselves on God's side and
the devil, while he may growl and snarl, is unable to snare us.

April 11

Victory through Worship

*And Jehoshaphat bowed his head with his face to the
ground: and all Judah and the inhabitants of Jerusalem fell
before the LORD, worshipping the LORD. And the Levites,
of the children of the Kohathites, and of the children of the
Korhites, stood up to praise the LORD God of Israel with a
loud voice on high* (2 Chron. 20:18, 19).

One of the classic examples of victory in Scripture is that of King
Jehoshaphat. We are told, *"It came to pass after this also, that the children
of Moab, and the children of Ammon, and with them other beside the
Ammonites, came against Jehoshaphat to battle"* (2 Chron. 20:1). The King
was in a pretty tough situation. It was three against one. These are difficult
odds to face.

However, Jehoshaphat took the matter to prayer. He led God's
people into a time of prayer and fasting (v. 3). Within his prayer he
reminded God of His promise, something I find to be a neglected aspect of
prayer among many Western Christians (vv. 7-9). After receiving a word of
assurance from the Lord that He would deliver them, we find King
Jehoshaphat worshipped God.

Please take notice that all Jehoshaphat had was a Word from God.
There was not yet any visible proof that they would be victorious over the
numerous enemies that they were confronted with. A Word from God is
sufficient evidence for worship. Jehoshaphat exhorts the people with these
words:

*And they rose early in the morning, and went forth into the
wilderness of Tekoa: and as they went forth, Jehoshaphat
stood and said, Hear me, O Judah, and ye inhabitants of
Jerusalem; Believe in the LORD your God, so shall ye be
established; believe his prophets, so shall ye prosper* (2
Chron. 20:20)

Jehoshaphat did not wait until he saw the victory before he
exhorted the people to believe. He exhorted them to believe God *before
they saw* (1 Cor. 5:7; Heb. 11:1). He told them, *"Believe in the LORD your
God, so shall ye be established."* Too many of God's people want to
reverse the order. They want to see themselves established before they will
believe God. For too many people, seeing is believing. However, true faith
in God believes and then it sees (Mark 11:22-24).

April 12

Worship Brings Victory

And when he had consulted with the people, he appointed singers unto the LORD, and that should praise the beauty of holiness, as they went out before the army, and to say, Praise the LORD; for his mercy endureth for ever. And when they began to sing and to praise, the LORD set ambushments against the children of Ammon, Moab, and mount Seir, which were come against Judah; and they were smitten (2 Chron. 20:21, 22)

After exhorting God's people to believe Him, Jehoshaphat once again *demonstrates* this faith by having a "praise and worship service" right in the midst of the battle. Notice the Bible says, *"And when they began to sing and to praise, the LORD set ambushments...."* It was this worship, done in complete faith in God, which moved God to work on their behalf. Too many of God's people are waiting to see God do something *before* they will worship Him. It is only after they see God work that they will worship Him. Nevertheless, faith and gratitude is expressed in worship first, and then God will work to bring victory and deliverance in our lives.

True faith in God is not based on visible results (Mark 11:22-24; 2 Cor. 5:7; Heb. 11:1). It is based on our confidence in God's integrity (Num. 23:19; Psalm 89:33-35; Titus 1:1, 2; Heb. 6:17, 18). Therefore, if we claim to trust God then we will worship Him even before we see tangible deliverances (Ex. 4:31; 2 Kings 18:22). It is by demonstrating our faith in God through worship that we will see God work on our behalf in giving us victory.

Many of God's people would find quicker deliverance from the bondages and trials that they face if they would learn to worship God. The Bible provides us with enough examples of this truth that it is amazing that so many are yet ignorant concerning this.

God wants to do so many things for His people but His hands are tied when we choose to worship the one who is keeping us in bondage. God cannot force His blessings upon us and that is exactly what He would be doing if we thought to receive anything from Him apart from worship. When we worship God we route the enemy who is attempting to ensnare and destroy us.

April 13

Lack of Worship Equals Lack of Victory

*But the LORD, who brought you up out of the land of Egypt with great power and a stretched out arm, **him shall ye fear, and him shall ye worship**, and to him shall ye do sacrifice. And the statutes, and the ordinances, and the law, and the commandment, which he wrote for you, ye shall observe to do for evermore; and ye shall not fear other gods. And the covenant that I have made with you ye shall not forget; neither shall ye fear other gods. **But the LORD your God ye shall fear; and he shall deliver you out of the hand of all your enemies. Howbeit they did not hearken, but they did after their former manner** (2 Kings 17:36-40)*

When we worship God, we are demonstrating faith in Him. We are also removing ourselves from the power of the enemy. Earlier, we saw in Psalm 106 that worship of idols, vice worshipping God, will snare, or trap us. Instead of victory we will live lives of utter defeat.

Understand beloved that defeat is never the will of God for anyone. It is His desire to deliver us from our enemies, but He would be unjustified in doing so if we will make an allegiance with them by worshipping them. God promised victory and deliverance to Israel but they stubbornly refused to meet His condition.

This is the sad conclusion in failing to fear and worship God. We often blame God's sovereignty for things in our lives that He does not want there. The favorite Christian mantra of our time is "God is in control." Yet we fail to understand that God has given a certain amount of control to us.

The Father seeks true (sincere) worshippers. This means that He will not, at this point, force us or coerce us to worship Him. Therefore worship is a heartfelt choice. If we refuse to worship Him and cling to our idols then we cannot expect deliverance from our enemies. The good news from 2 Kings is that we see the willingness of God to deliver His people if they will simply fear Him and worship Him.

Worship is warfare. We will all worship something whether we believe this or not. However, we have a choice in *who* or *what* we worship, and it is that choice that will determine victory or defeat in our lives.

Through His death, burial and resurrection, Jesus has defeated every enemy that would array themselves against us (Col. 2:15; Heb. 2:14; 1 John 3:8). We must accept the Lord's victory by faith and recognize that the devil is a defeated foe. Worship the Lord and demonstrate the defeat of the enemy.

April 14

Does Evil Proceed from God? (Part 1)

*"Who is he that saith, and it cometh to pass, when the Lord commandeth it not? **Out of the mouth of the most High proceedeth not evil** and good?"* (Lam. 3:37-38)

There are many who desire to make God the author of evil and they have cherry picked through the Bible to find texts that would make their case for this. The passage above is one of several. One of the problems with such an approach is that it starts out with a distorted picture of God and then looks for proof of that picture.

If the Bible is read with the known revealed character of God in mind then such passages, while admittedly still difficult for the average Westerner to grasp immediately, will not shake one's confidence concerning God's goodness. Certainly when the passage is left by itself, without the immediate context as well as the support of other passages of Scripture, it makes God appear to be a distributor of evil. However, when Lamentations 3 is read in its context we we do not find a God who wants to inflict evil upon people, but One who is doing His best to withhold from His people the suffering of evil:

> *It is of the Lord's mercies that we are not consumed, because his compassions fail not. They are new every morning: great is thy faithfulness. The Lord is my portion, saith my soul; therefore will I hope in him. **The Lord is good unto them that wait for him**, to the soul that seeketh him. It is good that a man should both hope and quietly wait for the salvation of the Lord* (Lam. 3:22-26)

Lamentations is a sad testimony to the consistent sin of Israel. They followed the idolatrous practices of other nations which included the sacrifice of innocent children. Their hearts became callous and murderous. Yet, God still showed Himself to be merciful and compassionate. It was because of His faithfulness and mercy that Israel had not been destroyed. In Lamentations 3, the same chapter that speaks of evil proceeding from God's mouth, we are given more insight into God's loving nature.

In light of God's revealed character in Lamentations 3, we must come to a better understanding of verses 37 and 38. Tomorrow we will learn from looking further at the context that this is possible.

April 15

Does Evil Proceed from God? (Part 2)

"Who is he that saith, and it cometh to pass, when the Lord commandeth it not? **Out of the mouth of the most High proceedeth not evil** *and good?"* (Lam. 3:37-38)

What does God mean by the statement above? Does He personally and actively distribute good and evil? Does He exert His power to bring evil to pass? When the Bible is studied in its context and read from the perspective of Hebrew way of speaking, especially in light of their permissive idiom, God is seen to be the One actually trying to save people from the impending evil that they are bringing upon themselves:

> **For the Lord will not cast off for ever:** *But though he cause grief, yet will he have compassion according to the multitude of his mercies.* **For he doth not afflict willingly nor grieve the children of men** (Lam. 3:31-33)

After sending numerous prophets to warn His people, who responded by ignoring or persecuting them, God *unwillingly* afflicted Israel because of their horrible sinful practices. He did not do this by exerting His power but by "casting off the Israelites".

Other translations of Lam. 3:31 say, *"For the Lord does not give a man up for ever"* (Bible in Basic English) and *"For the Lord does not abandon anyone forever"* (New Living Translation). Basically, God removed His protection and gave Israel over to the natural consequences of their rebellion. This is repeated in chapter five:

> *Wherefore dost thou forget us for ever, and* **forsake us** *so long time? Turn thou us unto thee, O Lord, and we shall be turned; renew our days as of old.* **But thou hast utterly rejected us;** *thou art very wroth against us.* (Lam. 5:20-22)

God causes grief or "brings about evil" by *casting off* (giving up, abandoning) those that reject Him; by forsaking, rejecting and leaving them unprotected and open to the consequences of their rebellion. This is how He exercises His wrath. God is not the *direct cause of evil in that He actively brings it about.* Even in His "casting off" He does it unwillingly. People force God's hand and He is left with no other choice.

April 16

Does God do Evil? (Part 1)

Shall a trumpet be blown in the city, and the people not be afraid? ***shall there be evil in a city, and the Lord hath not done it?*** *Surely the Lord God will do nothing, but he revealeth his secret unto his servants the prophets.* (Amos 3:6-7)

As we study the Bible carefully we learn that God is often said to do the thing that He allowed to occur after He has removed His protection from a person or nation. However, this protection is only removed when *the person or nation has removed themselves from His protection.* God persistently begs and pleads with people to return to Him before He finally and reluctantly "gives them up."

Before He speaks about His responsibility for the evil done in a city God asks, *"You only have I known of all the families of the earth: therefore I will punish you for all your iniquities.* ***Can two walk together, except they be agreed?"*** (Amos 2:2-3). Due to their constant sinning Israel was not in agreement with God and therefore was not walking with God. Like every other passage of this type, Amos 3:6 is *permissive* in that God is *allowing* men the consequences of their choices.

Commenting on Isa. 45:7, Amos 3:6, and other passages that contribute evil to God, Daniel Waterland writes, "God sees fit to execute vengeance he unties the hands of wicked men and lets them loose to commit all uncleanness and iniquity with greediness. He withdraws his protecting arm for a time from those whom he has once determined to chastize."[19] Some of the church Fathers such as Irenaeus (125-202 AD) agree:

> "Upon all those who separate themselves from Him, God inflicts the separation that they have chosen. Now separation from God is death; separation from light is darkness; separation from God means the loss of all good things that come from Him."[20]

The Lord "does evil" by removing His protection from those who reject Him. Stay in Christ and remain protected.

---

[19] Waterland, Daniel "A Thanksgiving Sermon" **The Works of the Reverend Daniel Waterland** (Oxford, Clarendon Press, 1843), p. 452

[20] Quoted by Faryna, Rev. Deacon Michael The Theology of Illness and Death, https://www.umanitoba.ca/colleges/st_andrews/profiles/MichaelFarynaArticle.html (Last accessed: Dec. 19, 2012).

April 17

Does God do Evil? (Part 2)

Shall a trumpet be blown in the city, and the people not be afraid? ***shall there be evil in a city, and the Lord hath not done it?*** *Surely the Lord God will do nothing, but he revealeth his secret unto his servants the prophets.* (Amos 3:6-7)

Yesterday we learned that God cannot walk with those who are not in agreement with Him. Therefore, His method of inflicting evil is to remove His protection and allow those who reject Him to suffer the consequences of their rebellion. The Israelites had forsaken Him. After much pleading God is said to have finally forsaken them:

Hear ye this word which I take up against you, even a lamentation, O house of Israel. The virgin of Israel is fallen; she shall no more rise: ***she is forsaken upon her land;*** *there is none to raise her up.... For thus saith the Lord unto the house of Israel,* ***Seek ye me, and ye shall live:*** *But seek not Bethel, nor enter into Gilgal, and pass not to Beersheba: for Gilgal shall surely go into captivity, and Bethel shall come to nought....* ***Seek good, and not evil, that ye may live:*** *and so the Lord, the God of hosts,* ***shall be with you,*** *as ye have spoken. Hate the evil, and love the good, and establish judgment in the gate: it may be that the Lord God of hosts will be gracious unto the remnant of Joseph.* (Amos 5:1, 2, 4, 5, 14, 15)

Notice the mercy of the Lord as shown in these passages: He does not do anything to Israel (the evil or disaster that He permits as a cause of their rebellion) without first warning them through His prophets, thus giving them a chance to repent. He gives Israel a chance to turn back to Him so that He can be gracious to them and offer His hand of protection in spite of how they have treated Him. ***What a loving and gracious God!!!***

Israel is not *actively* being punished by God. He is punishing them by withdrawing His presence and protection (*forsaking* Israel). However, Israel is given an opportunity to turn this whole thing around by seeking God. If they return to Him then He will protect them. God is the source of life (John 14:6; Acts 3:15; 1 John 1:1-2). His withdrawal means that Israel will be open to death and its consequent destruction. Lack of life means death. Therefore, Israel is encouraged to turn back to the source of life.

April 18

Does God Frame Evil against People? (Part 1)

"Now therefore go to, speak to the men of Judah, and to the inhabitants of Jerusalem, saying, Thus saith the LORD; Behold, **I frame evil against you,** *and devise a device against you: return ye now every one from his evil way, and make your ways and your doings good."* (Jer. 18:11)

All Scripture of this nature must be interpreted in the light of other Scripture in order to understand the actual mechanism by which God is said to have framed evil against Israel. Jeremiah himself, in other places, explains what he means by God "framing evil" against His people:

Cut off thine hair, O Jerusalem, and cast it away, and take up a lamentation on high places; **for the LORD hath rejected and forsaken** *the generation of his wrath. For the children of Judah have done evil in my sight, saith the LORD: they have set their abominations in the house which is called by my name, to pollute it. And they have built the high places of Tophet, which is in the valley of the son of Hinnom, to burn their sons and their daughters in the fire;* **which I commanded them not, neither came it into my heart.** (Jer. 7:29-31)

I have forsaken mine house, I have left mine heritage; I have given the dearly beloved of my soul into the hand of her enemies. (Jer. 12:7)

For I have set my face against this city for evil, and not for good, saith the LORD: **it shall be given into the hand of the king of Babylon,** *and he shall burn it with fire.* (Jer. 21:10)

God *frames evil* by removing His protection from the recipients of evil. Words and phrases such as "rejected," "forsaken" "left" and "given into" show us that God is not actively exerting energy to bring about evil but is merely removing the umbrella of protection from over the people.

God is not the author *of* evil. He is the protector *from* evil. However, our rebellion may leave Him no choice but to remove that protection and when He does, He takes responsibility for what happens as a result as if He Himself had done it. Stay in Christ and stay protected.

April 19

Does God Frame Evil against People? (Part 2)

*"Now therefore go to, speak to the men of Judah, and to the inhabitants of Jerusalem, saying, Thus saith the LORD; Behold, **I frame evil against you**, and devise a device against you: return ye now every one from his evil way, and make your ways and your doings good."* (Jer. 18:11)

As with all of the passages we have studied, we pointed out yesterday that God only frames evil by removing His hand of protection and allowing one to suffer the consequences of their rebellion. However, Jeremiah makes it clear that this is not an arbitrary act on God's part, but it is actually due to God's people *removing themselves from His protection*:

*For my people have committed two evils; **they have forsaken me the fountain of living waters**, and hewed them out cisterns, broken cisterns, that can hold no water.* (Jer. 2:13)

Hast thou not procured this unto thyself, in that thou hast forsaken the LORD thy God, *when he led thee by the way?* (Jer. 2:17)

Thine own wickedness shall correct thee, and thy backslidings shall reprove thee: *know therefore and see that it is an evil thing and bitter, **that thou hast forsaken the LORD thy God**, and that my fear is not in thee, saith the Lord GOD of hosts.* (Jer. 2:19)

*A glorious high throne from the beginning is the place of our sanctuary. O LORD, the hope of Israel, all that forsake thee shall be ashamed, and they that depart from me shall be written in the earth, because **they have forsaken the LORD, the fountain of living waters**.* (Jer. 17:12-13)

Hence, we see that the "evil" that God is "framing" against the people is to remove His protection from them and allow them to reap what they have sown in a morally ordered universe. Nonetheless, the people removed themselves from God's protection first and continually rebelled against Him, leaving Him no choice in the matter. We must always remain in Christ if we are to enjoy the benefits of His protection from evil.

April 20

Does God Frame Evil against People? (Part 3)

*"Now therefore go to, speak to the men of Judah, and to the inhabitants of Jerusalem, saying, Thus saith the LORD; Behold, **I frame evil against you**, and devise a device against you: return ye now every one from his evil way, and make your ways and your doings good."* (Jer. 18:11)

As we look at the Scriptures we have been studying the past several days we might get the impression that God just easily gets disgusted with His people and removes His protection from them. However, this is far from the case. In the context of Jeremiah 18, God offers to refrain from "bringing" evil if the people would just repent.

*At what instant I shall speak concerning a nation, and concerning a kingdom, to pluck up, and to pull down, and to destroy it; If that nation, against whom I have pronounced, turn from their evil, **I will repent of the evil that I thought to do unto them.** And at what instant I shall speak concerning a nation, and concerning a kingdom, to build and to plant it; If it do evil in my sight, that it obey not my voice, then I will repent of the good, wherewith I said I would benefit them.* (Jer. 18:7-10)

*If so be they will hearken, and **turn every man from his evil way, that I may repent me of the evil**, which I purpose to do unto them because of the evil of their doings.* (Jer. 26:3)

Therefore now amend your ways and your doings, and obey the voice of the LORD your God; and the LORD will repent him of the evil that he hath pronounced against you. (Jer. 26:13)

This shows us that it is not the will or desire of God that people suffer evil in any form: God offers His people a way out. He does not want to remove His protection from them nor does He want to leave them hopeless. He only warns us of impending punishment so that we will turn away from the actions that could bring it upon us. When we turn from sin, God will always change His plans for removing His protective presence.

April 21

God's Actual Plans for His People

For thus saith the LORD, That after seventy years be accomplished at Babylon I will visit you, and perform my good word toward you, in causing you to return to this place. For I know the thoughts that I think toward you, saith the LORD, thoughts of peace, and not of evil, to give you an expected end (Jer. 29:10-11)

Despite how serious Israel's rebellion was and God reluctantly having to remove His protection and turn them over to their enemies, God still lovingly tells them that He has plans of good for them. He says that His thoughts for Israel were for "peace" and not "evil." Some Hebrew experts define the word "peace" as used in this passage as "completeness, safety, soundness (in body), welfare, health, prosperity, quiet, tranquility, and contentment."

What a tender loving God who wants to give hope to people even though they ill-treated Him and forsook Him. Here we see the unconditional love of God in operation. These people told God that they want nothing to do with Him. They have committed horrific acts against God and humanity. They have treated their own citizens in shameful ways. They have sacrificed their innocent children to demonic forces, and they have broken every major law of God that was meant to protect them and their nation. They rejected Jeremiah's warnings about impending judgment and listened to false prophets who told them that they could continue in their sin and no disaster would come upon them.

God, from the natural standpoint, had every right to say, "Good riddance! I don't need these people any more. I have the power to raise up another nation who can represent me on the earth." Yet He did none of those things. Instead He gave His sinful people hope. He told them that even though they put themselves in the predicament that they were in, He hadn't completely given up on them. He would come to them again and rescue them from their captivity. Daniel would later take this same Word from God and pray for the release of His people (Daniel 9-10).

Whatever situation we find ourselves in, even if we caused it by our own neglect or stupidity, we can rest in God's love. We can go to Him in repentance and He will not turn us away nor will He continually throw our wrong in our face. He will rescue us and turn our situation around. He is unconditional love and His love and His plans for our good continue even when we have wronged Him. What a wonderful God we serve.

April 22

Must We Accept Evil from God?

*"Then said his wife unto him, Dost thou still retain thine integrity? curse God, and die. But he said unto her, Thou speakest as one of the foolish women speaketh. What? **shall we receive good at the hand of God, and shall we not receive evil?** In all this did not Job sin with his lips."* (Job 2:9-10)

There are a number of Biblical texts that appear to attribute evil to God. When they are thoroughly examined we learn that God is only taking responsibility for the evil that is done when He removes His protection.

There is no clearer example of this than what we find in Job. Job had no knowledge of all that was transpiring in the spirit realm. He had no knowledge of Satan or his evil ways. Job only knew about God and so he attributed the good and the evil to Him. Job did not sin in doing this because even God took responsibility for what Satan had done to Job (see Job 2:3). However, the reader of Job's historical account is allowed to get a glimpse behind the scenes and see the true source of his misfortunes:

"Hast not thou made an hedge about him, and about his house, and about all that he hath on every side? thou hast blessed the work of his hands, and his substance is increased in the land. But put forth thine hand now, and touch all that he hath, and he will curse thee to thy face. And the LORD said unto Satan, Behold, all that he hath is in thy power; only upon himself put not forth thine hand. So Satan went forth from the presence of the LORD." (Job 1:10-12)

God is only said to have brought evil to Job because He removed His hand of protection, something that He did reluctantly. Satan had just accused God of buying Job's worship and accused Job of only worshipping God for what he could get out of Him. Satan denies that anyone has unselfish motives. The most perplexing thing about Job 2:9-10 is how people quote this passage in an effort to comfort those who are sick, who lost a child, or experienced some other tragic event. It is almost as if they forgot to read the chapter and verses before Job's statement. While Job had an excuse for blaming God (the culture of his times and the lack of light concerning Satan), modern believers have no excuse for taking Job's words when we have been given much more light.

How to Bring Comfort Concerning Evil

*"Then came there unto him all his brethren, and all his sisters, and all they that had been of his acquaintance before, and did eat bread with him in his house: and they bemoaned him, and **comforted him over all the evil that the LORD had brought upon him**: every man also gave him a piece of money, and every one an earring of gold."* (Job 42:11)

Here we are told that God is the direct cause of the evils that Job suffered. Job's friends and family did what they could to bring him needed comfort. However, when someone in our time has suffered a tragedy do we still believe that the way of comfort is to blame God?

Many people seem to believe such is the case. We hear statements like, "God knew what He was doing when He took your child. He knew that he or she might grow up and become evil," "All things work together for good," "The ways of the Lord are mysterious," "receive the evil as well as the good from God," "God is in control. Nothing happens apart from His will," or "God is sovereign. He has a purpose for everything that He does."

One would have to put away all common sense and become religiously blind in order to receive any comfort that an omnipotent God is the source of the evil inflicted upon them and that there is nothing that they can do about it. But, of course, this is exactly what how Job's friends attempted to comfort him.

Nevertheless, the book of Job is an excellent example of how we must interpret Scripture in light of its immediate and wide contexts as well as in light of God's known character of love. For example, in Job 2:7 we read, *"So went Satan forth from the presence of the LORD, and smote Job with sore boils from the sole of his foot unto his crown."* Here we see that the evil brought upon Job was directly inflicted by Satan. God's part was nothing more than removing His protection from Job and permitting Satan to do it (Job 1:10-12; 2:5-6).

God is not the direct-active cause of evil. He is only said to bring evil upon a person when He has lifted His protection from them. Satan is the actual cause of evil, to include disaster, calamity, and sickness.

Here we see one of the best examples of how to interpret Scriptures that attribute any type evil to God. Scripture should always be understood as God *permitting* evil rather than *causing* it. The Bible always explains itself rather than contradicts itself. ***What some claim to be a <u>contradiction</u> is actually an <u>explanation</u>.***

April 24

Satan's Defeat and Your Legal Rights (Part 1)

*"Giving thanks unto the Father, which has made us meet to be partakers of the **inheritance of the saints in light**: Who hath delivered us from the **power of darkness**, and hath translated us into the kingdom of his dear Son. In whom we have **redemption through His blood**, even the forgiveness of sins."* (Col. 1:12-14)

We are partakers of the inheritance of *light.* This is because we are no longer under the authority of darkness. According to Webster's dictionary an *inheritance* is something that we come into possession of or receive as a *right* or *divine portion*.[21] When Adam sinned against God he turned his God given dominion over to the devil (Gen. 1:26). Satan gained legal rights over us. When Jesus died as our substitute He destroyed all of Satan's legal rights and delivered us from his dominion.

Kenneth Wuest translates verse 13, *"....who delivered us out of the tyrannical rule of the darkness and transferred us into the kingdom of the Son of His love."* We were under Satan's tyranny but God rescued us and placed us into the kingdom of the Son He loves so much. There is not one iota of selfishness in God. He loved Jesus so very much yet He was willing to give Him to the world to purchase our freedom from Satan's tyrannical rule.

Paul says that those who are redeemed by the blood of Jesus and delivered from the authority of darkness are translated into a "kingdom"— the kingdom of God's dear Son. Here we have two authorities—two kingdoms that are opposed to each other. Jesus makes it clear that Satan has his own kingdom.

God has a kingdom and Satan has also set up a kingdom. Satan is a king who oppresses his subjects and keeps them in bondage. The reason why God's Kingdom, when it is proclaimed, becomes good news is that, when one embraces it they are released from the bondage inflicted upon them by Satan's kingdom (Matt. 12:22-29). No wonder Satan makes every attempt to blind men and keep them from receiving this good news (2 Cor. 4:3, 4). It is the good news that is the destruction of his evil works over our lives. Now that truly is "good news."

---

[21] Merriam Webster's Collegiate Dictionary, Tenth Edition (Springfield, MA: Merriam-Webster, Incorporated, 1997), p. 1008

April 25

Satan's Defeat and Your Legal Rights (Part 2)

*"Giving thanks unto the Father, which has made us meet to be partakers of the **inheritance of the saints in light**: Who hath delivered us from the **power of darkness**, and hath translated us into the kingdom of his dear Son. In whom we have **redemption through His blood**, even the forgiveness of sins."* (Col. 1:12-14)

Kingdoms represent governments and power. We are no longer under the reign of the kingdom of darkness; therefore, we have the right to be free from all of Satan's bondage. As citizens of a different kingdom, we have citizenship rights as well as inheritance rights.

God's kingdom includes healing for the body, deliverance from demonic oppression and possession, and protection from the attacks of Satan in all areas of our lives (Matt. 4:23; 10:7-8; Luke 9:2; 11:20; 12:32). As a citizen of the United States I possess certain rights and privileges. If this is true concerning USA citizenship then how much more as a citizen of the kingdom of our Lord Jesus Christ?

Satan can only do what *we* give him the right to do. The devil has often kept us in ignorance, attacking us and then blaming God for the attacks. We accepted what Satan has done to us because we believed God was behind it. We either believed that God Himself was bringing negative things upon us or permitting Satan to do it in order to test us. Yet God has redeemed us from Satan's government and taken away his rights to us.

As long as we remain ignorant of the fact that Satan no longer has any rights over us we will allow him to have his way. Once we begin to *see* the truth concerning our redemption in Christ then we will refuse to accept as normal every negative thing that comes our way. We will learn to challenge Satan in line with our redemption rights and privileges in Christ (Ps. 107:2; Heb. 6:12).

Once we leave the darkness and come into the *light*, we begin to *see* our inheritance. This has been made possible by the precious blood of Jesus. We have been redeemed from the curse that comes as a part of the kingdom of darkness. The curse included sickness, sin, poverty, and defeat in every area of life (Deut. 28; Gal. 3:13-14).

Father God did not only rescue us from Satan's evil dictatorship, but He also gave us "rights in Christ" that we are able to exercise when the enemy attempts to attack and overpower us. He *"has made us meet to be partakers of the **inheritance** of the saints in light."*

April 26

Inheritance available by turning to Christ

*"To open their eyes, and to turn them from **darkness to light**, and from **the power of Satan unto God**, that they may receive forgiveness of sins, and inheritance among them which are sanctified by faith that is in me."* (Acts 26:18)

The word "inheritance" is used by Paul in relationship to our rescue from Satan's dominion. This word is in reference to our "family rights". We gain these rights when we become a part of the family of God through the shed blood of Christ. For this very reason Satan keeps sinners in darkness through his lies and deceptions (2 Cor. 4:4; Eph. 4:18). If they could truly see what's available to them by entering into God's family, they would quickly change. He knows the potential that every soul redeemed from his kingdom has for bringing upon it further destruction.

The inheritance we are given as part of our redemption can be seen as our "rights in Christ". It is no coincidence that Paul connects our inheritance, or rather our "rights in Christ" to our freedom from satanic tyranny. The reason why we must emphasize *our rights* is because Satan constantly attacks our faith with His mischaracterizations of Father God. He tells us lies that those things promised us in God's Word may not be His will for us.

Even if He is unable to deceive us with this lie He will still fight hard against the provision coming into manifestation. These battles are designed to make us more inclined to give up from weariness (Dan. 7:25). If we recognize God's promises as our rights then we will not quit trusting for the full provision to come to pass despite lengthy delays and circumstances that appear to be contrary to what we have sought God for.

This is why God's people should not so quickly give up when they do not immediately see a manifestation of a promise that they have sought God to fulfill. We are told, *"That ye be not slothful, but followers of them who through faith and patience inherit the promises"* (Heb. 6:12). All of God's promises are given to alleviate some misery that Satan has placed on the world or on us as individuals. For example, the promises of the new birth and eternal life are meant to free us from Satan's tyranny of death. God's promises for Healing are meant to free us from the bondage of sickness and disease. This is one reason Satan will fight so hard to dissuade us from claiming them. But these promises are our inheritance and must be fought for.

April 27

Fighting for Our Inheritance (Part 1)

*According as his divine power **hath given unto us all things** that pertain unto life and godliness, through the knowledge of him that hath called us to glory and virtue: Whereby are **given unto us exceeding great and precious promises**: that by these ye might be partakers of the divine nature, having escaped the corruption that is in the world through lust* (2 Pet. 1:3-4).

We come into possession of our inheritance by claiming God's promises (Heb. 6:12). The present tense reality of our redemption means that we have a right to all that is accrued from it *in this life*. Many of God's people believe that this is something we receive *after* we get to Heaven. This is why they remain defeated. A. B. Simpson in his book, *"The Land of Promise: Claiming Your Christian Inheritance,"* writes:

> What is meant by the inheritance? First, Israel's inheritance was given them by promise. So our inheritance is all the fullness of God's exceedingly great and precious promises: all the unclaimed wealth of these 40,000 checks in the bank of the Bible-promises for the soul, promises for the body, promises for ourselves, promises for others, promises for our work, promises for our trials, promises for time and promises for eternity.... So our inheritance has been purchased by the Lord Jesus Christ. It includes all that He died for. There are redemption rights, for which He has paid the full, tremendous price.[22]

These are our "redemption rights". The primary reason why we must emphasize God's promises and provisions as our *rights* certainly has nothing to do with God. He is more than willing to bestow them upon us. So willing is He that Jesus shed His blood to ensure and secure them for us and the precious Holy Spirit was sent by Jesus to ensure that we have revelation of these rights (John 16:13).

The primary reason for emphasizing our rights in Christ is due to our ongoing warfare with Satan. If we do not recognize that we have a right to everything that God has promised then Satan will use his lies to throw off our faith, leading us to having a passive attitude towards God's promised blessings. So claim God's promises as your right. Precious blood was shed for that right.

---

[22] Simpson, Albert B. **The Land of Promise: Claiming Your Christian Inheritance** (Camp Hill, PA: Christian Publications, 1996), pp. 84, 85

April 28

Fighting for Our Inheritance (Part 2)

*According as his divine power **hath given unto us all things** that pertain unto life and godliness, through the knowledge of him that hath called us to glory and virtue: Whereby are **given unto us exceeding great and precious promises**: that by these ye might be partakers of the divine nature, having escaped the corruption that is in the world through lust* (2 Pet. 1:3-4).

According to one dictionary a *promise* is defined as, "a **legally binding declaration** that gives the person to whom it is made **a right to expect or to claim** the performance or forbearance of a specified act"[23] (emphases are mine). The fact that God states that His Word has promises is sufficient in itself to say that His Word is a recitation of our *rights in Christ*. When God, who cannot lie, made any promises to us then it automatically gives us the right to possess it as long as we have met His conditions. We overcome the enemy when we understand that we have a right to see him defeated in any area of our lives in which he attempts to put us into bondage and we stand on those rights against all opposition.

Nothing builds our faith more than to know that we have a right to the possession of a certain thing. When we know that something is rightfully ours then we will not so easily yield to enemies that attempt to keep us from possessing that which belongs to us. Many people suffer things that they need not suffer because Satan has used theologians and ministers to tell them that God is the cause of their suffering and that there is no guarantee that He will ever relieve them. However, when you discover that God is actually for you and not against you, that He is on your side, that there is an enemy that is opposed to both you and God but that God has defeated him and given you authority to take from him what is rightfully yours, you will usually get a different perspective. For most of us it will cause an unrelenting, persevering faith to rise up within us that will enable us to stand and not relent until we have obtained that which is ours by right of inheritance.

Having rights do you no good unless you stand against the opposing forces that wish to take your rights away from you. The whole purpose of having "rights in Christ" is to persevere against all opposition. Go through the Bible, learn what your rights are, and stand on them in Jesus' Name.

---

[23] Merriam Webster's Collegiate Dictionary, Tenth Edition (Springfield, MA: Merriam-Webster, Incorporated, 1997), p. 933

April 29

Fighting for Our Inheritance (Part 3)

*According as his divine power **hath given unto us all things** that pertain unto life and godliness, through the knowledge of him that hath called us to glory and virtue: Whereby are **given unto us exceeding great and precious promises***: that by these ye might be partakers of the divine nature, having escaped the corruption that is in the world through lust* (2 Pet. 1:3-4).

God, in the *past tense*, has *given* to us great and precious promises that enable us to escape Satan's domain and influence. The Good News Translation renders verse 4 as *"....**the destructive lust that is in the world, and may come to share the divine nature.**"* Remember that Satan is this world's present ruler (John 12:31; 14:30; 16:11; 2 Cor. 4:4; Eph. 6:10-12; 1 John 5:18-19). The lust in this world that brings about corruption and destruction is totally his doing. Since we are presently in the world where we must do battle with its satanic influence then we certainly cannot wait until the sweet by-and-by to possess the promises that we have inherited. They were given to us for the purpose of walking in victory over this world's corrupting and destructive lust.

God is not at fault for the way that this world is. He has nothing to do with it. Instead, God has given us His Word—His promises for overcoming the satanic lust that seeks to corrupt and destroy us:

*I have written unto you, fathers, because ye have known him that is from the beginning. I have written unto you, young men, because ye are strong, and **the word of God abideth in you, and ye have overcome the wicked one.** Love not the world, neither the things that are in the world. If any man love the world, the love of the Father is not in him. **For all that is in the world, the lust of the flesh,** and the lust of the eyes, and the pride of life, **is not of the Father**, but is of the world. And the world passeth away, and the lust thereof: but he that doeth the will of God abideth for ever* (1 John 2:14-17).

John states it plainly that God is not the cause of the evil that is in the world. This is all Satan's doing. However, we have promises for overcoming the destructive influence of the evil one. We need to claim these promises if we are to overcome him in every area of our lives.

April 30

Claiming our Rights

*Moses my servant is dead; now therefore arise, go over this Jordan, thou, and all this people, unto the land which I do give to them, even to the children of Israel. Every place that the sole of your foot shall tread upon, that have I given unto you, as I **said** unto Moses.... Be strong and of a good courage: for unto this people shalt thou divide for an inheritance the land, which I sware unto their fathers to give them* (Joshua 1:2, 3, 6).

The dictionary tells us that a promise is, "....**a right to expect or to claim** the performance or forbearance of a specified act." (Emphasis are mine). A "claim" means one has a right to that which is being claimed. Linguistically speaking, *rights must be claimed.* The book of Joshua shows us that an inheritance is worthless until it is claimed.

God told Joshua that the land had been *given* to Israel. This land was *sworn* to Joshua's forefathers. This means that God bound Himself to the fulfillment of His Word and His own righteous nature made it impossible to break covenant promises (Ps. 89:33-35; Heb. 6:12-19).

However, it is left up to Joshua and the Israelites to take possession of this inheritance. One can have an inheritance but it does them absolutely no good apart from taking possession of it. It was only when Joshua and the Israelites obeyed by *"Placing the sole of their feet on what God had given them"* that they had this inheritance in actual experience. It was already theirs by right but it was not theirs *experientially* until the soles of their feet tread upon it. This would be no easy task. There is warfare involved in claiming the promises that God has made available:

*So Joshua **took** the whole land, according to **all that the Lord said unto Moses**; and Joshua gave it for an inheritance unto Israel according to their divisions by their tribes. And the land **rested from war*** (Joshua 11:23)

The passage says that Joshua *took* the whole land. Why? The Lord *said* unto Moses—relayed His promises through Moses—that the land was their inheritance. It was their right to possess it. But it did not come without struggles because their enemies were not about to easily give up territory that they had been in possession of for so long. Do not for a minute think that the devil is going to just step aside and let you easily claim your inheritance. You must take possession through aggressive faith warfare.

May 1

Harsh Sayings of Jesus: Calling a Woman a "Dog"

But he answered and said, It is not meet to take the children's bread, and to cast it to dogs. (Matt. 15:26)

Around the time we first became Christians and began learning the Bible, I remember one evening sitting down with my wife in conversation and she had just read where Jesus called a woman a dog. Not being familiar with the passage I was shocked. I told, her, "No, Jesus could not have done that. You're probably reading it wrong. She showed me the passage and sure enough, that is what He called her. I could not believe that my loving Jesus who I was just coming to know would intentionally insult someone. Yet, there it was. I knew there had to be some explanation for this but at the time I did not even know where to begin to find it.

Later I learned that Jesus was not being intentionally harsh and insulting here. He was teaching several lessons to this woman and all others who would read the recording of this incident. The first lesson was for His *Jewish* disciples. A certain amount of racism existed in the hearts of the Jews. They believed that their race was superior and others inferior. To them Gentiles were nothing more than dogs. They needed to see that *anyone* who comes to Christ in faith will receive from Him. It is a lesson that they failed to learn when Jesus healed the servant of a Roman soldier who was one of the very people the Jews disdained as their oppressors (Matt. 8:1-13).

He also needed to teach all of us the necessary perseverance of faith. He insulted this woman with the common belief that was held by all Jews concerning her race. Instead of her feeling slighted and walking away in an angry huff, she replied, *"Truth, Lord: yet the dogs eat of the crumbs which fall from their masters' table"* (Matt. 15:27). Again, Jesus took this opportunity to show that faith and humility, not national origin, is the key to receiving God's blessings and miraculous answers to prayer.

Jesus did not actually view this woman as a dog. He loved and valued her but it was necessary to insult her in order to test her faith, bring a lesson about the love of God to His disciples, and rid them of racial prejudice in preparation for their ministry to **all of the nations** (Matt. 28:18-20). Perseverance of faith brings blessings and God's blessings are available to those, be they Jew or Gentile, who are not easily discouraged by seeming denials.

May 2

Harsh Sayings of Jesus: Causing Family Strife

Think not that I am come to send peace on earth: I came not to send peace, but a sword. For I am come to set a man at variance against his father, and the daughter against her mother, and the daughter in law against her mother in law. And a man's foes shall be they of his own household (Matt. 10:34-36)

How is it that the "Prince of peace" (Isa. 9:6) would be the cause division? Would He exert His omnipotent power to manipulate families into hating one another? Some might read it this way. However, this is another case of the Hebrew idiom in which **God is said to be the cause of that which He merely allowed to happen.** One old commentary, in its section on idioms, explains this well:

> These words, if understood as ordinary English, express the very opposite of the real design of our Lord's coming. He came to unite the whole human family in love to God, and in love one to another. At his birth the angels sang, "Glory to God in the highest, on earth peace, good-will towards men." When He, the Prince of Peace, shall reign universally, the "nations shall beat their swords into plough stares, and their spears into pruning-hooks, and shall learn war no more." Yet his coming did cause sons to rise up against their fathers, and daughters against their mothers. Whenever a member of a Jewish family professed himself a disciple of Christ, he soon experienced the fulfilment of his Master's words, "They shall put you out of the synagogues; yea, the time cometh that whosoever killeth you will think that he doeth God service" (John xvi. 2). The *result* of our Lord's coming was, in all these cases, the very opposite of his intention; yet his words, if interpreted literally, declare that his *object* in coming was to produce variance and strife.[24]

When we understand the language of Scripture, our Lord's "harshness" does not appear to be so harsh after all.

---

[24] Spalding, Thomas **Scripture Difficulties, Explained by Scripture References: Or, The Bible Its Own Interpreter** (London: Daldy, Isbister, and Co., 1877), pp. 316, 317

May 3

Harsh Sayings of Jesus: Hate Your Relatives

*If any man come to me, and **hate** not his father, and mother, and wife, and children, and brethren, and sisters, yea, and his own life also, he cannot be my disciple.* (Luke 14:26)

Is Jesus telling us that we must literally *hate* our family members in order to be His disciple? This would clearly contradict all that we are taught elsewhere in Scripture where we are explicitly told to honor our parents that it may go well with us (Deut. 5:16; Eph. 6:2-3). Jesus Himself recognized the ongoing validity of this commandment (Matt. 19:19) and rebuked the Pharisees for giving people an excuse for violating it for their personal financial gain (Matt. 15:3-9).

Therefore Jesus is either contradicting Himself or we are misunderstanding His Words. I opt for the latter. It goes back once again to learning the cultural idiomatic language that was used by the people of that time. "Hate" as used in the context of Jesus' words is not being used in the same manner in which we might use it today. In this context it merely means to "give less value to." More clarification is giving in Matt. 10:37 where Jesus says, *"He that loveth father or mother more than me is not worthy of me: and he that loveth son or daughter more than me is not worthy of me."* Jesus was not saying, "Hate your relatives and love only me." He was saying, "I am first. All others must come *after* me." Otherwise there is a tendency to have a family idolatry in which we would easily violate God's Word to please our family members.

The erroneous idea that Jesus wants us to have the modern understanding of hate towards our family is disproven by John, who was there when Jesus spoke these words. John later wrote, *"If a man say, I love God, and hateth his brother, he is a liar"* (1 John 4:20a). John goes as far as to say that the person who hates his brother is of the devil and has no eternal life abiding in him. He uses Cain as an example of someone who actually hated his flesh and blood brother and killed him (1 John 3:10-15). The lesson here is that when we truly love God then we will learn to love our family members the way that *He* loves them.

When we fail to allow the Bible to interpret itself it becomes easy to cast aspersions upon God's character and picture Him as a monster who demands that we have murderous intentions towards our own loved ones. However, when we learn what our loving God is really saying, we will reflect His character of love by loving Him first which will in turn enable us to love others the right way.

May 4

Harsh Sayings of Jesus: Calling Peter "Satan"

But he turned, and said unto Peter, Get thee behind me, Satan: thou art an offence unto me: for thou savourest not the things that be of God, but those that be of men. (Matt. 16:23)

Jesus' rebuke of Peter in the passage above seems overly harsh. Jesus had just spoken of His impending death at the hands of satanically inspired men. Peter, seemingly concerned about his Lord, took Him aside and rebuked Him. He told Jesus that these things were *not* going to happen to Him.

Now most of us would have put a hand on Peter's shoulder and said, "Listen my son, I know you love me and you are concerned about my welfare, but this is something that simply has to be done for your salvation and the rest of the world. You may not understand now but one day you will." We consider this "walking in love." However, Jesus did not only seem to harshly rebuke Peter for his concern but referred to him as the source of all evil, Satan himself.

How do we explain such a seemingly harsh action on the part of Jesus? Commentators throughout the centuries have differed on how to approach this, but it has always boiled down to two primary views: Jesus was actually calling Peter a "satan" (adversary) or He was addressing the actual person of Satan (who may have been influencing Peter's actions). I opt for the latter. In 1 Chron. 21:1 we read, *"And Satan stood up against Israel, and provoked David to number Israel."* Godly men have occasionally yielded to influence by Satan to oppose God's purposes.

Even more, Jesus is addressing the malicious spirit behind Peter in the exact same manner in which He dealt with Satan in the wilderness temptation: *"And Jesus answered and said unto him, **Get thee behind me, Satan**: for it is written, Thou shalt worship the Lord thy God, and him only shalt thou serve"* (Luke 4:8). Therefore it is not Jesus referring to Peter himself as Satan but dealing with the evil influence working through Peter.

This should help us when we are attacked and hurt by people, especially those closest to us. It is easier to forgive and deal with the situation if we recognize that our battle is not against flesh and blood but against satanically inspired forces working behind the scenes to influence people against us (Eph. 6:10-12; 2 Cor. 10:3-5). This is why Jesus could pray, *"Father, forgive them; for they know not what they do"* (Luke 23:34). When we recognize that Jesus was dealing with the spirit influencing Peter rather than Peter himself, it takes away the sting of his response to an otherwise sincere, though misguided, concern.

Harsh Sayings of Jesus: Telling People to Mutilate Themselves

And if thy right eye offend thee, pluck it out, and cast it from thee: for it is profitable for thee that one of thy members should perish, and not that thy whole body should be cast into hell. (Matt. 5:29; see also Matt. 18:9)

This passage was difficult for me when I first became a Christian. I really had an eye for the ladies. After reading the Lord's words about how one can commit the act of adultery by simply looking upon a woman with lust and then reading this passage, I became very concerned. After all, I did not want to go to hell and I might be willing to go blind to keep from going there, but I was scared of pulling my eye out of its sockets.

I spoke with an older Christian friend about my concern and after laughing at my ignorance he assured me that Jesus was only speaking spiritually and not literally. That did assuage my fear and I began to work on my lust issues by studying God's Word. However, I wasn't totally convinced that Jesus was only speaking figuratively here. I am convinced today that He was speaking *literally*.

Now, before you pluck out any eyes or cut off any limbs allow me to give you some good news. Jesus was stating that the eternal horrors of hell are not worth those members of our body that we are unable to control. He is saying it would be better to dismember ourselves than to spend eternity in an unending fire where one is tormented day and night forever. No body parts are worth that.

Nonetheless, Jesus has provided us a better way through the power of the Holy Spirit. Paul writes, *"This I say then, Walk in the Spirit, and ye shall not fulfil the lust of the flesh"* (Gal. 5:6). It is by the power of the Spirit that we are able to "mortify our members" (Col. 3:5) and yield them for righteousness rather than sin (Rom. 6:13, 19).

While there is a certain amount of discipline involved in resisting sin and temptation, the Holy Spirit's enablement can help us succeed. Apart from the indwelling Holy Spirit it is indeed better to cut off some limbs and pluck out some eyes than to go to hell in a full body. However, this is unnecessary if one is born again by the Holy Spirit and is yielded to His direction for our lives.

When we study this in full, we see that Jesus was more concerned about our eternal destiny and not about our self-mutilation. He needed us to understand the severity of sin. But He also provided us an alternative to slicing off our body parts, and that is to yield to the Spirit of God.

May 6

Are Only a Select Few Ordained to Eternal Life?

And when the Gentiles heard this, they were glad, and glorified the word of the Lord: and as many as were ordained to eternal life believed (Acts 13:48)

There is a system of theology known as Calvinism, named after the 16th century Protestant reformer, John Calvin. Through this false system of theology much evil has been attributed to God. One of the worse is the idea that, before God created any human being, He had already decreed the fall of man, and then ordained some to eternal life and others to eternal damnation. Calvinists use numerous Bible "proof-texts" to make their case.

Acts 13:48 appears to make a case for God ordaining a select few to eternal life. However, what kind of deity that claims to be love would ever decide to damn trillions of souls to an eternal hell before ever creating them? The good news is that God does no such thing. The original Greek language in which the passage is translated from disproves this false idea.

While I am not a Greek scholar, one online interlinear Greek New Testament gives this literal rendering: "Hearing yet the nations they-joyed and esteemized the saying of the Master and believe as-many-as were having-been-set into life eonian." When read in the Greek, the order is correct: they believe *first* and *after* they believe then they are set into life eternal. Other translations, such as The **Power New Testament**, which is a transliteration from the Greek translates Acts 13:48: *"And while the heathens were hearing, they were rejoicing and glorifying the message about the Lord and as many as were believing were being set into eternal life."*

So in the Greek, the "believing" comes BEFORE being *set* into eternal life. However, there is no better proof of this than to interpret Scripture with Scripture itself. In Ephesians 1:13 we read:

*In whom ye also trusted, after that ye heard the word of truth, the gospel of your salvation: in whom also **after that ye believed, ye were sealed with that holy Spirit of promise.***

The Bible is clear that the order is AFTER ONE BELIEVES, and not BEFORE. It is impossible to read the Scriptures and believe that God has only selected a few for salvation and that regeneration (new birth, salvation, eternal life) precedes faith.

May 7

Did God Create Some People to be Reprobates? (Part 1)

The LORD hath made all things for himself: yea, even the wicked for the day of evil (Prov. 16:4)

Proverbs 16:4 has become a standard proof-text for the erroneous belief that God decrees some to reprobation before they were even born. Of course, if read this way, we would have to believe that God intentionally created some to be wicked and then believe that he created them this way for the express purpose of sending them to hell.

Again, if the isolated text is left alone, it might appear to make a good case for the Calvinist dogma. Nonetheless, it would also be a direct contradiction of other equally authoritative Bible texts:

> *Lo, this only have I found, that **God hath made man upright**; but they have sought out many inventions.* (Ecc. 7:29)

> *This is the book of the generations of Adam. In the day that **God created man, in the likeness of God made he him**; Male and female created he them; and blessed them, and called their name Adam, in the day when they were created. And **Adam** lived an hundred and thirty years, and **begat a son in his own likeness, after his image**; and called his name Seth*: (Gen. 5:1-3)

God created man UPRIGHT. God created man in His image and likeness. To say that God created any man to be wicked is blasphemous since man is created in God's image and likeness. To say that God created any man to be wicked would be to call God wicked since man is created in His image and likeness.

It was Adam, not God, who introduced sin into the world (Rom. 5:12; 1 John 2:16) and had sons in his own image and likeness. So God could not have created anyone for the express purpose of being wicked so that He could punish them. Hence, the Calvinistic understanding of Proverbs 16:4 is clearly wrong. Tomorrow we will look at even more Biblical proof concerning this.

May 8

Did God Create Some People to be Reprobates? (Part 2)

The LORD hath made all things for himself: yea, even the wicked for the day of evil (Prov. 16:4)

As we stated yesterday, followers of Calvinist theology, a doctrine that teaches that God created some people for salvation and others for damnation, uses isolated texts like the one above to make their case. Some of them seem to derive a perverted joy from the idea that they are one of the "elect" and millions of others have been created by God to be wicked so that He can damn them.

It is teaching of this kind that turns men into atheists (though Calvinists would tell us that God decreed that such people would become atheists). Can a God who does this be considered as "compassionate" or "loving" in the true sense of the word? What does such a thing say about God's character? From a common sense standpoint this makes God appear to be worse than the devil.

Proof that God did not create wicked people for the express purpose of punishing them is seen in Ezekiel where God tells us that he takes no pleasure in the death of the wicked:

> *Say unto them, As I live, saith the Lord GOD,* ***I have no pleasure in the death of the wicked;*** *but that the wicked turn from his way and live: turn ye, turn ye from your evil ways; for why will ye die, O house of Israel?* (Eze. 33:11, see also Eze. 18:23, 30, 32)

If God decreed that a person should be wicked and created him thus for the express purpose of punishing him, then the above would make no sense. God says that he has no pleasure in the death of the wicked but that the wicked would turn from his evil way and live. God does not afflict willingly (Lam. 3:33), so God obviously does not get some perverted pleasure out of roasting people.

Therefore, the ideas presented by Calvinism via this text are in direct contradiction to God's full revelation concerning Himself. Nonetheless, how should one interpret Proverbs 16:4? We will look at this tomorrow.

May 9

Did God Create Some People to be Reprobates? (Part 3)

The LORD hath made all things for himself: yea, even the wicked for the day of evil (Prov. 16:4)

Given the biblical evidence that we have presented the past two days that counters the false Calvinistic interpretation of Proverbs 16:4, how then should we understand the passage? We should understand it as men **willingly working themselves to a day of evil** and that, through God's laws of sowing and reaping, He has established that anyone who persists in wickedness and refuses to repent will be destroyed.

The Young's Literal Translation helps us to understand it in this manner: *"All things hath Jehovah wrought for Himself, And also the wicked worketh for a day of evil."* The Young's LITERAL translation is straight from the Hebrew and conveys a thought that is consistent with what the rest of the Bible teaches.

God did not create anyone wicked just to destroy them, but He did decree that if one is going to *choose* to be wicked then they will be reserved for punishment. Peter also teaches this and shows us why these individuals have been *reserved* (not *created* or *decreed*):

> *The Lord knoweth how to deliver the godly out of temptations, and to* **reserve the unjust unto the day of judgment to be punished:** *But chiefly* **them that walk after the flesh in the lust of uncleanness,** *and despise government. Presumptuous are they, selfwilled, they are not afraid to speak evil of dignities....* **Which have forsaken the right way, and are gone astray,** *following the way of Balaam the son of Bosor, who loved the wages of unrighteousness* (2 Pet. 2:9, 10, 15)

We can see that God does not make anyone wicked (Eze. 18:23, 32; Eze. 33:11; Ecc. 7:29; Gen. 5:1-3). However, if men will persist in their wickedness and will not receive the provision for salvation that God has made through Jesus Christ then they will reap the natural and eternal consequences of their rebellion.

In conclusion, I say that Proverbs 16:4 has been grossly misunderstood and misinterpreted by Calvinists. Furthermore more, since it is one of the foundational passages for their doctrine then we must further assume that Calvinism is not a biblical system of theology.

May 10

Does God Prepare Some to be Vessels fit for Destruction?

What if God, wanting to show His wrath and to make His power known, endured with much longsuffering the vessels of wrath prepared for destruction, (Rom 9:22; NKJV)

Here we find another passage in which God is said to have created certain individuals for the primary purpose of destroying them. The usual reading is that God Himself fitted these vessels of wrath for destruction. Nonetheless, this passage is not in reference to a "decree" in which God Himself reprobate some while damning others.

Most unbiased Greek scholars believe that the word that is translated as "fit" is a passive verb. This mean that men (especially in Pharaoh's case within the context) made themselves fit for destruction. A number of English translations remove God as the One actively bringing people to the point of destruction. Phillip's New Testament is one of several: *"May it not be that God, though he must sooner or later expose his wrath against sin and show his controlling hand, has yet most patiently endured the presence in his world of **things that cry out to be destroyed?** "*

This is the only understanding that makes sense. How is it that if God decreed the destruction of these vessels that He would have to "endure them with much longsuffering?" If He had already decreed that such is the case then there is no need to *endure* them because He already has their destiny planned.

So in light of the usual absurd Calvinist understanding of all things, we can see that the vessels fitted themselves, or "cry out," for destruction of their own free choice. God endured them with longsuffering because:

> *The Lord is not slack concerning his promise, as some men count slackness; **but is <u>longsuffering</u> to us-ward, not willing that any should perish**, but that all should come to repentance.* (2 Pet. 3:9)

God *endured* them because He wanted them NOT to perish. This is the true character of God. He is loving and wanting to save these vessels from destruction. However, He will not violate their will to do so. Calvinist teaching would have us to believe otherwise, thus casting aspersions upon God's loving reputation.

What is "the Counsel of God's Will"?

In whom also we have obtained an inheritance, being
predestinated according to the purpose of him who worketh
all things after the counsel of his own will (Eph. 1:11)

In teaching their doctrine of hyper-sovereignty Calvinists often point to this passage as proof that all things happen as the result of God "willing them" to happen. This false idea includes God preordaining sickness, tragedies, crime, war, natural disasters and other evils, but the focus is often primarily on His decree to save some and damn the rest before any man was ever created.

However, the context of the passage in Ephesians 1 is dealing with God's plan for the believer who by faith is already saved. Let's look at this passage in conjunction with verse 12:

In whom also we have obtained an inheritance, being
predestinated according to the purpose of him who worketh
all things after the counsel of his own will: **That** *we should*
be to the praise of his glory, who first trusted in Christ.
(Eph. 1:11, 12)

The key to this passage is the word "that" in verse 12. This word is connecting the two verses in order to finish the thought that had begun in the previous verse. "That" follows "the counsel of His own will." This verse further explains God's plan which is that He willed or predestined "**That** *we should be of his glory, who first trusted in Christ*" (v12). Believers are to bring glory to God and this was the purpose of His plan or what God elected for those that would believe

The "all things" that were worked "after the counsel of his own will" are all those things mentioned in the preceding verses (verses 3 to 10). This is NOT in reference to everything that happens or has happened on the earth since God makes it clear in His Word that many things are not of Him and that some people do things that He did not command or even think about (1 John 2:15-17; Jer. 7:31; 19:5; 32:35)..

Do not accept the false teaching that everything that happens is "the will of God". The Bible nowhere supports this notion. Ephesians 1:11, when read in its context, offers no support for this doctrine. God is a good God and is not the One causing problems in our lives. He is *for* us, not *against* us.

May 12

God has not Given a Spirit of Fear

*For God **hath not given** us the spirit of fear; but of power,
and of love, and of a sound mind* (2 Tim. 1:7)

There are some who claim that all things come from God's sovereign hand, regardless of what it is. They claim that nothing happens apart from His will. Many of them even claim that the acts of the devil cannot occur apart from God's permission and that they all fit a divine (though mysterious) purpose.

If what these folks are saying is true then that would mean that God is responsible for fear. Yet Paul tells Timothy the exact opposite. He tells us that God has *not* given us a spirit of fear. On the contrary, we are told, *"There is no fear in love; but perfect love **casteth out fear**: because fear hath torment. He that feareth is not made perfect in love"* (1 John 4:18). God's love casts out fear. Here is something that definitely does not come from the "sovereign hand of God."

Why is this important to note? We do not put up a resistance against anything that we believe comes from God's hand. If we are fearful then we may accept the lie that it is God who is making us afraid. Yet, this is the same God who says repeatedly throughout Scripture, "fear not," "do not be afraid," "be anxious for nothing," and "have faith." Therefore, if we are fearful in any of life's circumstances, God is not the source of it.

The Bible actually identifies the true source of fear: *it is a spirit.* This spirit is obviously not sent by God but by the ruler of all rebellious spirits of torment, Satan:

Forasmuch then as the children are partakers of flesh and blood, he also himself likewise took part of the same; that through death he might destroy him that had the power of death, that is, the devil; And deliver them who through fear of death were all their lifetime subject to bondage (Heb. 2:14-15)

God does not bring us fear but has sacrificed Himself to deliver us from it. We must always keep in mind that there are two kingdoms operating in this world and both are attempting to influence human lives. This is Satan's kingdom and God's kingdom. Therefore, resist any circumstance that produces fear and recognize its source. Then stand in God's Spirit of power, love and a sound peaceful mind.

May 13

Is God behind all of Life's Events?

*This time, you will be founded and grounded on right thought, speech, and action. And no one will trouble you, abuse or oppress you; you will know no fear and have no worries. **If a nation marches against you, know that I am not behind it.** Anyone foolish enough to challenge you will fall to you* (Isaiah 54:14-15; The Voice)

Some tell us that nothing in this universe happens apart from God's will. This implies that God is the one behind every sickness, disease, war, child rape, kidnapping, police brutality, communistic regime, poverty and starvation, and every other horrendous activity that is taking place on the earth. No wonder many of the people who believe this lie are very afraid of God. Some even hate God with a passion because of this teaching.

Yet, the idea that God is behind it all contradicts so much of the Bible, most notably the passage above. God does not give things that cause us fear and worry. If He did then He would be the source of our worries. All His admonitions to "be anxious for nothing" and to "be careful for nothing" and to "take no thought for your life" would be nothing more than meaningless platitudes.

Thankfully we have it on record that God is not behind those things that would normally cause His people to be full of fear and worry. Not only is He not behind it but He tells us that anything that is foolish enough to challenge us will fall to us.

This should bring courage to every child of God. God is not the source of our problems but is the One who gives us the victory over them. Our problems must fall to us. Do not accept the false idea that a faithful Christian will walk through this life without challenges. On the contrary we should expect plenty of them when we are serving Christ.

Satan has an intense hatred for God which is inflected upon God's people. Furthermore, as we seek to advance God's kingdom this signals further decimation of Satan's kingdom. When the devil is threatened he will attempt to challenge the source of that threat. When his usual lie that God is the One behind those challenges has been refuted then his defeat is inevitable and he will fall to us.

Recognize that God is not behind any of life's negatives. Do not buy into the very lie that has caused Christians defeat in this life. Resist the challenges brought on by the kingdom of darkness and watch them fall to you because of your faith in God's powerful Word.

May 14

Is Everything that Happens Ordained by God?

And they have built the high places of Tophet, which is in the valley of the son of Hinnom, to burn their sons and their daughters in the fire; which I commanded them not, neither came it into my heart (Jer. 7:31)

In some of the most wicked "theology" I have read, a number of ministers have claimed that God has foreordained every life event to include *sin*. One man has had the utter audacity to write, "**It is even biblical to say that God has foreordained sin**. If sin was outside the plan of God, then not a single important affair of life would be ruled by God" (Edwin H. Palmer, *"The Five Points of Calvinism"*, p.82-83).

The word "commanded" in Jeremiah 7:31 is from the Hebrew word *"tsavah"* which, among several things, means "to command, appoint, ordain (of divine act)". Reading it with that definition we understand God as saying that He did not foreordain Israel's sin of idolatry. On the contrary He said that it never even came into His heart. God warned His people more than once to never do such a thing (Lev. 18:21; 20:20).

Not only does God care about the life of the children, He revealed very early on there are the evil agents that seek to destroy them: *"Yea, they sacrificed their sons and their daughters unto devils"* (Psalm 106:37).

Again, we see that Satan and his agents are involved in the sinful practices of men. One cannot sin without dealing with the evil spirits behind the sin:

*And he made his son pass through the fire, and observed times, and used enchantments, **and dealt with familiar spirits** and wizards: he wrought much wickedness in the sight of the LORD, to provoke him to anger* (2 Kings 21:6)

Satan has been able to cloak his work of evil behind the false teaching that everything that happens is foreordained by God, including sin. Yet the Bible reveals that there is a spiritual warfare taking place in which God and His angels are fighting on man's behalf against evil spirits. God asks us to cooperate in this war by not yielding to sinful enticements. So-called theologians must come to grips with this and stop blaming God for Satan's works.

May 15

Is God the Author of Everything?

*"For God is **not** the author of confusion, but of peace, as in all churches of the saints."* (1 Cor. 14:33).

There have been a number of men, usually in what is known as the "Calvinist" or "Reformed" camps, that taught the false idea that God is the author of everything that happens. This includes sin itself. One of the most influential has been the father of the Calvinist doctrine, John Calvin himself. Calvin wrote, "But the objection is not yet resolved, that if all things are done by the will of God, and men contrive nothing except by His will and ordination, **then God is the author of all evils**" (John Calvin, *Concerning the Eternal Predestination of God*, p.179).

What a horrible deceptive lie. The only logical conclusion to the false idea that God ordains all things to include what "men contrive" is that God is the author of all evils. Such double-talk cannot defy the God created laws of logic nor the teaching of God's Word.

In contrast to Calvin, God's Word says that He is not the author of *confusion*. When we examine how the Bible uses the word "confusion" then Calvin's statement is easily repudiated. For example, men and women engaging in bestiality and incest is described as *confusion* (Lev. 18:23; 20:12), and James compares confusion to *evil works* (James 3:16).

Confusion, which, Biblically speaking, equates to sin and *evil*, is not credited to God as its author. The Bible says that He is the author of *peace* and the divine record refuses to acknowledge Calvin's false teaching here. The Bible does say, *"And being made perfect, he became the **author** of eternal salvation unto all them that **obey him**"* (Heb. 5:9). God wants men to obey Him and has authored salvation for them. He did not author the disobedience that would keep them from salvation as Calvin teaches above.

Satan has worked through reformers and modern theologians alike in order to castigate God's character, remove all resistance to his kingdom agenda, lull men to sleep, and push forward his destruction of mankind through blatant sin. "Why resist," he will say, "God is the one who authors everything that happens in life, including evil."

The beginning of a holy and victorious life is to see God in a different light. This can only come from a consistent study of what the Scriptures say, unfiltered by the canonized protestant reformers of yester-year or any of their spiritual descendants today. Sin leads to death and destruction. God is the author of neither.

May 16

Is God the Source of this World's Problems?

For all that is in the world, the lust of the flesh, and the lust of the eyes, and the pride of life, is __not__ of the Father, but is of the world (John 2:16)

Quite often God gets the blame for every event that occurs in the world in which we live. Even people who claim to believe the Bible put God at fault for all that is in the world. This is consistent with their ideas of what it means for God to be sovereign. For them, sovereignty means absolute control of every single event that occurs. If there is one thing that occurs that did not have God's mysterious hand in it then, in the scenario of some, God simply cannot be sovereign.

As usual, Scripture teaches something altogether different than what so many other people claim. We are told in the above passage that all of the sinfulness that is in the world does not have its source in the Father. If God is not the source of the sinfulness in our world then He certainly is not the author of the consequences that come from these things, at least, not in a direct way. God is only responsible as far as *allowing* the physical and spiritual laws in this world to take place with very little interference on His part.

We must keep in mind that this world is not the original world that God created. It is now a fallen world and is actually hostile to God and those who follow Christ (John 1:10; 15:18-19). God even considers this world His enemy (James 4:4; Rom. 5:10). Because Adam yielded to Satan sin was brought into the world. Satan has become the world's prince and ruler (Rom. 5:12; 1 John 3:8; John 12:31; 14:30; 16:11; Eph. 2:2; 6:10-12; 2 Cor. 4:4). Scripture tells us that the world is under Satan's control, at least temporarily (1 John 5:18, 19; Rev. 12:12).

Since Satan is the world's ruler then we can expect him, demons, and people under his influence to bring problems our way. Problems are the results of a world full of the lust of the flesh, the lust of the eyes and the pride of life (John 16:33). These things are a part of our spiritual warfare. Yet, we are not in a hopeless situation. God has given us every resource for dealing with problems in our lives (2 Pet. 1:3-4; 1 John 4:4; 5:4-5).

Nonetheless, if we are to walk in victory over the issues and problems that we encounter in this world then we must not look at God as the source of any of it. All that is in the world is not of the Father. He loves us and wants to deliver us from the world's deadly effects.

May 17

God does not Give Devilish Wisdom

*But if ye have bitter envying and strife in your hearts, glory not, and lie not against the truth. **This wisdom descendeth not from above**, but is earthly, sensual, devilish* (James 3:14-15)

The idea that everything that happens in life somehow comes from the hand of God is a popular teaching in the majority of Christian circles. This has caused many to try to look for some mysterious good or some divine purpose in any negative circumstance in life. Some reason that perhaps the circumstance was sent by God to strengthen their faith and make them a better Christian.

The majority of the painful things we face in life often come from other people. Some of the people who have hurt us most have been professing Christians. People have hurt us through bitterness, envy, and strife. They have gossiped about us, soiled our reputations, and have caused us insurmountable pain. People have divorced, lost jobs, churches have split and families have been destroyed due to bitter envying and strife. Yet when these things happen we hear the phrase intended to bring comfort: "God is in control. He knows what He is doing."

Regardless, James tells us that these things are *not* from God. The source of the bitter envying and strife that brings confusion and every evil work has Satan as its author. We should never look for a divine reason or some expected good to come from sin. Like Joseph, God can turn everything around for our good when we cooperate with Him (Gen. 50:20; Rom. 8:28), but we should not see good in the sin itself.

The source of this "wisdom" is devilish. The only thing we are to do with devilish ideas is cast them down and resist them (2 Cor. 10:3-5; James 4:7). We must remember that we are dealing with an enemy and we are not to take a passive position in dealing with his machinations. We especially must reject his constant lies about God that puts Him at fault for the very things that Satan and demons are doing.

James says, *"Every **good gift** and every perfect gift is from above, and cometh down from the Father of lights, with whom is no variableness, neither shadow of turning"* (James 1:17). Accept only that which we know to be good. Accept no devilish substitutes.

May 18

God does not show Prejudicial Favoritism

*Then Peter opened his mouth, and said, Of a truth I perceive that **God is no respecter of persons**: But in every nation he that feareth him, and worketh righteousness, is accepted with him* (Acts 10:34-35)

There is a false idea that has been prevalent in the church for centuries. The false idea is that God picks and chooses particular people for certain blessings based solely on His mysterious sovereign decision. Within this teaching God has chosen to save some and has rejected others. He has chosen to prosper and heal some but has decided that others should be poor and sick. This teaching claims that God gives some faith while leaving others destitute in unbelief.

While this is supposedly "orthodox teaching" and is accepted as "evangelical doctrine" in numerous churches, it is not only in contradiction to the plain teaching of God's Word, but it maligns God's loving and gracious character. The Holy Spirit inspired Peter to teach us that God is not a respecter of persons. He does not pick and choose people for salvation and blessings while rejecting others. He tells us that *"....he that feareth him, and worketh righteousness, is accepted with him."* That means anyone can get in on what God is giving if they meet the conditions.

This is just as true of divine healing of the body as with any other blessing. Right in the same message Peter says:

*How God anointed Jesus of Nazareth with the Holy Ghost and with power: who went about doing good, and healing **all** that were oppressed of the devil; for God was with him* (Acts 10:38).

Note the word "all" in that verse. God is not selective in who He wants to heal, deliver, bring to Heaven or any of these things. He wants all men to be saved (1 Tim. 2:4) and He wants to heal all who are being oppressed by Satan in their mind, body or finances. That includes YOU! Get in on the blessings that God delights to bestow on all who receive them willingly.

God is not Unrighteous

*For **God** **is** **not** **unrighteous** to forget your work and labour of love, which ye have shewed toward his name, in that ye have ministered to the saints, and do minister* (Heb. 6:10)

"Why am I going through all of this? Why is God letting this happen to me? Has God forgotten all that I have done for Him? I have tried to obey Him in everything He has asked but I am still suffering? I don't understand?" If God forgets our work and our labor of love then based on His written Word He is unrighteous. This is impossible. If God were unrighteous then there is entirely no hope for us or this universe.

The word "righteous" basically means "to be right". It is not a mysterious or esoteric word. It simply means that there is no crookedness or darkness in God. Unrighteousness on the other hand is anything that is the opposite of what is right. John said, *"All unrighteousness is sin"* (1 John 5:17a). For God to forget our work and labor of love would be a sin on His part. Can we imagine God being referred to as a "sinner"? But some will protest and say, "Well, God is God. He can do whatever He wants and whatever He does would not be a sin."

That is not entirely true. God Himself specifically said that if He performed certain actions that this would make Him unrighteous, thus making Him a sinner. In this case, God says that He would be a sinner if He forgot our work and our labor of love. That means that God cannot just simply "do whatever He wants" and still be holy and righteous. Even God must do what is righteous in order to be righteous.

This should give us confidence in the fact that God could never do us wrong or any harm. He brings us this assurance because we have a tendency, when things are tough, to think that God has forgotten about us and our sacrifices. This is exactly what was happening during the time that Hebrews was written. Many of the Jews who converted to Christianity suffered strong persecution for leaving Judaism. They went through hard times and thought that God had forgotten them. They were tempted to reject Christ and go back. God assures them that they weren't forgotten.

Take your stand on this truth when you are facing tough situations and the devil whispers his lie, "God has forgotten about you and all that you have done." Tell him, "No devil. If God did that it would make God unrighteous like *you*. And He isn't."

May 20

God is Not Willing that Any Should Perish

The Lord **is not slack** *concerning his promise, as some men count slackness; but is longsuffering to us-ward,* **not willing that any should perish**, *but that all should come to repentance* (2 Pet. 3:9)

Again we find another "not" in the Bible that gives us some insight into God's wonderful and loving nature. Some theologians embrace a theological system that teaches the false idea that God has selected some for salvation and others for damnation. He had chosen to do this long before any man was ever born. This theology has come under several names – TULIP, Reformed, Augustinianism and Calvinism just to name a few. While this is supposed to be an "orthodox" position, it goes in direct contradiction to the Biblical revelation of God's loving character.

Peter tells us plainly that God is not willing that any should perish. It simply is not His will for anyone to die and spend an eternity in hell. I have never understood how anyone could embrace Calvinism or even sympathize with this system of theology when its teaching calls God a liar on this point.

While God truly is sovereign and is indeed all-power, according to 2 Pet. 3:9, God does not always get what He wants. This is because God's power is exercised through His love. He does not force or coerce men and women into doing what He wants, even though what He wants is far better for them. Yet, even in eternal decisions God is unwillingly to violate the free-will decisions of His creatures. They must choose for or against Him. But God is always hoping that people choose *for* Him because He does not want them to perish.

We have been told that God exercises an all-controlling sovereignty and He gets whatever He wants. This attitude makes God an unloving tyrant who uses power to coerce and even force His will upon people, making them nothing more than automatons. The Bible does not support this anywhere and often Scripture is taken out of context to teach this lie.

Nevertheless, the sad part for the sinner who dies without Christ is that they will go to an eternity of torment and torture, something that God does not want. It is important that we share the truth with the lost about how much God longs for them to know Him and escape eternal punishment.

May 21

Some Things Happen Outside of God's Will

*Even so it **is** **not** the will of your Father which is in heaven,*
that one of these little ones should perish (Matt. 18:14)

Some claim that nothing happens outside of God's will. Were this true then no one would be unsaved and suffer an eternity in hell. After all, it is God's will that all men be saved (1 Tim. 2:4). In this particular "not" concerning God, we see this truth made plain based on the fact that He does not want any of the little ones to perish.

The possibility of the little ones being lost is seen in the preceding verses of Matthew 18. In verses 12 and 13 Jesus has given a parable concerning a sheepfold that has 100 sheep in it. One of the sheep goes astray and the shepherd goes after it. When the sheep has returned we are told that this shepherd, who symbolizes God, rejoices over that sheep. As a matter of fact, he rejoices over the lost sheep being found more than the ones that remained.

Why is it that God would rejoice over a lost sheep that returns to Him? It is because it is not His will that any perish. Those that remain in the sheepfold are already safe. Those who stray endanger themselves both temporally as well as eternally. The fact that God may lose someone He loves for all of eternity brings aches and pain to His heart. To see that sheep return to Him and removed from eternal damnation brings Him overwhelming joy.

Strangely enough, the warped theological systems that emphasize an idea about God's sovereignty in which everything that happens is His will ignore these basic truths. By ignoring passages such as Matthew 18:14, not only is God's character unreasonably maligned but He appears to be untrustworthy.

The plain teaching of His Word cannot be trusted when it is read through the filter of an all-controlling dynamic. Based on this method of interpretation, Matt. 18:14 may as well read as follows: "Even so it *is* the will of your Father in Heaven that *some* of these little ones should perish." If we accepted some of the things that are taught about God's will then we would have no need for evangelism or intercessory prayer.

What places a strong desire in believers to pray for and win the lost to Christ? Knowing that this is what God longs for. It is not His will that any be lost. We love God so we want what He wants.

God is not the God of the Dead

I am the God of Abraham, and the God of Isaac, and the God of Jacob? **God is not the God of the dead, but of the living.** *And when the multitude heard this, they were astonished at his doctrine* (Matt. 22:32)

Whenever a truth about God has been revealed that goes contrary to lies that have been taught about Him, people are often astonished. This astonishment can be good and bad. Some are astonished by the fact that someone would even dare to teach anything contrary to what they have traditionally understood to be the truth about God. It is a "how dare you!" type of astonishment. Others, who were in bondage to a lie about God that made Him anything other than loving are astonished but relieved to have revealed to them a truth concerning God that paints a much better picture of Him.

In Matt. 22:23 we discover that the people during Jesus time were being given a false portrayal of God, *"The same day came to him the Sadducees, which say that there is no resurrection."* From there they attempted to ask Jesus a trick question. One might wonder how denying the resurrection of the dead could possibly malign God's character. One of the problems is the false idea that when a person's body has died that this is the end of their existence. Some believe that death means annihilation or extinction. For some, there is no hope of an after-life.

What is the need for living righteously in this life if this life is all that there is? Isn't this the false belief today that moves people to have as much fun as they can before they die? Isn't this the false belief that moves people to commit suicide because they believe that by doing so that this ends all of their pain and suffering?

What an insult to God to say that He is the God of the dead. He has referred to Himself as "....the God of Abraham, and the God of Isaac, and the God of Jacob." To say that these men are dead would imply they are separated from God, thus making God a liar. How are we to believe that Christ truly rose from the dead if this is true? How can we believe that through Jesus we will be resurrected? Because God is the God of the living, we can be sure that He will and has rescued us from the power of death.

May 23

Christ's Kingdom is not of this World

Jesus answered, **My kingdom is <u>not</u> of this world***: if my kingdom were of this world, then would my servants fight, that I should not be delivered to the Jews: but now is my kingdom not from hence* (John 18:36)

For years I thought that Jesus was complaining that no one had fought to keep the Jews from taking Him captive. Yet this did not make sense. When Peter cut off the ear of one of the soldiers taking Jesus prisoner, Jesus rebuked him and restored the soldier's ear (Matt. 26:51-52).

Jesus also told His followers that if He really needed someone to fight for Him, He could pray and His father would send a legion of angels for this task. However, the scriptures needed to be fulfilled concerning His redemptive death, burial, and resurrection (Matt. 26:53-54). Therefore, Jesus could not have been complaining about no one having fought for Him to keep Him from being taken captive. He willingly laid down His life for us (John 10:17-18).

So then what is Jesus saying here? Jesus was answering Pontius Pilate's question, "Art thou the King of the Jews?" (John 18:33). Jesus never denied that He is a king but He clarified the fact that His kingdom does not operate on the same self-seeking principles found in earthly kingdoms, most of which are satanically influenced.

Very few kings would ever willingly give their lives for their people. Most would not even give any thought to dying for their enemies (Rom. 5:6-10). These kings would expect their soldiers to give their own lives to save the king and keep him from being captured. Jesus was explaining to Pilate how the system in this world operated, a system Pilate was quite familiar with.

Jesus' kingdom is not of this world because it does not operate on the same principles that the world does. This world is ruled by Satan. He is the god of this world and has men blinded to the truth. The world operates on the principle of selfish hatred. The kingdom of our Lord operates on the principle of others-focused love.

Jesus stopped Peter from fighting for Him and denied Himself His right to angelic protection because His death was necessary for our redemption. Had Jesus acted as an earthly king and allowed Himself the privilege of protection from Jewish capture, the rest of us would have no hope. We would die in our sins. Jesus died to save us from sin and its consequences. In this He was demonstrating the principle of unselfish love. Truly His kingdom is *not* of this world.

May 24

The Lord is not Furious

*In that day sing ye unto her, A vineyard of red wine. I the Lord do keep it; I will water it every moment: lest any hurt it, I will keep it night and day. **Fury is not in me:** who would set the briers and thorns against me in battle? I would go through them, I would burn them together* (Isa. 27:2-4)

We hear much these days about the "wrath of God." It is a truth that must be proclaimed but I do not believe that most of the church understands it fully. We seem to have two opposite extremes on this subject. Some teach that the wrath of God applies only to the Old Testament. Since He supposedly poured out His entire wrath upon Jesus while He was on the cross, God is said to no longer operate in wrath.

On the opposite extreme are those who do recognize that the New Testament teaches the wrath of God but proclaim it in a way that makes God appear to be very angry and vindictive. Many of these same people seem to believe that there is a disconnect between God's wrath and God's love. He can operate in one or the other but not both. That means God can be loving sometimes and other times He can be wrathful.

However, if we grasped the truth about God's wrath we would learn that it is not disconnected from His love. When the Scripture is read carefully, we can see that God's "fury" or "wrath" is something that is outside of Him:

But he, being full of compassion, forgave their iniquity, and destroyed them not: yea, many a time turned he his anger away, and did not stir up all his wrath. For he remembered that they were but flesh; a wind that passeth away, and cometh not again (Psalm 78:38-39)

Note that due to His love (compassion) He did not "stir up all His wrath". There is no disconnect between God's love and "fury". The New Living translation says, *"Many times he held back his anger and did not **unleash** his fury!"* In Psalm 78:49 we are told that how He unleashes this fury when left with no choice: *"He **loosed** on them his fierce anger—all his fury, rage, and hostility. He dispatched against them a band of destroying angels."* The fury is *not* in God Himself. We open ourselves to fury when we rebel against God and open the door for Satan to attack us.

The Lord's Hand is not Shortened

Behold, **the Lord's hand is <u>not</u> shortened,** *that it cannot save; neither his ear heavy, that it cannot hear: But your iniquities have separated between you and your God, and your sins have hid his face from you, that he will not hear* (Isa. 59:1-2)

I have taken a very keen interest in a theological discipline called theodicy in the past several years. This is an aspect of theology that is meant to defend God's goodness in the light of evil. Many have asked that if God is good then why so much evil. Theologians and philosophers who specialize in this area attempt to answer that question.

Some who set out to defend God's goodness attempt to do so by questioning whether or not He is omnipotent. Many theologians who embrace a God of coercion place emphasis on His omnipotent power. Others have reacted to this by diminishing or altogether removing this important aspect of God's nature.

Denying God's omnipotence is not the way to resolve the seeming contradiction between His omnipotence and the overwhelming truth that evil is running rampant in the world—at least, not if we are going to base our beliefs on Scripture. The Bible states that there is evil in the world. The Bible also teaches us that God is very good and hates evil in all of its variations. However, the Bible never denies that God is all-powerful.

This being true, why doesn't God exercise His omnipotent power to stop evil? First, God could never stop all evil without positively destroying all of the free agents that cause evil—to include you and me. He must allow a lot of the evil to take place because His does not use His power to coerce or to override our free-will.

Secondly, God does work to stop evil in our personal lives and in our nation but He requires our cooperation (2 Chron. 16:9). He is well able to save us from the hurt and harm that evil intends to do to us but we often hinder Him from working on our behalf through our own sin and iniquity. When we sin we take the side of evil and the evil one. When we do that we separate ourselves from God and lose His protective presence. He cannot hear or answer our prayers when we choose to rebel against Him. God is not lacking in power to save. He is lacking in *our permission* to let Him save us.

Can God be Embarrassed?

But now they desire a better country, that is, an heavenly:
*wherefore **God is not ashamed to be called their God:** for*
he hath prepared for them a city (Heb. 11:16)

Can God be embarrassed or ashamed to be claimed as someone's God? Can God be proud of His people? If you believe that there is an ongoing war between God and Satan then the answer should be "yes" to both questions. Satan is constantly attempting to malign God's character before men and angels (Gen. 3:1-7; Job 1-2). Satan's primary arguments, as seen from Scripture, are that God is an egotistical selfish being who bribes men and angels to worship Him. There is no man on the earth who would worship God and live holy for the mere purpose that he or she loves God.

Sadly, Satan has been able to prove this to be true in far too many cases. Quite often God's own people have embarrassed Him in front of the universe and among the heathen who are looking for excuses not to serve Him (2 Sam. 12:13, 14; Rom. 2:23, 24). Satan wants everyone to believe that God is unjust, unloving, and unfair and that no one can actually live up to His standards of holiness.

Paul's advice to widows demonstrates how our conduct is important in the warfare between God and Satan (1 Tim. 5:14-15). The conduct of the widows gave the devil and those who follow him occasion to slander and blaspheme. Their conduct led them to deny God and follow Satan. Jesus said:

> *"Whosoever therefore shall be ashamed of me and of my*
> *words in this adulterous and sinful generation; of him also*
> *shall **the Son of man be ashamed,** when he cometh in the*
> *glory of his Father with the holy angels"* (Mark 8:38)

We must keep in mind that we are God's representatives on the earth (2 Cor. 5:17-21) and in the heavens (Job 1; 1 Tim. 5:21; 1 Pet. 1:12). What we do can have an effect on the salvation of others. On the other hand, we can certainly make God proud by how we conduct our lives when we do it for His glory (Matt. 5:14-16).

God is not a Liar

God is <u>not</u> a man, that he should lie; neither the son of man, that he should repent: hath he said, and shall he not do it? or hath he spoken, and shall he not make it good? (Num. 23:19)

God is not trying to be insulting. He is making a statement of *reality* here. Every human being (except Jesus) has sinned and by sinning has taken on the nature of Satan (John 8:44). Therefore we are subject to lying because we at one time possessed the nature of the original liar. Due to this we have lied to one another and we have reneged on our promises.

God had this statement recorded so that we would be able to trust Him. He was telling us that He won't fail us like men would. We are susceptible to doubting God's Word based on our experience with men. Men have lied to us and have failed us. But God is nothing like us in that regard. Recognizing God's integrity is the foundation for faith. The Scripture says, *"So then faith cometh by hearing, and hearing by the word of God."* This is meaningless unless we are confident that God would never lie to us.

It was this questioning of God's integrity that caused man to fall in the beginning (Gen. 3:1-7), kept His people out of the promised land for forty years (Num. 13-14) and causes people today to sin without repentance, to fail to persevere in prayer, to make confessions that are not in line with God's Word, and to simply fail to claim His innumerable promises for the spirit, soul and body.

When we begin to recognize that God is holy, is not by any means subject to the same failures as fallible men, is not arbitrary or vindictive, is loving and longing to do things for us, then we will better grasp the fact that He is nothing like men who can easily lie. We lie when the truth is inconvenient for us and we break promises when they become a burden to keep. We then inflect this unloving characteristic on God. Yet God says, *"....thou thoughtest that I was altogether such an one as thyself: but I will reprove thee, and set them in order before thine eyes"* (Psalm 50:21).

We have no legitimate reason for failing to believe God's promises or to obey His commands. On the contrary, we have every reason to trust Him. Understanding that God never lies empowers us to counter the true liar, Satan, who is constantly whispering doubts in our ears concerning God's Word. Anything that contradicts God's Word is a lie, because God is not a man that He should lie.

May 28

The Lord Kills People and Makes People Poor? (Part 1)

The Lord killeth, and maketh alive: he bringeth down to the grave, and bringeth up. The Lord maketh poor, and maketh rich: he bringeth low, and lifteth up (1 Sam. 2:6-7)

Is the Lord responsible for death and poverty? Is He the one that determined that Howard Hughes and Bill Gates would be rich while decreeing that many people in third world countries would suffer poverty and starvation and the diseases inherent in such conditions?

There are some who became rich by lying, cheating, and stealing. Many of them have oppressed others to gain wealth (Prov. 22:16). Is this God's *sovereign hand* bringing this about? (Unfortunately, some Calvinists would actually answer "yes" to this question.) Then there are those who have become poor as a result of bad choices (Prov. 6:10-11; 11:24; 13:18; 20:13; 23:21; 24:33-34; 28:19, 22).

The same is true concerning sickness and diseases (Mark 2:5; John 5:13-14; James 5:14-16). Certain choices we make can either prolong or shorten our days on the earth (Eccl. 7:17; Eph. 6:2-3; 1 Pet. 3:10). While some of us are born into conditions beyond our control, much of our destiny has a lot to do with *us*. God should not bear the responsibility for these things.

Passages such as 1 Samuel 2:6-7 are often quoted to prove that God has ordained all of life's events, both good and evil. Yet this misreading of Scripture contradicts Jesus' words in John 10:10 which He says, *"The thief cometh not, but for to steal, and to kill, and to destroy: I am come that they might have life, and that they might have it more abundantly."* Jesus, who is the exact representation of the Father, says that the thief (Satan) comes to kill. Jesus' mission is to give *life*. Furthermore, we are told that Satan was the one who had the power of death (Heb. 2:14-15).

In other passages God tells us that He takes no pleasure in the death of the wicked but that they should live (Eze. 18:23, 32; 33:11). It is only Satan who seems to get a joy and a delight from killing and destroying people (Job 1-2). Therefore, 1 Sam. 2:6-7 cannot be looked upon as support for the idea that every single death, case of poverty, wealth, or any other event has been somehow manipulated by God via His sovereign hand. Much of the negatives we experience in life are due to sin having come into the world (Rom. 5:12).

So how do we read such passages as the one above? How do we understand them without questioning the divine inspiration of the Scriptures? We will learn how to do this in tomorrow's devotion.

May 29

The Lord Kills People and Makes People Poor? (Part 2)

The Lord killeth, and maketh alive: he bringeth down to the grave, and bringeth up. The Lord maketh poor, and maketh rich: he bringeth low, and lifteth up (1 Sam. 2:6-7)

Yesterday we saw how the idea that God arbitrarily kills and makes people poor goes in direct contrast with other passages of Scripture, including Jesus' contrast with His and the devil's work (John 10:10). That being the case, how do we resolve this tension without questioning the integrity of Scripture?

We must interpret Scripture with Scripture to resolve these problems. Moses makes a similar statement in Deuteronomy, but the context clarifies what God is saying:

*To me belongeth vengeance and recompence; **their foot shall slide in due time: for the day of their calamity is at hand,** and the things that shall come upon them make haste. For the Lord shall judge his people, and repent himself for his servants, when he seeth that their power is gone, and there is none shut up, or left. And he shall say, Where are their gods, their rock in whom they trusted, Which did eat the fat of their sacrifices, and drank the wine of their drink offerings? **let them rise up and help you, and be your protection.** See now that I, even I, am he, and there is no god with me: **I kill, and I make alive; I wound, and I heal:** neither is there any that can deliver out of my hand* (Deut. 32:35-39)

The context of Moses' teaching states that God kills from a "sowing and reaping" aspect (Gal. 6:5-7). At some point God must remove His protection and allow the consequences of rebellion take place. That is when "their foot shall slide in due time" and the day of their calamity will come. Then God asks if the false gods that the people begin to worship will give them the protection from the calamity that He gave.

In verse 30 God says, *"How should one chase a thousand, and two put ten thousand to flight, unless **their Rock had sold them,** and **the Lord had given them up?**"* (Revised Standard Version) God's method of making people poor and killing is to "sell them over" and "give them up" to the consequences of their sin when they rebel and refuse to repent.

154

May 30

How God Killed King Saul

So Saul died for his transgression which he committed against the Lord, even against the word of the Lord, which he kept not, and also for asking counsel of one that had a familiar spirit, to enquire of it; And enquired not of the Lord: ***therefore he slew him****, and turned the kingdom unto David the son of Jesse* (1 Chron. 10:13-14)

For the past two days we have looked at the passage in 1 Samuel 2:6-7 that tells us that "God kills and makes alive". Some have concluded from the passage that every killing and every death has come from God's hand. There is no shortage of proof-texts to help promote this idea. The inspired text telling us that the Lord killed King Saul is one of many. Sadly, it is also a text that makes God appear to be vindictive since He killed Saul for seeking guidance from demons instead of Him.

However, a proof-text must always be interpreted in the light of the context surrounding it as well as other passages on the subject. For example, several verses before God is said to have killed Saul, we read that Saul *committed suicide*:

Then said Saul to his armourbearer, Draw thy sword, and thrust me through therewith; lest these uncircumcised come and abuse me. But his armourbearer would not; for he was sore afraid. ***So Saul took a sword, and fell upon it. And when his armourbearer saw that Saul was dead****, he fell likewise on the sword, and died* (1 Chron. 10:4-5)

Does God use His divine energy to override the will and push people to kill themselves or is God simply taking responsibility for a free will choice? What does it say about free will if God is the one who pushes suicide? What does this say about His character? How could He present Himself as the moral judge of the universe if He moves people to sin, including self-murder?

The only conclusion is to remember that God's Spirit had already departed from Saul, thus removing His comfort and protection and turning him over to his own machinations. Without God's restraint upon Saul he took his own life. In the Old Testament God is often said to do the thing that He did not prevent. It is in this sense that God killed Saul. When we serve God, His restraint keeps us from self-destruction. Stay connected to Christ and He will keep you.

Did God or Israel Kill the Benjamites?

*And **the LORD smote Benjamin before Israel: and the children of Israel destroyed of the Benjamites that day** twenty and five thousand and an hundred men: all these drew the sword* (Judges 20:35)

For the past several days we have been looking at some of the Old Testament passages that some misinterpret to teach that God is an arbitrary killer. We have learned that when Scripture is interpreted in light of its immediate context as well as with other passages, we get a totally different picture of God and His character is vindicated.

I am going to remind you of a simple Hebrew idiom, one that has been affirmed by numerous students of the Hebrew language for several centuries: *"In the Hebrew language God is often said to do the thing which He permitted or allowed."* This idiom is affirmed in numerous places in the Bible. This same truth is identified in the above passage in which God is said to have killed the tribe of Benjamin. However, look at what God says to Israel's leader, Phineas:

*And Phinehas, the son of Eleazar, the son of Aaron, stood before it in those days,) saying, Shall I yet again go out to battle against the children of Benjamin my brother, or shall I cease? And the LORD said, Go up; for to morrow **I will deliver them into thine hand*** (Judges 20:28)

Notice that the Lord "killed" Benjamin by removing their protection and turning them over to Israel. After a few difficulties in seeing the Lord's words come to pass, we finally read the following:

*And **the men of Israel turned again upon the children of Benjamin, and smote them with the edge of the sword**, as well the men of every city, as the beast, and all that came to hand: also they set on fire all the cities that they came to* (Judges 20:48)

Now, which one smote Benjamin? Was it the Lord or was it Israel? Did the Lord directly smite Benjamin? When God's protection was removed from Benjamin, the Israelites were able to kill them. God's method for killing the rebels was to give them into the hands of their enemies.

June 1

Offence is Inevitable in a Wicked World

Woe unto the world because of offences! for it must needs be that offences come; but woe to that man by whom the offence cometh! (Matt. 18:7)

An "offence" is sin. This expression of sin does not only affect the *offender* but others as well. Adam's sin, which affected all of mankind, is said to be an *offence* (Rom. 5:16-20). For centuries people have been asking, "If God is good and all powerful then why does He not use His power to stop people from sinning?"

Jesus said that offences *must* come. They are inevitable and cannot be avoided. God simply cannot stop them from happening at this point in time. Man has been given the freedom of choice. Sadly men are continuing to abuse that freedom on a daily basis. Islamic terrorists are kidnapping individuals and groups of people. They are holding them hostage and demanding ransom money from families and governments.

People are driving drunk and killing others. People are robbing, raping and murdering others for their own selfish gratification. However, God could not wisely prevent any of this without violating the will of those who commit these horrible selfish acts. Once God made the decision to give men the freedom of choice rather than making them automatons, He could not revoke this without violating His own covenant to man. To do so would violate God's integrity as well. That is why, in a world run by selfish self-seekers, offences must come. They are inevitable and bound to happen.

But in all of this Jesus says *woe* to the man by whom the offence comes. A "woe" is an affliction or a calamity (Rev. 8:12-13; 9:1-12; 11:13-14). These woes are not inflicted by God but by Satan (Rev. 12:12). It is on the basis of the sowing and reaping process: *"Woe unto their soul! **for they have rewarded evil unto themselves**.... Woe unto the wicked! it shall be ill with him: for the reward of his hands shall be given him"* (Isa. 3:9b, 11).

Therefore, we must expect offences in this life, but let us not be the offenders. Let us love even those who offend us and pray for their salvation. God loves even our offenders and persecutors and desires their salvation. However, He is not the author of offenses or of its punishment. The offenders open themselves up to their own destruction.

God Delivers from Persecution

Persecutions, afflictions, which came unto me at Antioch, at Iconium, at Lystra; what persecutions I endured: **but out of them all the Lord delivered me.** *Yea, and all that will live godly in Christ Jesus shall suffer persecution* (2 Tim. 3:11-12)

Most of us have learned by now that there is no such thing as a problem free life. On the contrary, if we are going to live godly lives we should keep in our minds that persecution is inevitable. It is bound to happen. I have often said that if a Christian is not being persecuted then that is the time that they should check to see if they are living godly or have strayed from the faith.

We are to love every human being because Jesus loves them. Yet, we are not to compromise holiness nor are we to conform ourselves to the world. Our lifestyles must be different. We cannot share in dirty talk or worldly festivities. This stringent stand for godliness will often cost us. It may mean losing promotions and bonuses. It may even mean a loss of friends and ostracism. In countries outside of the USA it could mean torture and death.

This all appears to be gloomy but Paul did not write an isolated text when he warned about godliness guaranteeing persecution. Paul spoke about the multitude of things he had to endure for the sake of the gospel but he also adds, *"but out of them all the Lord delivered me."* Persecution is inevitable. Godly people are guaranteed to suffer it. But we can receive deliverance from all of them just as Paul did.

People mistakenly believe that Paul suffered persecution without any relief whatsoever from God. They believe that certain things are their lot in life and that they must endure them without any expectation of deliverance. Paul certainly endured persecution, but not without a breakthrough.

God receives no joy from seeing His children suffer in any respect. Being persecuted in and of itself is not pleasing to God. However, God is very pleased with our faith (Heb. 11:6). He is pleased when we live godly despite the persecution it will bring. He is pleased when we love our persecutors despite their cruelty. He is pleased when we endure the persecution without thoughts of retaliation. Yet, He is also pleased to deliver us when we ask Him. God will deliver us from persecution. Expect deliverance the next time you get persecuted for living godly.

June 3

According to His Will (Part 1)

And this is the confidence that we have in him, that, if we ask any thing according to his will, he heareth us: And if we know that he hear us, whatsoever we ask, we know that we have the petitions that we desired of him (1 John 5:14, 15).

There are some who believe that this passage leaves answers to prayer at the mercy of a mysterious sovereign will of God. The way that some interpret this otherwise powerful teaching on prayer is by the idea that we can ask God for something, but we could never really know for sure if what we are asking for is God's will. The reasoning goes that if it is His will, we will get it. If it is not, then we won't.

The passage, when kept in context, is far from teaching a lack of certainty concerning answers to prayer. It actually teaches how we can experience answers rather than mere "hits and misses." The passage should be interpreted from both the immediate context as well as with other passages of Scripture. First let us deal with the immediate context:

*If any man see his brother sin a sin which is not unto death, he shall ask, and **he shall give him life** for them that sin not unto death. There is a sin unto death: I do not say that he shall pray for it.* (1 John 5:16).

One of the definitions in the Random House Unabridged Dictionary for the word *shall* is "will have to, is determined to, or definitely will." In essence, it is the will of God for us to pray for the one that is not sinning unto death and *expect God to give that person life*. This is the revealed will of God. This is God's will made very clear and there is no need to pray for one sinning unto death and wonder if the prayer was in accordance with His will.

The word of God in verse 16 makes God's will on the matter very clear. The instruction in this verse is that we are not to even waste time praying for it. Therefore, verses 14 and 15, when kept in context, is not asking us to "pray and guess" the will of God. It is not asking us to pray and take chances. According to verse 16, we are to know the will of God on the matter *before* we set out to pray.

June 4

According to His Will (Part 2)

And this is the confidence that we have in him, that, if we ask any thing according to his will, he heareth us: And if we know that he hear us, whatsoever we ask, we know that we have the petitions that we desired of him (1 John 5:14, 15)

We need to recognize that God's Word is the primary revelation of God's will. When we have Bible promises and commands stating clearly what God wants from us and what He intends to do for us, we can pray with confidence and expect an answer. The late Presbyterian Evangelist, William Edward Biederwolf commented on today's passage:

> How, then, may I know the will of God? I may know it through the Word of God. The Word is full of general promises which we have only to apply to the particular circumstance of our own life in order to ask within the limits of the revealed will of God. Such are the general promises of deliverance and protection and provision, and if special favor we crave be so covered by the Word, what better guarantee of its bestowal could we reasonably expect?[25]

This truth is brought out in many passages of Scripture. One of those is found in Ezekiel where we read, *"Thus saith the Lord GOD; I will yet for this be enquired of by the house of Israel, to do it for them; I will increase them with men like a flock"* (Eze. 36:37)

God made a promise to increase Israel with men. However, the condition is that they enquire of Him to do it. God makes His will known through the prophet and expects it to be prayed for. Notice the two "I wills" in the Ezekiel passage. Here is a simple rule of Bible interpretation: Whenever you see God saying, "I will" this is a clear indication of "His will."

Clearly God reveals His will *before* we pray and expects us to pray in line with His will. Prayer is not a "chance lottery" in which we hope to pray enough prayers and perhaps we might just hit on the will of God in at least one of them and get an answer. Prayer is taking the known will of God to Him in prayer and expecting Him to fulfill it.

---

[25] Biederwolf, Wlliam E. **How Can God Answer Prayer?**, p. 188, copyright, 1906-1910

June 5

Are all Elected Officials ordained of God? (Part 1)

Let every soul be subject unto the higher powers. For there is no power but of God: the powers that be are ordained of God. Whosoever therefore resisteth the power, resisteth the ordinance of God (Romans 13:1-2)

Many Christians in the United States believe that every elected official, no matter how godly or ungodly, was placed in office by God. This is despite the fact that the USA has elections to choose their leaders. This idea is often based on a faulty understanding of our opening passage.

In the USA our elected officials are where they are by THE WILL OF MAN and not God. Romans 13 is speaking about the fact that God ordains the AUTHORITY, or rather, the POSITION and not necessarily the PERSON. If we believe that every single person in a position of authority was there by God's divine will then God is responsible for murderers such as Mussolini, Hitler, Stalin, Hussein, Kim Jong Il, Idi Amin Dada, and numerous other dictators who tortured people and massacred others. We are in essence saying that it was the will of God that leaders who advocate policies that go directly against God's will (abortion, homosexual marriage, etc.) were placed in office by Him. If it was God's will to have certain liberal politicians in office then it is also God's will to have baby killing continue and homosexual marriage promoted as well as have taxes so high that one would have less to support the gospel with. Those are all God's will *if* God is the One who put these individuals in office.

In the context of the passage God set up authority for the purpose of law and good being done in the land, *"**For rulers are not a terror to good works, but to the evil.** Wilt thou then not be afraid of the power? **do that which is good, and thou shalt have praise of the same: For he is the minister of God to thee for good.**"* (Rom. 13:3-4a).

In the context it is not saying that every person placed in authority is ordained of God, unless one wants to contend that there is some mysterious good in killing and starving the people you are ruling over, or aborting children and promoting the legalization of gay marriage. No, the office of PRESIDENT is ordained of God. The office is ordained of God. The one who sits in the office is not always ordained of Him. However, we are required to pray for **everyone** that is authority (1 Tim. 2:1-6)

June 6

Are all Elected Officials ordained of God? (Part 2)

Let every soul be subject unto the higher powers. For there is no power but of God: the powers that be are ordained of God. Whosoever therefore resisteth the power, resisteth the ordinance of God (Romans 13:1-2)

Those who misinterpret the above passage to teach that every elected official who is in office has been placed there by God often tell us that to deny this belief and resist ungodly policy such as the murder of innocent unborn children, homosexual marriage, unnecessary spending and tax increase are actually resisting God Himself.

However, I have challenged them with this question: "When the authorities tell us to stop preaching in Jesus Name, should we humbly submit to the powers that be?" This is exactly what the "powers" did to the apostles in the early church. Notice their response:

*And when they had brought them, they set them before the council: and the high priest asked them, Saying, **Did not we straitly command you that ye should not teach in this name?** and, behold, ye have filled Jerusalem with your doctrine, and intend to bring this man's blood upon us. Then Peter and the other apostles answered and said, **We ought to obey God rather than men*** (Acts 5:27-29)

Now were Peter, John and the rest of the apostles in disobedience to God? Should they have disobeyed God and obeyed men and in that way they would be obeying God by disobeying Him? What if the authority tells us to bow down to a false deity? Should we humbly submit? Shadrach, Meshach, and Abednego seemed to disagree with modern day ideas as they actually resisted the powers. Yet, God blessed them for this resistance of authority (See Dan. 3:13-18). It was not God's will for these boys to "obey God" by submitting to the king's request.

We must interpret Scripture with Scripture in order to get its correct and fullest meaning. Too many theologians attempt to build a doctrine on only one passage, and usually based on *eisegesis* of that text. This too often mischaracterizes God and makes Him responsible for the ungodliness happening in our government systems. On the other hand, God's people should become politically active in our nation and always vote for candidates whose values are closest to those advocated by Scripture.

June 7

Jesus' Miracles: The Results of His DEITY or Reliance upon the Holy Spirit?

*Ye men of Israel, hear these words; Jesus of Nazareth, a man approved of God among you by miracles and wonders and signs, **which God did by him** in the midst of you, as ye yourselves also know:* (Acts 2:22)

One of the teachings that promotes modern unbelief in the church is to believe that all of Jesus' works were the result of His being God. Some theologians will tribute to Jesus during His earthly life the attributes of God such as ominiscience, omnipotence, and even omnipresence in His earthly walk.

As a result these unbelieving theologians conclude that because we are not God, we could not do those things that Jesus did. Many theologians have taught that Jesus healed, prophesied, casted out devils and other miracles only *to prove that he was God.* When pressed about the fact that His apostles, who were mere men, worked miracles as well, we are told that they were given special powers and worked miracles that would cease after the completion of the Biblical canon. Thus, miracles, in the estimation of these theologians, were only to prove Christ's deity and a substitute for the written Word of God.

It certainly is essential that we affirm the deity of Christ since the Bible is clear that Jesus co-existed with the Father and the Holy Spirit from eternity past. Yet, it is also essential to affirm that while Jesus was on earth, He lived as a MAN who heavily relied upon the power of the Holy Spirit to perform the miraculous (Luke 4:18-19; Matt. 12:22-28; Acts 10:38).

In order to fight against unbelief in the church and the lack of miracles that we are seeing in this age, it is essential that we start to understand exactly how Jesus performed miracles on earth and then exactly how He in turn expects us to fulfill the commission that He has given to us (Mark 16:15-20; John 14:12).

Erroneous beliefs always lead to UNBELIEF. Knowing the truth is what will strengthen our faith and help us to reach the heights commissioned to us by God. We must do away with intellectual theology that finds ways of rationalizing away the present day miraculous and look to God to manifest Himself as he did through our Lord and savior, the Messiah.

June 8

Does God author Temptation?

*And again the anger of the LORD was kindled against Israel, and **he moved David against them** to say, Go, number Israel and Judah* (2 Sam. 24:1)

When we read the rest of the chapter we discover that God punished David for the sin that we are told that He moved him to commit. Based on the plain reading of this passage, God tempted David to sin and then punished him for yielding to the temptation. Seems unfair doesn't it? Yet, the New Testament tells us that God is not the One who entices people to sin: *"Let no man say when he is tempted, I am tempted of God: for God cannot be tempted with evil, **neither tempteth he any man**"* (James 1:13).

Does the Bible contradict itself? Is God schizophrenic? I reject both of those ideas. What we must understand is that the Bible is PROGRESSIVE REVELATION. There was very little knowledge of Satan in the Old Testament, especially in the beginning. While Satan is not absent from the Old Testament, knowledge of his activities were revealed by God *progressively* throughout Jewish history.

In the cases of David, 1 Chron. 21:1, which was written many centuries after 2 Samuel 24:1, speaks about the same incident but this time makes Satan the tempter: *"And **Satan stood up against Israel, and provoked David to number Israel."*** This is a clear example of the Hebrew idiom of permission in which God is very often said to do the thing which He allowed or permitted.

Keep in mind that in the Bible there are no *contradictions*, only *explanations*. The explanation for the seeming disparity above is to apply the simple principle in which SCRIPTURE AFFIRMS THE TRUTH THAT **GOD IS OFTEN SAID TO DO THAT WHICH HE MERELY ALLOWED OR PERMITTED.**

This principle is the secret to understanding many of the harsh and difficult statements about God found in the Bible, primarily in the Old Testament. Failure to interpret Biblical statements such as the opening passage in the light of this truth has led to many erroneous views about God. Some of these views have turned men into atheists, have caused many Christians to blame God for everything in their lives, and have turned many theologians into cold logicians who focus on scientific attributes about God rather than understanding the dynamics of an intimate relationship with Him. When God is seen as purely good and nothing but good, then we are able to trust Him to deliver us in the face of temptation.

June 9

Is Evil in Our Lives our Choice or God's Ordination?

*See, I have set before thee this day life and good, and death and evil.... I call heaven and earth to record this day against you, that I have set before you life and death, blessing and cursing: **therefore choose life**, that both thou and thy seed may live* (Deut. 30:15, 19)

Some years ago I read about a preacher who believed that every detail of our lives, both the good and the bad, was ordained by God before we were ever born. One day he broke his leg and his response was, "Well, glad that's over." The implication is that long before this preacher was born God had ordained that at a certain time and place he would break his leg. Now that this occurred he was glad to get past this thing God had established for his life.

While there are many things that come to us in life that are not our own choice, Scripture teaches us that God has no desire to see us suffer painful events such as broken legs. In Deuteronomy 28 God gave a list of blessings that He desired to see His people walk in and within that same chapter He gave an extensive list of curses that would come upon them if they choose to forsake Him. In chapter 30 we see Him summarizing all of this. He tells His people that they have the power to make a choice but then tells them to "choose life." He was implored them to make the *right* choice.

In this passage we see that "life and good" are synonymous with blessing while "death and evil" are synonymous with cursing. "Life and good" are synonymous with the *blessings* listed in Deuteronomy 28 such as health, fruitfulness, prosperity, victory, etc. "Death and evil" are synonymous with the curses in this chapter which includes sickness, defeat, poverty, deprivation, etc.

Not once does God confuse these curses with being something that is good nor does He confuse the blessings with something that is evil. Yet so many people are calling "good" what God has clearly called *evil, death*, and a *curse*. Furthermore, since God tells His people to choose life—that which is good and does not harm—then He could not be the One who ordained that the evil would come into their lives. If He did then He was being dishonest in telling His people that they had genuine choices.

If you are suffering any type of evil today, do not accept it as coming from God. Call it what God calls it: *death*, *evil*, and a *curse*. Stand against it in Jesus' Name and then tell the Father that you choose life instead of this. God is able to change one's circumstance but one must first believe that God did not author it.

Rejecting the Merciful God

But ye are they that forsake the LORD, that forget my holy mountain, that prepare a table for that troop, and that furnish the drink offering unto that number. Therefore will I number you to the sword, and ye shall all bow down to the slaughter: because when I called, ye did not answer; when I spake, ye did not hear; but did evil before mine eyes, and did choose that wherein I delighted not. (Isa. 65:11-12)

One of the ways that God is blamed for evil is by the idea that everything He wills comes to pass and nothing He intended for our lives can be resisted. We are told that "God does what He pleases". Yet the prophet Isaiah tells us that there were a group of people who *"did choose that wherein I delighted not."* It seems that we can actually make choices that displease God and that bring Him no delight. Therefore His will is not irresistible as some claim.

In Isaiah's prophecy we learn that these choices brought defeat and hardship on Israel. God told them, *"Therefore will I number you to the sword, and ye shall all bow down to the slaughter."* God was telling them that He has no choice but to give over into the hands of their enemies (Psalm 81:10-14). But note that this is due to the fact that when He called they would not answer Him. God makes every effort to reach out to people who are destroying themselves. It is their refusal to answer God's call that remits His protection and causes them to suffer defeat in life.

God equates our choices against Him with forsaking Him. He wants to bless us, protect us, and keep us from all that harms. However, He has given us the freedom to accept or reject those things He desires to do for us. It is this rejection that places us in a position to be destroyed rather than God actively bringing punishments upon us.

We live in a very hostile world with evil all around us. We are surrounded by spiritual and physical enemies that would destroy us quickly if given a chance. Most of us will never know how much we owe to God's protection until we stand before Him and He shows us all that could have happened and all that He has saved us from. However, when we make choices that remove us from God's hand, we forsake Him, thus forsaking all that He is to us. People often see this as God actively punishing us, but in reality we are the ones who forsook our protective refuge.

Choose that which God delights. Your choices delight Him as well and bring victory in your life.

June 11

When God Refuses to Answer Prayer

*Because I have called, and ye refused; I have stretched out my hand, and no man regarded; But ye have set at nought all my counsel, and would none of my reproof: I also will laugh at your calamity; I will mock when your fear cometh; When your fear cometh as desolation, and your destruction cometh as a whirlwind; when distress and anguish cometh upon you. Then shall they call upon me, but I will not answer; they shall seek me early, but they shall not find me: For that they hated knowledge, **and did not choose the fear of the LORD**:* (Prov. 1:24-28)

Notice how God offers Himself but He is refused. The people chose against God and refused to fear (reverence and worship) Him, thus turning away from Him to worthless idols. It is this behavior that leads to calamity, fear, desolation, destruction, distress, anguish, and *unanswered prayer*. None of these things that come upon God's people are things that He wants for them.

Sadly, many people will blame God and make Him the direct result of these calamities. However, it is not God who directly brings these things upon them. They come as a natural result of His withdrawing His protective presence and refusing to answer prayer. Hosea says, *"They shall go with their flocks and with their herds to seek the LORD; but they shall not find him; **he hath withdrawn himself from them**"* (Hos. 5:6).

If Prov. 1:24-28 is not read carefully it makes God appear to be vindictive because He refuses to answer prayer and is said to laugh at their calamity. Scripture of this nature should always be understood in the light of God's character as revealed in other portions of Scripture. For example, God takes no pleasure in the death of the wicked (Ezek. 18:23-32; 33:11) and He is *"not willing that any should perish, but that all should come to repentance"* (2 Pet. 3:9b).

If people continue to rebel, He will *allow* them to fall and *be* mocked (Judges 16:25; Eze. 22:1-5; Isa. 14:15-19). In that sense God is said to do that which He *allows* or *permits* to be done by others. The same is true with His refusal to answer the prayer of rebellious people. Keep in mind that sin separates people from God, thereby, preventing Him from being able to *legally* answer prayer (Psalm 81:10-14; Isa. 59:1-2).

If we want continued streams of answered prayer we must make right choices. If we fail to make those choices then God cannot and should not be blamed for the accruing results of what we have chosen.

June 12

Eating the Fruit of our Own Way

*They would none of my counsel: they despised all my reproof. Therefore shall they eat of the fruit of their own way, and be filled with their own devices. **For the turning away of the simple shall slay them, and the prosperity of fools shall destroy them. But whoso hearkeneth unto me shall dwell safely, and shall be quiet from fear of evil.*** (Prov. 1:29-33)

God calls but is not answered. He reaches out but is rejected. God does not give up immediately but when continually told "leave us alone", He honors our free will (Job 21:14; 22:17). He has no choice but to leave us to the consequences of our rebellion. Since He is responsible for what happens after His protection is removed, the Hebrew idiomatic expression appears to be *causation* to the Western mind.

Notice the phrase, *"Therefore shall they eat of the fruit of their own way."* The Bible often uses the "fruit" metaphor to speak about the results of one's lives and actions. It also uses the word "seed" in the same metaphorical sense because our words, actions, and conduct are the seeds that we plant that produce the harvest in our lives. Since fruit comes from planting seeds then we can say that the results that we see in our lives are based on the seeds that we have planted of our own choosing (Gal. 6:6-8).

If I plant apple seeds and it sprouts apple trees then should I blame God because I really wanted some watermelons? If I wanted watermelon then that is what I should have planted. Scripture and practical experiences attests to the truth that *"the fruit tree yielding fruit after his kind, whose seed is in itself"* (Genesis 1:11b).

From a spiritual standpoint, God often protects us from the bad harvests that *we* plant. He keeps us from receiving the full consequences of our own choices. Sadly, people mistake this for "getting away with sin". When God attempts to reprove it is easy to turn a deaf ear to Him because nothing bad seems to happen.

Continued rejection of God's Word and warnings eventually removes the protective hedge that God places around us. The results, as we see in today's passage, leads to being slain and destroyed. It is not God personally doing the destroying. It is the seeds we planted that brought forth destructive fruit. But the positive side of this is that those who listen to God will dwell in safety—will have His loving protection in our lives. Evil will not harm us. Isn't it better to listen to God than to reject Him for sinful pleasures that destroy?

June 13

Understanding God's Lovingkindness

*Whoso is wise, and will observe these things, even they shall **understand the lovingkindness of the Lord.*** (Ps. 107:43)

Scouring a few English Bibles I saw that the word "lovingkindness" has been translated as "faithful love," "steadfast love," "gracious love," "constant love," "acts of loyal love," "blessings," "mercies," and "kind acts." Basically the word comes from a Hebrew word which is a combination of "love" and "kindness". This should be no surprise to us since we are told by Paul that *"Love suffers long and is kind"* (1 Cor. 13a; NKJV).

The Psalmist tells us that it is a wise man who will observe certain things and come to an understanding about this aspect of God's beautiful character. Psalm 107 lists a number of things that God did for His people such as redeeming them from the hand of their enemy, delivering them out of their distresses, filling their hungry souls with goodness, delivering them from the darkness and death that they brought on themselves through their own rebellion, healing them from sickness and delivering them from the destruction brought on by their own iniquities, calming dangerous storms, and ensuring that their cattle doesn't decrease.

If you look at the negative portions of Psalm 107 in which people suffer, it is always due to their sin and rebellion. The people push God away and then suffer the consequences for it. However, each and every time they cry out to Him, God is said to not only deliver them from the results of their own rebellion but to also give them blessing and increase. God never takes a "you made your own bed so lie in it" attitude towards them. He rescues them each and every time when they cry out to Him.

We are told that wisdom dictates that we understand this truth about God. Failure to understand certain things about God has kept too many people in bondage. Christians wallow in condemnation and unforgiveness because they believe that God is mad at them and He is punishing them for their sins. Others do not believe that God is willing to heal, deliver, and meet all needs (spiritual and material). These poor saints do not understand His lovingkindness..

Wisdom, which generates faith in God, begins with observing God's past acts and then coming to an understanding of His faithful, loyal, gracious, constant, steadfast love and in turn receiving His mercies and blessings.

June 14

Unreaping the Bad Seeds We Have Sown

Be not deceived; God is not mocked: for whatsoever a man soweth, that shall he also reap. (Gal. 6:7)

God often gets the blame for the negative things that comes into our lives. However, in many cases, we are simply experiencing the law of "sowing and reaping". This law is just like gravity. Both laws were established for our good but both can work against us when we fail to adhere to them properly. Jump from a tall building and the law of gravity, which was meant to keep you from floating into outer space, will work against you. The law of sowing and reaping was meant to benefit us *positively*, but when we sow into sin, we reap corruption (v. 8).

Because of the law of sowing and reaping, we are primarily responsible for the good or the evil that comes into our lives. It is not the will of God for us to receive evil. But because of this law we will reap it if we sow it. Nevertheless, God is so loving that even for this He has made a provision. If we *repent* of the evil that we have done then we can change the situation. An example of this is found in James:

> *"Is any sick among you? let him call for the elders of the church; and let them pray over him, anointing him with oil in the name of the Lord: And the prayer of faith will save the sick, and the Lord shall raise him up; and if he has committed sins, they shall be forgiven him. Confess your faults one to another, and pray for one another, that ye may be healed."* (James 5:14-16a)

When we sin, it can cause problems in our health, finances, relationships, and many other areas. It is not the will of God that we sin, therefore, neither is it His desire that we reap the results of our sins. However, if we are experiencing difficulty in any area, we need to confess and forsake that sin. God promises that when we do this we will have mercy (Prov. 28:13).

If we have sinned and strayed from the will of God then we must repent. Repentance automatically puts us back into God's will. When we are back in His will we receive the results of being in His will. If you are in sin, don't just accept your situation. Repent to God and any other person that you have to and by doing this you can change your situation.

June 15

God's Goodness Leads Sinners to Repentance

*Or dispiseth thou the riches of his **goodness** and forbearance and longsuffering; not knowing that the **goodness of God leadeth thee to repentance**.* (Rom. 2:4)

Years ago during an evening of street ministry, I handed a young man a gospel track. On the front of the track it had an ugly picture of the devil with an evil grin on his face and he was standing in the midst of flames. There were words in big bold letters that said, "HELL: 1000 DEGREES HOT AND NOT A DROP OF WATER."

This young man began to shake from fear and said, "Man I'm scared. I don't want to go there." I replied, "You don't have to go. Jesus died so that you won't have to go. All you need to do is accept Him as your savior and repent of your sins." Still shaking, he told me, "I'm not ready to do that yet, but I'm still scared." I tried persuading him but though he was afraid of hell, he refused to make a decision for Christ. I saw from this incident that fear of eternal punishment does not always lead one to repent.

In another incident when I was in the Air Force working for a supply unit, I walked into the office and met with one of my co-workers. He appeared to be depressed. I asked him to tell me why he was so down. He explained that he had a bump on a certain part of his body. He had gone to see the doctor and he thought that it might be cancerous.

I took him outside and shared the gospel with him. I then laid hands on him and prayed for him (Mark 16:18), and I rebuked the lump attacking his body in Jesus' Name (Luke 10:17-20). He visited the doctor some days later and found that the lump had disappeared. He, his wife, and another couple accepted Jesus Christ as their savior that following weekend in my living room.

In the first incident we saw that fear did not lead to repentance. No doubt that we MUST warn people about hell. But as we tell them the truth concerning hell we must remember to tell them about God's goodness and His provision for their redemption and deliverance. Fear of punishment has a tendency to wear off after a while. Yet gratitude can last a lifetime. Many people turn to God, not because of fear of punishment, but because they find out that He is the only solution to their problems. It is important for us to know God's goodness and not despise it as so many do. After all, it is His goodness that leads people to repentance.

June 16

Who Hardened Pharaoh's Heart?

*And Yahweh said unto Moses, When thou goest to return to Egypt, see as touching all the wonders which I have put in thy hand, that thou do them before Pharaoh - but, I, **will let his heart wax bold,** and he will not suffer the people to go.* (Ex. 4:21; The Emphasized Bible by J. B. Rotherham)

The King James rendering of the latter portion of this passage says, *"...but I will harden his heart, that he shall not let the people go."* This is pretty much how it is rendered in most English translations. Is Rotherham justified in translating it in a *permissive* rather than a *causative* sense?

Robert Young, who was a Greek and Hebrew scholar known primarily for his concordance and his own literal Bible translation, also wrote a Bible commentary (which is out of print but can be found on Google books). In his comments on the hardening of Pharaoh's heart in Exodus 10:1 Young writes, "....the causative (or Hiphil) form of the Hebrew verb is often simply *permissive* or declarative, as has been already repeatedly noticed, and as is universally admitted by all Biblical critics."[26]

In plain English, this means that God was not going to prevent Pharaoh from exercising his free will to act stubborn but would instead use it as an occasion to demonstrate His power to redeem His people. God does not use divine energy like a puppet master and make people sin just so that He can punish them for it. God already knew Pharaoh's arrogance and decided to permit him to act according to his nature. The Scriptures themselves confirm this truth: *"But when Pharaoh saw that there was respite, he hardened his heart, and hearkened not unto them; as the LORD had said"* (ex. 8:15; see also 8:32; 9:34).

Atheists have used the idea that God hardened Pharaoh's heart in order to cast aspersions on God's character. Some other Christians have used it to teach a false doctrine of divine reprobation. However, when studied correctly in the light of God's love, we cannot see God doing such a thing. What Pharaoh did, he did to himself and reaped the sad consequences of it. God does not author sin and should not be blamed.

---

[26] Young, Robert **A Commentary on the Holy Bible, as Literally and Idiomatically Translated out of the Original Languages** (New York: Fullton, McNabb & Co., 1868), p. 51

June 17

Is The Old Testament Still Relevant?

And the Father himself, which hath sent me, hath borne witness of me. Ye have neither heard his voice at any time, nor seen his shape. And ye have not his word abiding in you: for whom he hath sent, him ye believe not. **Search the scriptures; for in them ye think ye have eternal life: and they are they which testify of me** (John 5:37-39)

There are a number of Christians who are troubled by what they believe is the Old Testament portrayal of God. Their solution is to discount the Old Testament as being relevant for Christians in this present dispensation. Too many of these Christians seem to believe that the God in the Old Testament is different than the One in the New Testament. The idea that Jesus reveals the true heart of God and how He actually is has strangely made people to believe that the God of the Old Testament did *not* act like Jesus. However, Jesus said that the Old Testament testifies of *Him*.

The Old Testament testifies of Jesus. Paul's epistles had not been written when Jesus made this statement. All they had at that time was Genesis to Malachi. Yet, Jesus said that it was these books that testified of Him. To reject the Old Testament is to reject Jesus Himself.

Most "New Testament only" Christians will not say that the OT is NOT the Word of God, but when teaching (such as tithing) is presented using Old Testament passages then some just quip, "Well, that's the Old Testament" and this intended to end the argument.

While I firmly believe that the New Testament interprets for us the Old Testament, and thus a doctrine cannot be built solely on OT Scripture alone, neither should we dismiss OT passages with a wave of the hand without fully examining their relevance for today. After all, the apostles preached Jesus Christ and the message of salvation strictly from the OT. The early church NEVER had a problem with the Old Testament except when Jewish leaders used it to practice legalism.

Obedience was required in the OT and it is still required in the new. Furthermore, you find God issuing judgment in *both* testaments. Nonetheless, God has never ceased to be a loving and merciful God from Genesis to Revelation. God did not change when the New Covenant was made through the blood of Jesus (Mal. 3:6; Heb. 13:8). He was loving in the Garden of Eden when He warned Adam about the consequences of disobedience. He was loving when, even after Adam and Eve sinned, He killed an animal, thereby shedding blood to atone for their sin, and then clothe them. God's love permeates the whole of Scripture. Therefore, none of it should be rejected.

June 18

Maligning God's Character

*And **he shall speak great words against the most High**, and shall wear out the saints of the most High, and think to change times and laws: and they shall be given into his hand until a time and times and the dividing of time* (Dan. 7:25)

When the Satan controlled anti-Christ is manifested one of his first acts will be to speak *against* the Most High. This has been Satan's modus operandi since the time he first rebelled against God. Satan attempts to discredit God in order to exalt himself and his system of rule.

Satan's most effective weapon is the use of words. Words can be used to paint a picture of a person in the minds of others. This picture may be a true or a false one. Either way, words are the most effective way of building or destroying someone's character. Since Satan's man will be speaking great words against God, we know that he will be using false information to malign God's character.

Satan first used this tactic to convince a third of the angels to rebel with him against god and he later used this same tactic to bring down Adam and Eve in the Garden of Eden. Since this has been proven to be an effective method for turning people against God, Satan continues to use it to this day. Satan has told the world that all of the children starving in third world countries is God's doing. He has told them that God is the One who sends tornadoes, hurricanes, avalanches and other deadly weather disasters. Outbreaks of sicknesses such as AIDS and Ebola are said by Satan to be God's punishment upon sinful men.

For the more scientific mind, Satan has used the natural evil that he has brought into this world to convince intelligent men and women that there is no God. For the believers in God, Satan often paints a picture of a harsh arbitrary deity who demands unquestioning servitude rather than loving relationship. No wonder Daniel is told that his speaking against god will wear out the saints of the Most High.

If we are to win our warfare against Satan we must ever keep in mind that a major part of the battle is to fight against dark ideas presented by Satan about Him. Those words spoken to us against God that he is unkind, unloving, uncaring, and the source of all of our trials and problems must be immediately dealt with and put away. It does not matter the source of these words spoken against God. Even if they come from a "Christian" pulpit, book, television or radio program, they must be rejected. Otherwise, Satan will succeed in wearing us out.

June 19

What is Blasphemy?

*And he opened his mouth in **blasphemy against God, to blaspheme his name**, and his tabernacle, and them that dwell in heaven. And it was given unto him to make war with the saints, and to overcome them: and power was given him over all kindreds, and tongues, and nations* (Rev. 13:6-7)

Yesterday we learned from Daniel how Satan will use words spoken against the Most High in order to wear out the saints. John repeats this exact same truth in Revelation as he prophesies concerning the anti-Christ making war on the saints by speaking blasphemies against God and against His name.

In religious circles we have limited our ideas about blasphemy to the idea of offending God through irreverent insults. While this is true, religion has painted God's reaction to blasphemy as violent and vindictive—a "how dare you speak irreverently against me" attitude.

Yet, the God represented by Jesus is not concerned about blasphemy simply because He is offended. He is concerned about it because it paints a false picture of Himself. Notice that the satanically controlled anti-Christ will *blaspheme his name*. This means that Satan will use words to cast aspersions upon God's character. He will present a distorted view of God that will cause men to hate and despise Him. The type of deity presented to the world by Satan already is one that many men hate and do not want to worship. Others who do worship Him do it out of fear of retribution rather than loving reverence.

By doing this Satan will make war on the saints. Already we see in our day how Satan has presented God as a hater of homosexuals simply because he is supposedly offended by them rather than His concerned that they are living self-destructive lifestyles. God is pictured as one who delights in torturing and killing them. The backlash has been on Christians. Christian businesses are being sued and financially destroyed, people are being fired from their jobs for saying what the Bible says about it, and in some countries one is threatened with jail time for publicly acknowledging homosexuality as sin. This is due to satanic blasphemy concerning God's character. He is presented as mean and arbitrary rather than having a loving concern for those who are engaging in destructive behavior.

God is concerned about blasphemy because it is a tool of Satan to keep people from Him and the salvation He desires to offer. This is why the truth about God's loving character is an important message to the world.

June 20

The Destructive Power of Sin

The way of the Lord is strength to the upright: but ***destruction*** *shall be to the workers of iniquity.* (Prov. 10:29)

God does not hate sin because He desires to restrict us and take away our "fun". On the contrary, God is deeply in love with us. He knows the destructive consequences of sin and that is why He commands us not to do it.

Much of what we think of as God personally bringing punishment and retribution upon us as a result of His wrath and anger for our sins is actually *the sin itself that brings destruction*. There is a law of sin and death that works the exact same way as the law of gravity (Rom. 8:2). When you violate this law, the law itself works against you. Every sin contains within itself its own seeds of destruction (Gal. 6:7-8). The late S. D. Gordon, famous for his excellent "Quiet Talks" books, gave some valuable insight on this:

> Let it be remembered that God is not punishing men in the sending of pain and affliction. God is not dealing with men in judgment; if He were the case would be settled at once for all of us. Judgment is reserved for future final settlement. And even then punishment is not a thing that God chooses to be meted out to us as a judgment for our misdeeds. It is something included in the sin itself. The worst thing God could do to any man would be to leave him utterly alone to the working out of his sin. In great graciousness He does not do that. But He does keep hands off in part, and permits much of the result of sin to work its way out. And so pain comes through the break in the natural order.[27]

So God is not in Heaven waiting for us to sin so that He can strike us down. On the contrary He is doing all that He is able to do to protect us from sin's power to destroy. Jesus died to set us free from sin and its destructive power. Stay free from sin and stay free from its painful consequences.

---

[27] Gordon, Samuel D. **Quiet Talks on Personal Problems** (New York: Eaton and Mains, 1907), p. 133

June 21

How to Keep from being Judged

*But let a man examine himself, and so let him eat of that bread, and drink of that cup. For he that eateth and drinketh unworthily, **eateth and drinketh damnation to himself, not discerning the Lord's body.** For this cause many are weak and sickly among you, and many sleep. **For if we would judge ourselves, we should not be judged.** But when we are judged, we are chastened of the Lord, that we should not be condemned with the world* (1 Cor. 11:28-32)

Many ministers sternly warn their people about taking these elements with unrepentant sin in their life. They teach that by doing so one can incur God's judgment. How does God bring about the judgment or chastening for taking the Lord's Supper in an unworthy manner? Does God personally inflict sickness and death as a result of this sin? The key is found in the statement that the one who does it sinfully *"eateth and drinketh damnation **to himself**, not discerning the Lord's body."*

The Message Bible paraphrases verse 29, *"If you give no thought (or worse, don't care) about the broken body of the Master when you eat and drink, you're running the risk of serious consequences."* Basically a person who takes the Lord's Supper while living in unrepentant sin is showing that he or she has no real regard for Christ in the first place.

The communion becomes nothing more than an empty ritual. They are in effect pushing Christ out of their lives, forfeiting His protection and leaving themselves open to the consequences of their rebellion. God is not actively punishing them but He is *permitting* the consequences.

The same individuals who are able to bring judgment upon themselves also have the God-given authority to prevent it. Paul's divinely inspired advice is that if *"we would judge ourselves, we should not be judged."* We are told to do self-examination. When we examine ourselves and we repent and weed out those things that would otherwise make us unworthy of partaking of the body and blood of our Lord then there is no need for God to judge and chasten us.

The time of communion is a beautiful divinely instituted tradition. It is meant to keep us in memory of the great sacrifice that Christ has made on our behalf. It enables us to appropriate the benefits of that sacrifice by faith, one of them being the healing of our bodies. However, when we treat it as something worthless, then we forfeit such benefits and instead open ourselves up to just the opposite. Therefore judge yourself and you will never have to worry about being judged.

June 22

Submission to God's Will or to Satanic Circumstances?

Submit yourselves therefore to God. **Resist the devil,** *and he will flee from you* (James 4:7)

One of the primary reasons why we must emphasize the truth about God is so that we can learn to stand against the evil circumstances that we confront in our lives. So often we have been taught that God is controlling the circumstances of life, that everything that happens is His will and we must submit to it.

However, James makes a sharp distinction between submission to God and resisting the devil. If there is a point in which we must resist the devil then that means that his acts are not God's will and are not to be submitted to. It behooves the child of God to learn his or her Bible, find out what is from God's hand and what is from Satan's and from there we will learn what we must submit to and what we must resist.

Does the trouble and problems that come into my life come from God or the devil? Charles Cuthbert Hall notes:

> There is much submission to God's will, as it is called; though often the term "God's will" is applied to troubles which are the Devil's will rather than "God's will." There is much reverent wonder at the reasons why afflictions are sent by God upon men, when of many of those afflictions it is certain God did not send them, but that they were instead the direct result of human carelessness, or of human extravagance, or of human hatefulness, or of human lustful* ness. And there is far down in many a heart that has suffered a deep-set, though surreptitious protest against "the will of God," as it is called, which sent this sickness, or that loss of property, or this disappointment, or that bereavement; when not one of those sorrows, the sickness, the loss of property, the disappointment, the bereavement, came from God's will, but from that broken and bruised and halting and sin-stricken order of the fallen creation which broke away from God's dear will, and pierced itself through with many sorrows.[28]

Let us stop blaming God for the problems of life. Let us go after the true source of our problems, which is the devil. Submission to God's loving will gives us the authority to resist Satan's destructive will.

---

[28] Hall, Charles Cuthbert **Does God Send Trouble?** (Boston: Houghton, Mifflin, and Company, 1894), pp. 7, 8

June 23

God's Surprising attitude Towards Rebellious Children

When Israel was a child, then I loved him, and called my son out of Egypt. As they called them, so they went from them: they sacrificed unto Baalim, and burned incense to graven images. I taught Ephraim also to go, taking them by their arms; but they knew not that I healed them. ***I drew them with cords of a man, with bands of love:*** *and I was to them as they that take off the yoke on their jaws, and I laid meat unto them. He shall not return into the land of Egypt, and the Assyrian shall be his king, because they refused to return* (Hosea 11:1-5)

We often get the impression that under the Old Testament God was harsh. We are taught by some that when a person rebelled against God during this period judgment was quick and forgiveness, if it ever came at all, was rare. Yet, Hosea presents us with an altogether different picture.

God is in serious emotional pain over Israel's rebellion. They sacrifice to false gods but He still wants them back. He calls to them and wants them to return to Him but they refuse. He loves them and draws them with cords of love. He heals them. He releases them from bondage. Despite all of this, Israel continues to reject God. Finally, God has to say that they will be in bondage to heathen nations due this rejection. God cannot be blamed since He has done all that He could to win His people to Himself. However, He has to allow them their choice *and* the consequences of it.

In some classic theologies such as Calvinism, we are taught that God uses an "irresistible grace" to bring people who were "predestined" for salvation. Jesus' words are often used to support this erroneous notion, *"No man can come to me, except the Father which hath sent me **draw him**"* (John 6:44a). However, when we compare this passage to Hosea's statement we see that God's drawing of men to Him is not an irresistible grace for a predestined few. It is an attempt to bring sinners to Him by His love. This drawing does not override the will. Love does not compel or force its way. It expresses its desire for the person and gives them the choice as to how he or she will respond.

Today God is still attempting to draw all men to Himself by His love (John 12:32). Sadly the majority of men reject Him. Therefore, anyone who rejects Christ rejects Him of their own volition. However, when we share the gospel, let us be sure that we present to the sinner a God who loves them and is attempting to win them by love. His desire is not to bring judgment but to rescue everyone from impending judgment.

The Cost of Refusing God

O Jerusalem, Jerusalem, thou that killest the prophets, and stonest them which are sent unto thee, how often would I have gathered thy children together, even as a hen gathereth her chickens under her wings, and ye would not! Behold, your house is left unto you desolate (Matt. 23:37-38)

As he put the gun in his pocket, his mother begged him not to go. She grabbed him and held on to him. She pleaded with him to stay home and turn away from his life of crime. He pushed her arms away from him and told his mother, "A man's gotta do what he's gotta' do." As he walked out the door his mother warned, "Son, this life of yours is going to put you in an early grave." He met up with his friends and they drove to the bank to rob it. The police arrived and a hostage situation ensued. After a standoff that lasted several hours, the young man was shot dead, his life wasted.

Did this mother kill her son? Of course not. She warned him. She gathered him up in her arms. She pleaded with him not to make choices that would eventually destroy him. Yet, he refused her love and her warnings. He died as a result.

Jesus, who expresses the Father's heart and intent, wanted to be a similar type of mother to Jerusalem. He tried to hold them in His loving arms and protect them. However, they rejected Him for the temporary excitement of doing things their own way. Jesus said that their refusal of Him has left their house desolate. The word "desolate" comes from the Greek word *"eremos."* One of its meanings is "deprived of the aid and protection of others, especially of friends, acquaintances, kindred" (studylight.org).

All that happened to Jerusalem in later years as a result of their sins was not due to God's direct involvement but due to His lack of involvement. By refusing God, Israel pushed God away and was deserted. Jerusalem lost God's protective presence and, as history has shown, were destroyed by their enemies in 70 AD as Jesus accurately warned them (Matt. 24:1-2; Luke 19:41-44).

Again, this was not God's doing. Like a mother He warned His children about the sad consequences of their rebellion. However, they pushed His arms from themselves and persisted in their sins. By leaving and rejecting God's presence they forfeited His protection, leaving themselves vulnerable to the destruction that they later suffered. It is always our choice to stay in God's protective presence.

June 25

Know the Time of Your Visitation

*And when he was come near, he beheld the city, **and wept over it**, Saying, If thou hadst known, even thou, at least in this thy day, the things which belong unto thy peace! but now they are hid from thine eyes. For the days shall come upon thee, that thine enemies shall cast a trench about thee, and compass thee round, and keep thee in on every side, And shall lay thee even with the ground, and thy children within thee; and they shall not leave in thee one stone upon another; because thou knewest not the time of thy visitation* (Luke 19:41-44)

Jesus heart is broken over the impending judgment of Jerusalem. Here God is actually crying because of what is about to happen to His people. This certainly is not the picture of the capricious arbitrary deity presented to us from some pulpits. God weeps over sinners destroying themselves. Twice Jesus says that ignorance brought destruction upon Jerusalem. In verse 42 Jesus said:

Exclaiming, Would that you had known personally, even at least in this your day, the things that make for peace (for freedom from all the distresses that are experienced as the result of sin and upon which your peace—your security, safety, prosperity, and happiness—depends)! But now they are hidden from your eyes. (The Amplified Bible)

They did not know the things that would keep God's protective presence and all that comes with it. What happened to Jerusalem was totally unnecessary and could have been avoided. Jesus also said, *"....because thou **knewest not** the time of thy visitation"* Truly it is a lack of knowledge that destroys people (Hosea 4:6).

The word "visitation" is the same word used concerning the office of an overseer, elder or a bishop in the church who is assigned by God to feed and protect His people. God was overseeing His people and offering them an opportunity to be helped and saved, but they refused Him. Therefore, in 70 AD Jerusalem was destroyed.

God offers all of us the opportunity to repent and be delivered from sins that bring destruction. However, this opportunity, if rejected too often, will be lost. Let us not be ignorant of the time of our visitation.

June 26

Sin Pays its Own Wages

*What fruit had ye then in those things whereof ye are now ashamed? **for the end of those things is death.** But now being made free from sin, and become servants to God, ye have your fruit unto holiness, and the end everlasting life. **For the wages of sin is death**; but the gift of God is eternal life through Jesus Christ our Lord* (Rom. 6:21-23)

The majority of Christians are conflicted about the idea that God actively punishes people for their sins. There are some who believe that God Himself sends cancer, AIDS, car accidents, and numerous other painful maladies in order to judge people for their iniquities. Then there are people who teach that God punishes sin but are quite reluctant to tell anyone suffering from a sickness or tragic event that God sent it as a punishment. This latter group insists that God actively punishes sin but they are afraid to state this in relation to individual cases of suffering.

We all have experienced suffering that was not our fault. Most of us know that all of the negatives in life are the result of someone's sin, even if not our own. Certainly the sin of Adam and Eve is ultimately responsible for all of our suffering. Most of us would never dare tell anyone that God is personally inflicting them for the sin of another including our first parents.

What about situations where there is a clear connection between the sin and the consequences? For example, a loose sexual life which eventually brings a venereal disease, a smoker who gets lung cancer, eating sugary foods and getting diabetes, a drunk driver driving off of a bridge, a drug addict overdosing? Is God actively involved in these consequences?

Let's take it a step further. Someone who is unwilling to forgive past hurts and is bitter towards others is suffering from cancer or severe arthritis? Someone who has shot and killed others and is finally shot and killed like an animal? Someone who has spread rumors and gossiped about others is finally being lied on and gossiped about? Are these active punishments from God?

While the Bible, especially in the Old Testament, has often used punitive language to describe the relationship between sin and its effects, the progressive revelation of God clearly demonstrates that it is the sin itself that brings forth death. Death separates us from God and dishes out its own penalties. Sin pays its own wages. God has no need to actively bring about sins results. Therefore, instead of blaming Him for what sin has done, we must run to Him to be rescued from the consequences of our sin. He's waiting for us (1 John 1:9).

June 27

Each Sin Contains its Own Seed for Destruction

But every man is tempted, when he is drawn away of his own lust, and enticed. Then when lust hath conceived, it bringeth forth sin: and sin, when it is finished, bringeth forth death (James 1:14-15)

Many who believe that God actively punishes sin have a difficult time understanding how we can say that sin brings about its own punishment. The answer to this is the fact that each sin is a seed. God has decreed that every seed would automatically produce after its own kind: *"And the earth brought forth grass, and herb yielding seed after his kind, and the tree yielding fruit, whose seed was in itself, after his kind"* (Genesis 1:12a).

Once God established this law then there was no need for Him to necessarily be involved hands-on in the process of every seed and its production. He placed the power of life itself in each seed to bring forth a harvest. The apple seed, when planted and cultivated correctly, will bring forth a harvest of apples. The same for orange seeds, grape seeds, watermelon seeds, etc.

This is true of the human and animal kingdoms. Human males cannot plant sperm in gorillas and produce anything. Neither can lions have sex with dogs and bring anything into being. Human males can only copulate with human females, lions with lions, and dogs with dogs. Each seed-sperm produces after its own kind without any supernatural intervention from God.

Lust and sin are seeds as well. The Greek word for "bringeth forth" in James 1:15 is *tikto*. According to the Strong's Concordance this means, "....to produce (from seed, as a mother, a plant, the earth, etc.)." James goes on to tell us that when the seed has been planted it produces, on its own, a harvest of death (or births "death" into being). Deuteronomy 28 gives us a long list of what is meant by the death that comes as the results of unrepentant sin.

Therefore it is correct to say that sin contains within itself its own seeds for destruction. This truth is vitally important to understanding God's loving character. If we believe that God Himself is inflicting upon us the punishment we deserve then we will either be angry with Him for what we perceive as vindictiveness, which will drive us further away from Him, or we will only come to Him out of fear, looking for mercy from One we perceive to be a tyrant. However, when we see that God is not the One who actively punishes, but is trying to save us from our sins, we will be more willing to repent and look to Him for salvation.

Adultery's Destruction of the Soul

But whoso committeth adultery with a woman lacketh understanding: **he that doeth it destroyeth his own soul.** *A wound and dishonour shall he get; and his reproach shall not be wiped away* (Prov. 6:32-33)

In our world today promiscuity seems to be the norm. Gay sex is on the rise, fornication is encouraged, pornography is considered "healthy" by some and adultery is not looked upon as badly as it has been in the past. In our technological age adultery has become easier with dating websites that especially cater to those who desire to cheat on their spouses.

Sadly, the person who listens to the multitude of sexual "experts" in society who are dragging us to the depths of sexual looseness is said to *lack understanding*. The adulterer believes that he is enjoying himself and gratifying a need not met by his spouse. However, he lacks the understanding that he is destroying his own soul.

Some seem to misunderstand this passage to teach that a person who commits sexual sin is obliterating themselves from existence. This would be funny if this was not such a serious issue. Man's spirit and soul will continue to exist forever either in heaven (with Jesus) or in hell (if Jesus has been rejected or we persist in unrepentant sin). Obliterating oneself from existence would be merciful compared to what actually occurs in both this life and after we depart from this life. The Hebrew word used for "soul" (*nephesh*) is translated 117 times in the King James Version as "life". In essence, the one who commits adultery is *destroying his own life*.

Verse 33 tells us how the adultery will destroy a person's reputation and credibility in this present life. No matter what happens, the person will always be viewed as an adulterer by some. In some cases it can hurt a career. In numerous cases it has destroyed marriages and families. Furthermore, failure to repent of it can even lead to sickness and tribulation (Rev. 2:22).

Failure to repent of it in this life leaves us subject to eternal consequences in the next life as adulterers will by no means inherit God's kingdom (1 Cor. 6:9). God does not want to lose *anyone* for an eternity, to include an adulterer. Therefore He calls for repentance.

Here we see that God is not a destroyer. He simply warns us of the inevitable destruction that we bring upon ourselves through our own sinful choices. It is sin itself that destroys. Let us learn to flee sexual immorality and keep ourselves from destruction. If you are in adultery then go to God in repentance and He will save you from the inevitable destruction to come.

June 29

Sin gives Satan Opportunity to Defeat Us

"When you are angry, don't let that anger make you sin,"
and don't stay angry all day. Don't give the devil a way to
defeat you (Eph. 4:26-27; Easy to Read Version)

Christians have to get settled into the fact that we are engaged in a constant spiritual warfare. Both God and our enemy are warring for our souls. If God were the only player when it comes to dealing with the human race then our need to avoid sin would only be a matter of trying to appease God's wrath. We would be afraid of God rather than sin itself. We would not think of sin as the harmful element that it actually is but we would be thinking of sin as breaking God's rules, offending His ego, and then incurring His harsh judgment.

When we recognize that there is an actual enemy who introduced the concept of sin into the universe, and that living in sin is giving him open access to destroy our lives then we will begin to have a whole different idea about God's role and why He is so strict concerning it.

Whenever we sin we are automatically placing ourselves under Satan's authority (Rom. 6:12-16; 1 John 3:8). By our sins we place ourselves in enemy territory. When one is in Satan's territory then they are at a disadvantage and are bound to suffer defeat. God recognizes that we will have emotional reactions to some injustices done to us but we are not to stew over it and sin by taking vengeance. If we do, we give Satan opportunity to hurt us further.

I have been told that there is no such thing as a person being sinless. We are told that we must sin every day. This is a teaching among those who claim to be born again. What people do not realize is that *if we must sin then that means we must remain in bondage to Satan.* That means we must live continually defeated lives when God has promised that we could live in perpetual victory (Rom. 8:37; 1 John 5:4-5).

It really is our choice as to whether or not we live defeated lives. God has given us the ability to resist sin and its proprietor, Satan (James 4:7). Our failure to do so will place us in Satan's hands.

We must distinguish between the works of God and the devil. When Satan attacks we must be careful not to blame God. We must not charge Him directly for Satan's work nor even claim that He *allowed* Satan to test us. If we are living in defeat we need to do an examination of ourselves and be sure that we did not give Satan any place in our lives (Eph. 4:26-27). If we did then we must repent and we can rest assured that the Lord will deliver us from our sins and from Satan who works through sin.

June 30

Opening the Door for Satan

If thou doest well, shalt thou not be accepted? and if thou doest not well, sin lieth at the door. And unto thee shall be his desire, and thou shalt rule over him. And Cain talked with Abel his brother: and it came to pass, when they were in the field, that Cain rose up against Abel his brother, and slew him (Gen. 4:7-8).

While we get some glimpses of Satan in the Old Testament, he was pretty much veiled. It is only in the New Testament that we get a concrete understanding that Satan is the actual serpent who tempted Eve, thus bringing the first couple under his dominion (Luke 4:6-8; Rev. 12:9). If one starts out with Genesis before ever reading the New Testament they may not realize that God was actually warning Cain about Satan.

God tells Cain that *"sin lieth at the door and unto thee shall be HIS desire."* Notice that a personal pronoun is being used in relation to sin here. If sin were merely an evil action on the part of the sinner then God would have had to use different grammar. Since God is using a personal pronoun then He is describing a person. The New Testament confirms that this person is Satan:

*"In this the children of God are manifest, and **the children of the devil:** whosoever doeth not righteousness is not of God, neither he that loveth not his brother. For this is the message that ye heard from the beginning, that we should love one another. **Not as Cain, who was of that wicked one, and slew his brother.** And wherefore slew he him? Because his own works were evil, and his brother's righteous."* (1 John 3:10-12)

Sin and Satan is the exact same person. No wonder that we are told that the one who sins is of the devil (1 John 3:8). It was Satan who moved Cain to murder Abel. Satan is the original murderer (John 8:44).

Yet, Cain did not have to open the door to Satan. God told Cain that he could rule over Satan. The same is especially true for those who have been redeemed by the blood of Jesus. Satan may knock at our door but it is our choice to let him in. He cannot break the door down without having to deal with God Himself. Therefore he can only knock and hope that we are foolish enough to give him entrance. Keep the door closed to Satan by not yielding to sin. You can rule over him.

July 1

Did God know that Man Would Fall?

And the LORD God called unto Adam, and said unto him, Where art thou? And he said, I heard thy voice in the garden, and I was afraid, because I was naked; and I hid myself. And he said, Who told thee that thou wast naked? Hast thou eaten of the tree, whereof I commanded thee that thou shouldest not eat? (Gen. 3:9-11)

For centuries theologians have assigned certain attributes to God in order to explain to their listeners and readers what constitutes perfection or flawlessness in God. One of these man-made attributes was the idea that God possesses divine exhaustive foreknowledge of all future events. This includes the idea that regardless of the time, energy and care that God had put into the creation He already knew beyond a shadow of a doubt that man would disobey Him and plunge everything into death and chaos.

One group of theologians have taught that God has this exhaustive foreknowledge of all future events because He has decreed every single event that will ever take place in history down to the minutest detail. This includes the spider you might find and kill tomorrow as well as the next Muslim terrorist attack. Every one of these events was known by God before He created because He planned and wanted them to happen.

Another theological premise on this is that God exists outside of time as we know it. While He does not want or desire many of the events that have occurred and continue to occur in history, He created the earth and the first couple with full and complete knowledge that they would fall and become responsible for billions of souls who would later suffer eternal torment. He was also fully aware of the horrendous acts that they would commit on each other. Yet, He chose to create any way for a greater purpose, which most claim to be the redemption of mankind.

I have found both ideas to be problematic and both make God appear to be a hypocrite (actor) in the passage above. God seems to be completely unaware of what Adam has done. He only realizes it after Adam tells Him why he is hiding. It is then that God is shocked and asks if Adam had eaten the forbidden fruit.

The Bible presents no proof that God knew all along that man would fall. Some like to excuse their sin with the false idea that says, "I'll sin anyway since God already knows what I am going to do so He is not surprised." God is always shocked and hurt by our rebellion because He loves us and knows the damage it does to us and others. Let us stop taking comfort in sin by traditional but unbiblical ideas about God.

What is this that Thou Hast Done?

And the LORD God said unto the woman, What is this that thou hast done? And the woman said, The serpent beguiled me, and I did eat. And the LORD God said unto the serpent, Because thou hast done this, thou art cursed above all cattle, and above every beast of the field; upon thy belly shalt thou go, and dust shalt thou eat all the days of thy life: (Gen. 3:13-14)

Many have stated that God is not asking Adam and Eve questions to gather information but to garner a confession. That could be true but it does not seem that God's method has rendered the type of confessions that He usually desires—confessions that lead to admitting one is wrong about their sin and that would bring repentance (Prov. 28:13; 1 John 1:9).

Adam and Eve begin to blame others. Adam blamed God and his wife and Eve blamed the serpent (who we know is Satan in disguise – Rev. 12:9). Regardless of God's intents, the question remains: did God know that the first couple would commit such an egregious act? Did He create with full knowledge of this eventuality?

According to the majority of Christians God created with full exhaustive foreknowledge of every future event. Yet, if this is true, God is doing a very good job of play-acting with Adam and Eve. If we can read God's tone into the passage above He appears to be shocked and hurt by their actions. He also appears to be extremely angry with the tempter as He begins to pronounce judgment upon him.

Why all of the painful emotional reactions if God had exhaustive foreknowledge of all that would happen? Furthermore, if God knew this all along then He appears to be a very good actor here. In God's question to Eve He is basically asking "Do you realize what you have unleashed and the problems that you have caused?" God does not seem to see any rational reason for Eve's behavior here?

Contrary to popular theology, the fall of man was not in God's original plan and it was not something He desired. The Scriptures teach that God's original plan for man was disrupted by Adam's fall into sin. God had a great purpose for the first couple and mankind as a whole that was disrupted by sin.

Quite often we disrupt God's wonderful plans for our lives by our constant failings. However, we can take heart in the fact that God is a God of redemption and restoration. He will get His plan for our lives back on track if we will go before Him in humility and repent of our rebellion.

July 3

God Regrets Creating Man

And the Lord regretted that He had made man on the earth, and He was grieved at heart. So the Lord said, I will destroy, blot out, and wipe away mankind, whom I have created from the face of the ground—not only man, [but] the beasts and the creeping things and the birds of the air—for it grieves Me and makes Me regretful that I have made them (Genesis 6:6-7; The Amplified Bible).

Many Christians believe that God created man with the full knowledge that he would later fall and bring wickedness upon God's good creation. Yet, if this is true then why did God become so grieved about mankind's wicked actions? Why does God regret having created Him? To "regret" something is to feel *disappointment* and dissatisfaction with the object of one's regret. If God knew all along that man would fall then why the disappointment?

Along with the idea that God has full foreknowledge of all future events, some theologians have taught that God is *impassible* – that He is without passions, feelings, and emotions. These ideas were meant to promote man-made definitions of what it means for God to be perfect and flawless. Yet, the divine inspired Word of God teaches that God is passionately dissatisfied with grief over what man has become.

We question the integrity of God with some of our traditional ideas about Him and His Word cannot be taken seriously. Furthermore, we make God a dishonest play-actor who regrets something He supposedly knew beyond a shadow of a doubt would occur, and according to some theologians, secretly decreed would happen and brought it about by His omnipotent manipulation.

Even more, we make God culpable for man's wickedness. Verse 5 says, *"And GOD saw that **the wickedness of man was great in the earth**, and that every imagination of the thoughts of his heart was only evil continually"* (KJV). To say that God knew and decreed all of these future events makes God fully the author of man's wickedness. This would be a blight upon His righteous and loving character. In essence, God would be behind every murder, child rape, drunk driver, unjust war, handicap and every other tragic event of this world.

God can be trusted based on the fact that He neither planned nor wanted man's wickedness. All of this was contrary to His plan. He is a totally good God and regrets the hurt and pain that we suffer and that we inflict upon one another. Let us see the God who has enough passion to be hurt by our sin is also one who can passionately love us.

The Person Responsible for Sin in God's Creation

Wherefore, as by one man sin entered into the world, and death by sin; and so death passed upon all men, for that all have sinned (Romans 5:12).

There are a number of theologians who knowingly or unknowingly cast aspersions on God's character with their ideas of what it means for Him to be perfect. Some believe that God must know every single future event that will ever occur and nothing should ever get past Him. Furthermore, God must be in absolute control of every single detail of each event because He is omnipotent and all powerful.

These theologians claim that if God is ever unknowledgeable of any future event then He is not all knowing. They say that if He is not controlling the minutest detail of every single thing that ever happens in the world then He is not sovereign or all powerful. Yet we can affirm the Bible's teaching about God as One who is all wise, all knowledgeable, all powerful and sovereign without having to be bullied into accepting the ideas of what this mean forced upon us by intellectual elites.

First, everything that God does is governed by His love, holiness and integrity. There is not one person or thing that is more powerful than God and there is not one creature in the universe that knows more and is wiser than God. However, God is not insecure like fallen men and fallen angels who must use their power to manipulate. God has given His creatures the freedom to choose and governs them by love. Furthermore, rather than micromanaging them, He puts His trust in them, assured that they will do the right thing since there is never any reason to do the wrong thing.

Sadly, the first man betrayed the love and trust of His Creator and plunged the world into sin and death. The Bible makes man responsible for the world being the way it is. The so-called "mystery of evil" or "problem of evil" is partially resolved by seeing that man used His God-given freedom and authority to bring evil into the world. God is not responsible either through negligence (creating while knowing full well it would happen) or by manipulative power. The passage above exonerates God from the evil in our world and makes man fully culpable.

Be careful about blaming God for the evil that occurs in this world. He is not the One who brought evil. He is the loving God trying to bring us out of the evil that we inflict on ourselves. We are at fault but He still loves us and longs to deliver us.

July 5

Sin's Relationship to Sickness

And he that was healed wist not who it was: for Jesus had conveyed himself away, a multitude being in that place. Afterward Jesus findeth him in the temple, and said unto him, Behold, thou art made whole: sin no more, lest a worse thing come unto thee. (John 5:13-14).

For years I have met many people who have blamed God for sickness. This has made some very bitter towards God and others simply accept it as God's will for their lives without any attempt to seek His relief. I have often been saddened by God getting blamed for the results of sin, be it our personal sin or someone else's.

Before going any further, it is essential to state that not all people are sick due to *personal* sin. A baby born with AIDS due to promiscuous parents is not at fault nor is any person who has been crippled due to the negligent behavior of another. Nonetheless, we cannot dismiss the truth that there is a clear relationship between sickness and sin. For the most part, we are reluctant to admit that much of the sickness suffered by so many may have its roots in sin and this is why they remain sick.

Jesus is very clear in his statement to this man that his sickness was the result of sin. He warned him that if he used his new found health to return to a life of sin that the consequences will be worse than before. Jesus, in His warning, made a very solid connection between sin and its harmful results.

When we sin we risk opening the door to so much pain and hurt in our lives. God's prohibition against sin is not so much an attempt to set up boundaries as it is to set up safeguards that will protect us from sin's unmerciful judgments upon us. Sin entices us to selfishly pleasure ourselves and then repays us with sickness and other tragedies.

Jesus' healing ministry both then and now is given to undo the results of sin upon our lives. We have rebelled against God's righteous laws, disrespected Him, separated ourselves from Him, placed ourselves in Satan's territory and reaped the results. Yet God still reaches out and completely heals the sick one despite what brought sickness in the first place. Truly there is no love that compares to this and there is no god of any religion who loves so unconditionally as the Father of our Lord Jesus Christ. He did not tell this man, "You made your own bed, now lie in it." Instead, He displays divine love through healing. But He also lovingly warns the man to stay away from that which would cause worse sickness.

July 6

The Power of God's Forgiveness

But that ye may know that the Son of man hath power on earth to forgive sins, (he saith to the sick of the palsy,) I say unto thee, Arise, and take up thy bed, and go thy way into thine house. And immediately he arose, took up the bed, and went forth before them all; insomuch that they were all amazed, and glorified God, saying, We never saw it on this fashion (Mark 2:10-12)

Some of our perspectives on God's reaction to sin makes many of us afraid to run to Him for help when we are suffering the consequences of our rebellion. If we believe that God is the One who personally inflicts upon us the results of our wrong behavior then we will look at Him more as a disease-inflictor rather than a loving healer. But when we begin to see that sin itself pays its own wages (Rom. 6:23) and has its own seeds of destruction (James 1:13-15) then we may be less reluctant to see how our loving Heavenly Father can deliver us.

If sickness is the result of sin then the first thing we need is to receive *forgiveness* from God. There are a number of definitions that one can find for the word forgive but the one I like best and that fits today's passage is this, "….to free or pardon (someone) from penalty; to free from the obligation of (a debt, payment, etc.)" (dictionary.com).

Many people in today's "grace movement" do not believe that one needs to confess sin or ask God for forgiveness when they sin. They believe that because God is loving and gracious that He no longer requires it due to the redemptive work of Christ.

What these people fail to understand is that when we sin we place ourselves under the power of that sin and of Satan who holds the power of death (Rom. 6; 1 John 3:8; Heb. 2:14-15). We need God's help in releasing us from the bondage and penalties that we have put ourselves under. We are not asking God to forgive us because He is angry at us and is holding resentment. He is already ready to forgive before we ever ask Him (Psalm 86:5; Neh. 9:17; Micah 7:18). Yet, until we receive the forgiveness that God is so ready to bestow we will continue to suffer the penalties accrued from our sin.

The good news is that Jesus demonstrates His power to forgive sins by bringing about supernatural healing to the one who sinned. That same authority to forgive also brings healing. We don't have to settle for one and not the other. Sin often brings about sickness but forgiveness of sin brings healing to the one willing to receive it. What a gracious God.

July 7

Jesus' Rescue Mission

*And she shall bring forth a son, and thou shalt call his name JESUS: for **he shall save his people from their sins*** (Matt. 1:21)

Since Satan has been unable to stop the spreading of the truth that Jesus died on the cross in order to save mankind, he has decided to twist and distort the truth in order to malign God's character. Satan, through some well-meaning people, has made Jesus' sacrifice one in which *He saves us from the Father.*

However, this is not true. The Father loved the world so much that He actually sent the Son Himself (John 3:16). It was *sin* that held us captive and gave Satan access to destroy us (1 John 3:8; Eph. 2:1-5). *Jesus came to rescue us from sin and Satan, not from God.*

The Greek word for "save" is *sozo* which means, "to save, that is, deliver or protect (literally or figuratively): - heal, preserve, save (self), do well, be (make) whole." (Strong's Dictionary) Another dictionary says it means, "....to save, keep safe and sound, to rescue from danger or destruction a. one (from injury or peril); to save a suffering one (from perishing), i.e. one suffering from disease, to make well, heal, restore to health; to preserve one who is in danger of destruction, to save or rescue; ....to deliver from the penalties of the Messianic judgment." (Studylight.org).

The Orthodox Jewish Bible gives us this translation, *"And she shall bear BEN (Son) and you will call SHMO (his name, Zech 6:12) YEHOSHUA (Zech 6:11-12) because he will bring his people yeshuah (rescue, salvation, deliverance) from their peyshaim (rebellions)."* God sent Jesus to deliver us from the POWER of sin so that it would no longer be able to involuntarily control us. He also rescued us from the CONSEQUENCES of our sin.

God shows us how much He loves us by giving His very life to rescue us from the power and consequences of our own sinful choices. If we fail to see this truth and take a distorted view of the sacrifice of Christ in which He saves us from an angry wrathful Father, then our "salvation" will be fear based rather than love and faith based. Recognizing that it was sin that was destroying us and not God helps us to see that the redemptive work of Christ was a rescue mission that involved the whole Godhead. Only a loving Father could risk the life of His only Son to rescue people who rebelled against Him.

July 8

Forgivenesees and Mercies

O Lord, to us belongeth confusion of face, to our kings, to our princes, and to our fathers, because we have sinned against thee. To the Lord our God belong mercies and forgivenesses, though we have rebelled against him (Daniel 9:8-9)

The word "confusion" in the passage above is a Hebrew word that actually means "shame". The Israelites were invaded by Babylon and many of them were taken as captives to this country. God had warned them time and time again to repent of their sin so that He could protect them from this dangerous foreign power but they refused Him. He was left with no choice but to let their enemies have their way. Now the great nation of Israel was brought to shame.

Daniel was saying that because of Israel's sin they deserved "shame of face" before God. Daniel was confessing to God that His people deserve to be painfully embarrassed by how they have treated God after He extended mercy upon mercy upon mercy. However, Daniel also recognized something wonderful about God's character: He saw that despite the rebellions of God's people, God was full of forgivenesses and mercies.

The word "mercies" means "compassion" and "tender love". Despite the sinful rebelliousness of God's people, He still had compassion and tender love for them. No matter what we do, God just can't seem to stop loving us. Oh how easily we humans hate people who wrong us, yet God's divine nature finds it impossible to turn off the love.

This "tender love" that is a predominant aspect of God's nature does not mean that we will not suffer the consequences of persistent rebellion. However, when we do, we can look at another aspect of His loving nature which possesses *forgivenesses*. Forgiveness means "....to free or pardon (someone) from penalty; to free from the obligation of (a debt, payment, etc.)" (dictionary.com).

In response to his prayer, God sent Gabriel the archangel to Daniel to give him further understanding of the prophecies and to tell him of the coming Messiah who would soon free Israel from her sins. God not only offers us His tender compassion, but He will give us the forgiveness we need – the release from the penalty we deserve, by taking upon Himself the penalty for our sin. That is what Jesus did. Now, we can declare ourselves free from sin's power and penalty because of what Jesus has done on our behalf.

July 9

Prayer and God's Character

O my God, incline thine ear, and hear; open thine eyes, and behold our desolations, and the city which is called by thy name: for we do not present our supplications before thee for our righteousnesses, but for thy great mercies. O Lord, hear; O Lord, forgive; O Lord, hearken and do; defer not, for thine own sake, O my God: for thy city and thy people are called by thy name (Dan. 9:18-19)

Many of God's people experience failure in prayer for a variety of reasons. One of them is a failure to know God's true character in relation to their own shortcomings. Some people realize that they are unworthy and undeserving to receive anything from God, to include His forgiveness. Yet, because they focus on themselves and not on God they fail to receive what He is more than willing to bestow.

Others seem to think that they are righteous due to their works and believe that they fully deserve to receive from God. They go before God emboldened by their self-righteousness and are later perplexed that they get no response from Him. Again, the focus is on themselves rather than on God.

If there was a man who lived a righteous life, it was Daniel. But Daniel also recognized that He had failures and shortcomings that left Him undeserving of receiving anything based on personal merit. Yet, as we read His prayer we learn a powerful principle for guaranteed answers to prayer: it is to focus on God's character and not our own whether we think our characters are righteous or unrighteous.

Daniel told God, *"....we do not present our supplications before thee for our righteousnesses, but for thy great mercies. O Lord, hear; O Lord, forgive; O Lord, hearken and do."* This is a reverent but very bold prayer. Daniel reverently demanded that God listen to him and act upon his request. When one reads further in the 9th chapter of Daniel we see that God did what Daniel requested.

The secret: Daniel stated that they were not coming to God based on their personal righteousness. They confessed and acknowledged their sin and the sin of their nation. But then He appealed to God's mercies—His tender love and compassion. By knowing the character of God Daniel was able to have boldness in prayer and to pray with expectation.

July 10

Did God Endorse Rahab's Lie?

*And the city shall be accursed, even it, and all that are therein, to the LORD: only Rahab the harlot shall live, she and all that are with her in the house, **because she hid the messengers that we sent**.... And Joshua saved Rahab the harlot alive, and her father's household, and all that she had; and she dwelleth in Israel even unto this day; **because she hid the messengers, which Joshua sent to spy out Jericho** (Joshua 6:17, 25)*

An attempt to slander God by Bible critics, and unintentionally by some well-meaning Christians, is the erroneous idea that God endorsed the lie that Rahab told to the king of Jericho after hiding two spies from Israel (Joshua 2:1-7). When we read the story it does appear that Rahab's actions are portrayed as noble. She is commended in both the Old and the New Testaments and even honored by her place in the lineage of the Messiah Himself (Matt. 1:5).

Does this mean that the God of Truth who finds it impossible to lie occasionally endorses lying for noble reasons? Solomon tells us that God hates lying and finds it abominable (Prov. 6:16-17). God hates lying so much that two people died for it at the beginning of the church (Acts 5:1-11). Even worse, the Lord points out the fact that liars will see their part in the lake of fire (Rev. 21:8). With this much hatred for lying, can we use Rahab's lie to justify the idea that lying can be good?

Rahab's lying is no more commended than her life of prostitution. The lie she told is never once given an endorsement in Scripture. Scripture commends her for the act of hiding the two spies. In the New Testament, Rahab is mentioned again as an example of great faith. It is her faith in receiving the spies and helping them that she is given recognition for (James 2:24-25; Heb. 11:31).

Rahab could not be expected to know everything that displeased God in such a short period of time. God is gracious where light concerning the truth is lacking (Luke 12:47-48; John 9:39-41; 15:22-24; Acts 17:30; Rom. 7:7-9; James 4:17; Heb. 10:26). Some time ago I heard about a man who received Christ. During his prayer he used a number of expletives, or what we might call "curse words" or profanity. Yet, God honored the faith of that man and saved him. Does this mean that God endorses profanity? No (Eph. 4:29; 5:4; Col. 3:8). This man would learn in time that God does not endorse foul language. The same grace was shown to Rahab. Those who know the truth cannot be excused for lying under any circumstances.

July 11

A Large Time Gap between Genesis 1:1 and 1:2

*In the beginning God created the heaven and the earth. And **the earth was without form, and void; and darkness was upon the face of the deep**. And the Spirit of God moved upon the face of the waters.* (Gen. 1:1-2)

In Christian circles today many have embraced what has become known as "Young Earth Creationism." This is the idea that the earth is only 6000 to 8000 years old. However, a number of problems in relation to God's character and the origin of evil in our universe appear with this teaching.

One of the problems with "YEC" is its lack of consistency with scientific data. For example, where did the dinosaurs come from? What about the geological age of the earth? Adam and Eve to present day only accounts for 6000 to 8000 years. Yet, geological studies appear to put the earth at millions of years old. Sadly, in response to some of these scientific problems some YEC proponents say that the earth was created with the APPEARANCE of age. Doesn't this make God a partaker in active deception and the author of confusion?

Others have attempted to answer these problems with what has been called "Old Earth Creationism". This is the belief that that the six days of creation or restoration in Genesis 1 are not 24 hours days but are 1000 years each. Some who hold this believe in a "Christianized Darwinism" or "Theistic evolution". What is most important is that this idea cannot be supported by the plain teaching of Scripture. The most reasonable answer to the scientific conundrum is in the gap between Genesis 1:1 and 1:2. It accounts for the dinosaurs, prehistoric animals, and the geological evidences concerning the earth's age.

However, the primary objective for believing any teaching is not how it reconciles with scientific facts but whether or not it is Biblical. Furthermore, does the teaching vindicate God in relation to evil or does it make Him to be culpable for it? Our main concern in studying the gap between Genesis 1:1 and 1:2 is to learn how evil came into existence and invaded our world. But as a bonus we can also see how the gap between Genesis 1:1-2 coincides with science *facts* and dispels the evolution *fiction*.

The GAP teaching sort of "fills in the gap" (pun intended) concerning the problem of evil, the origin of Satan, and why Satan is so obsessed with the earth. While the issues of the age of the earth, dinosaurs, and geology is secondary, the GAP answers those questions way better than "young earth" and "theistic evolution" does.

Did God Create the Earth Chaotic and Ruined?

Created by the Elohim were the heavens and the earth. Yet ***the earth became a chaos and vacant, and darkness was on the surface of the submerged chaos.*** *Yet the spirit of the Elohim is vibrating over the surface of the water.* (Concordant Literal Translation - Emphasis are mine)

The phrase "without form, and void" in the traditional King James Version comes from a Hebrew phrase, "tohu va bohu". The phrase actually indicates a ruin and an empty wilderness. Another English translation reads, *"In the beginning, God created the heavens and the earth. Now, **the earth, had become waste and wild, and darkness, was on the face of the roaring deep**,—but, the Spirit of God, was brooding on the face of the waters"* (Rotherham Emphasized Bible - Emphasis are mine)

The late German theologian, Johann August Dathe, believed the passage should read, "In the beginning God created the heaven and the earth, but afterwards the earth became waste and desolate." Another late Bible scholar named Arthur Custance translates Genesis 1:1-2 as following: "IN A FORMER STATE GOD PERFECTED THE HEAVENS AND THE EARTH. BUT THE EARTH HAD BECOME A RUIN AND A DESOLATION, AND THE DARKNESS OF JUDGMENT WAS UPON THE FACE OF IT."

Did God, who made everything beautiful and whose work is perfect (Deut. 32:4) create the earth into a chaotic mess? According to Isaiah the answer is an emphatic "NO!"

For thus saith the Lord that created the heavens; God himself that formed the earth and made it; he hath established it, ***he created it not in vain****, he formed it to be inhabited: I am the Lord; and there is none else* (Isaiah 45:18)

The same Hebrew phrase, "tohu va bohu" used in Genesis 1:2 is found in the above passage. Why would God say that He did not create the earth as a "tohu va Bohu" here in Isaiah but many claim that in Genesis 1:2 that is exactly what He did? God does not create anything chaotic or ruined. To do such is simply not consistent with His character. The earth was not created in the way that it is described in Genesis 1:2 but it *became* that way due to the fall of Lucifer (now known as "Satan").

Unformed and Unfinished?

I beheld the earth, and, lo, it was without form, and void; *and the heavens, and they had no light. I beheld the* *mountains, and, lo, they trembled, and all the hills moved* *lightly.I beheld, and, lo, there was no man, and all the* *birds of the heavens were fled. I beheld, and, lo, the fruitful* *place was a wilderness, and all the cities **thereof were*** ***broken down at the presence of the Lord, and by his*** ***fierce anger*** (Jeremiah 4:23-26)

In Genesis 1:2 we find that after God has created the heavens and the earth, the earth is said to be "without form and void". Some who embrace "young earth creationism" claim that this only means "unformed and unfinished". Yet, Genesis 1:1 says that in the beginning God created the HEAVENS and the earth. I believe it is only correct to ask why is it that verse 2 only mentions the earth being "unformed and unfinished" as some claim and not the heavens?

Actually "unformed and unfinished" is not the way "tohu va bohu" is used in the Hebrew Scriptures and cannot be confirmed by a clear study of the phrase as it is used in the Bible. *Tohu va bohu*, when used in Isa. 45:18 and other places in the Hebrew Bible describes something that is completely out of order, is contrary to God's intended purposes, and is under divine judgment. This is made clear in Jer. 4:23-26 quoted above.

Far from speaking about being "unformed and unfinished" this phrase speaks of judgment and destruction. That is how the phrase "tohu va bohu" is always used. There is no legitimate reason for making Genesis 1:2 the exception. It is obvious that from the common use of the phrase that Genesis 1:2 is speaking of a judgment.

A deeper look shows that in Genesis 1:2 God is correcting something that was caused by Satan's rebellion: *"The realm of the dead is naked before God; **Destruction [Abaddon] lies** uncovered. He spreads out the northern skies over **empty space [tohu]**; he suspends the earth over nothing"* (Job 26:6, 7).

According to Rev. 9, Abaddon is Satan the destroyer. God was fixing what Satan destroyed in Genesis 1:2. No other explanation is sound or reasonable without questioning God's ability to create perfectly. No other explanation can help us to understand the beginnings of evil in our universe and why the earth would later become the center of the ongoing battle between God's forces of light and good and Satan's forces of darkness and evil. Other models of creation offer no Biblically viable explanation for Satan's fall and his interest in the earth in particular.

Satan Thrown to the Earth

Your heart was filled with pride because of all your beauty.
You corrupted your wisdom for the sake of your splendor.
***So I threw you to the earth** and exposed you to the curious*
gaze of kings. (Eze. 28:17; NLT)

There are some, primarily in the "Young Earth Creationism" camp who believe that Satan fell right after Adam was created. If someone can easily learn the art of deception and is able to persuade a third of the angels to follow him after what may have been millions of years in God's holy and loving presence, then angels are exceptionally stupid and Satan got evil pretty quick. That simply is not the normal experience. It takes time to be persuaded and deceived after knowing the truth for so many centuries.

Others who believe in YEC will tell us that Satan fell *before* the creation of the earth. However, this would make no sense in light of the fact that Satan was immediately thrown to the earth upon his fall. Ezekiel records this and so does Isaiah: *"How you are **fallen from heaven**, O shining star, son of the morning! **You have been thrown down to the earth**, you who destroyed the nations of the world"* (Isa. 14:12; New Living Translation). It is due to Satan being thrown to the earth that we find it a chaos and a ruin in Genesis 1:2. Erich Sauer writes:

> "But with the fall of Satan there must have been associated the ruin of the region over which he ruled, as is evidenced by the organic connexion between spirit and nature, and by the later and resembling fall of man, though this last to a smaller extent (Gen. 3:18). World and earth catastrophes occurred as counter-workings of the righteousness of God against this cosmic revolt. The creation was subject to vanity (Rom. 8:20, 21)."[29]

We believe that after Satan was thrown to the earth he and his followers began to set about ruining it. Without God's presence and protection over this region they quickly realized how desolate it had become. God created a good universe full of love and unselfishness. There was nothing but joy and happiness in God's creation until one day, a rebellion ensued which brought the first catastrophe in history. This rebellion was caused by Satan and his followers. The origin of evil begins, not with God, but with the devil.

---

[29] Sauer, Erich **The Dawn of World Redemption** (Grand Rapids, MI: Wm. B. Eerdmans Publishing Co., 1994), pp. 34-35

July 15

Faith is Believing that God is Everything that He Says He Is

*But without faith it is impossible to please him: for he that cometh to God must **believe that he is**, and that he is a rewarder of them that diligently seek him* (Heb. 11:6)

Many translations of the Bible take the phrase, "must believe that He is" and interpret it as "We must believe that He exists". We are led to believe that the writer of Hebrews is referring to faith in God's existence. This might be true but two things cause me to doubt it. First, the epistle was written primarily to Jewish Christians and not to unsaved people. Second, the passage in question is in reference to faith that is confident in receiving an answer to prayer. Therefore, the statement, "He is" implies more than just believing in God's existence. After all, the Bible has never attempted to *defend* God's existence. It has always *assumed* it.

Compare Hebrews 11:6 to to Exodus 3:14 which says, *"And God said unto Moses, I AM THAT I AM: and he said, Thus shalt thou say unto the children of Israel, I AM hath sent me unto you."* This is God's covenant name which being interpreted means "Whatever you need me to be, I will be." From that we understand that God is our healer, need-supplier, righteousness, sanctification, victory-banner, etc.

Now here are some questions that should further strengthen our faith: Should this not include everything that God is NOT? Is He the One responsible for sickness, disease, and other types of evil? If I am unsure that God is behind my problem then is my faith able to work in standing against a circumstance that in the back of my mind I might believe that God has something to do with it?

Are we able to exercise faith in God if we believe Him to be anything but the supplier of that which is good? Some actually believe that God is the creator of evil. Can you truly exercise faith in God if you believe that He dispenses both good and evil? Can faith accept a schizophrenic view that God is both the healer and sickness bringer? The one who sends the devil and also gives you victory over him? The one who tests with sin while still being your sanctification?

Many people cannot believe God to bring them out of a situation because they believe that He is the one who brought the situation on them. Some believe that He does it for mysterious but beneficial purposes and others believe that He is punishing them for some sin in their life. Isn't it important to understand God's character if one can truly have the type of faith that actually gets answers to prayer and changes circumstances? The answers to these will strengthen or weaken one's faith in God.

July 16

God is a Rewarder

*But without faith it is impossible to please him: for he that cometh to God must **believe that he is**, and that **he is a rewarder** of them that diligently seek him* (Heb. 11:6)

Looking at Hebrews 11:6 we see from the passage itself that the phrase "He is" has something more to do with God than just merely His existence. We are told that we must believe that *He is* a Rewarder of those who diligently seek Him. Australian Pentecostal scholar, Dr. Ken Chant, gives us a very insightful interpretation of what it means for God to be a Rewarder:

> Notice that the word is a noun, not a verb (as it is translated in some versions). He did not say merely that God "rewards," but rather that God's very name and nature is "Rewarder." He is giving us a new name for God. We already call him Father, Saviour, Healer, Redeemer – now we can also call him *Rewarder*. Furthermore, he links this name with a verbal structure that coveys the idea of continuity. That is, God is not just an *occasional* Rewarder; rather, it is his *habit* to reward those who seek him. He continually proves himself to be the Rewarder. He is always showing himself in that character. He can never be any other. Faith perceives this. Faith rejoices in it. Faith depends upon it. Faith never doubts that there is a vast generosity in God.[30]

Chant concludes, "Unhappily, most people have a problem with that concept-either because they have a poor opinion of themselves, or a poor opinion of God, or both." If what Chant is saying is true then this tells me that it is essential to understand the character of God if we are to have fully developed faith that is able to receive from Him. It is essential that we understand who God claims to be, and also what He plainly says that He isn't. He tells us that He is our Rewarder. This goes against the satanic idea that God is stingy and often withholding from us for mysterious unknown purposes.

---

[30] Chant, Ken **Faith Dynamics: God's Way to Move Mountains** (Ramona, CA: Vision Publishing, 1989), p. 82

July 17

He IS A Very Present Help in Trouble

God is our refuge and strength, a very present help in trouble. Therefore will not we fear, though the earth be removed, and though the mountains be carried into the midst of the sea (Psalm 46:1-2)

We have learned from Hebrews 11:6 that we must "believe that He IS". God can only reward our faith when we believe that *He is* exactly what He says that He is to us. The written Word of God contains a vast record of those things that God says that *He is* to His people. In Psalm 46, we discover that God *is* our refuge and strength and that He *is* a very present help in trouble. This discovery removes fear despite whatever circumstances we find ourselves in.

The word "trouble" in the Hebrew means, "adversary, adversity, affliction, anguish, distress, tribulation, trouble." (Strong's Dictionary) In our day there are many people that teach that God Himself sends us trials, tribulations, afflictions and adversity to make us strong. However, if we compare this traditional idea with Psalm 46 then we get a picture of a schizophrenic deity who sends trouble only to help us in it.

The problem with many of these people is the failure to recognize the Biblical truth that God's people are engaged in warfare between the forces of good and evil. As long as we remain on the earth we will find ourselves as combatants in enemy territory. God is not the one who brings us trouble; He is the one who is a very present help in the trouble brought to us by the adversary. Peter says, that it is *"your adversary the devil, as a roaring lion, walketh about, seeking whom he may devour"* (1 Pet. 5:8). He also tells us that the devil is responsible for the afflictions that many of God's people suffer (v. 9).

Failure to distinguish between the works of God and the works of Satan has caused many people to lose their faith in God. Our failure to learn and believe who God says that He is has caused us to wrongly accuse Him of doing things that He would never do and attribute to Him the things that the devil does to us.

When we recognize the true source of trouble and then recognize that it is God who will give us refuge from it, shield us from it, and help us in trouble then we won't just simply allow ourselves to be beaten down by it but will run to Him in faith and embrace all that He is to us. This is why faith, if it is to be properly rewarded, must believe all that God *is*, which will help us to also recognize that which He is NOT.

July 18

Understanding and Knowing God: Foundation for Faith

But let him that glorieth glory in this, that he **understandeth and knoweth me**, *that I am the Lord which exercise lovingkindness, judgment, and righteousness, in the earth: for in these things I delight, saith the Lord.* (Jer. 9:24)

Some seem to believe that faith in God works whether or not we understand Him. However, the Bible disputes this idea. If we have wrong ideas about God then this will lead us to accepting many things that never come from His hand. Notice that God is One who exercises *lovingkimdness*. He is both loving and kind. He is not mean, capricious, and vindictive. He wants to love on us and show us kindness.

He also executes *judgment*. We need not be afraid of this word. In our modern culture we limit the truth about judgment to the ideas of crime and punishment. This is only one aspect of judgment. In the passage above God is not speaking about judging His people for their sins but judging on behalf of His people in order to bring them victory and salvation against those who oppress them (Psalm 18:47-48; 94:1-14; Matt. 12:20-21). We are to actually rejoice and be glad for God's judgment (Psalm 48:11; 149:1-9). When we understand God's judgment then we will cry out for Him to judge the earth (Psalm 82:8).

We are to also understand God's *righteousness*. His righteousness is an aspect of His character by which we can be sure that He will keep His promises (Neh. 9:8; Isa. 45:21-25). The Father so longs for fellowship with His sinful creatures that, through the blood of Jesus, we can receive God's righteousness which empowers us to live holy and also gives us "right-standing" in God's presence (2 Cor. 5:21; 1 John 1:7-9).

Satan has so distorted our understanding about God that we easily skip over His lovingkindness and begin to focus on negative ideas about judgment and righteousness. Many believe that understanding God is unessential to faith. On the contrary, they have difficulty believing anything other than a God who is shrouded in mystery.

God is not the author of "mystery religion". It is Satan who darkens the understanding of people (Eph. 4:18; 2 Cor. 4:3-4). God expects His people to both understand and know Him. Many people are afraid of God and many hate Him because they have been taught a distorted concept of His nature. To know God is to love Him. In order to truly know Him we must understand Him. Just like us, God does not want to keep being misunderstood. Let His children at least understand Him so that we can help the world understand Him.

God's <u>Wonderful</u> Works

Oh that men would praise the Lord for his goodness, and for his wonderful works to the children of men! (Psalm 107:8, 15, 21, 31)

Four times we are told in Psalm 107 that we should praise the Lord for His goodness and His *wonderful* works to mankind. The word "wonderful" means something extraordinary or marvelous. It has a "You have to see it in order to believe it" connotation. Furthermore, each of the four verses couples God's wonderful works with His *goodness*.

When the average person hears the word "wonderful" their mind automatically relates it to something positive (as it should). Therefore, describing God's works as wonderful is important because too often God is blamed for "works" that are anything but wonderful. People and insurance companies too often blame God for natural disasters such as tornadoes, hurricanes, typhoons, drought, and other hurtful events. Even well-meaning preachers claim that God sends these things as acts of judgment against sin. These works that are attributed to God could not be considered "wonderful" by the average human intellect.

Sickness and disease is often considered by some to be a work of God and some sincere Christians, due to a warped understanding of God's nature, will praise Him for sickness. The surrounding context of Psalm 107 speaks directly against this idea, giving credit to sin for bringing sickness and also telling us that it is God who sends His Word to heal us. It is for the wonderful work of deliverance and healing that God is to be given praise for and rather than the results of sin (see verses 17-21).

Part of our failure has been our inability to distinguish between the works of God and the works of Satan. The Bible tells us that Jesus was manifested in order to destroy the *works* of Satan (1 John 3:8). Satan has *works* and his works are destructive (Job 1-2; Luke 13:16; John 8:44; 10:10; Acts 10:38).

On the other hand the Bible speaks about the works of Jesus. The Lord promised that believers will not only do these works, but even greater (John 14:12). Certainly Jesus was not expecting His followers to bring natural disasters. He rebuked some disciples for thinking in such a manner (Luke 9:51-56). Furthermore He did not consider our ability to do greater works than Himself as inflicting people with sickness and disease. If we as His disciples cannot see Jesus, who is God in the flesh, doing certain things or expecting them of us then how dare we attribute them to God? When we grasp the truth about God's works we will be able to see them as truly wonderful and praise Him for them.

July 20

Judgment unto <u>Victory</u>?

Behold my servant, whom I have chosen; my beloved, in whom my soul is well pleased: I will put my spirit upon him, and he shall shew judgment to the Gentiles.... A bruised reed shall he not break, and smoking flax shall he not quench, till he send forth judgment unto victory. And in his name shall the Gentiles trust. (Matt. 12:8, 20-21)

A picture is shown of an angry Jesus coming through the clouds. Underneath is the caption, "HERE COMES THE JUDGE!" Not the most comforting picture for most people. True that those who remain in their sins and reject the mercy of Jesus have need to be afraid, not because Jesus is harsh or cruel, but because His judgment will only allow them to see that their rejection of His sacrifice on their behalf will cost them an eternity of painful torture—torture He so badly wanted to save them from.

On the other hand, God's children have no need to be afraid of judgment. The righteous judge is coming to render judgment on our behalf. He is not coming to judge us for those sins that He has already cleansed by His blood and for which we have turned away from. He is coming to give us judgment unto victory. As a matter of fact He has already come and rendered this judgment. He has judged Satan as a defeated enemy and has given His victory to those who have aligned themselves with Him.

Perhaps we have thought completely wrong about what it means for God to judge. Man judges for the purpose of punishment and condemnation. Prosecutors work hard to get a victory and to ensure that a judge condemns a person. However, defense attorneys work hard to gain a victory on behalf of a client in order to ensure his or her freedom from condemnation.

Judges in most courtrooms attempt to remain unbiased. They only want to listen to the evidence from both sides. The one with the most convincing evidence is the one who gets the victory. Jesus is a very biased judge. He is both your advocate and your judge. It is His full intention to give you a victory. Take note that *God judges us in order to bring us victory over the works of the devil.*

It is Satan who led us into sin and kept us in bondage to it. It is Satan who attempts to accuse the brethren before God day and night. It is Satan who roams to and fro throughout the earth attempting to find something by which he can justifiably condemn us before God. Yet, it is God Himself who looks for and has even provided for Himself the opportunity to render us a judgment unto victory. Here comes the judge— He has come to give us victory. HALLELUJAH!!!!

July 21

How God Judges the Wicked

The heathen are sunk down in the pit that they made: in the net which they hid is their own foot taken. **The LORD is known by the judgment which he executeth: the wicked is snared in the work of his own hands.** *Higgaion. Selah. The wicked shall be turned into hell, and all the nations that forget God* (Psalm 9:15-17)

Verse 16 tells us that God is known by the judgment He executes. It goes on to show us exactly *how* He executes judgment on the wicked. Those who look at God as a harsh stern judge believe that God personally inflicts wicked people with sickness, diseases, tragedies and eventually He personally throws them into the lake of fire.

This poses no problem for those who want to see God finally deal with those rotten sinners, forgetting, of course, that apart from the blood of Jesus, we were all rotten sinners. For others who have come to know that God is compassionate and patient, intensely desiring the repentance and salvation of sinners, the idea that He must eventually judge those who reject Him is difficult if seen from the aspect of judging and then personally handing out a sentence which He carries out Himself.

Our understanding of God's love for the wicked becomes easier when we understand that God's judgment is to remove whatever protection He has held over them and allow them to be snared in the work of their own hands. It is the sinner that makes the pit that he eventually sinks down into and it is his own net that he lays for others that catches him. It is the results of their free-will choices that God will finally let them suffer.

God continually tries to protect everyone from the full consequences of their rebellion. He is consistently attempting to woo the wicked to His side. He uses His goodness to lead sinners to repentance. Sadly, many would rather enjoy the temporary pleasures of wickedness than to embrace a loving God who constantly warns them about their unnecessary travel on the road to destruction. Finally, at some point He must allow them to sink in their own pit, get their foot caught in their own trap, and be snared by the works of their own hands.

God's love towards the wicked is much more easily understood when we see that, though He must eventually judge, He is not personally carrying out the sentence of their judgment. God must eventually allow sinners to receive the consequences of their own choices. He loves them but He must allow them their freedom regardless of what it brings them. But from this we see that God is not personally throwing lightning bolts to destroy those who offended Him.

The Punishment for Idolatry

Israel hath cast off the thing that is good: the enemy shall pursue him. They have set up kings, but not by me: they have made princes, and I knew it not: of their silver and their gold have they made them idols, that they may be cut off (Hosea 8:3-4)

Quite often God is accused of either having foreordained all that comes to pass, both good and evil, or He is said to have known from eternity past all the evil that men would commit. The above passage refutes both ideas. God says that His people set up idolatrous kings but it was not by His ordination or direction. He said that they made rulers but He knew nothing about it. God simply is not culpable for the evil that men freely choose to do either by foreknowledge or divine ordination.

God vindicates His character further in this passage by stating that those who make idols cut themselves off from Him and His protection. They leave themselves open to being pursued by their enemy. Basically, when we commit the sin of idolatry and suffer for it, no one can justly shake their fist at God and claim that they are suffering by His vindictive hand. It is their decision to cut themselves off from God and remove themselves from the place of safety. In His excellent book, *We Become what We Worship*, G. K. Beale offers us this insight into the subject of idolatry:

> A number of biblical passages.... express the idea that instead of worshiping and resembling the true God, idolators resemble the idols they worship. These worshipers became as spiritually void and lifeless as the idols they committed themselves to. We will see that people are judged as their idols are; ironically, people are punished by means of their own sin: "Do you like idols? Then you will be punished along with them." It is difficult to distinguish between being punished like the idol and becoming identified with the character of the idol.[31]

When we cut ourselves off from God and look to the protection of our idols we suffer their fate. Basically it is our own sin that does us in. This is especially true in the fact that most sin is basically idolatry in some form or another.

---

[31] Beale, G. K. **We Become what we Worship: A Biblical Theology of Idolatry** (Madison, WI Intervarsity Press, 2008), p. 16

July 23

Did God Bring Diseases upon Egypt?

*And said, If thou wilt diligently hearken to the voice of the Lord thy God, and wilt do that which is right in his sight, and wilt give ear to his commandments, and keep all his statutes, I will put none of these diseases upon thee, which I have **brought** upon the Egyptians: for I am the Lord that healeth thee (Ex. 15:25, 26)*

It is wonderful that God proclaims to be "Jehovah Rophe" which is translated in this passage as "I am the Lord that healeth thee". However, God also tells Israel, *"I will put none of these diseases upon thee, which I have **brought** upon the Egyptians"*. Many people who advocate the idea that God personally inflicts people with cancer, AIDS, and other forms of sickness and disease use this passage to promote it. Is this what God is saying here?

What can be worse than a mad scientist who uses his genius to spread a virus and then demands our obedience if we want the cure? That is the picture of God that we get without fully studying this passage in the light of other Scripture. However, when we compare Scripture with Scripture we discover that God is merely taking responsibility for what He permitted to be done to Egypt.

The book of Job offers one of the best explanations for the use of this type of language. In Job 1-2 we find that God permitted Satan to afflict Job by killing his children, destroying his property, and inflicting him with disease. In Job 2:7 we read, *"So went Satan forth from the presence of the LORD, and smote Job with sore boils from the sole of his foot unto his crown"* (Job 2:5-7). Yet, when we get to the last chapter of Job we read that Job's friends and family *"comforted him over all the evil that the LORD had **brought** upon him"* (Job 42:11b). The same word "brought" in Job 15:26 concerning God bringing diseases on the Egyptians is used again concerning the afflictions of Job.

From this we see that in Exodus 15:26 God is simply speaking to Israel using the idioms of their own culture in which He is said to do the thing that He only allowed or permitted. God does not afflict with sickness because sickness is the result of death. God is life and has no death in Him. Satan is the author of death and its fruit which is sickness and disease. God is only said to bring death and inflict with the consequences of death by removing His life giving presence and protection and allowing the results to take place. Hence, God is our healer, not our sickness bringer. Trust Him to heal you in Jesus' Name.

July 24

How God Afflicted the Egyptians

He cast upon them the fierceness of his anger, wrath, and indignation, and trouble, **by sending evil angels among them.** *He made a way to his anger; he spared not their soul from death, but* **gave their life over to the pestilence;** *And smote all the firstborn in Egypt; the chief of their strength in the tabernacles of Ham* (Psalm 78:49-51)

In order to understand how God *"brought upon the Egyptians"* diseases as we saw yesterday in Ex. 15:26 we must first understand the need to interpret Scripture with Scripture. In Psalm 78:50 we read, *"....but* **gave their life over** *to the pestilence."* This is expressing *permission* and not *causation*. God "brought" diseases on Egypt by permitting satanic evil angels to have their way.

The Hebrew word for "cast" in verse 49 is *"shalach"* which means "allow" or "permit". The original Hebrew word "sending" does not mean "sending" but "mission," "host," or "band". The Revised Standard Version of verse 49 reads, *"He* **let loose** *on them his fierce anger, wrath, indignation, and distress, a company of destroying angels."*

A question that often arises concerning this passage is s whether the "evil angels" in Psalm 78:49 are God's angels or Satan's. Those who believe that God personally inflicts sickness and other evils upon people have no trouble believing and teaching that these are God's angels.

However, I believe that the Bible makes a stronger case for these being Satan's angels. Satan also has angels (Matt. 25:41) and they are at war with God and humanity (Rev. 12:7-9). God does not work alongside Satan or his angels but he does permit them to perform certain acts upon unrepentant men, to include hurting and tormenting them with plagues and diseases (Rev. 9:1-15). Therefore, there should be no doubt that it is Satan's angels that are being referenced in Psalm 78.

Finally, we must understand the phrase, "the fierceness of his anger". This is always the language used in the Bible in relation to God's punishment of sin in which God, "gives some up" to the consequences of their sin (Psalm 81:10-16; Hosea 11:7-9; Rom. 1:24-28). This principle is prevalent throughout the Old Testament (Deut. 31:17-18; 1 Kings 14:15-16; 2 Kings 17:17-20; 2 Chron. 29:6-8; Ezra 5:12; Psalm 5:10-12; 9:15-16; Isa 54:8; 57:17; Jer. 33:5; Eze. 22:30-31). Therefore, God is only said to inflict sickness and disease or having "brought it upon the Egyptians" by giving them up to the demonic forces that they themselves worshipped. God is your healer, not the One who inflicts you.

God's Protection of Israel during Egypt's Plague

*And Moses said, Thus saith the LORD, About midnight will I go out into the midst of Egypt: And all the firstborn in the land of Egypt shall die, from the firstborn of Pharaoh that sitteth upon his throne, even unto the firstborn of the maidservant that is behind the mill; and all the firstborn of beasts. And there shall be a great cry throughout all the land of Egypt, such as there was none like it, nor shall be like it any more. But against any of the children of Israel shall not a dog move his tongue, against man or beast: that ye may know how that **the LORD doth put a difference between the Egyptians and Israel** (Exodus 11:4-7)*

God said He would go into the midst of Egypt and their firstborn will die. We learned in previous devotions that God did this by releasing Satan and his evil angels to kill them. However, God told Pharaoh that He would protect Israel from the sickness that would kill Egypt's firstborn. He said that there would be a "difference" between the two nations. This word "difference" is used several times in Exodus. In some places the word is translated "sever". For example, in Exodus 8 concerning a swarm of flies that were to attack Egypt, God says:

*Else, if thou wilt not let my people go, behold, I will send swarms of flies upon thee, and upon thy servants, and upon thy people, and into thy houses: and the houses of the Egyptians shall be full of swarms of flies, and also the ground whereon they are. And **I will sever in that day the land of Goshen, in which my people dwell, that no swarms of flies shall be there**; to the end thou mayest know that I am the LORD in the midst of the earth (Ex. 8:21-22).*

The word "difference" in Exodus 11:7 and "sever" in Exodus 8 are the same Hebrew word (*palah*). The word "send" in Exodus 8 comes from the Hebrew word *"shalach"* which means "allow" or "permit".

God was going to allow the swarm of flies to attack Egypt but if He did not sever Israel from Egypt then they would share their fate. God removed the protection and checks on nature that kept Egypt from being bombarded by flies and allowed them to suffer the consequences of their rebellion. Psalm 91:7-8 certainly holds true for Israel here as well as for believer today.

What Does "Passover" Really Mean?

*"For the LORD will pass through to smite the Egyptians; and when he seeth the blood upon the lintel, and on the two side posts, **the LORD will pass over the door, and will not suffer the destroyer to come in unto your houses to smite you.**"* (Ex. 12:23)

Some who advocate a belief that God is the actual inflictor of all sickness, disease and accidents ignore or reject the important truth taught in our opening passage that the destroyer is some distinct from God. They believe that the word "destroyer" should be a "verb" rather than a "noun" ("destroying" rather than "destroyer"). In this view the Lord is the direct cause of the destruction and no other agent is involved. Many of these same people also claim that this is a reference to a destroying angel who actually works *for* the Lord and not *against* him (and they cite the following passages to support this idea: 2 Sam. 24:15-17; 1 Chron. 21:12-27; 2 Kings 19:35; Isa. 37:36; Acts 12:23).

Thankfully, for those of us who believe Jesus' words in John 10:10 that Satan is the destroyer and not God, there is another view that sees the "destroyer" in Exodus 12:23 as a malevolent being that God must oppose. The key to understanding this truth is to understand the word "Passover" as used in this passage. This misunderstood word, once clarified, gives a whole new understanding to Exodus 12:23 that is consistent with our Lord's teachings about God:

The Hebrew word for "passover" is the same word used in Isaiah 31:5: *"As birds flying, so will the LORD of hosts defend Jerusalem; defending also he will deliver it; and **passing over he will preserve it.**"* Therefore "Passover" should not be misunderstood as God simply *skipping* the house that had blood. It should be understood as God *guarding, preserving and protecting that house from the destroyer.*

As one commentary says, "Here it is possible to see as the destroyer of the firstborn of Israel, not God, but some other power whom the Lord opposes and from whom He protects the Israelites."[32] Instead of the *destroyer* working alongside God as an agent of destruction, it seems that God is merely allowing him free access to the Egyptians due to Pharaoh's failure to comply with God's demands. Yet He opposes this destroyer to protect Israel, as He does for the child of God today when we obey and stand on His Word.

---

[32] Dunnam, Maxi D., Oglivie, Lloyd (Ed.) **The Communicator's Commentary: Exodus** , ©1987, Waco, TX: Word Books, p. 149

July 27

Protection from the Wicked Ones' Reward

*Thou shalt not be afraid for the terror by night; nor for the arrow that flieth by day; Nor for the pestilence that walketh in darkness; nor for the destruction that wasteth at noonday. A thousand shall fall at thy side, and ten thousand at thy right hand; but it shall not come nigh thee. Only with thine eyes shalt thou behold and see **the reward of the wicked*** (Psalm 91:5-8)

The word "reward" in this passage can mean "requital" or "retribution" and is usually associated with some criminal act or an act of evil done to someone or against God. When we read this Psalm we do not see anywhere that God personally inflicts the punishment but instead it is something that is an automatic consequence for wickedness. We are told about *"the destruction that wasteth at noonday"*. This psalm tells us that sin has a destructive power that sooner or later affects the one sinning.

For the child of God who has decided to walk with Christ, we are promised that despite what happens around us, despite those who may fall due to sickness and disease, the destruction will not come near us. We have no need to be afraid because God has severed us from the world and has made a difference between the world and us.

God never inflicts with sickness and disease. The world is already full of it. Man disobeyed God and gave death entrance into the world. The earth was cursed because of sin and this gave place to much sickness and disease. Now microbes that were originally created for our good have become distorted and corrupted by sin and they culminate in germs that eventually bring forth sickness and disease. These corrupted microbes are all around us. There is no need for God to "create" sickness. Men and Satan are doing a very good job of bringing forth sickness on their own by distorting God's good microbes.

God, in His deep and overwhelming love for all of mankind, constantly seeks to protect us from the inevitable consequences of sin. No doubt that if God was not still working in men's lives things would be far worse than what we presently see. However, there comes a point where men continually push God away through their constant acts of wickedness and He eventually must allow them to receive their *requital* and *retribution* for these acts—their *reward*.

The good news is that those who continue to make God their refuge and fortress have nothing to be afraid of because God promises in this wonderful Psalm to keep His protection over us. Claim God's protection so that you will not suffer the reward of the wicked.

Why Does God Care about Man?

*When I consider thy heavens, the work of thy fingers, the
moon and the stars, which thou hast ordained; What is
man, that thou art mindful of him? and the son of man, that
thou visitest him?* (Psalm 8:3-4)

The psalmist, after observing the wonderful marvels of God's
creation, began to wonder why God keeps His mind on mankind. Why does
He remain involved with us? The Revised Standard Version's translation of
verse 4 says, *"What is man that thou art mindful of him, and the son of man
that thou dost care for him?"*

This is a very good question to ask in the light of man's rejection of
God. So many in this world live and act as if there is no God. Many may
believe in Him intellectually but their lives and conduct express the
opposite of what they profess to believe. Furthermore, man continues to
ruin and destroy God's creation in multiple ways through pollution, killing,
waste, neglect and other means of blatant destruction. The people that God
cares so much about have not been very good stewards of His great
creation. Yet, God continues to care for man and keep us on His mind.

This truth flies in the face of some deistic ideas that God just
created everything and left it running all on its own. While God has
established certain laws that automatically operate in this world, He
continues to superintend numerous aspects of His creation. He does not
superintend in the "Calvinistic sense" in which everything that happens is
His doing but He does continue to show tender care of the universe on
man's behalf. We should be glad that He does. As we continue to violate
God's established laws, He continues to work to override much of our
"anti-creation".

Furthermore, we as individuals should stop believing the lie of the
devil that God has no concern for us. The passage does not only mean that
God cares about mankind collectively, but He cares about each one of us
individually. He is mindful of us and cares even about what we might think
are the small trivial concerns of our life. God is not "too busy running the
universe to care about your little needs" as the saying goes. He is busy
running the universe precisely because He cares about all of our little
needs.

God has been given such a bad rep. Either He is painted as a
sadistic monster who desire to do harm to everyone for some mysterious
good or He is made out to be an uncaring deity to such insignificant dust
balls as us. Neither is true about God. He really cares about man.

Does God Send "Evil Spirits"?

When Abimelech had reigned three years over Israel, ***Then God sent an evil spirit between Abimelech and the men of Shechem****; and the men of Shechem dealt treacherously with Abimelech:* (Judges 9:22-23)

There are some troublesome passages where God is said to have personally sent an evil spirit to do His bidding. These need to be examined in order to further vindicate God from the accusation of authoring evil. One of the earliest recorded incidents concerns Abimelech.

In Judges 9 God is said to have "sent" an evil spirit to cause strife between Abimelech and the men of Shechem. Abimelech, who was actually the self-appointed king of Israel, had been very wicked and murdered a number of his own brothers. However, does this justify God Himself sending evil spirits to deal with the problem?

Some have attempted to soften this by saying that the meaning here is that God did not send a "demon" but "an evil disposition". That really does nothing to vindicate God since it only means that He exercised divine irresistible power to cause men to get into strife and go to war with each other. The Hebrew word for "sent" in the passage above is *"shalach"*. This word means to "allow" or "permit". Some commentators suggest this is the actual understanding of the passage:

> The meaning is, as it is explained in the following words, God permitted Abimelech to be deceived and dealt treacherously with by the men of Shechem, that his cruelty, and the blood which he had shed, might come upon him. It is nothing more than an acknowledgment of the justice and wisdom of Providence, in suffering wicked men to be judicially blinded, that they may fall according to their own deserts. *Dr. S. Clarke.* This is an usual form of speech in Scripture, and denotes, not any positive action, but a permission only, or at most a direction from God. *Stackhouse.*[33]

Whether it is actually a demon or just an evil spirit, God's only part in this is *permission* and not *causation.*

---

[33] George D'Oyly, Richard Mant **The Holy Bible According to the Authorized Version** (London: Society for Promoting Christian Knowledge, 1839), p. 545

July 30

Why did God Permit an Evil Spirit in Judges 9?

That the cruelty done to the threescore and ten sons of Jerubbaal might come, and their blood be laid upon Abimelech their brother, which slew them; and upon the men of Shechem, which aided him in the killing of his brethren (Judges 9:24)

Yesterday we saw that God had *permitted* (the correct interpretation of the word "sent" in Judges 9:23) an evil spirit to cause trouble between Abimelech and the Shechemites. Yet why would He permit this? One thing that is clear throughout Scripture is the fact that there is a sowing and reaping process that is at work. Abimelech murdered Gideon's children and never repented for his actions.

Even a dastardly deed such as murdering and asserting oneself as king over God's heritage can be forgiven if one is sincerely repentant. God is loving, kind, merciful and ready to forgive even the worst of sinners. No doubt that Abimelech was given plenty of space to repent—at least three years. His failure to repent meant that God had to permit the consequences of sin to take place. Since sin usually opens the door for Satan to attack (Eph. 4:26, 27) then I have no doubt that the "evil spirit" in Judges 9:23 is a reference to a demonic spirit.

Most important is the reason why this evil spirit was permitted. We are told *"That the cruelty done to the threescore and ten sons of Jerubbaal might come, and their blood be laid upon Abimelech"*. I like the way that The Message Bible paraphrases this: *"Violence boomeranged: The murderous violence that killed the seventy brothers, the sons of Jerub-Baal, was now loose among Abimelech and Shechem's leaders, who had supported the violence."*

Jesus was very clear when He said, *"Put up again thy sword into his place: for all they that take the sword shall perish with the sword"* (Matt. 26:52). Violence begets violence. If one achieves his status through violence then he can be sure that it will be a continuous cycle that will sooner or later bring his own downfall.

This explains why God had no choice but to permit the evil spirit to cause strife and bloodshed between the two warring factions. When we fail to repent and seek God for mercy, and arrogantly remain in our sins, God will have no choice but to allow Satan and his demonic forces to go through the door that we have opened for ourselves and bring forth the results of our rebellion.

July 31

Is God to Blame?

Some people ruin themselves by their own stupid actions and then blame the Lord (Prov. 19:3; Good News Bible)

I have often found it strange throughout the years that I have been walking with the Lord how often His own people blame Him for EVERYTHING! God gets blamed for rapes, murders, accidents, miscarriages—well, EVERYTHING! We use out-of-context Scripture such as Romans 8:28 ("all things work together for good") or Matthew 6:10 ("Thy will be done"). We use our favorite "Christian catch-phrases" ("God is in control," "God is sovereign," "God's ways are mysterious," etc.) No matter how "biblical" or "pious" it sounds, we are in effect blaming God.

One dictionary definition of "blame" is "the act of attributing fault". According to dictionary.com, some synonyms of "blame" are "reproach, reprove, reprehend, criticize, censure, condemn, imply finding fault with someone or something; To blame is to hold accountable for, and disapprove because of, some error, mistake, omission, neglect." From an etymology standpoint, the word "blame" comes from a Latin word which means "to blaspheme." Do we realize what we are doing when we claim that God is the instigator of the negative circumstances of life?

Some of the more openly bitter people who blame God are a little more honest with their feelings when they tell God, "This is all your fault!" Others believe that they must simply "kiss the rod". But no matter what attitude we use when we express it, to find fault with God for the events in life that are primarily the result of sin and death in this world is nothing less than blasphemy.

While not everything that happens to us is due to personal sin in our lives many people do have a tendency to blame God for problems that are the result of their own decisions. We must remember that sin has its own built-in consequences (Rom. 6:23; James 1:13-14; Gal. 6:5-6). Each sinful act contains within itself its own seed of destruction. Don't blame God for the results of your decisions. Turn to Him so that He can rescue you from them (James 5:14-16; Mk 2:1-12).

Remember also that we are engaged in warfare with the powers of darkness and that they are responsible for the spread of evil and misery in this world (Eph. 6:10-18). It is unfair to blame God for the devil's work (1 John 3:8). As a matter of fact, it is downright blasphemous. Let us stop blaming God for evil. It's a stupid thing to do.

August 1

Who Destroys Body and Soul in Hell? (Part 1)

And fear not them which kill the body, but are not able to kill the soul: but rather fear him which is able to destroy both soul and body in hell. (Matt. 10:28)

This passage presents what appears to some as a harsh view of God. It seems that we are given a choice to be afraid of what men can do to us versus what God will do to us if we do not comply with his wishes.

In order to soften the seeming harshness of this passage some groups believe that Matthew 10:28 is in reference to a doctrine called *annihilation*. This is the belief that all sinners will someday be removed from existence. While I wish that this were true, much of the Biblical evidence tends towards hell being a literal place with literal fire that continues throughout eternity.

There are others who fall into both the *annihilationist* and the *eternal hell* camps that believe that the one who is to be feared in this passage is Satan. However, this cannot be true since the Bible tells us that Jesus conquered Satan. He is a defeated foe and nowhere in Scripture is anyone told to fear him. We are told to resist him, stand against his wiles, cast him out, give him no place, and to use our authority over him. Never are we told to fear him.

Therefore, the only person left for Jesus to be speaking about is God Himself. But are we to be afraid of God? The word fear comes from a Greek word which means "to reverence, venerate, to treat with deference or reverential obedience" (Studylight.org). While it can mean "afraid" when applied to the men that can kill, it should be understood as "reverence" when it pertains to God.

This is the same Greek word translated "reverence" in Ephesians 5:33 where Paul writes, *"Nevertheless let every one of you in particular so love his wife even as himself; and the wife see that she **reverence her husband**"*. If Paul is commanding a wife to be afraid of her husband then he is dispensing some of the worse marriage advice ever. Thankfully, the KJV translators had enough foresight to know that this could not be what Paul meant and translated the word as *reverence*.

Jesus is telling us not to fear those who persecute believers and can kill only the body but reverence God and can destroy body and soul in hell. However, understanding our attitude towards God is only half the problem. Does God literally destroy body and soul in hell? We answer this tomorrow.

August 2

Who Destroys Body and Soul in Hell? (Part 2)

And fear not them which kill the body, but are not able to kill the soul: but rather fear him which is able to destroy both soul and body in hell. (Matt. 10:28)

Yesterday we learned that this passage can be understood to read, "Don't be afraid of those who kill the body.... But rather reverence him which is able to destroy both soul and body in hell." However, is it easy to reverence someone who is threatening to personally torment and destroy you?" Only if you understand exactly how God is said to "destroy".

In Matthew 7:13 Jesus tells us that each person who goes to hell does so through their own free-choice: *"Enter ye in at the strait gate: for wide is the gate, and **broad is the way, that leadeth to destruction,** and many there be which go in thereat:"* When people make this choice of their own free-will God tells them to *"depart from me"* (Matt. 7:23; 25:41). God destroys people by removing them from His protective presence, by "giving them up" and "delivering them" to the results of their choices:

> **How shall I give thee up, Ephraim? how shall I deliver thee, Israel?** *how shall I make thee as Admah? how shall I set thee as Zeboim? mine heart is turned within me, my repentings are kindled together. I will not execute the fierceness of mine anger,* **I will not return to destroy Ephraim:** *for I am God, and not man; the Holy One in the midst of thee: and I will not enter into the city* (Hosea 11:8-9)

God's method of destroying is to depart from the unrepentant sinner, thus removing His protective presence, and allowing the automatic choices of the sinner to take effect (Exodus 12:12, 13, 23; 2 Kings 13:23; 2 Chron. 12:7; Job 2:3-7; Psalm 5:10; 73:27-28; Isa. 34:2; Jer. 7:29-31; 18:7-10; Eze. 21:31; 22:30-31; 32:12-13; Hosea 4:5-6; 11:8-9).

In Luke's version of this teaching Jesus talks about denying those who deny Him (Luke 12:4-9). In hell, those who wanted nothing to with God will receive their choice. Sadly, that choice comes with destruction. This is the "sowing and reaping" process at work here. Therefore, God "destroys" by no longer stopping the reaping from taking place (Ps. 9:15-17).

August 3

The Word of God Judges Us

*And if any man hear my words, and believe not, I judge him not: for I came not to judge the world, but to save the world. He that rejecteth me, and receiveth not my words, hath one that judgeth him: **the word that I have spoken, the same shall judge him in the last day*** (John 12:47-48)

There are many people who only see God as a harsh judge ready to condemn them for their sins. Jesus said that it is not His purpose to judge but to save. Yet, Jesus also says that our rejection of Him and His salvation will still leave us open to judgment. His *Word* will bring this judgment.

What does it mean for God's Word to judge us? God warns us about the destructive power of sin. He warns us about Satan's desire to destroy our lives. He invites us to come to Him to save us from the bondage and power of sin and His victory over the evil one. Yet, most of the world has chosen to reject this salvation for the temporary pleasures of sin. A day will come when a person receives the temporal and eternal consequences of their sin. The Words of warning that God had given to save them from trouble will be there to judge and condemn them in their sin.

I can warn a young lady not to go down a certain street at a certain time of night because there is a danger that she can be raped, tortured and murdered. However, there may be a dangerous product she feels that she desperately desires that can only be purchased on that dangerous street at that dangerous time of the night. Her desire for the pleasure of the product outweighs her sound judgment. Ignoring my words she goes down that street. Being young and alone she is surely beaten, raped and murdered. My word in which I tried to save her from this horror comes back to her as she suffers the devastating results of her choice. My words have judged her.

God does not give us some of those tough "thou shalt nots" in His Word in order to scare us into compliance with His demands. He is warning us of the dangers of going down that broad road that leads to destruction (Matt. 10:28). He is trying to save us from temporal and eternal pain and misery. Sadly, many people look at God as trying to control them and put boundaries on them. They want their "freedom" and its "pleasures." Yet, when their sin finds them out and begins the process of destruction, it is God's Words that will judge them. If they die without Jesus then God's Word will judge them unto eternal death. The Word judges us by reminding us that we had another choice but chose destruction. The Word God gives with the full intention to save us will judge the one that rejects it.

August 4

Does God actually Hate Sinners?

The foolish shall not stand in thy sight: **thou hatest all workers of iniquity** (Psalm 5:5)

I have seen this and a number of other passages used to refute the teaching that *God hates the sin but loves the sinner*. The response is to say that this statement is unbiblical because Psalm 5:5 (and other passages) says that God actually *hates* sinners.

When people teach this doctrine of God's divine hatred of sinners, they have failed to apply the principles of correct Biblical interpretation. The first is to *interpret everything in light of equally important but seemingly contradictory Scriptures.* For example, doesn't our Bible tell us, "But *God commendeth* **his love toward us, in that, while we were yet sinners***, Christ died for us*" (Rom. 5:5)? Is there a contradiction between Psalm 5:5 and Romans 5:5? Does the Bible contradict itself?

This brings us to our second principle of interpretation which is to *interpret all Scripture in the light of God's character.* Nowhere in the Bible do we ever read that "God is hate". Oh, God certainly does hate sin, but sin is not a natural part of His creation. But concerning people, we read, *"He that loveth not knoweth not God; for God is love"* (1 John 4:8). God is love and He expects those of us who claim to be His to love others as well.

Which leads to the third principle which is *interpret God's acts in the way that He expects* **us** *to act.* Jesus said, *"But I say unto you, Love your enemies, bless them that curse you, do good to them that hate you.... Be ye therefore perfect, even as your Father which is in heaven is perfect"* (Matt. 5:44a, 48). God tells us that to be perfect like Him we must love sinners as He does. If God hates sinners then so should we. But He loves them and we are to do so as well.

The first three Biblical principles build the foundation for the fourth principle which is *interpret all passages such as Psalm 5:5 in light of Hebrew idiomatic expressions.* Failure to understand this truth has led to many erroneous teachings, such as the false idea that God hates sinners. Jesus said, *"If any man come to me, and* **hate** *not his father, and mother, and wife, and children, and brethren, and sisters, yea, and his own life also, he cannot be my disciple"* (Luke 14:26). Yet the Bible commands elsewhere that we are to honor and love these people. "Hate" as used here simply means not to put family above Jesus. That is the way "hate" is used in Psalm 5:5. God does not put workers of iniquity above His holiness. He cannot, so He must *hate* them in the proper way that the idiom is understood.

August 5

Did God Kill the Israelites with Quail?

And while the flesh was yet between their teeth, ere it was chewed, the wrath of the LORD was kindled against the people, and the LORD smote the people with a very great plague (Num. 11:33)

The story begins with the "mixed multitudes" among the Israelites complaining about the manna that God gave and longing for the meaty delicacies that they enjoyed in Egypt. Moses prayed, God answered and promised to give them plenty of meat for a whole month (Num. 11:4-32). Yet, we read that the Lord smote the people with sickness while the meat was still between their teeth.

This might seem to strange to anyone who is not a causal reader of Scripture. After all, God had provided quail in previous times along with the manna and it was considered to be a blessing to the people (Exodus 16:11-13; Psalm 105:40). So why is it that in this particular case God is angry enough to "smite" the Israelites with a plague? Doesn't He appear vindictive here?

Interpreting Scripture with Scripture will help us understand this better and vindicate God's character. In Psalm 106:14-15 we read, *"But lusted exceedingly in the wilderness, and tempted God in the desert. And he gave them their request; but sent leanness into their soul."* The word "sent" used in Psalm 106:15 is from the Hebrew word *"shalach"* which can be translated as "allow, permit, forsake, give over to". This means that God did not personally smite the offenders but gave them over to the "leanness" or sickness. It means that He removed His protection from them due to their complaining and their lack of appreciation for His provision.

R. A. Torrey explains, "They despised the manna, calling it light or innutritive food. God gave them flesh as they desired, but no blessing accompanied it; and, in consequence, they did not fatten, but grew lean upon it; and many, surfeited by excess, died of disease" (Treasury of Scripture Knowledge, E-Sword Edition),

God promises, *"And ye shall serve the LORD your God, and he shall bless thy bread, and thy water; and I will take sickness away from the midst of thee"* (Ex. 23:25). God will bless our bread and water when we worship and serve Him. When we go against Him we forfeit this promised protection and we can no longer claim that sickness will not be in our midst. This is the removal of God's protection (Psalm 91:4-8). God simply cannot bless rebellion so the rebellious quail eaters suffered the automatic consequences of sin (Rom. 6:23).

August 6

How God the Father Deals with Our Rebellion

And the younger of them said to his father, Father, give me the portion of goods that falleth to me. And he divided unto them his living. And not many days after the younger son gathered all together, and took his journey into a far country, and there wasted his substance with riotous living. And when he had spent all, there arose a mighty famine in that land; and he began to be in want (Luke 15:12-14)

Jesus was telling the famous parable about the prodigal son to help us understand how God relates to sinners and wayward children. This young man was an essential part of the family business and enjoyed the loving provisions and protection of his father. But one day he demanded that his father give him his inheritance. This was a slap in his father's face and an insult but the father did as he asked.

The young then left his father's home and began to live a sinful life. After wasting all of the blessings that his father gave him and being out from under the protection of his father the boy began to suffer from the circumstances around him. A famine hit the land where he was at and he had no source of provision. He ended up having to feed pigs (a Jewish boy and pigs don't mix) and he was so hungry that he was willing to eat pig slop. Finally, he remembered that he enjoyed safety at his father's house and decided to return.

Please understand that the father neither kicked the young man out of his house nor did the father manipulate the circumstances that caused the young man the suffering and pain that he experienced later. The young man left his father's home of his own free will and went as far away from his father's presence as he could. All that this young man suffered, he suffered due to having left his father's protective presence. This is the part of the parable that is seldom expounded upon in any detail.

This parable shows exactly how the Father deals with our rebellion. He allows us our free-will decisions, no matter how heartbreaking and insulting that they are to Him. Nonetheless, He also allows us to suffer the consequences of those free-will decisions. He does not sovereignly manipulate circumstances. He does not need to. There is enough wrong in this sinfully fallen world. When we leave the umbrella of God's protection we will be open to the difficulties already present. He deals with our rebellion by allowing us the consequences of our choices.

August 7

How the Father Deals with the Penitent

And he arose, and came to his father. But when he was yet
a great way off, his father saw him, and had compassion,
and ran, and fell on his neck, and kissed him (Luke 15:20)

Jesus is teaching the famous parable about the prodigal son to tell us how God relates to sinners and backsliders. In this portion of the parable Jesus shares the Father's reaction to those who return to him after a lengthy time of living in rebellion.

Many of us would have let the young man walk the miles up the road. We would not have even been outside. We would have waited for the boy to beg to come into the house to see us. After making them wait a lengthy amount of time we would have let them in and let them grovel at our feet.

After much groveling and begging for forgiveness we would have given the young man a good tongue lashing and let him know the embarrassment and disgrace that was brought on our good name because of his actions. We would have met his "humble" request to be a hired servant by making sure that is all that he became, at least until he showed himself worthy of anything else. We would have made him suffer far more humility and embarrassment than we received by his actions.

Oh how we would have enjoyed the vengeance upon our ungrateful child. Of course we would justify this act of vindictiveness as "teaching the boy a lesson" and "ensuring he doesn't repeat the same mistake twice by rebelling against us." Personally, as one who has been a sinner and one who has rebelled more than once after becoming a child of God, I am so glad that God does not act like us.

God actually stands outside looking for us to come back to Him. When He sees us far down the road He runs down to meet us, hugs us, and won't even listen to our prepared speeches. He is just so glad that we have come back. He is so deeply in love with us that He restores us back to full status as sons immediately.

This is our Heavenly Father. This is the Father that Jesus wanted us to know. He is not the mean vindictive deity ready to strike us down unless we grovel at His feet and beg His forgiveness for our rebellion. He is the One who runs to us and meets us and restores us. WOW! What a wonderful God!

August 8

Did God Ordain Wickedness Upon Jesus?

Him, being delivered by the determinate counsel and foreknowledge of God, ye have taken, and by wicked hands have crucified and slain (Acts 2:23)

When Adam and Eve fell God knew that the second person of the Triune Godhead would have to come and rescue man from the captivity that they had placed themselves under. It was prophesied in Isaiah that Jesus would suffer a painful and tormenting death because of our (not His) iniquities (Isa. 53:3-10). Jesus would later reveal what Isaiah's prophecy meant, which was that He would be betrayed by wicked men and crucified (Matt. 17:22; 20:18; 26:2, 24).

Sadly, some theologians, by misinterpreting words such as "determinate counsel" and "foreknowledge" have taught people that God ordained and controlled the actions of these wicked men who killed our Lord. Many of them have drawn the false conclusion from this that God ordains all the actions of all wicked men. In other words, *God ordains sin*.

How sad that these theologians (primary the Calvinistic ones) take the wonderful sacrifice of Christ on our behalf, derive ideas from it that are not there, and then twist it to teach that this is God's "modus operandi" for all of the events in life. Yet just because Jesus was bruised for our iniquities does not mean that God wills the murder and death of everyone. Does Jesus predestined death as the Lamb of God for the sins of the world mean that God also ordains abortion, child rape, and murder? Does our Lord's predestined death for the sins of man imply that God is responsible for the atrocities of Mussolini, Hitler, Hussein, Al Qaida, and ISIS? Jesus death served a purpose. God was behind it and *allowed* sinful men to crucify His Son because of the beneficial outcome.

Notice the phrase "delivered up" in the passage. This means that God *gave up* His Son for this purpose. Jesus said no man takes my life but I give it. He could have called for a legion of angels to rescue Him from it but He preferred to endure the death of the cross. Babies being aborted are not volunteers for death. Children being raped and murdered are not dying for any purpose. Kurds being cruelly gassed by sadist tyrants such as Husssein are not being slain for the sins of the world. Jesus murder and death had a purpose. The majority of atrocities committed today have no purpose and should not be blamed on God's sovereignty. Many of these people die without Jesus and go to an eternity in hell. This does not please God who wills that all men be saved (1 Tim. 2:4; 2 Pet. 3:9).

August 9

Was Redemption Planned Before the Creation of the World?

And all that dwell upon the earth shall worship him, whose names are not written in the book of life of the Lamb slain from the foundation of the world. (Revelation 13:8)

The majority of theologians, no matter what theological persuasion they hold to, tell us that God planned redemption *before* He created because He foreknew the fall of man. Revelation 13:8 is a foundational text for this belief. They believe that God looked through the corridors of time, saw the fall of man, made a covenant with the second member of the Triune Godhead to die for them, and went on ahead and created.

However, if God knew beyond a shadow of a doubt that Adam and Eve would fall and plunge us into this catastrophe then He is fully culpable for the evil that is in the world. Furthermore, God, just before the flood of Noah, begins to grieve over man's sin, is very heartbroken, and regrets that He ever created them (Gen. 6:5-7). None of this makes sense at all if God exhaustively knew that man would fall and that Jesus would be slain for it.

Perhaps we need to reexamine Rev. 13:8. The word for "foundation" in the Greek is *katabolē*. The problem with this verse is that in the majority of English translations, the word "foundation" is used. However, this is not the best translation of *katabolē*. The Harper Collins dictionary says that the root meaning is a "destructive metabolism". W. E. Vine, while acknowledging its use in Scripture, says that *katabole* literally means, "a casting down" (Vine's Expository Dictionary of Biblical Words, p. 254).

Some literal Bible translations recognize the true meaning of *katabole*: *"And all who are dwelling on the earth will be worshiping it, everyone whose name is not written in the scroll of life of the Lambkin slain from **the disruption of the world"*** (Rev. 13:8; Concordant Literal Version).

While some believe that this "disruption of the world" occurred during the gap between Genesis 1:1 and 1:2 (which I believe is the time period in which Satan fell), I believe that Rev. 13:8 is connected to Genesis 3:15. It was when man sinned, brought a curse on God's good creation, thus disrupting the world, is when God decided that Jesus would die on his behalf. In this respect Jesus was slain from the disruption of the world, or when sin brought death into the world (Rom. 5:12).

August 10

God Does Whatever He Pleases?

"But our God is in the heavens: he hath done whatsoever he hath pleased." (Psalm 115:3)

Calvinists often cite Psalm 115:3 in support of their understanding of God's sovereignty in which He controls everything that happens down to the minutest detail. The Calvinist teaches that God is the "first-cause" of everything, that He is controlling everything to include the actions of men, good and evil, and that nothing happens apart from Him ordaining it. When a non-Calvinist naturally protests against such blasphemy, the Calvinist appeals to the above text (usually strung along with a number of other out-of-context quotes) and retorts, "God can do whatever He pleases."

However, when we compare Scripture with Scripture, Psalm 115:3 speaks *against* the Calvinist dichotomy. For example, "God has no Pleasure in the death of the wicked." He says, *"For I have **no pleasure** in the death of him that dieth, saith the Lord GOD: wherefore turn yourselves, and live ye"* (Eze. 18:32; Eze. 33:11).

Furthermore, God says, *"For **thou art not a God that hath pleasure in wickedness**: neither shall evil dwell with thee"* (Psalm 5:4). God could not have decreed sin because he has no pleasure in it. If the Calvinist understanding of Psalm 115:3 is accurate then they must do away with the doctrine of decreed sin since God does what He pleases and sin does not please Him, only uprightness pleases Him: *"I know also, my God, that thou triest the heart, and **hast pleasure in uprightness**....* (1 Chron. 29:17a).

In His love God is pleased with our prosperity, *"Let them shout for joy, and be glad, that favour my righteous cause: yea, let them say continually, Let the LORD be magnified, **which hath pleasure in the prosperity of his servant**"* (Psalm 35:27). Not all of God's people are prospering. Many are failing. Is God responsible for this? Our failures do not please God so He cannot be behind them. He is only pleased with our prosperity.

Finally, the Bible teaches that there are things we can do to please the Lord and displease Him. If Psalm 115:3 is a passage teaching unilateral sovereignty, then Scripture would not teach that God is able to be pleased and displeased by what the actions of His creatures. Learn what it takes to please God and set out to do it. Do not buy into fatalistic theology.

August 11

God's Working and Our Free-Will

Wherefore, my beloved, **as ye have always obeyed,** *not as in my presence only, but now much more in my absence,* **work out your own salvation with fear and trembling.** *For it is God which worketh in you both to will and to do of his good pleasure* (Phil. 2:12, 13)

In some of the Free-will vs. Calvinism debates that I have been a part of, verse 13 has been used to deny the free-will of the Christian. Some Calvinists claim that verse 13 teaches us that any good that we do is because of God doing it through us, not by *influence*, but by *control*. This is meant to support the concept of an all-controlling God who controls our every action.

However, if verse 13 denied free-will then there would be no need for Paul to tell them to obey and to work out *their own* salvation. The preceding verses also dispute the denial of free will in that passage. In light of the context we need to understand Phil. 2:13 as teaching *divine enablement* rather than *divine conctrol*. Rotherham's Emphasized Bible, which is a literal translation, says, *"For it is, God, who energiseth within you, both the desiring and the energising, in behalf of his good pleasure."*

The word "work" being used in the KJV is from the Greek word *Energeo* and means, *to be operative, be at work, put forth power; to work for one, aid one.* This is better conveyed in the following translations:

Yes, God is working in you. God ***helps*** *you want to do the things that please him. And he gives you the power to do these things.* (Easy to Read Version)

because God is working in you to ***help you*** *want to do and be able to do what pleases him.* (New Century Version)

So yes, God does indeed work His desires in us, but He is not overriding our will. It is still left up to us to obey or disobey. If that were not so then Paul would not have to exhort us to do just that before and after verse 13. NO TRUE Christian should ever want to sin if he has the Holy Spirit living in him. Neither does anyone *have to* sin because they have been given supernatural divine assistance.

August 12

Does God Send Lying Spirits?

And there came forth a spirit, and stood before the LORD, and said, I will persuade him. And the LORD said unto him, Wherewith? And he said, I will go forth, and I will be a lying spirit in the mouth of all his prophets. And he said, Thou shalt persuade him, and prevail also: go forth, and do so (1 Kings 22:21-22)

During an online debate with a Calvinist, this passage was cited to me as proof that God sovereignly controls all that happens, including sin. However, we must learn to *read* Scripture and not *read into* Scripture. God was asking His counsel of angels (Job 1) about how they should go about dealing with Ahab. A spirit "came forth" and volunteered his service just as Satan did in Job 1. In neither case was the spirit summoned by God. In both cases he came on his own.

God did not command this spirit to become a lying spirit. The spirit himself came up with the idea. It was merely seeking *"permission"* to go about this task. Though God planned none of this nor did He command it, due to Ahab's persistent desire to receive false information, He *permitted* it. Walter C. Kaiser, in his book, *Toward Old Testament Ethics*, explains how the idea of permission can be understood from a Hebraic perspective:

> ….here in 1 Kings 22:22, "Go and do it" (i.e., deceive Ahab's false prophets) signifies only permission, not a command or sponsorship. What really took place was that God allowed a lying spirit to speak through the false prophets to Ahab, for that is what he had made up his mind he wanted to hear. The efficient cause of the deception was not God, but the lying spirit.[34]

In this situation God was merely allowing King Ahab what he wanted. However, if God really wanted Ahab to be deceived then he would not have allowed the prophet Micaiah to reveal what had actually occurred in heaven. This was Ahab's chance to repent, an opportunity that he refused. It cost him his life. God reveals things to us to keep us from wrong decision. Let us learn to heed His counsel.

---

[34] Kaiser, Jr., Walter C. **Toward Old Testament Ethics** (Grand Rapids, MI: Zondervan Publishing House, 1983), p. 256

August 13

Does God Put Lying Spirits in People's Mouths?

*Now therefore, behold, the LORD hath **put** a lying spirit in the mouth of all these thy prophets, and the LORD hath spoken evil concerning thee* (1 Kings 22:23)

Yesterday we studied verses 21 and 22 of this passage. Some believe from those verses that God commanded a lying spirit to go and deceive King Ahab. Upon careful examination was saw that this a *permission* rather than a *command*. Nonetheless, we still have the troubling passage that says that God personally *put* a lying spirit in the mouth of the false prophets.

The word "put" comes from the Hebrew word *"nathan."* This word is translated "permit" and "allow" in other passages of Scripture. During the Passover in Exodus God promised the obedient Israelites, *"....and he will not **permit** the destroyer to enter your houses and strike you down"* (Ex. 12:23; New International Version). The word "permit" is the same word as "put" in 1 Kings 22:23.

Is there any reason why the Hebrew word *"nathan"* cannot be understood as "permission" in 1 Kings 22:23? Some writers seem to think it should be understood in this exact same way:

> *"The Lord hath put a lying spirit in the moutk of all these thy prophets."* This is the common translation, "But the original Hebrew does not sanction such a rendering. For it makes Jehovah the author of this sin, by exerting an influence over the minds of the idolatrous priests to persuade Ahab to ascend to Ramoth-gilead, that he might destroy him." "The word *naathan,* is rendered *hath put* i.e. *the Lord."* But it is perfectly proper that the passage should receive the same rendering, as in other places.[35]

The writer believes that the Hebrew word "nathan" should be rendered "permit" just as it is in other places. One would have to ask themselves why so many of our English translations translate the word in a "causative" manner. Still, we learn from these examples that God only permits what we permit by our rebellion against Him.

---

[35] Thornton, R. & Billings, J **Expounder of Primitive Christianity Volume 2** (Philadelphia, 1846), p. 346

August 14

Loving a Lie more than the Truth

That this is a rebellious people, lying children, children that will not hear the law of the LORD: Which say to the seers, See not; and to the prophets, Prophesy not unto us right things, speak unto us smooth things, prophesy deceits (Isaiah 30:9-10)

For the past two days we have been studying 1 Kings 22 concerning the lying spirit that deceived Ahab. We learned that God *permitted* the lying spirit to deceive Ahab. He was not the cause of it. However, saying that God permitted the sin rather than causing it is not enough to vindicate Him. We still must ask why would God permit such a thing.

When we look at the history of Ahab, we can understand why God finally allowed the lying spirit to influence do as it did. It is exactly what Ahab wanted. His heart is revealed in how the false prophets went free while the one who spoke the truth was thrown into prison. If God truly wanted to deceive Ahab, He would not have allowed Micaiah to tell him the truth. Ahab received the truth and ignored it, demonstrating his desire for deception. Ahab accurately fits the description found in Isaiah's prophecy.

God has given all of His people freedom to choose between right and wrong and good and evil (Gen. 4:7; Deut. 11:26-28; 30:19; Joshua 24:15, 22; Isa. 66:3; Jer. 3:22; Matt. 11:28; 19:17; 23:37; John 5:40; 7:17; Acts 17:30-31; Rom. 2:14-15; 6:16-17; Heb. 7:25; James 4:5-8; Rev. 3:20 and many others). God will do all that He can possibly do to persuade us to choose that which is right, but will not force our choices. If we persist in rebellion and we persist in believing lies, then God is obligated to permit us to have the very thing we have chosen. Paul wrote:

*And with all deceivableness of unrighteousness in them that perish; **because they <u>received not</u> the love of the truth**, that they might be saved. And **<u>for this cause</u> God shall send them strong delusion**, that they should believe a lie:* (2 The. 2:10, 11)

God sent the truth but Ahab preferred the lie. The same is true in these end times. People prefer lies and deception over the truth. For God to force anyone by His omnipotent power to receive the truth is to rob them of the freedom of choice that He gave them, and God does not rob people of the gifts that He gives (Rom. 11:29).

August 15

Did God Give Saul an Evil Spirit

*"But the Spirit **of** the LORD departed from Saul, and an evil spirit **from** the LORD troubled him"* (1 Sam. 16:14; see also 16:16; 19:9).

Notice the distinction between the "Spirit of the Lord" and "evil spirit from the Lord." Readings of some English dictionaries distinguish between "of" and "from". "Of" means "the cause, source, means, author or agent bestowing." "From" implies, "departure" and "moving to a distance." The Spirit *of* the Lord was upon Saul by God's direct agency.

On the other hand, the evil spirit *from* God is driven away or put at bay by David (who is now anointed with God's Spirit) playing music. Furthermore this evil spirit moved Saul to attempt to kill David. This spirit *from* the Lord was *not* sent by His direct agency.

The evil spirit *from* the Lord that tormented Saul is exactly like the one in Micaiah's vision that he related to Ahab and Jehoshaphat who volunteered to trouble Saul and was given *permission* by God. This was due to Saul's persistent rebellion (1 Sam. 13:11-14; 15:19-23). This is affirmed by a number of Bible expositors. F. B. Meyer writes:

> The evil spirit is said to have come from God. In the bold language of Scripture, because He permitted it, and so constituted the laws of the human mind, that when a man gives himself up to any kind of sin, it always opens the door to Satan and to further and more desperate acts. When we refuse God's Spirit, we surrender ourselves into the power of the devil. When men do not wish to retain God in their knowledge, He gives them up (Rom. 1:28).[36]

When the Spirit of the Lord departed from Saul this left him without divine protection from Satanic onslaughts (Luke 11:24-26). We are warned not to give any place to the devil through our sin (Eph. 4:24-27; 2 Cor. 2:10, 11; 2 Tim. 2:24-26; 1 Pet. 5:8). We are also taught that when we persist in sin that God will turn us over to Satan (Matt. 18:32-35; 1 Cor. 5:1-5; 1 Tim. 1:20), which implies removing His protection from over us and allowing Satan to have his way in our lives (Job 1:9-12). This is not something that God does arbitrarily but *permits* after He has given us numerous warnings and we yet persist in rebellion.

---

[36] Meyer, F. B. **Choice Notes on Joshua-2 Kings** (Grand Rapids, MI: Kregel Publications, 1985), pp101, 102

August 16

Is Confident Prayer being Presumptuous?

Come now, you who say, "Today or tomorrow we will go to such and such a city, spend a year there, buy and sell, and make a profit"; whereas you do not know what will happen tomorrow. For what is your life? It is even a vapor that appears for a little time and then vanishes away. For that ye ought to say, If the Lord will, we shall live, and do this, or that. (James 4:13-15)

There are some who believe that there is no way of knowing what God is willing to do for us in prayer. Many who are against the Biblical truth that we can pray and boldly declare specific answers from God usually appeal to this passage. Their premise is that those who teach God's people that they need not pray "if it be thy will" concerning healing and other material needs are teaching presumption.

There is "faith" and there is "presumption." If we have no direct word from God concerning our plans from day to day then we have no right to presume that God will bless our efforts. While we are not to presume upon God's will for tomorrow, neither does He leave His will in a vacuum, causing us to guess or to believe that whatever happens the next day is His will (James 1:5-7).

On the contrary, He tells us to ask Him for wisdom and He will indeed give it. God makes His will known concerning His desire to impart wisdom. He tells us to simply pray and He is will give it. We need not pray "If it be thy will Lord, please give me wisdom" when He has clearly made His will known on the subject. To pray such a prayer demonstrates unbelief and the person who prays in such a manner cannot expect to receive anything from the Lord.

Furthermore, James was not advocating the idea that we must pray, "if it be thy will" or "thy will be done" concerning divine healing as some teach. Ironically, in this same epistle, James tells us that healing is certain when we ask for it (James 5:14-15).

Notice that James 4:15 says, *"For that ye ought to say, If the Lord will, we shall live, and do this, or that"* but in James 5:15 we are told, *"And the prayer of faith shall save the sick, and the Lord shall raise him up."* There is a difference between presuming that God will bless our *personal* plans and desires that have no basis in his Word and actually asking with complete confidence that God will heal our bodies in answer to prayer. Confidently expecting God to heal is not presumption because he promised to do it. There is no need to pray "if it be thy will" when His will has already been revealed.

August 17

It is Impossible for God to Lie

*Wherein God, willing more abundantly to shew unto the heirs of promise the immutability of his counsel, **confirmed it by an oath**: That by two immutable things, in which it was <u>impossible for God to lie</u>, we might have a strong consolation, who have fled for refuge to lay hold upon the hope set before us* (Heb. 6:17-18)

How could we ever doubt the Word of God when we have His *oath* that He will do what He promised? How could we be so powerless in prayer when we have numerous promises from God? When we go before God and ask Him to bless us based on His Word, we should have absolute assurance that it is done.

Sadly, not all believe this and they continued to spread their unbelief to others. For example, one man wrote, "....God is no further bound by his general promise to hear the prayers of His people, than to give such things as in his wisdom he shall judge most suitable in the case."[37]

With teachings like this is it any wonder that people cannot trust God? Yet God wants us to be so assured of His honesty and integrity that, contrary to the beliefs of the writer above, He *makes an oath*. To "make an oath" means "to bind oneself." That means "obligation." An oath is "a statement by which people give assurance that they have spoken the truth or by which they obligate themselves to perform certain actions.

We are told that it is *impossible* for God to lie. There is no possibility that He can lie to us. God's limitations are beneficial to us. Notice how we are given revelation of God's inability to lie in relation to His promises. Yet, God loves us so much and so wants us to trust Him that he even goes "beyond the call of duty." God not only makes promises, but in order to give us unwavering assurance, He binds Himself to them and obligates Himself to their fulfillment.

God has gone out of His way to strengthen and ground our trust in Him by binding Himself with an oath. It should have been enough for God to say, "I cannot lie." However, God knows how frail our faith is and, out of the deepest unimaginable love He says, "If you still have trouble trusting me, I'll bind myself to my promises by an oath to you. I will obligate myself to do what I have said so that you can make a demand on me."

---

[37] M'Laren, John F. (Editor) **The Christian Magazine, Volume 1** (Geneva: Associate Reformed Presbyterian Church, 1832), p. 277

August 18

Abortion is MURDER!

*Lo, children are an heritage of the LORD: and **the fruit of the womb is his reward**. As arrows are in the hand of a mighty man; so are children of the youth* (Psalm 127:3-4)

The Bible, which is God's infallible Word, is clear that the pregnant woman is carrying a real human being (Luke 1:39-44). It does not matter what scientists or the medical profession says. Christians are to go by the Scriptures. They are our authority. Therefore, if we kill the fruit of the womb then we are committing a murder and aligning ourselves with the original murderer, Satan.

There are so-called experts who tell us that the fruit of the womb is only tissue. It is not a real person. Any "expert" that contradicts the Bible is to be rejected and regarded as satanic. Satan has been contradicting God's Word with worldly wisdom since the beginning and it has only led to DEATH (Gen. 3:1-5; 1 John 2:15-17; Rom. 5:12).

Abortion is no different than the disgusting child sacrifices that the ancient nations lured the Israelites into (Jer. 7:31; 19:4-6; 32:35-36). While these nations sacrificed to false gods of wood and stone, the abortions that are done today are sacrificed to false gods of convenience, career, and endless sex with no repercussions. These are just as much idols as the ones worshipped during ancient Israel.

Every Abortion "doctor" is a High Priest and Tool of Satan. He or she is a propagator of Satan's agenda to destroy those created in God's image. This is more than just breaking a law of God. This is more than just another thing that offends God. Satan has an agenda to destroy mankind. He hates God and therefore hates human beings since we were created in God's image. He does everything he can to destroy those creatures that God loves. Furthermore, he is able to drag into hell every person that participates in this murder.

God, on the other hand, not only cares about the unborn babies being murdered. He cares about the abortion doctors who perform the abortions. He cares about the mothers who allow the abortions to be performed on them. He cares about the callous fathers who push women to get abortions so that they are not burdened with a new financial responsibility. The love of God cares about each person involve because, in the long run, abortion destroys everyone involved.

Satan gives no one a free ride. We may think that we are freeing ourselves from a burden, but abortion puts all participants in bondage to Satan and gives him access to destroy their lives both temporally and eternally. Stand against the abortion agenda in Jesus' Name.

August 19

The Cursing of the Ground

*And he said to the man, "You listened to your wife and ate the fruit which I told you not to eat. **Because of what you have done, the ground will be under a curse.** You will have to work hard all your life to make it produce enough food for you. It will produce weeds and thorns, and you will have to eat wild plants* (Gen. 3:17-18; Good News Translation)

Before the fall, the ground would have given man no trouble in producing its fruit, but after the fall, this would change. God said, *"....cursed is the ground **for thy sake**"* (KJV): God did not, by some act of supernatural power, make the ground become more difficult. Adam was given dominion and his actions affected the earth (Gen. 1:26-28). By yielding to satanic influences and rejecting God (the only one able to sustain life) Adam himself caused the earth to be cursed. Adam, and not God, brought this on the world (Rom. 5:12; Deut. 30:15, 19).

Many people, including God's own people, do not understand how powerfully destructive sin is. Sin not only affects us personally, but it affects the environment around us. This is seen in numerous passages of Scripture, one of the clearest being found in the book of Hosea:

*By swearing, and lying, and killing, and stealing, and committing adultery, they break out, and blood toucheth blood. **Therefore shall the land mourn**, and every one that dwelleth therein shall languish, with the beasts of the field, and with the fowls of heaven; yea, the fishes of the sea also shall be taken away* (Hosea 4:3)

Quite often we want to find scientific and secular ways to save our environment. However, the best way, though it is the most rejected way, is to repent of our sins and invite God back into the environment. He has promised that when we pray, seek His face and turn from our wicked ways that He will heal the land (2 Chron. 7:14).

Environmental regulations will not solve the problem. Campaigns to save the whales and placing heavy fines for destruction of rare wild-life will not fix our issues with our environment. The problem with our environment is a *sin* problem. It started with Adam and we have made it worse. We have pushed away God and this means pushing away His life giving protection. Let us pray for repentance and healing to go throughout the land.

August 20

Making the Land Sick

Defile not ye yourselves in any of these things: for in all these the nations are defiled which I cast out before you: And the land is defiled: therefore I do visit the iniquity thereof upon it, and the land itself vomiteth out her inhabitants (Leviticus 18:24-25)

Many people do not understand how their actions affect the environment around them for good or for ill. Therefore, God gets the blame for all that happens as a result of our sin. Yet, it is our sins that destroy the earth and makes it sick.

This is also another reason for the "holy wars" that the Israelites were engaged in with the other nations. These nations simply would not repent and were destroying the land that they occupied. God had to remove them before there was permanent destruction—a destruction that would have had much more far reaching effects than just their areas of occupation.

In Leviticus 18, God lists a number of sins that were being committed by the heathen nations that He was sending Israel in to remove. Among them were incest, bestiality, homosexuality, adultery, murder, and child sacrifice. All of the natural disasters experienced by nations is due to the land becoming sick and vomiting. As God said through Isaiah:

The earth mourneth and fadeth away, the world languisheth and fadeth away, *the haughty people of the earth do languish.* **The earth also is defiled under the inhabitants thereof; because they have transgressed the laws,** *changed the ordinance, broken the everlasting covenant.* **Therefore hath the curse devoured the earth,** *and they that dwell therein are desolate: therefore the inhabitants of the earth are burned, and few men left* (Isa. 24:4-5).

The curse is devouring the earth because of the numerous sins listed above. Sadly, this list and more fits the United States of America today as well as the nations in Europe. Our nation is definitely moving away from its foundation of being "One nation under God." In order to explain the bad weather patterns that come as a result of sin we make a new science called "global warming." Others simply blame God for the disastrous results of our nation's rebellion. The fault lies with us and nothing can save our nation apart from national prayer and repentance. Let us pray for this nation.

August 21

Did God Personally Destroy Sodom and Gomorrah? (Part 1)

Then the Lord rained upon Sodom and upon Gomorrah brimstone and fire from the Lord out of heaven; And he overthrew those cities, and all the plain, and all the inhabitants of the cities, and that which grew upon the ground (Genesis 19:24-25)

Quite often the Bible portrays God as personally engaging in destructive behavior. While the Bible is the divine inspired Word of God, God spoke using the language and idioms of the people of those times in which the Bible was being written. When Scripture says that God engaged in destruction, it does not necessarily mean He used His power to destroy. It means that He stopped protecting those who push Him away.

In the case of Sodom, the area around it called Siddim was full of dangerous slime pits: *"And the vale of Siddim was full of slimepits"* (Gen. 14:18a). God makes note of this fact for a reason. The area surrounding Sodom was full of what many archaeologists have noted were petroleum gases, which is what these "slimepits" were. These pits were ready to explode at any moment. It was God's protection that kept them from doing so (Rev. 7:1-3). When no repentance from Sodom was forthcoming, God had to release His protection. One minister explains the science of this:

> Nothing is more certain than that science supports the Bible. Prof. G. F. Wright, of Oberlin College, a man who stands high in the ranks of scientists, shows clearly in his volume, "Scientific Aspects of Christian Evidences," that the whole region about the Dead Sea has the appearance now of being an abandoned "oil district," and that all the conditions for the catastrophe described in the Bible were present in the inflammable accumulations of oil and gas reservoirs. We have only to suppose that at the time of the destruction quantities of gas and petroleum existed below the plain; then their escape through a fissure would produce the results described. (Robert Stuart MacArthur, **Bible Difficulties and their Alleviate Interpretation - Old Testament**, pp. 213, 214)

MacArthur concludes, "We see here how God can punish sinners with physical forces associated with their own sin" (p. 216). In other words, God rained down fire on Sodom and Gomorrah by removing His protection and allowing the natural consequences of their sin to take effect through those "slimepits." God is not a destroyer in the literal sense. We bring about our own destruction when we push God away through our sin.

238

August 22

Did God Personally Destroy Sodom and Gomorrah? (Part 2)

What happened to Sodom and Gomorrah and the cities near them is an example for us of the punishment of eternal fire. The people of these cities suffered the same fate that God's people and the angels did, because they committed sexual sins and engaged in homosexual activities (Jude 7; God's Word Translation)

In yesterday's devotion we learned that the area surrounding Sodom was covered by slimepits and the Bible makes special note of this: *"And the vale of Siddim was full of slimepits"* (Gen. 14:18a). Scientists who have made it their goal to prove the Bible to be an accurate historical record, have noted that these slimepits were pits full of petroleum gases and that they were ready to explode.

It was something supernatural keeping this from happening. It was the continuous unrepentant sin of Sodom and Gomorrah that cause God to remove this supernatural protection and allow the destruction of these cities to take place. This is affirmed by Hosea:

*How shall I <u>give thee up</u>, Ephraim? how shall I <u>deliver thee</u>, Israel? how shall I make thee as Admah? how shall I set thee as Zeboim? <u>mine heart is turned within me</u>, my repentings are kindled together. I will not execute the fierceness of mine anger, **I will not return to destroy Ephraim**: for I am God, and not man; the Holy One in the midst of thee: and I will not enter into the city* (Hos 11:8-9)

Admah and Zoboim were in the same region as Sodom and Gomorrah and were connected together in the same sins, which included homosexuality (Gen. 10:19; 14:2, 8; Deut. 29:23). Therefore, God removed His protection over that region and allowed the brewing slime pits (full of destructive gases) to have their way, thus destroying those cities. **God's method of destruction is to remove His hand of protection (which is to give the person or nation up) and deliver the person or nation to the consequences of their choices**.

God "destroyed" Sodom and Gomorrah by "giving them up" and "delivering them" to the consequences of their rebellion. Let us take heed to this. If God gives up a person or nation then it is in serious trouble. But when He does give us up, we cannot blame Him for the trouble that we experience. Let us repent of our sins and invite God back in to help us and protect us.

The Results of Korah's Rebellion

And it came to pass, as he had made an end of speaking all these words, that the ground clave asunder that was under them: ***And the earth opened her mouth, and swallowed them up****, and their houses, and all the men that appertained unto Korah, and all their goods* (Num. 16:31-32)

In this passage it appears that God has engaged in destructive behavior. After all the passage says, *"But if the LORD make a new thing, and the earth open her mouth...."* (v. 30). Certainly this was a new and "creative" way of bringing about punishment, but is this the first time the earth has ever opened her mouth?

In Genesis 4:11, God speaking to Cain after he murdered his brother Abel says, *"And now art thou cursed from the earth,* ***which hath opened her mouth*** *to receive thy brother's blood from thy hand."* Here we see that the earth had a mouth even from the beginning and that she opened it. However, the earth did not open its mouth to punish Cain as it did Korah since, despite his dastardly deed, God's protection remained on him (Gen. 4:15). However, Cain's sin affected the earth to the extent that it would no longer easily yield its strength to him.

In the book of Revelation we learn that the earth will again open her mouth but it will do so to protect God's people: *"And the earth helped the woman, and* ***the earth opened her mouth****, and swallowed up the flood which the dragon cast out of his mouth"* (Rev. 12:16). Here we see warfare between Satan and the earth and the fight is over the people of God.

Jewish tradition taught that God had created the earth with a mouth at the beginning. James L. Kugel writes, "A widely held rabbinic tradition held that.... the 'mouth of the earth' that swallowed up Korah and his followers was no figure of speech but an actual opening in the earth that had been created by God at the time of creation" (Traditions of the Bible, p. 791). *If* this is true then no wonder we read where sin makes the earth vomit (Lev. 18:24-28; 20:22), causes her to mourn (Isa. 24:4-5; Hosea 4:3), and to groan, travail in pain and long for its redemption (Rom. 8:18-22).

When we read that the earth opened her mouth to swallow the people it does not say that God *personally* did it but that the earth itself did it. This language is always used to describe Korah's rebellion and the results (Num. 26:10; Deut. 11:6). Sin continually causes problems for the earth, makes her sick, and vomit up stuff that we refer to as "natural disasters." It was *sin* that destroyed Korah and his followers, not God.

August 24

How God Expresses His Anger

*They made Him angry with their sinful places of worship. And they made Him jealous with their false gods. God was very angry when He heard them, and He hated Israel. **He left the holy tent at Shiloh,** the tent He had set up among men. **And He let His strength be taken.** He put His greatness into the hands of those who hated Israel. **He allowed His people to be killed with the sword.** And He was very angry with those who belong to Him.* (Psalm 78:58-62; New Life Version)

Many times God is said to have sent nations to destroy Israel because of their sins or He is said to have destroyed them Himself. Regardless of which way God is said to have done it in some portions of the Bible, other portions of it explains the language. God's punishment of Israel is always in the *allowing sense* and not the *causative sense*.

In the passage above we learn that God "left the holy tent at Shiloh". This means that He departed from Israel. Usually it takes a very long time before God does this because He is often pleading with His people to stop doing what they are doing. However, after a lengthy period of time in which God is rejected and false gods are accepted, God leaves.

Along with the lifting of His presence is the departure of His strength. The Bible says, *"He let His strength be taken".* It was His strength that kept Israel safe. Once His strength is gone from His people then those who hate them have easy access to them. We must always keep in mind that it is God who strengthens us. Arrogance and idolatry begins when we forget this truth. Forgetting this truth has deadly consequences.

Once God removes His presence and His strength He allows the enemy to have his way. We are told that He *allowed* His people to be killed with the sword. From this we can see that it is not God using supernatural power to stir up hatred against His people as punishment for their sins. He does not have to. The enemies already hate God's people and would have already killed them if they could have. It was only God's presence and strength that prevented that. Once that was gone then the enemy had easy access and was allowed to kill and destroy.

God is not at fault for what happened to Israel when they were attacked. Israel began to worship false gods, thus pushing God away. We are in danger of doing the same thing when we push God away with our idolatry of sex and perversion. When we do, let us not blame God but ourselves. Repent and turn back to Him and He will rescue us. He's that merciful.

August 25

Who Actually Makes Men Spiritually Blind?

He hath blinded their eyes, and hardened their heart; that they should not see with their eyes, nor understand with their heart, and be converted, and I should heal them. These things said Esaias, when he saw his glory, and spake of him (John 12:40-41)

John, quoting from Isaiah, says that Jesus came to blind men and to harden their hearts so that they would not be converted and healed. Those who embrace the Calvinistic ideas that God controls every single event and that there is no such thing as "free-will" get a lot of mileage from passages like this one. However, apart from an understanding of Hebrew idioms, this passage becomes troubling for those of us who know God to be loving, fair, and just.

In the context of John 12 Jesus is reminding them that He is the light sent from God and He exhorts them to walk in this light while it is still available to them (John 12:34-36). He even did miracles of healing and deliverance to demonstrate this light but they still did not believe Him (v. 37). Nowhere does it say that Jesus used divine power to harden and blind people. On the contrary He used divine power to set men free from satanic bondage. Yet, His use of divine power is said to be the fulfilling of Isaiah's prophecy that He would harden and blind.

This is simply the Hebrew idiom in which God is said to do that which He has permitted or has not prevented. The same sun that softens the ground can also harden the clay. God's intention is to soften hearts and open men's eyes but men love darkness rather than light (John 3:18-20). Due to this love of darkness, Satan is the actual agent that blinds and hardens men to the light: *"In whom **the god of this world hath blinded the minds of them which believe not**, lest the light of the glorious gospel of Christ, who is the image of God, should shine unto them"* (2 Cor. 4:4).

Therefore, when we read Scripture of this nature we must always remember to interpret them first, in the light of God's known and loving character in which we know that He does not literally do such things. Second, we must interpret such passages in the light of the Hebrew idiom in which God is said to do that which He merely permitted and did not prevent, and thirdly, within this same idiom He often takes responsibility for the work of Satan and evil men.

This truth, as we see above, is easily supported by interpreting Scripture with Scripture. Scripture is its own commentary and explains exactly what is meant by some of the troubling language we find in John 12:40-41.

August 26

Israelites bitten by Fiery Serpents

And the people spoke against God, and against Moses, Wherefore have ye brought us up out of Egypt to die in the wilderness? for there is no bread, and there is no water; and our soul loatheth this miserable bread. And **the Lord let loose** *against the people poisonous serpents, and they bit the people; and there died much people of Israel* (Number 21:5-6 Leeser Old Testament)

The King James Version renders verse 6, *"And the Lord sent fiery serpents among the people."* Just about every English translation uses the word "sent" in relation to God and the serpents except for the Leeser Old Testament. However, the word "sent" is a Hebrew word that can be easily translated as "allow" or "permit". Leeser's translation appears to be more accurate in how it renders it and more consistent with the Biblical evidence.

God did not "send" the serpents as we understand the word "sent". They were in the desert the whole time: *"Who led thee through that great and terrible wilderness, wherein were fiery serpents, and scorpions...."* (Deut. 8:15a). There was no need for God to "send" what was already there. God was protecting the people from these serpents.

However, when the people continued in incessant complaining, speaking against God and His appointed leadership, they began to push Him away. By pushing God away we forfeit His protective presence and we are left to the mercy of the circumstances around us. Our constant complaining demonstrates complete unbelief and we begin to speak words that will break the hedge of protection that God has placed around us: *"He that diggeth a pit shall fall into it; and whoso breaketh an hedge, a serpent shall bite him"* (Eccl. 10:8).

Therefore, God is said to have *let loose* the fiery serpents that He once kept bound. This was not His will or desire but when we complain about what He is doing and fail to appreciate all the good He has constantly done for us then what else can we expect of Him? We cannot blame Him for not protecting us when we are the ones that pushed Him away through our negative words of unbelief.

However, when we speak words of trust in His protection, He restores it: ***"Because thou hast said, The Lord is my protection,*** *the Most High hast thou made thy refuge.... Upon the fierce lion and asp shalt thou tread: thou shalt trample under foot the young lion* ***and serpent"*** (Psalm 91:9, 13; Leeser). Speak positive words about God. Speak His promises and keep His protective presence around you.

August 27

Does God Profane His Own Sanctuary?

*Speak unto the house of Israel, Thus saith the Lord GOD;
Behold, **I will profane my sanctuary**, the excellency of
your strength, the desire of your eyes, and that which your
soul pitieth; and your sons and your daughters whom ye
have left shall fall by the sword* (Ezekiel 24:21)

This is a tough statement coming from the mouth of the Lord. He says that He will profane His own sanctuary. This word "profane" means to "defile" or "pollute" and it is always the result of sin. It is the opposite of holiness (Ezek. 22:26). Furthermore, God specifically commanded that no one do such a thing to His sanctuary: *"Neither shall he go out of the sanctuary, **nor profane the sanctuary of his God;** for the crown of the anointing oil of his God is upon him: I am the LORD"* (Lev. 21:12).

How do we understand the language in Ezekiel in which God is said to profane His own sanctuary in light of the command in Leviticus? This can only be understood by applying the Hebrew permissive idiom in which God is said to be the doer of that which He actually only *permitted* to be done. This is how we must understand all language in relation to God saying that He will do things that violates His own laws.

The people of Israel had already profaned God's sanctuary through their idolatry, an idolatry that included sacrificing innocent children: *"For when they had slain their children to their idols, then they came the same day into my sanctuary to profane it; and, lo, thus have they done in the midst of mine house"* (Ezek. 23:39).

God continued to show them compassion by sending prophets to them day and night who warned them of the consequences of their sin. Yet, all they did was laugh at them and mock them (2 Chron. 36:15-16). Finally, they had pushed God so far that He allowed the King of Babylon to come and kill men, women and children right there in the sanctuary. This king also took all of the holy items and vessels from the sanctuary and burned it (2 Chron. 36:17-21).

The divine commentary on this is, *"....he [God] gave them all into his [The king of Babylon's] hand"* (2 Chron. 36:17c). In other words, God permitted His sanctuary to be profaned by a foreign king and allowed him to kill many of the Israelites. If we persist in sin, God will compassionately warn us time and again so that we do not suffer the wages that sin delights in paying (Rom. 6:23). But if we continue to ignore His warnings then sooner or later we will reap the sad results. However, when this happens, God is not responsible. Let us repent of sin and stay away from profanity.

Did God tell Shimei to Curse David?

And the king said, What have I to do with you, ye sons of Zeruiah? so let him curse, because the LORD hath said unto him, Curse David. Who shall then say, Wherefore hast thou done so? And David said to Abishai, and to all his servants, Behold, my son, which came forth of my bowels, seeketh my life: how much more now may this Benjamite do it? let him alone, and let him curse; for the LORD hath bidden him (2 Sam. 16:10-11)

A very good rule for Bible interpretation is to always see who is speaking, what they are saying, and if what they said lines up with God's commands and ways. The Bible is indeed the inspired Word of God and is a divine book given to us by God. However, within this divine book we have the statements of men, women, Satan, and demons accurately recorded.

We certainly do not quote Satan's words that are accurately recorded in the Bible and use them in a *positive* manner to support doctrinal truth. This being so, we should be careful about doing the same thing with men who are discouraged even though their words are recorded in holy Scripture, even great men. Both Moses and Elijah asked God to kill them when they were frustrated and discouraged. Do we build doctrines on those words? Thomas Pearce, a great theologian during the "age of Enlightenment" helps us to better understand David's words here:

If David's words concerning God's bidding Shimei be understood to be spoken by the common Hebraism, by which such verbs as are active in sound are only permissive in signification, all those horrible absurdities will be avoided; or if the Hebrew particle which we render *because,* were rendered *if,* as sometimes it signifies, it will then be no more than a mere conjecture arising out of David's guilty conscience ....In sundry respects the effect doth seem to be ascribed unto God, after the Hebrew custom of speech, and the phrases, *exciting,* or *bidding,* &c, are used figuratively or tropically of God Himself, when as yet He is so far from exciting or commanding, that He doth the contrary to them both (Pierce's **"Divine Philanthropy Defended,"** chap. iv., sec. 35. Edition of 1658).

We believe that Pearce has accurately pinpointed the problems with David's words. God is not the author of any sinful action though the idiom of the Hebrew is to attribute all things to Him.

August 29

God Delivers from Sin's Consequences

For thus saith the LORD, **Ye have sold yourselves for nought**; *and ye shall be redeemed without money* (Isa. 52:3)

When we sin and rebel against God what do we gain from it? Do we gain temporary pleasure? Fun? Do we gain the favor of a few friends or relatives who are happy that we have forsaken our morals to please them? God says that when we sin we have *sold ourselves*. The Hebrew word is often used in relation to someone being *sold as a slave* (Lev. 25:50; Psalm 105:15).

Scripture says that the one who sins becomes a slave to it (John 8:34; Rom. 6:16-20). By extension, we have become a slave to the one who is the master of all sinners, Satan (1 John 3:8; Eph. 2:1-2; Acts 26:18). When we sin we sell ourselves as slaves to Satan for nothing. We gain nothing really tangible or eternal from it except our own eternal destruction.

However, there is some good news in all of this. God, speaking through Isaiah, says that He will redeem us without money. This word means "to buy back." Those of us living under the New Testament understand very well that this is in reference to the blood of Jesus which paid the redemption price for us (Rev. 5:9; Gal. 3:13; Col. 1:12-14). This blood is more precious than silver or gold (1 Pet. 1:18-19).

Sometimes when we warn people about the natural consequences of sin, if we are not careful, we can leave them without hope. God's tender love and mercy is so overwhelming that He is willing and ready to bring redemption to the repentant sinner. He says, *"O Israel, thou hast destroyed thyself; but in me is thine help"* (Hosea 13:9).

God cannot be blamed for our sin or its results. We destroy ourselves. Oh but the greatness and graciousness of Christ is seen in His willingness to die for us and deliver us from both sin and its consequences. This is despite the fact that we have been willing to engage in it to our own eternal destruction.

We need to remember the heavy price that Christ lovingly and willingly paid to "buy us back" from sin's slave plantation. Do not allow Satan to deceive you with false ideas about grace and sell yourself back into this bondage. You been redeemed with precious blood. Don't sell yourself for nothing.

August 30

Did God Predestine Judas to Betray Christ?

I speak not of you all: I know whom I have chosen: but that
the scripture may be fulfilled, He that eateth bread with me
hath lifted up his heel against me (John 13:18)

There are several passages in the Bible that use the phrase "that it may be fulfilled" or that "the Scripture may be fulfilled" in relation to Judas and his betrayal of Christ (Mat. 27:9; John 13:18; 17:12; Acts 1:16-20). For centuries, teachers and theologians have taken this to mean that Judas' heinous crime and its results (eternal damnation) were predestined by God before the creation of the world and that He merely revealed glimpses of it to His servants in the Old Testament.

Others who find the idea that God would predestine anyone to sin is mischaracterizing God still teach a similar doctrine in which God looked down the corridors of time, saw that Judas would betray Christ, and then mystically worked it into His plan of redemption. Based on both models Judas simply did not stand a chance. He was either predestined by God or God saw the unchangeable future in which it was inevitable for Judas to do it so it happened as the future told God it would happen. The word "fulfilled" is supposed to be the concrete proof of this.

However, there is another way to understand this whole issue with Judas and vindicate God's character in the process. When the New Testament writers use such phrases as "that the scripture may be fulfilled," it is not always necessarily in reference to a specific prediction made concerning a particular person centuries before their birth. In many cases, it was simply a matter of *paralleling the past event recorded in Scripture with the event that was presently occurring.* The writer was showing how the event that was happening has its type in Scripture.

Jesus is making reference to Psalm 41:9 in His statement. In his notes on John 13:18, Albert Barnes writes, "'May be fulfilled.' The cases were similar; the same words would describe both events, and there was an exhibition of similar ingratitude and baseness in both cases, so that the same words would fitly describe both events" (Albert Barnes, *Notes on the Gospels*, p. 342).

An examination of the Old Testament texts is proof of this. The Old Testament passages when read apart from what we know about Judas, doesn't even hint at a reference to him. If Judas had not betrayed the Lord then there would have been no need to fulfill any of the Scriptures that are paralleled with his acts. Therefore "that the Scripture may be fulfilled" is not always the literal fulfillment of a particular prophesy concerning a specific person.

August 31

Judas' Betrayal of Jesus Due to Satanic Thoughts

"Then entered Satan into Judas surnamed Iscariot, being of the number of the twelve" (Luke 22:3)

Yesterday we looked at the case of Judas and saw that He was neither predestined to betray Christ nor was it something that was foreseen from eternity past as some claim. Judas was a genuine disciple and apostle of Jesus (Mat. 10:1-5; Luke 6:12-19; John 12:4). So how was it that Satan was able to "enter into Judas?" Like Ananias (see Acts 5), Satan planted a thought in Judas' heart. Judas, of his own free-will, acted on this horrible thought:

> Now before the feast of the passover, when Jesus knew that his hour was come that he should depart out of this world unto the Father, having loved his own which were in the world, he loved them unto the end. And supper being ended, **the devil having now put into the heart** of Judas Iscariot, Simon's son, to betray him (John 13:1, 2)

J. B. Phillips renders verse 2 this way: *"By supper-time, **the devil had already put the thought of betraying Jesus in the mind** of Judas Iscariot, Simon's son."* The God's Word Translation says that *"the devil had already put the **idea** of betraying Jesus into the mind of Judas"* and the Weymouth translation says, *"the Devil having by this time **suggested** to Judas Iscariot, the son of Simon, the thought of betraying Him, Jesus."* From these we understand that Satan was able to "enter into Judas" and control him through placing in his mind "thoughts, ideas, and suggestions."

If God had predestined Judas to betray the Lord and suffer eternally for this heinous crime, then why is Satan given the credit for God's work? The truth is that God had nothing to do with Judas' crime. This was totally Satan's doing. Judas willingly received and acted on the thought that was given to him by the devil. It was Satan who put the thought in Judas and not God. God is not a party to the sinful acts of men.

God's people must be very careful about the thoughts that enter their minds. Every sin and every reprehensible act begins with a thought. Learn to cast them down in Jesus' Name (2 Cor. 10:3-5).

September 1

Your Sin Will Find You

But if ye will not do so, behold, ye have sinned against the LORD: and **be sure your sin will find you out** *(Num. 32:23)*

Satan leads people to believe that they can sin and keep it from ever being exposed. They believe that they can get away with it. Just continue to go to church, act holy, and no one will ever know that you are caught up in some form of iniquity. There are some who even seem to believe that they can hide their sin from God Himself.

In our opening passage, Moses was speaking to a group of people who were plotting evil. Yet the statement was recorded by the inspiration of God for our profit (2 Tim. 3:16). We do not get away with anything. Regardless of whether or not any human being knows, God will know. God has no desire to expose us. Rather, He seeks our repentance and not our embarrassment. However, there comes a time when unrepentant sin will have to be exposed:

Therefore judge nothing before the time, until the Lord come, who both will bring to light the hidden things of darkness, and will make manifest the counsels of the hearts: and then shall every man have praise of God. (1 Cor. 4:5)

We must come to the realization that sooner or later our actions and motives will be exposed. Our Lord, in His abundant mercy, always gives us "space to repent" (Rev. 2:21). He is not waiting in Heaven to destroy us or embarrass us but to lead us to repentance. However, Satan, the Tempter, will deceive us into believing that God's patience in waiting for us is due to either God not knowing what we are doing or He has decided to let us get away with what we are doing. Either way, if we do not repent, run to Him for mercy, and seek His power to overcome, then someone is gonna' know. Several prominent internationally known ministers have discovered this the hard way in the past several years. Let us not continue in sin and have it find us.

September 2

Is God Against Us Having Fun?

*Charge them that are rich in this world, that they be not
highminded, nor trust in uncertain riches, but in the living
God, who giveth us richly all things to enjoy* (1 Tim. 6:17)

While some preach a licentious God who has no problems with
loose morals, others go to the opposite extreme of teaching a sour-puss
deity who frowns at the Christian having any enjoyment in this life. Satan
is skilled at taking Christians to opposite extremes. The unfortunate result
of the "God is against fun" extreme is that many Christians either serve
God legalistically or they simply quit serving Him because they can no
longer handle such a spoil-sport.

God is a loving parent who wants us to enjoy life. Scripture states
this truth in so many places that we could write a book on this alone. Paul
has already told us in today's devotional passage that God gives us things
in abundance to enjoy. God really wants us to enjoy ourselves. Peter tells us
that it is unnecessary to sin in order to enjoy life and good days:

*For he that will love life, and see good days, let him refrain
his tongue from evil, and his lips that they speak no guile:*
(1 Pet. 3:10)

God is the very One who gives us richly all things to enjoy. If God
did not want His people to have fun then why would He bother giving us
things that would enable us to have fun? Furthermore He provides
instructions for those who would "love life." God wants His people to love
life and to see good days.

God has been given a bad reputation for being a strict non-fun
loving God who is only interested in giving us a list of "dos" and "don'ts".
It is no wonder that so many people are uninterested in Christianity. We
have presented them with a stern idea about God who only wants us to
suffer hardships, be miserable, but at the same time smile and fake some
pseudo type of joy. My friend, God wants us to enjoy life, but He simply
wants us to do it without engaging in sin. Life is more enjoyable when we
are not under the bondage of sin.

September 3

Why God Gave Commandments

O that there were such an heart in them, that they would fear me, and keep all my commandments always, that it might be well with them, and with their children for ever! (Deut. 5:29)

God laments to Moses how He desperately wanted things to go well for His people. Sadly, He knew that these people did not have a heart in them to do it and would suffer as a result. But God cannot be blamed for the suffering. It is His intense desire that things go well for everyone but our yielding to destructive sinful practices can easily prevent that.

God knows that the only way that people can have things go well with them is for them to fear Him and obey Him. Obedience to God is never meant to destroy our need for fun and enjoyment of life. Obedience is meant to actually enhance fun. Fun without guilt is the best fun one can have. God wants us to hang out with family and friends, play games, eat delicious (but healthy) food, and enjoy clean entertainment (though such seems to be rare but we are thankful for the many Christians who are writing good novels, making entertaining films with godly themes, and even cartoons and video games).

God wants husbands and wives to enjoy one another. A healthy sexual relationship within the confines of marriage is ordained by God Himself. God wants us to even enjoy some material blessings that He is willing to provide. God is not against godly fun.

God doesn't even mind church being fun (as long as it does not become irreverent). Being in God's presence should not be something dull (if it is then it could not be God's presence). It should be enjoyed. These are just a small sample of the many ways we can have fun and enjoy life without sin. Obeying God is more fun than it is given credit for – and it comes without the Tempter's evil price tag.

Sadly, our fallen flesh tends to want things that cause us pain and destruction. For some people it is more fun to get drunk, to smoke, to do drugs, to engage in illicit sexual activity, and other things that bring condemnation rather than blessing. God wants things to go well with us but this is impossible if we engage in behavior that destroys. Have fun, but do it within the protective grid of God's commandments.

September 4

Why Didn't God Stop Peter from Sinning?

"Jesus said unto him, Verily I say unto thee, That this night, before the cock crow, thou shalt deny me thrice" (Mat. 26:34).

Some people believe that if God doesn't want us to sin then He can stop us. After all, He already knows what we're going to do anyway. Satan so often feeds us "half-truths." Satan neglects to tell us that God usually does not override our free will and does not usually intervene apart from our asking.

Peter swore that he was ready to die with Jesus even if the rest of the disciples denied Him. Yet, Jesus knew exactly what Peter was going to do. However, Jesus also knew that the future can be changed through the praying of His people. Jesus makes an attempt to teach this to Peter:

*And he cometh unto the disciples, and findeth them asleep, and saith **unto Peter, What, could ye not watch with me one hour? Watch and pray, that ye enter not into temptation**: the spirit indeed is willing, but the flesh is weak* (Mat. 26:40, 41)

Peter did not have to deny His Lord. Had he prayed as the Lord instructed him he would not have entered into temptation but would have been strengthened by God. Prayer can change future events because the God of the future answers prayer. Therefore, Peter's problem was his self-assurance. We have all failed in this regard.

The person who truly wants God to "stop him or her" will follow Scripture's teaching to go boldly to the throne of grace and get the help we need to overcome temptation (Heb. 4:15, 16). Unfortunately, when we have been hypnotized by Satan's enticement then we will not want God to really intervene but use His lack of intervention as our excuse to yield to the temptation.

God will not force His way and His will upon us (Matt. 23:37; Luke 7:30; Rev. 3:20; etc.) but will invite us to come to Him for help. If we want God to keep us from temptation then we must submit ourselves to Him and the Tempter will flee (James 4:7). Never let theological speculation about God's omniscience keep us from appropriating His promises of victory through prayer.

September 5

Does "Permission" mean "Control"?

And the Lord said, Simon, Simon, behold, Satan hath desired to have you, that he may sift you as wheat: But I have prayed for thee, that thy faith fail not: and when thou art converted, strengthen thy brethren. (Luke 22:31-32)

Quite often when discussing Satan's role in the universe those who advocate a sovereignty of God in which God controls everything will tell us that God has the devil under control. Some even imply that Satan is secretly doing God's bidding. When asked for Biblical proof of this we are shown Scripture where God grants permission for Satan to perform certain acts. However, when such passages of Scripture are thoroughly examined, we will find that this is not about "control" in the way that some use the word in relation to how God deals with Satan. Satan is actually the one who comes up with devious ideas. He is the initiator of those ideas and at times, due to certain limitations, he must seek permission from God in order to carry them out.

In the passage above Satan desires to sift Peter. This is not something that God commissioned Satan to do but one that Satan himself sought to do. The word "desire" means "to ask or beg for one's self, to ask that one be given up to one from the power of another" (Studylight.org). So Satan was seeking permission to have God give up Peter to Satan (since God's way of "judgment" is not to actively deal with the person but to remove His hand of protection).

However, God is NOT THE INITIATOR HERE!!! SATAN IS THE INITIATOR!!! It is not God's idea. He did not call a conference with Satan and say, "Hey buddy, I need to test Peter. Can you do me a favor and sift him as wheat?" NO! Satan, completely on his own initiative sought God's permission to sift Simon.

God certainly places limitations and overrules Satan, but it does not mean that God wanted Satan to do what he is doing or that it is some part of God's "secret mysterious divine plan." In Job we see the exact same thing (Job 1:8-12; 2:1-7). It was Satan who came up with the ideas of how to destroy Job. He initiated the tragedies and disasters. God did not have a conference with Satan to detail what Satan would do. He only told him his limits. Yet everything else that Satan did, he did totally on his own with no initiation or input from Yahweh.

So while God *limited* Satan He most definitely was NOT *controlling* him. God does not control Satan. He expects the born again New Testament believer to resist him (James 4:7; 1 Pet. 5:8-9).

September 6

Satan Does Many Things without God's Permission

*Thou wast perfect in thy ways from the day that thou wast created, till iniquity **was found in thee**. By the multitude of thy merchandise they have filled the midst of thee with violence, and thou hast sinned* (Eze. 28:15-16a)

It is a popular notion that God controls every situation. While this is often intended to bring comfort to those who have been the victim of some devastating circumstance, it can have the opposite effect with many who will then blame God for causing them the pain that they are experiencing. It is difficult to reconcile in one's mind how a loving God can plan such hurtful things to come upon His own children.

Even when we tell people that this was the work of Satan others are quick to chime in that God even controls Satan's actions. Their belief is that God is sovereign and in control and Satan can only do those things that God permits (as in "commission").

Ezekiel 28, which describes how the good angel that God created later fell and became Satan presents us with an irrefutable case demonstrating that Satan is NOT a God-controlled robot only fulfilling some secret will of God. Satan actually does numerous things without God's granted permission or desire.

If iniquity was *found* in Satan then this means that God did not put it there. You don't "find" something in a place where you knowingly put it. This "finding" of iniquity in Lucifer (later to be known as Satan) was a new discovery to God. This "internal violence" that God discovered in Satan was Satan's own doing and not God's.

Satan was the first creature ever to become violent. He then led numerous other angels to follow him in his criminal acts and since the fall of man he has been able to influence men and animals to become violent criminals like himself. Every act of violence from Cain killing Abel to the Jewish leaders killing Jesus can be attributed to Satan's doing (Gen. 4:7-8; 1 John 3:10-12; John 8:44). This was not God's ordained plan. Satan became a violent criminal completely on his own.

God is not controlling every action of Satan. If He were then God would not have found iniquity in Satan's heart. Satan put it there without God's consent. Therefore, we need to stop taking a position of fatalism towards Satan's activities and learn to resist him.

September 7

The Cause of Satan's Fall

*For **thou hast said in thine heart**, I will ascend into heaven, I will exalt my throne above the stars of God: I will sit also upon the mount of the congregation, in the sides of the north: I will ascend above the heights of the clouds; I will be like the most High* (Isa. 14:13-14)

Every sin begins with a thought. The thought, when continually meditated upon, usually leads to the action thought about. Sin began with Satan no differently than it does with us with one small exception: Satan had no tempter. Quite often for us, Satan and his demons plant evil thoughts within us. However, every free moral agent of God has the power to think his or her own thoughts, to accept or reject the suggestions of others, and the freedom to act on all thoughts without coercion.

In Isaiah we read that Satan said "in his own heart" how he planned to rebel against God. This means that God did not put it there. This was a totally free act of Satan with no permission from God whatsoever. Yet many theologians tell us that Satan can do NOTHING apart from the will of God. If this is true then this really would make God the author of sin and its consequences, a teaching that many "God is in control" advocates vehemently deny. If God is controlling Satan, then one could not draw any other conclusion than to say that God is the author of sin.

The fact that Satan can say and do things unauthorized by God is taught in John 8:44. Jesus said that things such as lying are things that Satan, *"When he speaketh a lie, **he speaketh of his own**: for he is a liar, and the father of it."*

Here we are told that whenever Satan lies he "speaketh of his own." God has nothing to do with it. God cannot lie and it is impossible for Him to do so (Titus 1:2; Heb. 6:18-19). The Bible says that Satan, and not God, is the "father" of lying. Satan is the father of lying and God (who is the "God of TRUTH") had no control over it, no part in it, and was not involved in birthing into the universe the thing called *lying*.

Satan's fall was not decreed, ordained, willed, or wanted by God. There was no special purpose or plan in Satan falling. This was a needless and unnecessary act that has done nothing more than to bring misery to the universe. We are thankful that the day is coming when God will rid the universe of Satan and sin. Until that day, let us not blame God for the work of the devil or his fall.

September 8

Satan the Author and Engineer of Evil

Another parable put he forth unto them, saying, The kingdom of heaven is likened unto a man which sowed good seed in his field: But while men slept, his enemy came and sowed tares among the wheat, and went his way. But when the blade was sprung up, and brought forth fruit, then appeared the tares also (Matt. 13:24-26)

The above is a parable but every parable is told by Jesus to illustrate a legitimate truth. In this parable we learn about God's role and Satan's role in the lives of men. God has planted nothing but good seed among men – seed that was meant to keep them in health, prosperity, and holiness. However, man has an enemy and this enemy planted bad seed that led to all things that harm men and women.

In some debates I have engaged in concerning Satan's ability to come up with new evil designs that were never before in existence, people have criticized me for assigning to Satan a "creative ability". It is not that Satan can create "ex-nihilo" as God can, but he is able to distort and reengineer things God has designed for good and use them to evil ends. Just as man has been able to manipulate seed, Satan has that ability as well.

Do we believe that God has created mosquitoes that suck blood and spread sickness? Do we believe that God created the parasites that kill? Do we believe that He created rats to spread diseases? Did God create scorpions that sting and kill? Did He create snakes to bite and give lethal injections to men and other animals?

It could very well be true that God created these animals but He did not corrupt them with disease and death. The Bible tells us that Satan is the one who held the power of death (Heb. 2:14-15). That power has to be something more than just symbolic. It obviously has the ability to corrupt and distort God's good creation for evil purposes.

Death began to reign in the world due to sin (Rom. 5:12). This can only mean that before sin, scorpions did not sting people, rats did not spread disease, snakes did not bite and spread poison, and lions did not pounce and kill their prey. All of this violence is the result of the satanic distortion of God's wonderful creation.

Jesus' parable tells us that it is Satan, and not God, who is responsible for the bad among the good. God created everything God and Satan corrupted it. Satan has distorted God's creation and brought suffering upon it. The evil in creation is not God's work since He only gave us the "good seed."

September 9

Placing God in Control

*The prophet went to Ahab and said, "The Syrians think the Lord is a god of the hills and not of the valleys. **So he has promised to help you defeat their powerful army. Then you will know that <u>the Lord is in control</u>.**"* (1 Kings 20:28; Contemporary English Version)

A prophet came to Israel's king, Ahab, with a warning: *"Later, the prophet[e] went back and warned Ahab, 'Benhadad will attack you again next spring. Build up your troops and make sure you have some good plans.'"* (1 Kings 20:22). The prophet admonished King Ahab to "build up his troops" and "have good plans".

How, in this instance, did God "control" the situation? Did He cause the Syrian army to attack Israel? Did He defeat the Syrian army apart from any cooperation from Israel? The answer to both of these questions is "no". God took control of the situation when Israel did their part. They obeyed by building up their troops, making good plans and then fighting when the time was right.

To prove that the Lord did not fully control the outcome in the sense that everything that happened was according to his will, all we need to do is read the rest of the chapter. It was obviously God's will that King Benhadad also be killed as part of the outcome of this war. Instead we read about Ahab's disobedience to God by letting Benhadad go free (1 Kings 20-23-34). God sent a prophet to Ahab to bring this to his attention:

The man quickly tore the bandage off his face, and Ahab saw that he was one of the prophets. The prophet said, "The Lord told you to kill Benhadad, but you let him go. Now you will die in his place, and your people will die in place of his people." Ahab went back to Samaria, angry and depressed. (2 Kings 20:41-43; CEV)

This appears to be a repeat of King Saul's disobedience when he let King Agag live (1 Sam. 15:8-33). It appears that the old axiom is true: "The only thing we ever learn from history is that we never learn from history." The main point here is that God being in control means that He has the power and authority to act on our behalf as we cooperate with Him. But it does not mean that He is the cause of every event nor do things necessarily always turn out the way He wants them to. We can disobey Him as Ahab did and keep God's temporal plans from fully coming into fruition.

September 10

God's Predestined Plan Dependent on Our Decisions

And Samuel said to Saul, Thou hast done foolishly: thou hast not kept the commandment of the LORD thy God, which he commanded thee: **for <u>now</u> would the LORD have established thy kingdom upon Israel for ever. But <u>now</u> thy kingdom shall not continue:** *the LORD hath <u>sought</u> him a man after his own heart, and the LORD hath commanded him to be captain over his people, because thou hast not kept that which the LORD commanded thee* (1 Sam. 13:13, 14)

Saul's descendants could have ruled Israel forever if he had obeyed God. It is possible that the Messiah, Jesus our Lord, would have come through his family line. If Saul had been obedient you possibly may never have heard of the shepherd boy named David. Contrary to popular teaching, David was not always in the plan of God for being king and being in the Messiah's lineage.

This is what the Lord is telling Saul here. His life could have been different. Things could have been different for him. His descendants could have enjoyed the monarchy forever and had the privilege of being in the ancestry of the Messiah Himself. His decision to obey or disobey the Lord determined his destiny and the destiny of his descendants. I am sure that if Saul could go back and do it again, he would do things differently. The decision we make in our present demonstrates where we are at with our faith and walk with God. Our decisions can have an effect on generations to come.

Scriptures such as this one cannot be reconciled with some of the current teachings on predestination that we find in some circles. I believe in predestination. However I believe in it in the way that the Bible presents it and not the way presented in some theological traditions. God had a predestined plan for King Saul. Saul forfeited that plan by his decisions. God said the same thing about the Pharisees: *"But the Pharisees and the experts in the law rejected God's plan for themselves by refusing to be baptized by him"* (Luke 7:30; International Standard Version).

It is possible to reject and forfeit God's predestined plan (Isa. 30:15; Matt. 23:37, 38). We can change destinies by our lives and actions. No future is set in stone (but if it is, God has a very powerful stone eraser). God has placed quite a bit of responsibility in our hands concerning the future.

September 11

Does God Stir up Enemies Against Us?

*And **the LORD stirred up an adversary unto Solomon**, Hadad the Edomite: he was of the king's seed in Edom* (1 King 11:14).

No king had it better than Solomon. His father David suffered much before God finally established his monarchy. While David made his mistakes, his heart was truly after God and never did he seek to replace Him or have Him compete with idols.

Solomon, on the other hand, enjoyed God's love, protection and peace. God's promise to David concerning Solomon was, *"Behold, a son shall be born to thee, who shall be a man of rest; and I will give him rest from all his enemies round about: for his name shall be Solomon, and I will give peace and quietness unto Israel in his days"* (1 Chron. 22:9). Solomon's only requirement from God was. *"....to keep my statutes and my commandments, as thy father David did walk"* (1 Kings 3:14).

Sadly, Solomon's lust for foreign women made that difficult for him and he fell into idolatry. God became angry with Solomon because he let his foreign wives turn him towards this sin (1 Kings 11:9-10). In reaction, God withdrew the peace and protection He once gave Solomon. Church father Tertullian taught that Solomon's sin opened the door for Satan to stir up Hadad against him:

> From Christ, too, God's mercy did not depart, whereas on Solomon even God's anger alighted, after his luxury and idolatry. **For Satan stirred up an Edomite as an enemy against him**. Since, therefore, nothing of these things is compatible with Solomon, but only with Christ, the method of our interpretations will certainly be true; and the very issue of the facts shows that they were clearly predicted of Christ.[38]

Tertullian held to the truth that God is often said in the Old Testament to do the thing that Satan actually does (compare 2 Sam. 24:1 with 1 Chron. 21:1). This includes taking credit for Satan sending enemy armies against His people (compare Job 1:15, 17 with 2:3). This is the proper way to interpret such passages of Scripture.

---

[38] 11. Tertullian, **Against Marcion, 3:20**, http://www.newadvent.org/fathers/03123.htm (Last accessed: March 3, 2015)

September 12

Can We Limit God?

*How oft did they provoke him in the wilderness, and grieve him in the desert! Yea, they turned back and tempted God, and **limited the Holy One of Israel**. They remembered not his hand, nor the day when he delivered them from the enemy* (Psalm 78:40-42)

We are told that the Israelites forgot how God had delivered them from their enemy. A faulty memory is one of the greatest hindrances to faith. In verse 32 we read, *"For all this they sinned still, and believed not for his wondrous works."* Miracles do not always convince people. Unbelief is not due to a lack of miracles but rather to questioning the veracity of God's Word. *Unbelief is a sin* and it is responsible for our inability to receive from God: *"your sins have withholden good things from you"* (Jer. 5:25).

It is not God's will that good things are withheld from His people. On the contrary it is His will that we love Him, fear Him and obey Him so that we can receive good things (Josh. 23:14-16). The responsibility is on God's own people to receive the good things that the Lord promises (Deut. 6:1-3, 17, 18; 30:15, 19, 20). God longs that His people have a heart to obey Him so that He can bless them (Deut. 5:29). However, the sin of unbelief limits what God is able to do in our lives

The word "grieve" in this passage comes from the Hebrew word *atsab* which means "to hurt, pain, grieve, displease, vex, wrest" (studylight.org). The word "limited" is similar and it means, "to pain, wound, trouble, cause pain." God is a God of passions and feelings. One who loves people as tenderly as He does can also be deeply hurt by our attitude towards Him. When He has put forth so much effort to bless us and we still call Him a liar, how can He not be hurt? God is not a god of stoicism. He is truly pained and hurt by our unbelief.

Unbelief is the product of our "forgetting." If we are not receiving good things from God, we should not blame it on His "sovereign will" but on ourselves. The problem with unbelief is a "memory problem." People so easily forget how God has taken them through crisis after crisis and they easily forget what He has done when they are confronted with a new crisis. Let us learn to "count our blessings" and stop limiting God's hand in our lives.

September 13

Unbelief Keeps Us from God's Blessings (Part 1)

"Thou wilt say then unto me, Why doth he yet find fault? For who hath resisted his will?" (Rom. 9:19)

Sadly, there are some Christians who claim that because God is sovereign, He can break His promises. They would never phrase it this way but when we encounter circumstances that contradict what He has promised they will say that nothing happens on earth apart from God's will because no one can resist it. Quite often they will appeal to Romans 9:19 to support this idea. As pious as this may sound, it still makes God out to be a liar.

The truth is that people appeal to such passages to excuse their unbelief. Yet, these passages can be explained apart from a deterministic bias. Israel felt that they were entitled to God's mercy simply because they were the "chosen race." Paul was refuting them by explaining that it was God's sovereign prerogative to decide who would receive salvation and its blessings. It was God's right to set the stipulations for receiving them.

In response, the Israelites raised an objection, *"for who hath resisted his will?"* We must understand that this was not Paul's question. Paul was repeating an insincere question by his objectors that was meant to dispute all that he had been saying about God's reasons for choosing the Gentiles and rejecting national Israel as the sole recipients of salvation. Therefore, Paul was setting the stage to address the objections of the Israelites.

God's extension of mercy to some and His rejection of others has nothing to do with a mysterious sovereign decree. It is extended to *anyone* who asks and receives it by faith. Therefore God's rejection of Israel was based on their failure to meet His conditions:

> *Wherefore?* **Because they <u>sought it not</u> by faith, but as it were by the works of the law.** *For they stumbled at that stumblingstone; As it is written, Behold, I lay in Sion a stumblingstone and rock of offence: and whosoever believeth on him shall not be ashamed.* (Rom. 9:32-33)

The word "because" explains the reason why Israel was rejected. It was not due to the sovereign will of God but it was due to Israel's failure to seek God by faith. Unbelief keeps us from the blessings God longs to give.

September 14

Unbelief Keeps Us from God's Blessings (Part 2)

"Thou wilt say then unto me, Why doth he yet find fault? For who hath resisted his will?" (Rom. 9:19)

Yesterday we looked at this passage and we learned how some use it to excuse their unbelief in God's Word and claim that everything in their lives is due to the sovereign will of God. By misapplying the passage in Romans 9:19, many have passively accepted circumstances that are contrary to the Word and will of God for their lives. They offer no resistance to the works of the devil because Satan has twisted this passage to lead them to believe that God is the one doing bad things to them (Eph. 6:10-12; James 4:7; 1 Peter 5:8-9).

However, Romans 9 is teaching about why Israel had been rejected by God. Paul explains in the context that this was not due to God's sovereign will but, *"Well; **because of unbelief** they were broken off"* (Rom. 11:20). The inspired writer of Hebrews said, *"But **without faith it is impossible to please him**: for he that cometh to God must believe that he is, and that he is a rewarder of them that diligently **seek him**"* (Heb. 11:6). The problem with Israel or anyone else that does not receive God's blessings has nothing to do with a sovereign choice on God's part to withhold such blessings, but the failure of the seeker to approach Him in faith. It is simply impossible to please God without it. Faith is obedience in approaching God's throne of grace in His prescribed way.

The good news is that Israel can be "grafted in" again under one condition: *"And they also, if they abide not still in unbelief, shall be graffed in: for God is able to graff them in again"* (Rom. 11:23). *Unbelief,* not "sovereign decrees," hinders God's revealed will in the lives of people. Contrary to some of our popular theology, people are indeed able to resist God's will for their individual lives (Psalm 81:11; Proverbs 1:24-30; Isa. 30:15; Isa. 65:12; Isa. 66:3, 4; Jer. 19:5; Jer. 32:35; Mat. 23:37; Luke 7:30; John 5:40; Acts 7:51; Rom. 10:21; Heb. 10:29).

Therefore unbelief has a negative power, not because it makes God weak, but because He respects our free choices. God is not a rapist who forces His will on people. God will allow people to die and go to hell if they choose not to believe Him (John 3:16-18). He certainly does not want this, but He respects us enough to allow us to destroy ourselves (1 Tim. 2:4; 2 Pet. 3:9). To disbelieve God is equal to making Him a liar. Let God be true. Choose to believe that God's Word is true and He will make it true in our lives. Choose to believe that it is not true and then we'll never see it come true in our lives.

September 15

A Good God Protects us in Trouble

"The Lord is GOOD, a strong hold in the day of trouble; and he knoweth them that trust in him." (Nahum 1:7)

The main reason many do not experience God's goodness is because they have no true revelation of it. They have sat in church and heard people say that God is good. Yet, in the same church they will hear that God allows sickness, pain, and misery to come into our lives to prepare us for glory. They will hear that God took their little baby or their little child because He wanted a little flower in heaven.

People hear such nonsense in the church and wonder how God could truly be good. Everything that they hear about God in religious circles contradicts their understanding of good. We attach religious explanations to it such as "God works in mysterious ways" or "God knows what is best for us." Yet such explanations serve to do nothing more than confuse the listener.

God's goodness is seen in the fact that He protects those who trust Him in a time of trouble. He has never taught us to view Him as good because He somehow mysteriously inflicts trouble on His people. As one writer noted:

> God desires our good - good for all people. A ghastly idea crept into religion at some point. Folks viewed God as a deity marked by anger and moved by an appetite for appeasement. If not pampered, begged, and cajoled, this God, according to these people, either ignores individuals or inflicts them with diseases and other difficulties. Such a view of God leads to a faith filled with fear, worship laced with anxiety, and a religious life that must be carried as a heavy burden.[39]

Basically, what the writer is saying is that if one will read the Bible, they will understand that God's true intentions for mankind are for good things and not the misery that so many people face. If preachers would preach the Bible more often and Christians would learn to study the Bible for themselves instead of taking the word of the preacher or their denominational creed then most of us would begin to have a better concept concerning God's goodness.

---

[39] Gaddy, C. Welton **Why Bother With The Bible? Understanding the Book of Faith,** © 1998 Judson Press, Valley Forge, PA, p. 12

September 16

Do We Get all Blessings in the "Sweet By and By"?

*I had fainted, unless I had **believed** to see the goodness of the Lord in the <u>land of the living</u>.* (Psalm 27:13)

It was not in the land of the "sweet by and by" that David believed to see the goodness of the Lord. In heaven, you are no longer "living" (on the earth). All who you leave behind on the earth when you depart this life consider you to be "dead" where *this* life is concerned. The land of the living is here on the earth. This Psalm shows us why so many people fail and give up. They do not believe that they will see God's goodness in *this* lifetime.

However, David believed to see God's goodness in the land of the living and he did. If you and I will believe God for the same thing then we will get the same results. This false idea of only seeing God's blessings in the "sweet by and by" is in contrast to David's inspired Psalm because it says that we will both receive all blessings such as healing, prosperity, and complete victory when we either get to heaven or during the millennium when Jesus is physically ruling and reigning upon the earth for a thousand years.

Yet it breaks the heart of God to watch such loving and faithful children suffer needlessly because they are denied all that has been made available in this life as well as the life to come. They suffer because they do not expect, and even believe that it is a sin to expect, any reward on earth.

The great teacher on prayer, E. M. Bounds, wrote, "Trust is not a belief that God *can* bless, that he *will* bless, but that he *does* bless here and now."[40] The primary reason for failing to see God's goodness is due to a lack of faith. Faith can only go as far as one's knowledge of God's Word. If one does not believe that God's goodness is available for them NOW, they will not step out in bold faith and claim what is rightfully theirs.

Other passages make it clear that we can receive all that God has for us while we are still alive on the earth: *"Behold the righteous shall be recompensed **in the earth**: much more the wicked and the sinner"* (Prov. 11:31). That which you sow is what you will reap, whether it is good or bad. You and I can have the joy that our reaping of righteousness will be done upon the earth in this age.

---

[40] Bounds, Edwards M. **The Complete Works of E. M. Bounds on Prayer**, Copyright © 1990 by Baker Book House, Grand Rapids, MI 49516-6287, p. 26

September 17

Is "Free-Will" a Myth?

And the times of this ignorance God winked at; ***but now commandeth all men every where to repent****: Because he hath appointed a day, in the which he will judge the world in righteousness by that man whom he hath ordained; whereof he hath given assurance unto all men, in that he hath raised him from the dead.* (Acts 17:30, 31)

Some who hold to the doctrine of "Calvinism," a doctrine that teaches that God controls every event and every human action, has disputed the terms "free-will" and "free-agency". They refer to these truths as "myths". The claim is that since God sovereignly controls everything then there is no such thing as "freedom of the will."

Arthur W. Pink, in his book, *The Sovereignty of God*, disputes the term, *free agency* along with *free will*. Pink writes: "To argue that man is a free moral agent and the determiner of his own destiny, and that therefore he has the power to checkmate his Maker, is to strip God of the attribute of Omnipotence."

Calvinists believe in man's *responsibility*, but they deny his ability to repent and believe the gospel. Yet this could not be true in the light of today's devotional text. God is never unjust to command men to do something that they have no ability to do. The very fact that they will be judged is due to the fact that they could have repented but refused to do so (see Luke 7:30 and John 9:39-41).

It would be ridiculous for God to hold men responsible for something that they cannot do. That would be similar to beating a 9 year old child for not driving his mother to the store so that she can go shopping. A parent would deservedly go to jail for that. Why would God punish people for something that they cannot do? Oh how the doctrine of Calvinism maligns God's righteous and just character. Thankfully, the Bible teaches that God is different than the way that He is presented by Calvinism.

The Bible defines the freedom of man's will in the following passages: Gen. 4:6-8; Deut. 11:26-28; 30:19; Joshua 24:15, 22; Isa. 66:3; Jer. 3:22; Matt. 11:28; 19:17; 23:37; John 5:40; 7:17; Acts 17:30-31; 26:20; Rom. 2:14-15 (NCV); 6:16-17; Heb. 7:25; James 4:5-8; Rev. 3:20 and many others. Therefore man is free to choose for or against God. God is just because He gives man a will that is free and one that He does not interfere with.

September 18

Repentance and "Irresistible Grace"

*Him hath God exalted with his right hand to be a Prince and a Saviour, for to **give repentance to Israel**, and forgiveness of sins* (Acts 5:31)

*When they heard these things, they held their peace, and glorified God, saying, Then hath **God also to the Gentiles granted repentance** unto life* (Acts 11:18)

Calvinists do not believe that men can repent apart from some irresistible grace. They cite Acts 5:31. One Calvinist wrote, "All men everywhere are commanded to repent yet the Bible says repentance is something God grants." This is in line with the idea that God chooses only a select few for salvation and those selected will have the irresistible ability to turn to Him. Those not chosen for salvation have no ability to repent of their sins.

However, these Scriptures could not be in reference to an elect few. Acts 5:31 does *not* say that God gave repentance to *some* in Israel, or the *elect* in Israel. It says that He gave repentance to *Israel* - PERIOD. The same would have to be true of Acts 11:18. It does not say that God granted repentance to *some* Gentiles or even the *elect* among the Gentiles. It says that God granted repentance to *the Gentiles*.

Therefore, the only way to understand these Scriptures is in relation to the rest of the Bible. The Good News translation renders Acts 11:18, *"When they heard this, they stopped their criticism and praised God, saying, 'Then God has given to the Gentiles also the <u>opportunity</u> to repent and live!'"* In light of the fact that one must hear the gospel and is commanded to repent and believe it, each person is granted the *opportunity* to do so.

God granting repentance means that He made repentance possible. That he offered repentance to the world as a choice. The Bible teaches that God granted repentance to the Jews and that He also granted repentance to the Gentiles. If that meant that He actually controlled and affected their repentance then all Jews and all gentiles *would have repented*, because God granted it to *everyone*. That's why the verse is understood to mean God granted it *as an option*, which also allows it to line up with the multitude of verses calling us to choose, to open up, to receive, etc.

God is a good God and He is fair. He will never pre-select anyone to be damned. He gives opportunity for all men to repent and leaves them with the choice to do so or not to do so.

September 19

How Does God Restrain Us from Sinning?

And God said unto him in a dream, Yea, I know that thou didst this in the integrity of thy heart; for I also withheld thee from sinning against me: therefore suffered I thee not to touch her (Gen. 20:6)

In Gerar Abraham was afraid that he would be killed because Sarah was his wife. Therefore he lied and told King Abimelech that she was only his sister. Abimelech then took her. God visited Abimelech in a dream and told him that he was a dead man. But because Abimelech's heart was sincere, God *withheld* him from sinning.

The Calvinist, based on false ideas of God's sovereignty, assumes that this withholding (or restraining) is automatically infringing upon Abimelech's will in some mysterious way. Yet, such a view does not explain why God would have to warn Abimelech not to do something when He could have just used a marionette puppeteer method.

Withholding someone from doing something is not taking over their will. God's restraint on Abimelech is explained by the fact that He visited him in a dream and warned him not to sin. In relation to this incident, Thomas Jackson explains:

> On this subject there is a peculiarity in the phraseology of Holy Scripture, which has not always been duly considered; and a meaning has been attached to particular texts which they were never intended to convey. It has been justly observed by John Howe, an unquestionable authority in the case, that in the inspired volume "God is said to do whatsoever creatures do; whatsoever second or subordinate causes do, while He has them in His hand, or in His power, either to restrain or let loose their inclinations and natural tendencies as He pleaseth; though He do not prompt them to this or that thing." The judicious Hooker also observes, that God "is said to cast them asleep whom He maketh not vigilant; to harden them whom He softeneth not; and to take away that which it pleaseth Him not to bestow."[41]

God's restraint of Abimelech does not deny free-will. It does wondrously demonstrate His protection over Abraham and Sarah as well as how He protected Abimelech himself from sinning.

---

[41] Jackson, Thomas **The Providence of God, Viewed in the Light of Holy Scripture** (London: John Mason, 1862),p. 293

September 20

Does Regeneration Precede Faith?

*That whosoever **believeth** in him should not perish, but have eternal life. For God so loved the world, that he gave his only begotten Son, that whosoever **believeth** in him should not perish, but have everlasting life* (John 3:15, 16)

A Calvinist doctrine that attempts to deny the freedom of man's will and teach that God preselects individuals for salvation apart from their accepting it is the false teaching that a person is regenerated by the Holy Spirit *before* they believe and receive salvation. This *regeneration* supposedly gives the sinner not only grace to be regenerated, but the faith to believe the Gospel.

A leading proponent of this doctrine, R. C. Sproul says, "We do not believe in order to be born again; we are born again in order that we may believe" (Chosen By God, p. 73). Sadly, these theologians do not realize how they denigrate God's character. Furthermore, this doctrine is diametrically opposed to Scripture. Observe the following:

*He that **believeth** and is baptized **shall be saved;** but he that believeth not shall be damned.* (Mark 16:16)

*But these are written, that ye might believe that Jesus is the Christ, the Son of God; and that **believing ye might have life** through his name.* (John 20:31)

*And they said, **Believe** on the Lord Jesus Christ, and thou shalt be save, and thy house.* (Acts 16:31)

In light of the Scriptures, regeneration, or the new birth, cannot precede faith. That would mean then that if a person is regenerated BEFORE they believe, then they have LIFE before they believe. Therefore we do not get eternal life, the new birth, apart from believing FIRST. Since so many passages teach that we are saved and receive new life AFTER we believe, then it stands to reason that regeneration does not happen until one believes God.

Let us share the gospel with all because Jesus died for all and God is willing to save all (1 Tim. 2:4; 2 Pet. 3:9).

September 21

God's Protection of His Prophets

And Elijah answered and said unto them, If I be a man of God, let fire come down from heaven, and consume thee and thy fifty. And the fire of God came down from heaven, and consumed him and his fifty (2 Kings 1:12)

Many Christians who embrace ideas of extreme pacifism have trouble with passages such as the one above. I am very sympathetic to most pacifist theology and agree with the majority of their concepts. However, like all truths they can be taken to unbiblical extremes. Some believe that God never, ever uses force to protect His own. Yet, we find a case with Elijah in which God does just that.

It is not God's normal "modus operandi" to use His omnipotent power destructively. Most passages, as we have learned in our devotional studies, that appear to cite God as engaging in destructive behavior, can usually be explained on the basis of the "permission principle" in which God is said to do that which He merely allowed to happen through other agents. We know that quite often Satan's work is blamed on God. Once Satan destroyed Job's sheep with lightning and this was referred to as "the fire of God" just as it is with Elijah in the passage above.

However, in this case, *Elijah* used his God-given dominion (Gen. 1:26-28; Psalm 8:5-6) to call down fire upon an army of men who came to arrest him for his negative prophecy to King Ahaziah. Some pacifists have explained this from a "dispensational perspective" in which God only acted this way under the Old Testament but would never engage in such behavior under the New Testament. However, the book of Revelation refutes this idea as it talks about the two end time prophets that oppose the anti-Christ: *"And if any man will hurt them, fire proceedeth out of their mouth, and devoureth their enemies: and if any man will hurt them, he must in this manner be killed"* (Rev. 11:5).

God does not change from one dispensation to another. He has always been loving, kind and just. He has always been unwilling to hurt and destroy. But on rare occasions, He sometimes allows His prophets to use their delegated authority destructively when He cannot reach His enemies through peaceful means.

But one must keep in mind that Elijah was not being vindictive in calling down lightning upon this army. In this particular case, He was engaging in self-defense as led by God. God does occasionally allow destructive judgment to defend His prophets. But keep in mind also that God only permitted this because Elijah exercised His delegated authority in this manner (Matt. 18:18-20).

September 22

The Mission of Jesus

*But he turned, and rebuked them, and said, Ye know not what **manner of spirit ye are of**. For **the Son of man is not come to destroy men's lives**, but to save them. And they went to another village* (Luke 9:55-56)

Jesus was headed towards Jerusalem and sought to pass through a Samaritan village. His attempt was met with ill-treatment. James and John became indignant with this utter disrespect of their Master and requested that they call down fire upon the village as Elijah did with the army of men sent by King Ahaziah (2 Kings 1:10-12).

Jesus rebuked the attitude of these disciples for this suggestion. Jesus was not being critical of what was done through Elijah, nor was He insinuating that God acts differently under a different dispensation as so many have insinuated. Jesus was merely pointing out the fact that James and John were operating under a different attitude than Jesus and Elijah. Elijah's calling down fire was for the purpose of protecting Himself. James and John, on the other hand, simply wanted vengeance for the way that Jesus was mistreated.

Jesus also pointed out the fact that His disciples lost sight of the Lord's primary mission. His mission is not to kill, steal, and destroy. This is the work of the evil entity named Satan (John 10:10). Jesus' whole purpose for coming to the earth was to save men from the destruction that they too often bring upon themselves *"O Israel, thou hast destroyed thyself; but in me is thine help"* (Hosea 13:9).

When Jesus came to earth He never gave sickness, tempted anyone to sin, called down famine, or brought natural disasters. On the contrary Jesus healed the sick, fed the hungry, delivered people from sin, and averted natural disasters. Jesus exhibited nothing but total love.

Jesus made it clear that He is *not* the One who sends adversity upon men. Jesus is *not* the destroyer. He did not want His Name or that of His Father's associated with destruction. The one who usually brings down fire upon people and subsequently blames it on God is Satan (Job 1:12, 16). Jesus' desire is to deliver us from destruction. Too many people, including God's own people, seem to believe otherwise.

Let us take on the character of Christ. Instead of looking for destructive judgment on those who offend us, let us seek ways to save them from destruction. In this we are being children of our Father in Heaven. To act any other way is to be influenced by a spirit other than the Holy Spirit.

God is a God of TRUTH

He is the Rock, his work is perfect: for all his ways are judgment: ***a God of truth and <u>without</u> iniquity,*** *just and right is he* (Deut. 32:4)

A God of truth can never have anything to do with iniquity, and lying is iniquity (Psalm 36:3; Isa. 59:3-4; Jer. 9:5; Hos. 10:13; Zeph. 3:13). If God had any ability to lie then truth could not be a part of His essential nature (1 John 2:21). The fact that He is a God of Truth makes it *impossible* for Him to lie (Heb. 6:18-19). He simply cannot do it. He is completely without iniquity. In contrast, Satan's very nature is one in which lying and deceit is intrinsic to it (John 8:44).

One's character determines their moral ability. Since truth is a vital part of God's nature, He cannot lie (Titus 1:1-2). Since there is no truth in Satan he cannot do anything but lie. One can only lie when the truth is not in them and is not a part of their nature (1 John 1:8; 2:4). Always remember that anything contradicting God's Word is a satanic lie. It is impossible for God to lie because He is a God of truth and it is impossible for Satan to tell the truth because the truth is not in him. God *is* truth and Satan *is* a liar.

This is why any promise or command given by God can be absolutely and implicitly trusted. The fact that God is a God of Truth helps us to understand what Paul meant when he wrote by the inspiration of God that faith comes by hearing, and hearing by God's Word (Rom. 10:17). It is by hearing the word of truth from the God of truth that faith is developed (Eph. 1:13). If we believe that God's Word is true, firm, reliable, beyond doubt, and irrefutable, then we would never worry. Instead His Word would lead us to commit all of our problems into His hands (Psalm 37:5; 55:22; 1 Pet. 5:7).

In order to have "faith" in someone or to "trust" in someone it is essential that we believe that they are completely honest and that they are always telling the truth. That is why the Christian that is going to walk in faith and claim God's promises must be convinced that everything that God says about them are true. In Psalm 31:5 the Psalmist writes, *"Into thine hand I commit my spirit: thou hast redeemed me, O LORD God of truth."* This statement is one of confidence and affirmation. It is a practical lesson in how we are to affirm all of God's promises.

September 24

Is God a Deceiver?

*And if the prophet be deceived when he hath spoken a thing, **I the LORD have deceived that prophet,** and I will stretch out my hand upon him, and will destroy him from the midst of my people Israel. And they shall bear the punishment of their iniquity: the punishment of the prophet shall be even as the punishment of him that seeketh unto him* (Ezek. 14:9-10)

Yesterday we learned that God is a God of truth. Yet here we find Him saying that He is personally involved in deceiving prophets. How can we trust Him if He has the ability to actively engage in deception?

The King James Version rendering of this passage leads us to believe told that God actually deceived the prophet, and the prophet in turn deceived the people. God then threatens to destroy the prophet for this deception. Is God so sadistic as to deceive people and then punish them for the deception that He brought on them? In his *Emphasized Bible*, Rotherham points out that it is the prophet that is allowing himself to be deceived:

*Yea the prophet himself **when he suffereth himself to be deceived,** and speaketh a word, Yahweh have suffered that prophet to be deceived, Then will I stretch forth my hand against him, and destroy him out of the midst of my people. Israel:*

If we were to read passages such as Ezekiel 14:9 apart from the Biblical permission principle, they would appear to contradict other portions of Scripture. Yet we know that Scripture *never* contradicts itself. God does not send false prophets to people and neither does he command them to deceive anyone. On the contrary, God always tries to protect His people from deception by making His truth known. However, if people persist in believing lies, after a time God will be left with no choice but to *give them up* to the deception. While His giving up people to their own sin is often seen as Him being the author of the sin, our studies have shown us that this cannot be the case. Therefore God can be trusted when we are sincerely seeking Him.

How Does the God of Truth "Send" Strong Delusions?

*....ye know **what withholdeth** that he might be revealed in his time. For the mystery of iniquity doth already work: only **he who now letteth will let, until he be taken out of the way.** And then shall that Wicked be revealed, whom the Lord shall consume with the spirit of his mouth, and shall destroy with the brightness of his coming: Even him, whose coming is after **the working of Satan** with all power and signs and **lying wonders** (2 Thess. 2:6-9)*

Many Bible critics latch on to the statement in 2 Thess. 2:11 which says, *"And **for this cause** God shall **send them strong delusion,** that they should believe a lie"* They question whether God can truly be a God of truth if He is involve in sending deceptions. Others who hold stringent views of sovereignty use this to prove their thesis that God ordains sin. But as we can see, both are proven wrong by the context.

How does the God of Truth send strong delusions? By no longer restraining or holding back the devil, the one who will actually bring delusion. Men exercise their free will and refuse God's truth and salvation. God protects men from satanic delusion, but when His love is continually rejected, He honor the wishes of rebellious men and allow them to have what they want (Rom. 1:24-28). Findlay notesthat this delusion, "comes about by what we now call a natural law." He further writes:

> In each case the result is inevitable, and comes about by what we now call a natural law. That persistent rejection of truth destroys the sense of truth and results in fatal error, is an ethical principle and a fact of experience as certain as any in the world. Now he who believes in God as the Moral Ruler of the Universe, knows that its laws are the expression of His will."[42]

As Edward Bird wisely put it, "For, pray take notice, God is said in Scripture to *send* what he *can* (but *doth not*) hinder from being *sent*."[43] God wants to protect men from evil, but due to free-will, He must allow them to have what they want, even if it is a delusion. The God of truth is only said to send what He merely permitted.

---

[42] Findlay, George Gillanders (editor) **The Epistles to the Thessalonians** (Cambridge: University Press, 1904), p. 152

[43] Bird, Edward **Fate and Destiny Inconsistent with Christianity or the Horrid Decree of Absolute and Unconditional Election and Reprobation Fully Detected** (London: Charles Rivington, 1726), p. 14

September 26

Homosexuality is Self-Destructive Behavior

For this reason God gave them over and abandoned them to vile affections and degrading passions. For their women exchanged their natural function for an unnatural and abnormal one, And the men also turned from natural relations with women and were set ablaze (burning out, consumed) with lust for one another--men committing shameful acts with men and suffering in their own bodies and personalities the inevitable consequences and penalty of their wrong-doing and going astray, which was [their] fitting retribution (Rom. 1:26-27; Amplified Bible)

In our time homosexuality has become so ingrained in our society that most states have made it legal for same-sex couples to marry and adopt children. Hollywood promotes this lie by airing dramas and sitcoms where families are same-sex couples. One can't even watch a cooking channel or a classic movie channel without having this sin promoted as normal.

Regardless of what the world tells us, homosexuality is not normal behavior and God is pained over how society has so easily given in to it. More and more we see Him beginning to lift the restraints. God is not the author of AIDS and other sicknesses, but when He abandons the sinner then these sicknesses will have their way. As Theodore H. Epp wrote:

"Men gave God up that they might indulge their own passions. So God gave them over to their vile and unnatural affections. Homosexuality is contrary to nature, and those who practice it are bound to suffer the consequences. Those people spoken of in Romans 1 paid for their own sins in the sense of reaping what they sowed."[44]

Once God lifts the restraints and abandons us as we have forced Him to then other destructive forces move in and take over. Epp wrote, "When God gives a person over to a reprobate mind (1:28), his mind is like an abandoned building which soon becomes the home of rats and other rodents."[45] Jesus Himself said almost as much concerning how demons operate (Matt. 12:43-45; Luke 11:23-26). Homosexuality opens the door for Satan to destroy. This is not God's desire for any man or woman.

---

[44] Epp, Theodore **How God Makes Bad Men Good: Studies in Romans** (Lincoln, NE: Back to the Bible, 1978), p. 35

[45] Ibid.

Homosexuality in Light of the Warfare between God and Satan

If a man also lie with mankind, as he lieth with a woman, both of them have committed an abomination: they shall surely be put to death; their blood shall be upon them.....
Ye shall therefore keep all my statutes, and all my judgments, and do them: <u>that the land</u>, whither I bring you to dwell therein, spue you not out (Leviticus 20:13, 22)

We must come to an understanding of the homosexual issue in the light of the ongoing warfare between the kingdom of light and the kingdom of darkness and evil. We cannot do this by allowing ourselves to be influenced by the world's acceptance of this lifestyle. Sadly even so-called Bible believing churches have begun to accept this lie.

We must look at it strictly from a Biblical viewpoint. The Bible will more than likely be in contrast with political correctness, popular opinion, and even so-called scientific data. Homosexuality is a serious issue that cannot be ignored and it is the reason that our own nation is in the turmoil that it is presently experiencing – and how it will get worse unless we repent.

God is indeed a God of love and tells us things for our own good rather than to simply assert His authority and get His way. This is the lying picture that Satan paints concerning God so that we will see nothing intrinsically wrong with sin except for the false idea that it makes God mad (Gen. 3:1-5).

Satan hides the fact that sin has consequences that God is actually trying to protect us from (Rom. 6:23). God is constantly trying to work against Satan for man's good but He needs our cooperation. If we refuse this cooperation then we as individuals or we as a nation will suffer the devastating consequences that come with God's abandonment. The very land that we live on will begin to vomit us out through sickness and natural disasters. God cannot be blamed for our reaping what we sow.

Satan's intent for man is his destruction, thus he spreads his delusions about the normality of homosexuality. The more he inserts these false ideas and convinces people that it is true, the more it is accepted and the stronger foothold he has. The church must pray, witness, and vote for moral leaders. Most of all, we must boldly proclaim the truth. Souls that God loves are at stake.

September 28

Does God Discipline Us by Hurting Us?

I will be his father, and he shall be my son. If he commit iniquity, I will chasten him with the rod of men, and with the stripes of the children of men: **But my mercy shall not depart away from him, as I took it from Saul,** *whom I put away before thee* (2 Sam. 7:14-15)

God can certainly teach us lessons from bad things. Years ago when my son was small and we had something baking in the oven we specifically told him not to touch the stove. Sadly, my son disobeyed our clear instructions. He touched the stove, burned his hand, and began crying in pain. I had to go our next door neighbor and borrow some medicine to relieve his pain. I was then able to teach him why he needed to listen to my instructions. I never had that problem with my son touching a hot stove since.

Please keep in mind that I did not put his hand on that oven nor did I want him to get burned. But when it was done, I used it to teach him some things. The God of Scripture most certainly chastens His children. However, if I disciplined my children by rigging their car to ensure that they get into an accident then most people would rightfully question my parenting skills.

On the other hand, if my children (speaking primarily of adult children) were to continue to persist in disobeying me and did things that I warned them against, then part of my discipline after some time is to allow them to suffer some of the consequences of their own rebellion. After they wake up and see what their disobedience has cost them (and me), then I do the sacrificial work of repairing the damage and rescuing them from their foolish mistakes.

Based on Scripture, this is often the way that God disciplines. In our devotional passage, God says that He will discipline David by allowing him to suffer the rod of men. However, He would not completely remove His protection from David as He did Saul. In this passage we can see the full meaning of what the Scripture meant when it says, *"But the Spirit of the Lord departed from Saul, and an evil spirit from the Lord troubled him"* (1 Sam. 16:14). God's mercy had completely departed from Saul because Saul never learned from his chastening. Therefore, he became a victim of Satan.

On the other hand, David's heart was right even though he made mistakes. Therefore, God chastened him by allowing him to reap some of the consequences of his sin, but God never took His mercy from David. Neither did God personally inflict pain on David or Saul.

276

September 29

God Loves those who He Chastens

*And ye have forgotten the exhortation which speaketh unto you as unto children, My son, despise not thou the chastening of the Lord, nor faint **when thou art rebuked of him**: For whom the Lord loveth he chasteneth, and scourgeth every son whom he receiveth* (Hebrew 12:5-6)

Many people have mistakenly claimed that God chastens us by personally inflicting upon us sickness, disease, and tragedy. It is true that God is said to chasten those in 1 Cor. 11:28-32 who irreverently took communion, however, this is not God personally inflicting consequences but rather allowing us to suffer the consequences that we bring on ourselves (see our June 21 devotional for a more detailed explanation).

God's primary method of chastening is through His *rebuke*. In other words, God primarily chastens *through His Word*. It is by the Word that we are given the needed correction that sets us on the straight and narrow path:

All scripture is given by inspiration of God, and is profitable for doctrine, for reproof, for correction, for instruction in righteousness (2 Tim. 3:16)

God gave us His Word to teach us, to reprove us, correct us, and instruct us. It is only when we fail to learn through the Word and when we continue to rebel against it is when we suffer so many of life's negative circumstances.

Blessed is the man whom thou chastenest, O Lord, and teachest him out of thy law; That thou mayest give him rest from the days of adversity, until the pit be digged for the wicked (Psalm 94:12-13)

Notice that God's way of chastening is to teach us out of His law—His Word. It is only those who persist in wickedness who have a pit dug for them. Solomon said, *"The law of the wise is a fountain of life, to depart from the snares of death"* (Prov. 13:14). Therefore, God does not chasten us by inflicting us with sickness and other difficulties. He chastens us via His Word. It is by ignoring His Word and remaining in rebellion that we then learn by the negative circumstances that we automatically reap.

Does God Have a Double Standard?

Be ye therefore perfect, even as your Father which is in heaven is perfect. (Matt. 5:48)

But as he which hath called you is holy, so be ye holy in all manner of conversation; Because it is written, Be ye holy; for I am holy (1 Pet. 1:15-16)

Many who advocate a Calvinistic view of God's sovereignty tell us that God is not subject to any of the laws that He created. We are told that He has no need to keep promises and that simply because He has established standards of righteousness for His creature does not mean that He is under any obligation to abide by them. Hence, God is able to excuse the reprehensible acts that He is often accused of under the guise of being "sovereign."

We are told that we must accept that He is a God of righteousness and is just no matter what He does. Regardless of what God supposedly does, even if it seems wicked to us, it is for a purpose and is righteous and just, even if we don't "get" it. This is all supposed to be a part of our exercising faith in His sovereignty. We are supposed to "trust" that the wickedness that was done is for a righteous purpose and we must tolerate it.

If I beat and bludgeon my children, one would rightfully have me arrested. But if God does it then to the Calvinistic sovereign doctrinaire this is "right" because, supposedly, everything He does is right even if it is *wrong*. This leaves us without any real standard of right and wrong when it comes to God. However, if this is true then it makes the righteousness and holiness of God into a FARCE.

Nevertheless, God has set a certain standard that He expects us to abide by. We are told by Jesus and His personally trained disciple Peter that we are to emulate God in His perfection and holiness. If God has a double-standard concerning holiness and righteousness then we have nothing by which to measure and the above passages are meaningless. However, based on the passages above, God does not give one standard for His creatures without being an example of how that standard is walked out.

When Jesus was on earth He railed against the Pharisees for their placing burdens on the masses and never lifting a finger to help them. He also presented a picture of God so unlike the one that the Jewish leaders presented that people were drawn to Christ's loving Father. Jesus is again telling us to put away this false deity of double-standards and embrace the God who is no law-breaker, but is righteousness in every way that we picture Him to be.

October 1

Does God Put Sickness in People's Houses?

*And the Lord spake unto Moses and unto Aaron, saying, When ye be come into the land of Canaan, which I give to you for a possession, and **I put the plague of leprosy in a house** of the land of your possession....* (Lev. 14:33-34)

God is often mischaracterized as the inflictor of sickness and disease. There is no shortage of Bible passages that could make a case for God being a sickness-sender when they are not interpreted properly. In Leviticus 14:34 God tells Moses and Aaron that He could possibly *put* a plague of leprosy on someone's house in Canaan.

"Put" is from the Hebrew word "Nathan". In his Expository Dictionary of Bible Words, Stephen D. Renn, says that *nathan* (or *natan*) in certain Old Testament passages "....expresses the meaning 'to let, allow,' in negative contexts of refusing to give permission."[46] Therefore, the passage could easily read, *"....and I **allow** the plague of leprosy in a house of the land of your possession."* One Bible expositor believed that this passage should be viewed in light of the common Hebrew idiom in which God is said to do what He permitted:

> In what this plague consisted is not known; see ch. xiii. 2. note. From this verse it has been inferred that the leprosy was something supernatural; but in the Hebrew idiom God is often said to do what he merely permits to be done.[47]

When this and other passages are read in the light of these linguistic truths then we can see that God is not the actual inflictor of sickness. Sickness is the result of the devil's work (Job 2:7; Luke 13:16; Acts 10:38). God is the protector from sickness and the healer of the sick. God is only said to inflict sickness by permission, usually by turning a rebellious person over to Satan (1 Cor. 5:5). However, He is not the actual direct inflictor of sickness. Don't blame God for sickness but trust Him to heal you.

---

[46] Renn, Stephen D. **Expository Dictionary of Bible Words: Word Studies for Key English Bible Words Based on the Hebrew And Greek Texts** (Hendrickson Publishers, 2005), p. 26

[47] Holden, George **The Christian Expositor; or, Practical Guide to the Study of the Old Testament** (London: J. G. and F. Rivington, 1834), p. 139

279

October 2

Satanic DNA Manipulation and the Roots of Evil

There were giants in the earth in those days; and also after that, when the sons of God came in unto the daughters of men, and they bare children to them, the same became mighty men which were of old, men of renown. And GOD saw that the wickedness of man was great in the earth, and that every imagination of the thoughts of his heart was only evil continually (Gen. 6:4-5)

If we understand that the "sons of God" here are in reference to the fallen angels who rebelled against God then we can begin to understand how DNA sequences have been corrupted and how evil has been bred into the earth.

Some people believe that the "sons of God" referred to in this passage is in reference to the sons of Seth while the "daughters of men" are in reference to Cain's female descendants. Yet we are told that this union produced giants (Hebrew: Nephilim). It is rather silly to believe that godly men marrying ungodly women can produce physical giants.

The only reasonable explanation for the giants would have to be that they were half-breeds (a mixture of angels and men). Furthermore, the phrase "sons of God" is always a reference to angels in the Old Testament (Job 1:6; 2:1; 38:7; Dan 3:25). Some of the apocryphal literature such as the book of Enoch concurs with this understanding and also describes the evil that came as a result:

> And when the angels, the sons of heaven, beheld them, they became enamoured of them, saying to each other, Come, let us select for ourselves wives from the progeny of men, and let us beget children.... And the women conceiving brought forth giants, Whose stature was each three hundred cubits. These devoured all which the labor of men produced; until it became impossible to feed them; When they turned themselves against men, in order to devour them; And began to injure birds, beasts, reptiles, and fishes, to eat their flesh one after another, and to drink their blood (Enoch 7:2, 11-14)

Here we see how satanic fallen angels distorted God's original plan, corrupted human DNA, and unleashed wickedness on the earth. Is there not a possibility that Satanic corruption of God's creation also results in disease carrying rats, animal violence, and other such wickedness? God certainly could not have created things this way though the sacrifice of Christ will redeem the whole creation.

October 3

Fallen Angels who Kept Not their First Estate

And the angels which kept not their first estate, but left their own habitation, he hath reserved in everlasting chains under darkness unto the judgment of the great day (Jude 6)

Jude wrote inspired Scripture. Within his Holy Spirit inspired epistle Jude quotes from the book of Enoch in verse 14 and 15. Jude tells us that there is a certain segment of angels that are being punished because they didn't keep their first estate. What could this mean? This means that they left the assignment given to them by God and began to corrupt His creation, to include teaching men evil. Justin Martyr, one of the earliest church fathers, explains:

> God, when He had made the whole world, and subjected things earthly to man, and arranged the heavenly elements for the increase of fruits and rotation of the seasons, and appointed this divine law— for these things also He evidently made for man— committed the care of men and of all things under heaven to angels whom He appointed over them. But the angels transgressed this appointment, and were captivated by love of women, and begot children who are those that are called demons; and besides, they afterwards subdued the human race to themselves, partly by magical writings, and partly by fears and the punishments they occasioned, and partly by teaching them to offer sacrifices, and incense, and libations, of which things they stood in need after they were enslaved by lustful passions; and among men they sowed murders, wars, adulteries, intemperate deeds, and all wickedness (Justin Martyr, *The Second Apology*, Chapter 5)

Church father Athenagoras also wrote about this angelic corruption: "For this is the office of the angels—to exercise providence for God over the things created and ordered by Him ....these fell into impure love of virgins, and were subjugated by the flesh, and he became negligent and wicked in the management of the things entrusted to him. Of these lovers of virgins, therefore, were begotten those who are called giants" (Athenagoras, *A Plea for the Christians*, Chapter 24).

This is what is meant by these angels having kept not their first estate—their first place appointed them by God. They then brought more rebellion and corruption upon the earth through half-breed children and satanic teachings. Evil was spread through them, and God chained them in order to protect man from further destruction by them.

October 4

The Disorder in this World is against God's Purposes

*At one time you did those wrong things, just like the people around you. You obeyed **the ruler who has the power over things in the air**. That ruler is the spirit who is working now in the people who do not obey God* (Eph. 2:2; Worldwide English New Testament)

The Bible in Basic English renders the latter part of Eph. 2:2, *"....the spirit who is now working in those who go against the purpose of God."* Satan uses his usurped power over the air to work against the purposes of God. He has deceived mankind into helping him to destroy the earth through sin and selfishness.

All of the so-called "natural evil" (hurricanes, tornadoes, volcano eruptions, earthquakes, and other disasters) are the workings of the one who has temporary authority over this world and its atmosphere. As William Matson notes:

> We have seen that Satan was the cause of the sin that is in the world. But sorrow and suffering are the consequence of sin, as are all the disorders of Nature. They are no part of the original plan and purpose. Search creation through, and you will find every creature and every part and organ of the creature made to subserve the purposes of use and happiness. You cannot find in the whole expanse of creation one being or part or organ or atom, even, that was created for the sole purpose of giving pain or producing sorrow. There are pain and sorrow in abundance, but nothing was ever created for the purpose of producing suffering. These, then, are the proofs of disorder,—a perversion, a distorting of what was made with some benevolent design. Public calamities are not the order of the universe, but its disorder.[48]

Upon completion of the earth, God declared that everything was *good* (Gen. 1:31). There was no chance of the earth experiencing the disorders that it now suffers before man fell and yielded it to Satan. Satan is now the one who controls the atmosphere and brings about evil. Let us stop referring to these "disorders" as "acts of God." Let us instead run to God for protection when these disorders occur.

---

[48] Matson, William A. **The Adversary, His Person, Power, and Purpose: A Study in Satanology** (New York: E.S. Gorham, 1902), p

October 5

Why God Smote Uzzah

And the anger of the LORD was kindled against Uzza, and he smote him, because he put his hand to the ark: and there he died before God (1 Chron. 13:10)

Uzzah seemed sincere in trying to keep the Ark from falling off of the ox cart. Yet, in his sincerity God smites and kills him. This looks more like the behavior of a cold dictator rather than a loving God.

In 1799, President George Washington woke up at 2 a.m. with a sore throat and breathing difficulties. He later called for medical assistance. He was unable to swallow any medicine so he ordered his doctor to perform a procedure called "bloodletting" in which they extracted blood from the body. They believed that this cured ailments. When Washington felt that they had not extracted enough he encouraged them to extract more. After extracting 40 percent of his blood, Washington died that evening.

Medical professionals today tell us that to extract that much blood from a person's body will kill them. Though medical knowledge was not as advanced as it is today, Washington did have his Bible which tells us, *"For the life of the flesh is in the blood"* (Lev. 17:11). It was the ignorance of this truth that led Washington to have the very life of his flesh drained to a large extent and kill him. David also discovered that this was the case concerning Uzzah: *"And the children of the Levites bare the ark of God upon their shoulders with the staves thereon, as Moses commanded **according to the word of the LORD**"* (1 Chron. 15:15).

The instructions for how to carry the ark were available all this time (Ex. 25:14-15; 37:3-5; Num. 7:9). God had already warned more than once that death would result in someone touching the holy things (Num. 4:19-20; Lev. 16:2). This is the specific reason for God having them *carry* the Ark in a prescribed way:

> *And when Aaron and his sons have made an end of covering the sanctuary, and all the vessels of the sanctuary, as the camp is to set forward; after that, the sons of Kohath shall come to bear it: but **they shall not touch any holy thing, lest they die*** (Num. 4:15)

It is a lack of knowledge that destroys God's people (Hosea 4:6). God did not want anyone to die so He gave specific instructions. However, ignorance killed Uzzah just as it is doing to so many of God's people today. God cannot be blamed for our ignorance when He has given us His clear Word that instructs us.

October 6

How God Smote Uzzah

*And when they came to Nachon's threshingfloor, Uzzah put forth his hand to the ark of God, and took hold of it; for the oxen shook it. And the **anger of the LORD** was kindled against Uzzah; and God **smote** him there for his error; and there he died by the ark of God* (2 Sam. 6:6-7)

Some read the smiting of Uzzah with the idea that God was being cold and vindictive. After all, Uzzah was trying to keep the ark from falling to the ground. However, as we learned yesterday, death was automatic for anyone who touched God's holy things.

So how did God smite Uzzah? Nothing within the context of the passage itself tells us the *how* of God's smiting. However, we have other Bible passages that explain exactly how God expresses His anger and how He smites. For example, the Bible often tells us the "anger of the Lord" is exercised by God removing His presence (departing) and "delivering" the objects of His anger into the hands of their enemies (Num. 12:9; Josh. 7:1-7; Judges 2:14; 2:20-23; 3:8; 2 Sam. 24:1/1 Chron. 21:1; 2 Kings 13:3; 24:19-20; 2 Chron. 25:15-20; Jer. 25:37-38; 52:3; Zeph. 2:1-4). He is also said to *smite* in this exact same way (Exodus 12:12, 23, 27, 29; Judges 20:28, 35, 48; 1 Sam. 4:2-3; 1 Kings 14:15-16; 2 Chron. 13:15-16; Isa. 53:4-5; 57:17; Jer. 14:19; 43:11; Hosea 9:15-17). In Psalm 78 we read:

*He **made a way to his anger**; he spared not their soul from death, but **gave their life over to the pestilence**; And **smote** all the firstborn in Egypt; the chief of their strength in the tabernacles of Ham* (Psalm 78:50-51)

God's *usual* way of expressing His anger and *smiting* sinners is by *giving them over* to the natural or supernatural consequences of their choices. In other words, God is often said to do the thing which He allows or permits to happen to others. Some possibilities concerning Uzzah is that the ark fell on him and crushed him, he suddenly fell sick and died, or any other number of things may have happened to him. The context itself does not say so we can only guess.

God is not looking to destroy us but is trying to protect us from destruction. This is why He gives us His Word. But we must *know* and be obedient to the Word. It is our ignorance of God's Word that destroys us as it was in the case of Uzzah. Therefore, know God's Word and receive His favor, presence, and protection.

October 7

Satan is behind all Evil on the Earth

Now there was a day when the sons of God came to present themselves before the Lord, and Satan came also among them. And the Lord said unto Satan, Whence comest thou? Then Satan answered the Lord, and said, From going to and fro in the earth, and from walking up and down in it (Job 1:6-7)

Due to false ideas about God's sovereignty many believe that all that happens in the world is due to some purpose that God has. This includes every evil and tragic event as well as every good one. Sadly enough, Job is often erroneously used to prove this. Yet a much more careful reading of Job teaches directly against this idea.

Satan, of his own initiative, and with no direction from God, is roaming the earth. If Satan was doing this by God's direction then the Lord would not have had to ask him the question concerning his whereabouts. Peter says that Satan *"....walketh about, seeking whom he may devour"* (1 Pet. 5:8a). Therefore, Job is telling us that Satan is the source of evil. J. Sidlow Baxter writes:

> ....we see from this passage that Satan is behind all the evils that curse the earth. In reply to the question, "Whence comest thou?" he says: "From going to and fro in the earth...." It seems clear that Satan has a special activity towards this earth. Genesis attributes the origin of sin in humanity to him, and the Scriptures make it progressively plainer that he is largely behind the evils that afflict our race. Satan's words: "going to and fro" and "walking up and down" indicate his restless and intermittent activity. His sinister genius is ever erupting malevolent strategems.[49]

Baxter adds, "We never get very far in dealing with social problems or in preaching or in praying until we realise that behind the world's evils is the energising and organising mind of a personal devil." Until this truth is understood, God will continue to be falsely blamed for the world's problems and progress will never be made from the Christian standpoint.

---

[49] Baxter, J. Sidlow **Explore the Book** (Nashville, TN: Zondervan, 1960), p. 38

October 8

Did God Instigate Satan's Attacks on Job

*And Jehovah said to Satan, **Have you set your heart against My servant Job,** because there is none like him in the earth, a perfect and upright man, one who fears God and turns away from evil?* (Job 1:8; Modern King James)

The classic KJV renders this passage, *"Hast thou considered my servant Job"*. This rendering, when not fully studied, has led people to the conclusion that God was bringing Job to Satan's attention. The usual teaching is that God needed to bring some humility to Job and so He decided to trick Satan into attacking him, thus fulfilling some secret plan of God's. Does God need Satan to tragically destroy the life of one of His choice servants in order to help him become more humble?

G. Campbell Morgan says, "'Considered' is a very strong word. It means, Hast thou been watching him? Hast thou been examining him? Hast thou been going round and round the citadel of this man's soul, trying to find some way to break in?"[50]

God was not attempting to bring Job to Satan's attention. On the contrary, God was exposing Satan's nefarious desire to destroy Job. Hence why I believe that the Modern King James renders the passage correctly when it says, *"Have you set your heart **against** My servant Job?"* J. Sidlow Baxter writes:

> ....we see here that even the dark mind of Satan is an open book to God. It might sound at first as though God's words ....were a provocation or incitement to Satan. God knew what was already there in that evil-designing mind, just as he knew all of Satan's goings to and fro before ever he asked, "Whence comest thou?" The questions are asked, not because God does not know but to compel confession on the part of Satan.[51]

The context states that Satan had been targeting Job all along. Immediately after God asks the question Satan responds with false accusations. God does not incite Satan against anyone. Instead He attempts to vindicate His children from the attacks of the accuser.

---

[50] Campbell, Morgan G **The Answers of Jesus to Job** (Fleming H. Revelll, 1935), p. 18

[51] Baxter, J. Sidlow **Baxter's Explore the Book** (Nashville, TN: Zondervan, 1986)

October 9

The Omnipotence of God

Is any thing too hard for the Lord? At the time appointed I will return unto thee, according to the time of life, and Sarah shall have a son (Gen. 18:14)

"Omnipotence" is a theological term that means that God is unlimited in power. The Bible teaches this truth though it does not necessarily use this word. However, the fact that God is unlimited in power means different things to different people.

Some theologians promote this truth but add to it the false idea that God controls everything that happens. To them, if anything in the universe is out of God's control and if He is not the first cause of the event then He cannot be sovereign or omnipotent. Omnipotence in this scenario means that God has a large ego and likes to flex His muscles. Therefore even evil things are supposedly His doing.

Another group of theologians have been distraught with the way that the aforementioned theologians have portrayed God's omnipotence so they have decided to deny His omnipotence altogether. In order to vindicate God from being charged with evil, their solution is to deny His omnipotence. Therefore, in this scenario, God is doing the best that He can, but is not able to do much because He does not have all power.

Either we have a God who uses His great power as a dictator to ensure that what He wants is done or we have a powerless God who is helpless. I find both concepts to be frightening. Perhaps when theologians stop attempting to define God intellectually and begin to embrace what God has revealed about Himself in Scripture then there would be much less confusion on the topic.

Power can be used to help or destroy. A strong young man can use his power to mug and hurt, and even possibly kill an old lady in order to get her money, or, he can use his power to help her cross the street and get her home safely. Also, the little old lady can reject the offer of his power, tell him to go away, walk by herself, and get mugged by someone who had less power than the one who offered his protection.

When God made the statement to Abraham He was not bragging about how powerful He is. He was attempting to build Abraham's faith in the possibility that He can give them a child in their old age. Whenever God makes statements about His unlimited power, it is not because He needs His ego swelled. He wants us to have confidence that He can accomplish on our behalf what we need. However, we must allow Him to use this power on our behalf because He respects our choices.

October 10

God's Power and God's Promises

He staggered not at the promise of God through unbelief;
but was strong in faith, giving glory to God; And being
*fully persuaded that, **what he had promised, he was able***
also to perform (Romans 4:20-21)

As we stated yesterday, there are some theologians who believe that God is all powerful but claim that He uses this power in a manipulative way, bringing about all circumstances that are both good and evil. Others, in an extreme reaction to such malignant teachings deny God any power at all. If God uses His power to bring about all events on this world then He is a monster who cannot be trusted.

If God is not all powerful then He still cannot be trusted. God has made a lot of promises recorded in Scripture. One diligent student is said to have found over seven thousand promises that God made to man. However sincere God may have been in making these promises, if He lacks the ability to bring them to pass then we cannot trust Him.

Thankfully the Bible (and experience) gives us the assurance that God is powerful but not manipulative. God's unselfish agape love governs how He exercises His omnipotent power. When God promised Abraham and Sarah a child in their old age, He was not pulling His hair out wondering how He was going to make it happen. He was not thinking that He may have over-promised on this one. God is confident in His ability to get things done.

The same is true about all the promises recorded in Scripture that we can claim. God is not sitting around worried about whether or not He can heal our bodies, protect us from danger, bless us financially, save our love ones from eternal damnation, or any of the other things He has promised to do on our behalf. He is confident in His ability to bring them to pass in our lives.

God wants us to have that same confidence. Like Abraham, He wants us to be fully persuaded that what He has promised, He is also able to perform in our lives. This is the primary reason why God has revealed in Scripture that He is an omnipotent God.

Men brag about their strength and abilities in order to impress and strengthen their own egos. Most do it from a selfish motive. They are not willing to sacrifice anything for others. They simply want people to know how great they are. This is not God, though some theologians have falsely painted Him this way. God wants us to know His power so that we will not be afraid to claim His promises.

October 11

God is Searching for People He Can be Mighty For

*For the eyes of the Lord run to and fro throughout the whole earth, to **shew himself strong in the behalf of them whose heart is perfect toward him**. Herein thou hast done foolishly: therefore from henceforth thou shalt have wars* (2 Chron. 16:9)

Note that God desires to display His power on someone's behalf, but He does not do this cheaply. He is searching for someone on the earth that He can work with. If God were someone whose only goal was to show off His greatness and omnipotence in order to impress (or bring fear) then we certainly would not read passages like this one.

Notice that God searches for someone *on the earth* to display His strength on their behalf. Believe it or not, by covenant right, God cannot just do anything that He wants on the earth. As far as power and ability are concerned, God certainly could do what He wants. However, God is a God that keeps covenant and in His integrity He will never use His power in a way that breaks covenant.

What is the covenant that has God searching on the earth for good men to utilize His power for? In Genesis 1:26-28 He gave man the dominion over the earth. Once He gave man this authority He respected it. Man became responsible for inviting God into the earth to intervene on his behalf. Quite often, men fail to pray and ask God to display His power and this is why we seldom see it. Hence God's eyes go to and fro throughout the earth looking for someone to invite Him in to intervene.

This is also the answer to the age old question that if "God is all good and all powerful, why does evil exist?" Evil exists because a good and all powerful God respected the covenant that He made with mankind despite the great pain He endures when He sees what we do with that covenant freedom.

Nevertheless, this passage shows us the love of God in how He uses His power on our behalf. He is searching for people that He can help. Satan, on the other hand, is looking for people to use the power he has usurped so that he can devour them (1 Pet. 5:8-9). In other words, while God wants to *use* His great power to help and bless, Satan wants to *abuse* the little power that he has to steal, kill, and destroy (John 10:10). Let us learn to yield to an omnipotent God who desires to show Himself strong on our behalf.

October 12

Your Power to Hinder God's Power

*And **he could there do no mighty work**, save that he laid his hands upon a few sick folk, and healed them. And he marvelled because of their unbelief. And he went round about the villages, teaching* (Mark 6:5-6)

In the passage above we read that Jesus *could not* do any mighty work there. It does not say that He *would not* do a mighty work there. "Would not" implies lack of willingness. "Could not" implies lack of ability. Did God all of a sudden lose His omnipotent power?

Actually this passage gives us a clear understanding as to *how* God uses His power. He will not force the use of His power for good on those unwilling to receive the blessings that He desires to bestow from it. God desires to use His omnipotent power to repair sick bodies, deliver people from oppressive demonism, and fix all that ails us. Yet, as powerful as God is, we can hinder Him from utilizing His power on our behalf.

Unlike some theologians who teach a doctrine of God's sovereignty in which He forces His will on us and we have no other choice but to sit back and let it be done, Jesus shows us the great respect and dignity that God has bestowed on His creatures. He simply will not force Himself on us, even for our good. We must "believe and receive" what He has to offer or wallow in unbelief and go without that which His power is fully capable of giving us.

It has been well said that faith is the hand that takes from God what He is so willing to give. On the other hand, unbelief is the hand that smacks God's hand away from it and says, "I don't trust you to do anything for me." While God is certainly omnipotent, His overwhelming love will allow us to reject His blessings and push Him away, and He will comply. Ah, but woe unto us when we do. Our unbelief leaves us at the mercy of the forces that desire to destroy us and they are waiting for us to act in our unbelief and push away that which is protecting us. No devil can stand against the omnipotent power of God. That is why Satan's temptations are aimed at maligning God's character.

It stands to reason that if a good and loving God does not use His power to force His good on us then why would He use it to force evil on us? He does not. The evil that we confront in our lives can be the result of rejecting God's power on our behalf through unbelief or failure to call on Him to work on our behalf. God does not use His power to destroy our lives. We do that to ourselves.

October 13

God's Power and God's Character

*And now, I beseech thee, **let the power of my lord be great**, according as thou hast spoken, saying, **The Lord is longsuffering, and of great mercy, forgiving iniquity and transgression**, and by no means clearing the guilty, visiting the iniquity of the fathers upon the children unto the third and fourth generation* (Num. 14:17-18)

Moses was concerned about two things in his prayer (and neither of those things concerned himself). First he was concerned about the people. They had sinned constantly against God and the Lord was ready to let them die a horrible death in the wilderness. Moses had the heart of God for the people and called to His mind His compassion, patience, and His willingness to forgive sin. Notice that in conjunction with these wonderful characteristics of God Moses prayed, "Let the power of my lord be great." Moses believed that God's omnipotent power worked in conjunction with, and is governed by His love, mercy, and His willingness to forgive.

Too many people are too willing for God to use His power to destroy their enemies. Some "Christians" would love for God to use His omnipotent power destructively to destroy the abortionists, the homosexuals, the Islamic terrorists, etc. Yes, all of these people who do not repent will eventually be destroyed. However, a Moses like prayer for them would aim towards their salvation.

A second thing we learn in this prayer is how Moses was very concerned about God's reputation. Moses told God that if He killed the people in the desert then His reputation would suffer with the nations that He was trying to reach. Moses said, *"Because **the Lord was <u>not able to</u> bring this people into the land** which he sware unto them, therefore he hath slain them in the wilderness"* (v. 16).

Moses believed that if God just killed His people then the nations would not think logically on the matter. They would not say, "Oh, He wanted to bring them and could have, but those folks kept disbelieving Him." On the contrary they would have begun to doubt God's omnipotence. Moses was zealous to defend God's character and reputation. Therefore, he prayed that God's power would be shown to be great as He exercised love, mercy, patience and forgiveness. That is how God governs His power. That is how we should pray that it be used on behalf of others.

October 14

The Reason for Evil in this World

*For we wrestle not against flesh and blood, but against principalities, against powers, against the **rulers of the darkness of this world**, against spiritual wickedness in high places* (Eph. 6:12)

The Bible tells us that darkness is synonymous with evil (Job 30:26; Isa. 5:20; John 3:19-20). This is why Satan and his kingdom are identified with darkness (Acts 26:18; Col. 1:12-14). The Word of God tells us that our battle in this world is against the forces that rule this darkness. The evil that is in this world is not from God. If it were from Him then we would not be told about a *wrestling match* with dark powers. We would be told to submit to the evil.

Sadly, this is exactly what some popular teachings call Christians to do. Instead of wrestling against the rulers of the darkness we are told that all of the evil in this world was ordained by God and that we must submit to it. Many tell us that "God is in control." Yet the Bible tells us, *"We know that we belong to God, **but the Evil One controls the whole world"*** (1 John 5:18; Easy to Read Version).

Some respond to this by saying, "But God even controls the devil's actions." If that were true then the Scripture should read differently. If God is controlling the actions of the evil one then what does that make God? Evil, of course. If Satan is not allowed to be, as the Bible plainly teaches, autonomous in his actions, then God is indeed the source of evil. If God is the source of evil then He is not good and we are without hope. I reject such a wicked theology on the grounds of the plain teaching of Scripture and my personal experiences with God.

The Bible tells us, *"God is light, and in him is no darkness at all"* (1 John 1:5b). If God is light and He has no darkness then He cannot be responsible for the darkness in this world. The Bible was written to reveal the actual source of darkness. In Ephesians 6 it has been shown to us that the demonic rebellious forces of Satan are ruling the darkness,

Every robbery, rape, murder, natural disaster, deprivation, sickness and other ills in life finds its source with the ruler of the darkness of this world. Every distortion of the social norm such as homosexual marriage, abortion, living together apart from marriage, pornography, and other sad things being accepted as the norm in our society finds its true source with the rulers of the darkness of this world.

God is not by any means sovereignly ruling over the darkness. On the contrary, He is at war against it. He desires to rescue us from it. He is indeed a good God in every sense of the word.

October 15

The Prince of this World

*Now is the judgment of this world: now shall **the prince of this world** be cast out* (John 12:31)

*Hereafter I will not talk much with you: for **the prince of this world** cometh, and hath nothing in me* (John 14:30)

*Of judgment, because the **prince of this world** is judged* (John 16:11)

Three times John recorded the words of Jesus in which He tells us who is presently ruling this world. Strong's dictionary says that the word "ruler" means "first in rank or power, ruler." Satan held this rank because he usurped the authority that God had given to Adam (Gen. 1:26-28).

Those who hold to stringent meticulous ideas about God's sovereignty give little place to Satan's role in the evil affairs in this world. Furthermore, they mischaracterize God by making Him the "first cause" of all things. The Bible tells us that Satan is the *first in rank* as it relates to evil.

The most egregious fact concerning the Calvinistic philosophy of God's sovereignty is how it minimizes the sacrifice that Jesus made on our behalf. Jesus had to actually engage in warfare with the prince of this world in order to rescue us. Notice Jesus' words in which the prince of this world has been "cast out" (defeated), had nothing in which to accuse Jesus, and was judged. All that Jesus did was to bring the rulership of Satan to an end.

After His resurrection Jesus said, *"All power is given unto me in heaven and in earth"* (Matt. 28:18b). Because He defeated Satan through His life, death, burial, and resurrection, Jesus could legally reclaim the authority once held by Satan. But this has to mean that if the authority was given to Him then He did not have it before then. This also means that all that was happening in this world was not in His control. Therefore He cannot be blamed for the evil in this world.

Jesus delegated the authority to His church and now we are to act on that authority in removing Satan's influence over the lives of others. It is now our duty to rescues souls from the domain of the devil as we proclaim the finished work of Christ. However, we must recognize who the true source of evil is if we are to do this successfully. We are not trying to rescue people from an "angry God" looking to roast people in hell, but from a sadistic devil looking to share his eternal fate with others. That's why we must remember who the ruler of this world is and confront him as we win the lost to Christ.

October 16

The Throne of Iniquity

*Shall the **throne of iniquity** have fellowship with thee, which frameth mischief by a law?* (Psalm 94:20)

The psalmist is referring to earthly rulers who abuse their power to do evil. God has no fellowship with such rulers. Since Satan is the evil spirit behind the actions of such men, there is much in this statement by the psalmist that gives us further insight into the so-called "mystery" and "problem" of evil in our world.

A throne is a place from which one rules. We are told that Satan is the ruler of this world (John 12:31; 14:30; 16:11; 1 John 5:18-19). This means that he has a throne. Note what Satan said:

*For thou hast said in thine heart, I will ascend into heaven, **I will exalt my throne** above the stars of God: I will sit also upon the mount of the congregation, in the sides of the north* (Isa. 14:13)

Indeed Satan has a throne. However, His throne is a throne of iniquity: *"Thou wast perfect in thy ways from the day that thou wast created, **till iniquity was found in thee"** (Eze. 28:15). From his throne of iniquity Satan frames mischief. To "frame" is "to fashion, make, determine, to form," and "to purpose."

Many religious people are often looking for a divine reason behind evil acts. Their belief is that God has some *purpose* in doing or allowing such acts. However, it is the "throne of iniquity" that determines and purposes mischief. The acts of evil in our world find their source in Satan and not God.

God cannot have any specific purpose for evil of any kind because the throne of iniquity has no fellowship with Him. As a matter of fact, Satan's purposes are in complete opposition to God's since he has determined to exalt his throne above the stars of God. Therefore, what Satan does, he does totally on his own.

The reason that evil has become such an unsolvable mystery to so many theologians is due to the fact that they have either left Satan out of the picture or have made him some unwitting tool of God. Very seldom has Satan been seen as an independent ruler with his own kingdom. Yet, this is exactly what Scripture teaches. When this is fully understood, we will stop blaming God for evil and place the blame where it belongs—at Satan's throne of iniquity.

October 17

The Will of Satan

*And the servant of the Lord must not strive; but be gentle
unto all men, apt to teach, patient, In meekness instructing
those that oppose themselves; if God peradventure will
give them repentance to the acknowledging of the truth;
And that they may recover themselves **out of the snare of
the devil, who are taken captive by him <u>at his will</u>** (2 Tim.
2:24-26)*

While all Christians agree that God is the sovereign ruler of the
universe, many of us differ with those who define sovereignty as ultimate
control. Many of these people turn men, angels, and devils into mere
automatons and puppets that only do as God had preprogrammed them.
They follow a predetermined role in a script written by God before creation.

These false ideas have been one of the reasons that evil has been
called a "problem" and a "mystery"—a puzzle that is difficult to solve.
Theologians and philosophers have wracked their brains for centuries
attempting to solve a difficulty *of their own making*. If the erroneous idea
that God controls the actions of all His creatures is abandoned, then evil is
no longer a "mystery" or a "problem".

When "God-control" philosophy is rejected then we will see that
not everything happens according to God's will. We will begin to
understand that there is more than one "will" operating in the universe.
Satan, for example, has a "will" that is separate from God's and is actually
opposed to it. He uses his will in his attempts to undermine God's purposes.

Our devotional text tells us that people who "oppose themselves"
open the door for Satan to entrap them. When they open the door then
Satan is able to take them captive *at his will*. These folks are not taken
captive by Satan at *God's will*, but are taken captive by Satan at Satan's
will. This is clear evidence from Scripture that Satan has his own will that
is not being controlled by God but is directly opposed to God's will.

Jesus' will for us is not *captivity* but *freedom* (John 8:31-32). Jesus'
will for man is in direct opposition to Satan's will for man. But those who
allow themselves to be taken captive are able to recover themselves by
acknowledging the truth. Satan cannot keep a person captive against their
will. Satan's will is *not* stronger than the person who acknowledges God's
truth. Acknowledgment of the truth enables a person to recover themselves
from Satan's trap. God's Word is truth (John 17:17). Therefore it is the will
of God for a person to be free from Satan and to be victorious over him.

October 18

Satan's Attempts to Undermine the Work of God

*For this cause, when I could no longer forbear, I sent to know your faith, lest by some means the tempter have tempted you, and **our labour be in vain*** (1 Thess. 3:5)

Some have asked, *"Is there Some Divine Plan that God has in 'using' Satan?"* My emphatic reply is NO! Satan's whole intent is to destroy God's plans. What kind of divine plan would God have by decreeing that His enemy seek to destroy His plans? If this appears to the reader to be ridiculous and counter-productive then you are getting the point. It is sad that so many well-educated men and women believe that God "uses" Satan and teach this idea. They tell us that God is using "the enemy" to mysteriously fulfill his plans.

Paul, an instrument by who God had His Word recorded, has a totally different take on this. Paul tells us that it is possible for Satan to successfully hinder and destroy what God is doing through His people. This is demonstrated in his concern for the Thessalonians in the passage above.

Paul tells us that it is possible for all of the work of God that we do in winning people to Christ to become worthless, empty, fruitless and void through the work of Satan, the Tempter. Therefore, it is borderline insanity for God to have a divine purpose in seeing His work and the work of His servants become empty, void, fruitless and undone by the work of the devil. The worse military strategist in our world would see this as asinine. Isn't God smarter than the world's BEST military strategist?

How sad that so many have submitted to the work of Satan with the false belief that they were submitting to some mysterious plan of God for their lives. We have seen churches close, effective ministries go down the tube, and people who once benefitted from these things have turned away and discontinued following Christ. Yet, some well-meaning person responds to this with the idea that "God is in control. He knows what He's doing." My friend, God is not into destroying churches and ministries and creating backsliders.

God's people will never rise up and stand against the forces opposed against the body of Christ if we hang on to these unbiblical ideas about the warfare between God and the devil. And this is exactly how Satan wants it. Satan has lulled the church asleep with these lies that all of his works against us have been authorized by God. To believe this keeps us from asserting our God-given authority over him. Recognize the fact that the tempter can indeed make our work vain if we do not stand against his wiles.

October 19

The Blessing of God's Holiness

*O Lord my God, I cried unto thee, and thou hast healed me. O Lord, thou hast brought up my soul from the grave: thou hast kept me alive, that I should not go down to the pit. Sing unto the Lord, O ye saints of his, and **give thanks at the remembrance of his holiness**. For his anger endureth but a moment; in his favour is life: weeping may endure for a night, but joy cometh in the morning* (Psalm 30:2-5)

Quite often when we hear about God's holiness it is too often in the context of dealing with the sin of man. While the comparison of God's holiness with the sinfulness of rebellious creatures is necessary to emphasize, the focusing on this alone has given us a very negative view of what it means for God to be holy. Our focus on such negativity has made us want to run from God out of fear of punishment rather than running to Him.

When we read the psalm above we are not told to cower in abject fear because God is holy. We are told to give thanks because He remembers to be holy. God's holiness certainly works against the rebellious ones who center their lives on doing evil, but to those who love God and desire to know Him, His holiness is beneficial to us and we are called to thank Him for it.

The psalmist says that when He cried to the Lord that he was healed. The holiness of God is there to heal us—to make us WHOLE. Holiness equals WHOLE-NESS. It is God's will to heal our physical bodies, our spirits and our emotions. Sickness of any kind is evil. Since holiness purges evil, then holiness heals. It does not make us sick.

Furthermore we learn from this psalm that holiness does not equal wrath, anger and retribution. While God certainly has emotions and is angered by evil and injustice, He is not a God sitting on His throne waiting to destroy sinners. Sadly, this is some people's idea of holiness. In the Psalm we learn that God's anger is only for a moment. He does not stay angry. In contrast, His favor towards people lasts a lifetime. In His holiness God would rather bestow favor than to express wrath and anger.

Isn't this a better picture of holiness than what some give us? Hence we can be thankful that God is a holy God. It is out of His holiness that He expresses unselfish love and kindness to His creation.

October 20

God's Holiness and His Covenant Promises

Nevertheless my lovingkindness will I not utterly take from him, nor suffer my faithfulness to fail. My covenant will I not break, nor alter the thing that is gone out of my lips. Once have I sworn by my holiness that I will not lie unto David (Psalm 89:33-35)

Indeed God is a holy God. Holiness and sin are opposed to each other. Sin is unable to survive God's holiness. This is why we have often emphasized the holiness of God when attempting to lead sinners to repentance. It is right for us to have done so and we should continue to do so since without holiness no man shall see God (Heb. 12:14).

Yet, an overemphasis on God's holiness in relation to sin (and the sinner) has caused us to miss some faith building truths. One of the many wonderful truths about God's holiness is that He, unlike man, cannot do evil nor sin in any manner. It is impossible for God to sin. The Psalmist tells us that in His holiness God will not lie to David. Lying is a sin and God's holiness prevents Him from lying. Dear reader, ***God's holiness means that God can be trusted.***

God has made numerous promises that are recorded in Scripture. These promises cover a myriad of things for our lives now as well as promises concerning eternity. We have been given promises of peace in the midst of trials, promises for deliverance from trials, promises to protect us in times of temptation and to make a way out of sinning, promises of divine forgiveness when we do sin, promises for material provision, healing of our bodies, and promises of a place reserved in heaven for those who stay in relationship with Christ. God has given many wonderful promises.

Unlike men and women who have let us down so many times, God says that He is holy and He will never break His covenant (promises). His faithfulness will never fail. We can count on Him and He will never let us down. To do so would be a question of His holiness. God will not have His holiness questioned.

This is a truth that should especially be kept in mind when we have delays in answers to prayer and have gone a lengthy time without seeing the fulfilment of God's promises. Instead of questioning the integrity of God, which is akin to questioning His holiness, we should stand, believing that we receive, until we see the manifestation with our physical eyes (Mark 11:24). Whenever we are tempted to doubt any promise from God, remember His holiness. Holiness is a faith-builder.

Stop cringing at the holiness of God and be thankful for it. It's because of His holiness that you can confidently claim His promises.

October 21

You Can be Holy Like God

But as he which hath called you is holy, so be ye holy in all manner of conversation; Because it is written, Be ye holy; for I am holy (1 Pet. 1:15-16)

Some years ago I was teaching a Bible study along the lines of perfection and holiness. I told the students that we are expected to be as perfect as God (Matt. 5:48). The shocks and protests were surprising. Despite my showing them exactly what the Bible itself says, many of the attendants complained that this could not be true. "God doesn't expect us to be perfect" many of them complained.

Perfection and holiness seems impossible to many people based on a false understanding of God and His Word. Some people believe that God puts impossible requirements in His Word so such passages must be understood metaphorically. However, God is a completely fair God and He never, ever commands us to be or do something without making the provision for it.

In 1 Thessalonians 3:13 we read, *"Then he will strengthen you to be holy. Then you will be blameless in the presence of our God and Father when our Lord Jesus comes with all God's holy people"* (God's Word Translation). God Himself will provide His supernatural strength to walk in holiness. He does not expect us to be holy in our own strength. This is impossible. He gives us His strength to be holy.

God does not require holiness on our part just because He likes pushing His weight around and asserting His authority. Everything God commands from us is for our safety and protection. John tells us, *"Blessed and holy is he that hath part in the first resurrection:* **on such the second death hath no power**, *but they shall be priests of God and of Christ, and shall reign with him a thousand years"* (Rev. 20:6).

God's desire is to protect us from the power that the second death has on those who refuse to live holy. It is God's will that all men be saved (1 Tim. 2:4; 2 Pet. 3:9). However, apart from holiness no man shall see God (Heb. 12:14). Those who follow Satan in any degree of his wickedness must share his eternal destiny (Rev. 20:10-15). This is not what God wants for anyone which is why He requires holiness from us. However, our loving God provides what He requires. Ask Him to strengthen you today to be as holy as He is.

October 22

The Real Reason why Jesus did Miracles

And Jesus went forth, and saw a great multitude, and was moved with compassion toward them, and he healed their sick (Matt. 14:14)

One author who denies that the supernatural power of God is present today in the church says, "Dispelling demons and diseases was Christ's way of proving that he was God in human flesh."[52]While the author does not deny the Biblical truth that Jesus did miracles out of compassion, he makes proving Christ's deity the primary focus of His miracles.

This idea could not be true for a number of reasons. First of all, when Jesus came to earth He "emptied Himself" of His divine attributes and prerogatives (Phil. 2:7) and became a man just as you and I (John 1:14; Heb. 2:14-18). Jesus could no longer perform miracles in His own power but relied completely upon the Father and the Holy Spirit to work the miraculous through Him (Matt. 12:27; John 5:19; Acts 2:22; 10:38). Therefore, though we fully affirm the deity of Christ, He was not acting in His deity when doing miracles. He was acting in His humanity. This is why He often referred to Himself as "the son of man."

Second, this idea that Jesus did miracles primarily to prove His deity makes Him appear to be egotistical, cold, and uncaring. It makes it appear as if He has no interest in men except to prove something about Himself. My friends, this was not Jesus' mission at all. Matthew 1:21 says that Jesus came to save men from their sins. His mission was not to point to Himself but to show us what the Father is really like and how He desires to save men from eternal destruction (John 3:16-18).

Two other things we need to factor in here. Jesus often delegated power to His disciples to perform miracles. He then told us that we can perform these same miracles today (John 14:12; Mark 16:15-20). Were His disciples doing miracles to prove *their* deity? This would be the only logical conclusion to such a false idea. Finally, Jesus did not always make public the miracles that He performed (Mark 1:43-44). If the purpose was to prove His deity then why keep some of these miracles quiet?

God is a very compassionate God. All of the miracles of healing performed by Jesus are attributed to His *compassion*. Sadly, the false doctrine of cessationism promoted by some theologians maligns the loving compassionate character of Christ.

---

[52] MacArthur, Jr., John F. **Charismatic Chaos** (Grand Rapids, MI: Zondervan Publishing House, 1992), p. 260

October 23

Does Sickness or Healing Glorify God

And immediately he received his sight, and followed him, glorifying God: and all the people, when they saw it, gave praise unto God (Luke 18:43)

Some have attached egotistical ideas to God's glory. God is said to do things for the express purpose of glorifying Himself. These things range from bestowing good gifts upon men to inflicting disaster, trials, and sickness. Many have claimed that sickness brings glory to God. Some have even twisted passages of Scripture to prove this teaching (John 9:1-5; 11:4). However, the passages often used actually show Jesus healing or raising from the dead those whose sicknesses were supposed to give God glory.

It is not *sickness* but *healing* that brings God glory. For example, a woman who had been bound by Satan for eighteen years was healed on the Sabbath day. The Pharisees were very angry about this alleged violation of the Sabbath law. Yet, Jesus called them out on their hypocrisy and told them that they were willing to rescue animals on the Sabbath so why begrudge the healing of one of God's own children on the day of rest.

We then read, *"And when he had said these things, all his adversaries were ashamed: and all **the people rejoiced** for all the glorious things that were done by him"* (Luke 13:17). Why did the people rejoice? They rejoiced because Jesus revealed an aspect of God's loving character that was seldom, if ever, taught by the religious leaders of His day. He showed them that God is not as much concerned about religious rituals, traditions, and laws as He is about people and their needs. The people needed a compassionate loving God since the deity presented by their religion was stern and lacked compassion. Jesus showed them that the true God is a God of love.

We need this same truth taught to us today. God is too often portrayed as the inflictor of sicknesses and very seldom portrayed as the healer. While God is said by these theologians to put sickness and disease on people for His egotistical glory, we are also told by them that He no longer works miracles of healing in our day. You must rely on medical science to relieve you of the pain that an all-powerful God has placed on you. Of course, medical science is not always successful in giving relief.

The Bible does not teach what these theologians claim it does. God's glory comes from the knowledge of His compassionate character (Ex. 33:18-19; 34:6-7). Jesus did miracles then, and He does miracles now for those who believe, for the primary purpose of love. It is the knowledge that He is a compassionate and loving God that glorifies Him.

October 24

Did Lazarus' Sickness Glorify God? (Part 1)

*Therefore his sisters sent unto him, saying, Lord, behold,
he whom thou lovest is sick. When Jesus heard that, he said,
This sickness is not unto death, but for the glory of God,
that the Son of God might be glorified thereby* (Jn 11:3-4)

Many have taken this passage out of context in order to prove that
all sickness, especially those suffered by a genuine believer, are given to
them by God for His glory. Nonetheless, a careful study of this passage
demonstrates that it was never the sickness that brought God glory, *but
what Jesus did about the sickness* that brought glory to God.

Of course someone may protest and say, "But the passage plainly
says that this sickness is for the glory of God that He may be glorified. It
does not say anything about the end result." That is true if we read only that
one statement. However, the protester must also explain why Jesus said,
"This sickness is not unto death..." and yet, several verses later, Jesus tells
His disciples, *"Lazarus is dead."* (John 11:14). In our day someone might
accuse Jesus of being a false prophet.

Yet we know that Jesus has never uttered one false word. Therefore
it is necessary to understand the language that Jesus is using. What does
He mean by the sickness not being unto Lazarus death? What does He
mean by the sickness glorifying God? Both of these are in relation to the
end result: Lazarus' healing and resurrection.

Notice the harsh criticism Jesus received when He finally went to
Lazarus' family: *"And some of them said, Could not this man, which
opened the eyes of the blind, have caused that even this man should not
have died?"* (John 11:37). The sickness and death of Lazarus was *not*
bringing God glory—it was bringing Him criticism.

Therefore, the language of Jesus was not meant to be taken in the
sense that God gets glory from sickness itself and that Lazarus would *never*
see physical death. It focused on the *end result* of the sickness and death.
God was to receive glory by how Jesus demonstrated His authority even
over death. The fact that Lazarus was sick is not what brought God glory. It
was what Jesus had done about the sickness that glorified Him.

Therefore, those who insist that Jesus taught that the sickness was
to the glory of God must also keep it in context by saying that the sickness
was not unto death. Using this method of interpretation then a person would
be accused of calling Christ a liar since Lazarus actually died. Yet, we
know that if we read the whole chapter and other Bible passages, our Lord
is vindicated from this horrendous accusation.

October 25

Did Lazarus' Sickness Glorify God? (Part 2)

Therefore his sisters sent unto him, saying, Lord, behold, he whom thou lovest is sick. When Jesus heard that, he said, This sickness is not unto death, but for the glory of God, that the Son of God might be glorified thereby. (Jn 11:3-4)

There have been a number of theologians who have mischaracterized God and maligned His character by claiming that He inflicts sickness on people for His glory. Since the Bible teaches no such thing we must conclude that they have misused and twisted passages such as the one above to make the case for their false teaching. Sadly, those who have not understood the Biblical language of faith have been easily duped into accepting this maligning of God.

As we emphasized yesterday, the language of Jesus in this passage was not meant to be taken in the sense that God gets glory from sickness itself and that Lazarus would *never* see physical death. His language was "faith language" in which a person does not go by what they see, but by what God says, even if what God says contradicts what we are seeing.

In John 11:40 Jesus asked Martha, *"Said I not unto thee, that, if thou wouldest **believe**, thou shouldest see the glory of God?"* They were to believe that **Jesus is the resurrection and the life**. Jesus did not want them to limit this truth only to some future event but He wanted them to recognize that resurrection and life was available *now* (Rom. 8:11). By placing their faith in this truth they would see the glory of God.

In verse 45 we are told that the Jews believed on Jesus. What caused the Jews to believe on Jesus? Was it the sickness and/or the death itself? No. The fact that the sickness was not healed caused some to criticize the Lord (John 11:37). It caused Martha to limit the power of God when she said, *"Lord, if thou hadst been here, my brother had not died"* (John 11:32). It caused the Jews to weep and cry instead of rejoicing that their Savior had come in the midst of them. This caused the Lord Himself to groan (John 11:33). Therefore it was not the sickness and death itself that brought Jesus glory.

The sickness was for the glory of God in this manner: it was an opportunity to demonstrate the power of God over sickness, disease and death itself. The sickness and death brought doubt, sadness, criticism, and grieving. Yet, when Jesus demonstrated resurrection power, this in turn caused many of the Jews to believe on Him. The demonstration of the power of God brought Jesus glory. This same resurrection power is still available to give life to your mortal body (Rom. 8:11).

October 26

Did God Make a Man Blind to Get Glory?

Master, who did sin, this man, or his parents, that he was born blind? Jesus answered, Neither hath this man sinned, nor his parents: ***but that the works of God should be made manifest in him.*** *I must work the works of him that sent me, while it is day: the night cometh, when no man can work.* (John 9:2-4)

Based on the punctuation in the KJV Jesus *appears* to be saying that a man was ordained to be born for the specific purpose of God's work being made manifest in him. Many fatalistic theologians have gotten a lot of mileage from the use of this passage and have led many to see a cruel God who brings sickness on people just so that He can show off His power.

What leads so many to this false conclusion is the *period* that our translators placed at the end of the Lord's sentence where He says, *"....but that the works of God should be made manifest in him."* The "period" is telling us that this is the end of the story and the end of any discussion on the matter. The man was born blind so that God would have a chance to work His works in him.

George Ricker Berry, in his introduction to **The Interlinear KJV** Bible writes, "There is no authority anywhere for the punctuation.... We have been obliged to punctuate for ourselves as we judged best."[53] The punctuation then should be replaced in a way that is consistent with God's known character of love. One English translation does this well:

Jesus answered, "Neither this man sinned nor his parents sinned. ***But that the works of God might be revealed in him,*** *we must work the works of him who sent me, while it is day. Night is coming, when no one can work."* (John 9:3-4; Common Edition New Testament)

What a difference a comma makes. The Common Edition's placing of a comma in the correct spot removes the fatalism easily found in the King James Version. When the *comma* is used instead of the *period*, we see that Jesus is not saying that the man was born blind in order to manifest God's work, but *since* he was born blind, Jesus says that the works of God must be made manifest in him. The difference is that God's desire is to relieve this man from a blindness that was not the fault of him or God.

---

[53] Berry, George Ricker **The Interlinear KJV: Parallel New Testament In Greek And English** (Grand Rapids, MI: Zondervan Publishing House) p. ii

304

October 27

Man Born Blind and Christ's Battle with Satan

I must work the works of him that sent me, while it is day:
the night cometh, when no man can work. As long as I am
in the world, I am the light of the world (John 9:4-5)

A number of theologians have taught from John 9 that God pre-ordained that this man be born blind so that one day He would be glorified by healing him. In yesterday's devotion we learned that a simple matter of repunctuating this passage removes the predestinarian fatalism often attributed to it. By this God is not made to appear like the cruel inflictor of blindness that He is falsely credited for.

A further investigation of this passage deals with the works of God that must be done while it is day. Jesus explains that the "day" represents His being the light of the world. The "day" continues while He was in the world and the "night" would come when His light was no longer in the world. Jesus was explaining that the situation with the blind man was a battle between light and darkness, good and evil.

Jesus, in referring to the works of God and using the metaphors of "light, day," and "night" was making a distinction between the works of God and those of the kingdom of darkness (Acts 26:18; Eph. 6:10-12; Col. 1:12-14). It is Satan and his demons who blind people both spiritually and physically (Matt. 12:22-28; 2 Cor. 4:4-5) and it is God who brings recovery of sight to the blind (Luke 4:18).

God was not responsible for this man becoming blind at birth. God did not punish this man for any sin he may have committed in some false "preexistence" nor did God inflict punishment on him as the result of a generational curse due to the sin of his parents. Even more, God did not pre-ordain that he be born blind knowing that one day He would display His mighty power in healing and then amaze the crowds. This is a warped theology that seems to charge God with intentional maliciousness.

The blindness of this man was fully the work of Satan and the healing was fully the work of God. The Bible's divine commentary on all of this is that God was with Christ healing all those who are oppressed of the devil (Acts 10:38). Jesus whole mission in life was to destroy the works of Satan (1 John 3:8). When we understand this truth then we can read stories such as this man being born blind under a new light. Rather than seeing God pre-ordaining sickness to boost His ego in healing it, we see it as Him coming to rescue those placed under satanic oppression.

October 28

Does God Put More on You than You can Bear?

There hath no temptation taken you but such as is common to man: but God is faithful, who will not suffer you to be tempted above that ye are able; but will with the temptation also make a way to escape, ***that ye may be able to bear it*** (1 Cor. 10:13)

One morning while talking to someone on the phone, the subject of their trials came up. As we discussed the issue the person, in an attempt to comfort herself said, "Well, God will never put more on you than you can bear." The implication was that God was responsible for the suffering that she was dealing with.

Having heard this statement made by Christians on many occasions I decided to challenge the congregation I pastored that same morning. I first asked everyone, "How many of you believe that the Bible says that God will never put more on you more than you can bear?" Many people raised their hands. I then asked them to please find me the chapter and verse where it says this. I heard pages rustling for several minutes as I waited patiently. After a few minutes and no one finding a chapter or verse I then asked them to turn to 1 Cor. 10:13 and I began to show them what the Bible *really* says.

1 Cor. 10:13, though often misquoted, tells us that the trials and temptations that we face are those that are common to man. In other words, nothing that we go through is so unique to us that others have never suffered it. However, nothing in the passage says that God puts these trials on us. On the contrary, the passage tells us that God is faithful in not letting us suffer anything above our ability to do so but makes a way of escape. God is not the One who brings the trial—He is the One who gives us an escape from the trial and temptation. By giving us this escape, we have the ability to bear it.

It is so sad that God has been blamed by His own children for giving them sickness, financial difficulties, relationship problems, marriage troubles, and even struggles with temptation and sin. How can God's people seek Him for the way of escape that He so clearly promises when they believe that He is the One who brought the trial and temptation in the first place?

When we read the Bible using traditional statements often we read into the Bible what it is not actually saying. This is how passages like 1 Cor. 10:13 can be distorted. This is also the reason that so many of God's people are weighed down by trials. They submit to trials rather than taking God's way of escape.

October 29

Satan, not God, is the Source of Tribulation

Fear none of those things which thou shalt suffer: behold, ***the devil shall cast some of you into prison, that ye may*** ***be tried; and ye shall have tribulation ten days****: be thou faithful unto death, and I will give thee a crown of life* (Rev. 2:10)

Satan has blinded so many of God's people with traditional ideas about God that are utterly false. Instead of reading the Bible and allowing this to change what tradition says about God, we read too many of our traditional ideas about God into the Scripture, thus distorting what the Scripture actually says about Him.

This is most true in relation to the trials and tribulations that God's people suffer, some even on a regular basis. God is too often accused of bringing trials upon His people. Yet the Bible makes it abundantly clear that Satan is the source of these things. How can we look to God for help if we continue to blame Him for the work of the devil?

Most of us are familiar with the persecution that Christians constantly suffer in Islamic and Communist countries. While some have erroneously (and blasphemously) claimed that Christians and Muslims worship the same God, there is no truth to this tall tale. Muslims reject Jesus as the Messiah and they are some of the biggest persecutors of Christians. It is a murderous religion influenced by Satan.

Communism claims to be atheistic, but this is also a lie. Richard Wurmbrand in his book, *Marx and Satan*, makes a strong case based on the evidence from writings and testimonies that the founders and leaders of Marxism were Satan worshippers and knew that they were doing Satan's bidding in spreading the communist and socialist agendas.[54]

Wurmbrand quotes a statement from a communist newspaper that reveals its true heart: "We do not fight against believers and not even against clergymen. We fight against God to snatch believers from Him."[55]

With this statement and many other proofs recorded in Wurmbrand's book, there is no doubt that trials, tribulations, and persecutions are Satan's method of warfare against God Himself. God is not the source of these things. He is our deliverer from them.

---

[54] Wurmbrand, Richard **Marx & Satan** (Bartlesville, OK: Living Sacrifice Book Company, 1986). The whole book is an interesting documentation of how Communists are revealed to be satan worshippers.

[55] Ibid, p. 77

October 30

Satan: the Afflicter of Trials and Persecutions

Be sober, be vigilant; **because your adversary the devil**, *as a roaring lion, walketh about, seeking whom he may devour: Whom resist stedfast in the faith, knowing that* **the same** *afflictions are accomplished in your brethren that are in the world. But the God of all grace, who hath called us unto his eternal glory by Christ Jesus, after that ye have suffered a while, make you perfect, stablish, strengthen, settle you* (1 Pet. 5:8-10)

When it comes to trials, tribulations, and persecutions most Christians believe that these are sent by God to chasten and/or strengthen His people. Though I disagree with it, it is the most common and popular position amongst most Christians. I believe that Scripture supports the opposite of the majority Christian view on this.

The Bible, in contrast with traditional teachings, reveals that the primary source of affliction is our adversary. If Satan is an adversary-enemy then that means that he is working his afflictions to DESTROY US. Satan certainly is not attempting to help us and strengthen us. Satan is not working with God in partnership to bring affliction to help us grow. His intention is to devour us.

The *grace of God is given to strengthen us*, perfect us, and to establish us. **The afflictions are not meant to do these things but the grace of God is.** So many people seem to have it backwards, but Scripture gets it right. So remember, afflictions are meant to devour us, but *the grace of God* is meant to stablish, perfect, strengthen, and settle us.

The Bible also teaches that Satan brings trials in an effort to hinder, disrupt and possibly bring to nothing the work that God is doing through His servants (1 Thess. 3:3-5). For example, in 1 Thess. 2:18, Paul writes, *"Wherefore we would have come unto you, even I Paul, once and again;* ***but Satan hindered us."***

God did not hinder Paul. *Satan did.* If God was using Satan to do these things, then God is working counterproductive to Himself and so is Satan. Jesus Himself once said that for Satan to do the work of God would be to divide himself and that his kingdom could not stand such a division (Matt. 12:24-26).

Satan does what he desires of his own initiative in order to destroy the work of God among God's people. We know it was men that brought suffering and affliction to Paul and his fellow workers. Yet, we need to recognize who our true enemy is and resist him.

October 31

God is <u>For</u> us, not <u>Against</u> Us

What shall we then say to these things? ***If God be for us,*** *who can be against us?* (Rom. 8:31)

Many of our teachings within Christianity have had a tendency to blame God for all of the ills that we face in this life. There have been various reasons for making God culpable for our problems ("God is punishing you for your sin," "God is testing you," "God is sending the trial to make you stronger," "God has a better purpose for you," etc.). It is no wonder that many sinners want nothing to do with God while many Christians live defeated lives.

In verse 35 of Romans Paul asks, *"Who shall separate us from the love of Christ? shall tribulation, or distress, or persecution, or famine, or nakedness, or peril, or sword?"* If God is responsible for our tribulations, persecutions and distresses then He would be *against* us. However, we are assured that God is *for* us. He loves us. He is not the One causing us problems. He loves you and cares for you deeply. The one causing you and I problems is the one that Peter refers to as our *adversary* (1 Pet. 5:8). *Adversity* comes from an *adversary*, not from the One who cares about us.

The Bible tells us that the devil, and not God, is our true enemy (see Matt. 13:24-25, 36-39; Luke 10:17-19). Thankfully, as we have already learned, Jesus has already defeated this enemy through His redemptive work on the cross (Col. 1:12-14; 2:14-15; Rev. 12:9-11). However, this is where I often run into another teaching that sometimes causes me some exasperation. There are some who will acknowledge that God is not behind the ills in life. They will acknowledge the fact that Jesus has even dealt a crushing defeat to Satan through His redemptive work. However, they seldom teach that God is willing to deliver them from the effects of satanic attacks in this life.

The idea is somewhat pacifistic where we do not aggressively confront satanic attacks but we instead allow God to simply use the attacks of Satan against us to help us grow and make us stronger. Eventually God will reward us in the next life for taking a beating from Satan.

This kind of teaching can still leave one hopeless, weak and defeated. Why would God tell us to allow our enemy to continually beat us down with no reprieve? Thankfully He did not. The weapon of God's Word and our delegated authority in Christ is able to confront and overcome every satanic attack thanks to the blood of Jesus (Eph. 6:17-18; 1 John 2:13-14; Luke 10:17-19; James 4:7).

November 1

The Millennium: God's Original Design for the Earth

The wolf also shall dwell with the lamb, and the leopard shall lie down with the kid; and the calf and the young lion and the fatling together; and a little child shall lead them. And the cow and the bear shall feed; their young ones shall lie down together: and the lion shall eat straw like the ox. And the sucking child shall play on the hole of the asp, and the weaned child shall put his hand on the cockatrice' den. They **shall not hurt nor destroy in all my holy mountain:** *for the earth shall be full of the knowledge of the Lord, as the waters cover the sea* (Isa. 11:6-9)

This passage is in reference to the future one thousand year reign of Christ in which He, along with His faithful saints, will come to physically reign on the earth during this period of time. The passage gives us a small description of how the animal kingdom will interact with humans and with each other during this period.

This is the way that it was always meant to be. Animal violence was never the will of God for the earth. Animal violence and the carnivorous nature of animals is the result of sin entering into our world. Sin brought death and death began reigning upon the earth (Rom. 5:12). Some of the results of death is the sad fact that we have animal violence. Animals hurt and kill each other as well as humans.

God says, *"They shall not hurt nor destroy in all my* ***holy*** *mountain."* Here we see the difference between the results of holiness and sin. Sin is destructive. Adam originally enjoyed peace and tranquility with all of the animals (Gen. 2:19-20). God warned Adam that disobedience to His simple command would have disastrous results (Gen. 2:15-17). As long as Adam walked in holiness before God, there was peace, safety, and tranquility with both Adam and the animals.

Sadly, Adam disobeyed God and one of the results of his sin was disharmony between man and beast (Gen. 3:14-15). However, Jesus' reign will show us how different it is when holiness reigns rather than sin. In His holy mountain, nothing will hurt or destroy. This is the way that it was always meant to be. The reason that it is not is due to sin.

When we look at the things in our world today that hurt and destroy, let us not blame it on God or claim that it is all under His control. The millennium is the period in which we will see the true control of God. It is in this time that we will experience pain free living on the earth, because God's mountain will become holy.

November 2

Why the Millennium will be a Wonderful Period

*And I saw an angel come down from heaven, having the key of the bottomless pit and a great chain in his hand. And he laid hold on the dragon, that old serpent, which is the Devil, and Satan, and **bound him a thousand years**, And cast him into the bottomless pit, and shut him up, and set a seal upon him, that **he should deceive the nations no more, till the thousand years should be fulfilled:** and after that he must be loosed a little season* (Rev. 20:1-3)

The millennial reign of Christ will begin once Satan has been shut up in a pit for a thousand years. What a joyous time on earth that this shall be. Christ will rule the earth with His saints, Satan and his demons will not be around to disturb His reign, and as He promised in Isa. 11:9, *"They shall not hurt nor destroy in all my holy mountain: for **the earth shall be full of the knowledge of the Lord**, as the waters cover the sea."*

This helps us to answer the age-old question as to why, if God is a good God, do we have evil and pain in this life. The present ruler of this world is blinding the minds of men and keeping them from the light of the truth concerning God's true character and nature (2 Cor. 4:4). He is currently deceiving the nations.

Muslim nations have been deceived into believing that God is a cruel killer who desires to bring constant Jihads against different people and nations. Communist and Socialist nations have attempted to deny God's existence and make every effort to oppress those who express faith in Him. Nations influenced by Hinduism put certain ones in a caste system so that some are privileged by their deities to have health and wealth while others are deservedly poor, sick and oppressed.

Finally, in many of our western cultures, worship of God has been replaced with worship of pleasure through illicit sex, drugs, and various types of ungodly entertainment. In this culture God is made out to be an old prude who is angry at people enjoying life, so He is to be avoided. All that is evil in this world is due to Satan's deception of nations and the lack of true knowledge concerning God. When Satan is no longer able to distort and malign the truth about God's character through His deceptions, the earth will be full of the knowledge of God. We will see that, while evil under the deceptive reign of Satan brought hurt and destruction, the true knowledge of God will reveal just the opposite which is no harm or destruction during His reign.

November 3

Why there is no Repentance for Satan

And when the thousand years are expired, Satan shall be loosed out of his prison, And shall go out to deceive the nations which are in the four quarters of the earth, Gog and Magog, to gather them together to battle: the number of whom is as the sand of the sea. (Rev. 20:7-8)

People often ask, "Is it possible for Satan to repent? If he repents would God forgive him?" Forgiveness and mercy is God's nature and character (Psalm 86:5; 145:8-9; Dan. 9:9; Micah 7:18). If it were possible for Satan and demons to repent, no doubt that God would forgive them.

The problem regarding repentance and mercy is not on God's part but on Satan and his followers. Due to His nature, God would have given Satan much time to repent (2 Pet. 3:9; Rev. 2:20-22). However, men and angels who persist in sin sooner or later get beyond the ability to repent. Satan became hardened as men do today, and is far beyond the ability or desire to repent (1 Tim. 4:1-2; Hosea 4:17-19).

The end of the millennial reign of Christ on the earth will remove all doubt concerning this truth. Jesus will have Satan bound for 1000 years and then released again. This will prove that Satan's character is so malignant that he could never repent. Theodore H. Epp writes:

> Why is it necessary to loose Satan after the 1000 year rule of Christ? ....it will prove he is still the same after the 1000 years of imprisonment. His evil nature will not change simply because he is confined for 1000 years. This demonstrates the justice of God in His final, eternal judgment of Satan.[56]

God attempts to reach out and reason with sinners (Prov. 1:24-30; Isa. 1:18-20; 65:2, 12; 66:3-4; Zech. 7:11-12). They reject His love so God eventually has to "give them over" to a reprobate mind (Rom. 1:28-32; Psalm 81:11-12). When someone is bound in sin then there is no desire to repent and there is nothing that God can do for them.

Some have taught "universalism" where it is said that everyone will be saved in the end, to include Satan. This is false and unbiblical because God honors the free-will of men and devils, even when that free-will leads the creatures He loves to eternal torment. However, Satan will not repent because he has gone beyond the ability and desire to do so.

---

[56] Epp, Theodore H. **Practical Studies in Revelation (Vol. II)** (Lincoln, NE: Back to the Bible, 1969), p. 362

November 4

An Enemy has Done This

*So the servants of the householder came and said unto him, Sir, didst not thou sow good seed in thy field? from whence then hath it tares? He said unto them, **An enemy hath done this**. The servants said unto him, Wilt thou then that we go and gather them up?* (Matt. 13:27-28)

After telling this parable, Jesus' disciples asked Him for more clarification. The Lord makes it plain that the sower of the tares (the bad seed) is the devil: *"The enemy that sowed them is the devil; the harvest is the end of the world; and the reapers are the angels"* (Matt. 13:39). It is made clear to us that all the evil that is done in this world has its source, not in God, but in the enemy.

Satan is an enemy to both God and men. Satan is not a servant of God nor is God mysteriously using Satan for some secret purpose. Satan is genuinely and without coercion, making every possible attempt to undermine the loving work of God towards man. This is seen in Jesus' parable in which Satan plants bad seed among God's good seed.

Seed is a powerful thing. It can be a tiny little thing starting out but can produce a large ongoing harvest. The seed that God plants is always good. God's good seed of love, forgiveness, peace, healing, and provision is all for the benefit of mankind and His other creatures. Satan's seed of turmoil, sickness, destruction, lack, and hatred is an attempt to break God's heart, undermine His credibility, and destroy mankind in the process.

Satan is able to take Good seed and distort and twist it as well the best of evil geniuses in our world have taken God's resources and used them in destructive ways. He has turned good into evil, love into hatred, health into sickness, abundance into lack, and truth into lies. He has done this by planting seeds of deception into the minds of men and angels. Therefore, every tragic event from airplane crashes to automobile accidents to mass murders are all his doing. God's hands are clean.

It is so sad how some well-meaning Christians have erroneously charged God with all of the misery in this world, claiming that He ordains it for divine benevolent purposes. What a malicious indictment of God's character to charge Him with the work of His enemy. The next time we are faced with tragic events, regardless of what they are, let us stop blaming God for them. Instead, say, "An enemy hath done this." To do so would be much more Biblical since God, as Jesus has stated in His parable, only plants good seed. God is not the author of evil of any kind.

November 5

Did God give His People Bad Laws?

*Because they had not executed my judgments, but had despised my statutes, and had polluted my sabbaths, and their eyes were after their fathers' idols. Wherefore **I gave them also statutes that were not good**, and judgments whereby they should not live* (Eze. 20:24-25)

For years this has been a favorite Scripture among atheists. They have this as their proof-text for rejecting the truth and existence of the God worshipped by Christians. After all, what kind of God is this who gives His own people laws that were not good seeing how such laws would lead them into sin and destruction?

Sadly, even Calvinists have turned to this passage to prove their twisted ideas about God's sovereignty. However, is the passage saying what atheists and Calvinists claim that it does? Interpreting Scripture with Scripture helps us to understand this better. In the psalms we read:

*The **law of the Lord is perfect, converting the soul**: the testimony of the Lord is sure, making wise the simple. The **statutes of the Lord are right, rejoicing the heart**: the commandment of the Lord is pure, enlightening the eyes* (Psalm 19:7-8)

In Ezekiel 20:25, the statutes that God supposedly gave the people led to them polluting their gifts (v. 26). In Psalm 19:7-8 God's laws and statutes converts the soul and are the subject of rejoicing. So which passage gives us the correct understanding of God's laws?

Look at the word "gave" in Ezekiel 20:25. It comes from the Hebrew word *"nathan"* Among its many meanings is to "permit" or to "give over" to something. The Holman Christian Standard Bible translates it correctly: *"I gave them over to worthless customs and laws."* It is similar to Paul's statement in Romans 1:28: *"And even as they did not like to retain God in their knowledge, God gave them over to a reprobate mind, to do those things which are not convenient."*

In Ezekiel 20:21 we learn that the Israelites refused to walk in the laws that God gave that were good and led to life. Therefore He *allowed* them to continue in the statutes of the heathen nations whose practices they adopted. After much pleading, God eventually removes all restraint and allows people to have what they want. However, this is *permissive* and not *causative*.

November 6

How Does God Smite?

*For **the LORD shall smite Israel**, as a reed is shaken in the water, and he shall root up Israel out of this good land, which he gave to their fathers, and shall scatter them beyond the river, because they have made their groves, provoking the LORD to anger. And **he shall give Israel up** because of the sins of Jeroboam, who did sin, and who made Israel to sin* (1 Kings 14:15-16)

Due to Solomon's marriage to multiple foreign women and subsequent fall into idolatry, God warned him that his kingdom would become divided as a result of his sins. Not too soon after his death Jeroboam returned from his Egyptian exile and led a delegation of disgruntled Israelites against the new king, Rehoboam, to demand relief from the heavy work placed upon them by Solomon.

Rehoboam, ignoring the advice of the elders, listened instead to the advice of young friends and threatened to act with more cruelty than his father. This nearly led to a civil war. Instead it gave Jeroboam control over ten of the twelve tribes of Israel. In order to prevent the Israelites under his control from going to Jerusalem for worship, Jeroboam set up golden calf idolatry in Bethel and Dan. In this manner Jeroboam made Israel to sin.

God became understandably upset by this. It is not only the lack of faithfulness to their covenant that hurts God but the destructive consequences that idolatry has on the idolaters themselves and those around them that brings Him grief and pain. Therefore, due to the sin of Idolatry, God threatened to *smite* Israel.

The word "smite" has a violent connotation and gives us a picture of an angry deity sitting on his throne with lightning bolts in both hands in which he is prepared to shoot the subjects of his wrath with accurate precision. This is often how we picture God, especially in the Old Testament, when He threatens to smite those He finds fault with. However, the Bible always explains such punitive language. God "smites" by "giving people up" to their sins.

Every sin contains within itself its own seeds of destruction (Rom. 6:23; James 1:13). When God "gives" people up, He removes His protection from them that would normally have kept evil forces at bay. God allows them to suffer the consequences of their sin. Therefore, God's "smiting" is not direct, but is a "turning over" of sinners to the very evil forces they have chosen for themselves.

November 7

Why God Cannot Always Intervene

*And I sought for a man among them, that should make up
the hedge, and stand in the gap before me for the land, that
I should not destroy it: but I found none. Therefore have I
poured out mine indignation upon them; I have consumed
them with the fire of my wrath: their own way have I
recompensed upon their heads, saith the Lord GOD* (Eze.
22:30-31)

What a sad passage of Scripture. God has no desire to punish Israel
for their sins despite how much they deserve it. Yet, unless someone stands
in the gap He is left with no choice but to allow the fire of His wrath to
consume them.

If God does not want to punish why does He *need* someone to tell
Him *not* to do it? Can He not just withhold the punishment? When we
understand the free-will covenant that God has established with men and
His method of punishing, this should remove the confusion.

God says, *"....their own way have I **recompensed** upon their
heads."* The word "recompense" in this passage comes from the Hebrew
word *"nathan"* which has several meanings, among them being "allow,
permit" and "to give over to".

In Ezekiel 22:31 there is a "sowing and reaping" process at work.
Other translations read, *"I have returned their way upon their heads"*
(English Standard Version), *"their own ways have I rendered upon their
heads"* (Good News Version), *"serve them with the consequences of all
they've done"* (The Message), and *"I will heap on their heads the full
penalty for all their sins"* (New Living Translation). God will *allow* Israel
to reap what they have sown since no one has stood in the gap.

Why must God *allow* this? God has given man dominion over the
earth (Gen. 1:26-28; Psalm 8:5). He can only intervene on the earth by
working through men who will work with Him (2 Chron. 16:9). He will
work through men who invite Him by standing in the gap before Him as
Moses did (Psalm 106:23).

This is a significant truth for our nation. Currently America has
fallen into sexual idolatry where homosexuality, fornication, adultery, and
pornography rules the day. People do not always connect the financial
problems, failure in foreign policies, wars, and natural disasters with these
sins and the loss of God's protection. Many "Christians" have become
apostate and genuine Christians have almost given up. However, we must
stand in the gap for our nation if we want to see things turned around.

November 8

How Does God Smite (Part 2)

*Now will I shortly pour out my fury upon thee, and accomplish mine anger upon thee: and **I will judge thee according to thy ways, and will recompense thee for all thine abominations**. And mine eye shall not spare, neither will I have pity: **I will recompense thee according to thy ways** and thine abominations that are in the midst of thee; and **ye shall know that I am the LORD that smiteth*** (Eze. 7:8-9)

Two days ago we asked, "How does God smite?" We learned from 1 Kings 14:15-16 that God smites, not by personally using His omnipotent power to bring harm, but by "giving Israel up" to the consequences of their rebellion. This, we learned, is the removal of His supernatural protection that holds back the evil forces waiting to bring about destruction.

In yesterday's devotion we learned that God does not always intervene unless He is asked. We learned from Ezekiel 22:30-31 that God really has no desire to give people over to the consequences of their sin. Therefore, He looks for a man to stand in the gap and invite Him to continue to protect the nation. However, since God could not find such a man, He allowed the nation to reap the consequences of their sin.

We learned in yesterday's devotion that the word "recompense" means to "permit, allow, and give someone over to" something. This comes from the Hebrew word *"nathan"* and it is the same word used in 1 Kings 14:16 in which we are told "he shall give Israel up" to the consequences of their rebellion. From the understanding of how this word is used in today's passage, we again conclude that God "smites," not by actively bringing about destruction to the nation, but by removing His protection and allowing people to have the very thing that they want, despite the fact that it leads to their demise.

If *"nathan"* had been translated consistently in this sense then Bible readers would not be so confused about God's character and would not depict the God of the Old Testament to be any less loving than the God of the New. Besides the fact that Jesus is the God of the Old Testament, the Bible does not depict two different deities—one loving and forgiving and the other vindictive and destructive. We find the same God in both testaments.

God's method of "smiting" is not to directly hurt and destroy. He has no desire to do that. God wants very much for people to turn from their rebellion and live (Eze. 18:32). However, when people are unwilling to do so, He allows them to reap what they sow.

November 9

God Permits what We Permit

*I promise you that **God in heaven will allow whatever you allow on earth, but he will not allow anything you don't allow.** I promise that when any two of you on earth agree about something you are praying for, my Father in heaven will do it for you* (Matt. 18:18-19; Contemporary English Version)

When I was young I was an avid superhero comic book fan. I especially loved a superhero called Spiderman. A young teenager named Peter Parker gains superhuman spider like powers after being bitten by a radioactive spider. Just before his death, Peter's Uncle Ben warns him that "with great power comes great responsibility." This philosophy, coupled with a serious tragic event, leads Peter to use his great power to fight for those who cannot fight for themselves.

In real life, God has actually given His people greater power than we realize. He tells King Asa, *"For the eyes of the LORD run to and fro throughout the whole earth, to shew himself strong in the behalf of them whose heart is perfect toward him"* (2 Chron. 16:9). It seems that due to God's covenant with man in which we were given dominion over the earth (Gen. 1:26-28; Psalm 8:5), He cannot intervene on the earth apart from someone on the earth asking Him to do so. God has to look in order to find someone who will allow Him to use His power on behalf of the earth.

This places a lot of power in the hands of men—and a lot of responsibility. God will only permit what we permit on the earth. God may instruct us as to what is right and wrong. He will plead with us to ensure that we make right choices. He will move us to seek Him for His intervention. However, a large part of what happens in the earth is completely determined by what we choose to do.

Once again we find that the Scriptures answer the age old "problem" or "mystery" concerning evil. It has been asked that if God is all good and all powerful then why evil? So many ridiculous philosophies have provided convoluted, nonsensical and distorted answers. However, the Bible provides the simplest of answers. God gave authority to men and His intervention on the earth is completely dependent upon them. If men fail to seek God then what evil forces do upon the earth is not His fault.

Every consequence of sin that we suffer is due to our permitting the consequences. When God gives people up and permits them to suffer from their rebellion, He is only permitting what we have permitted. Our failure to repent and pray brings these things upon ourselves (Jer. 2:17-19; 5:25).

November 10

God Punishes but Does not <u>Personally</u> Punish

They sacrifice upon the tops of the mountains, and burn incense upon the hills, under oaks and poplars and elms, because the shadow thereof is good: therefore your daughters shall commit whoredom, and your spouses shall commit adultery. I will not punish your daughters when they commit whoredom, nor your spouses when they commit adultery: **for themselves are separated with whores, and they sacrifice with harlots: therefore the people that doth not understand shall fall** (Hos. 4:13-14)

Isn't strange that God says that He will not punish His people for their sins? We are used to reading in Scripture how God says that He will personally bring about punishment for the sins of the people.

Nevertheless, in these passages God is simply stating a principle that can be found even in the very passages in which He says that He will "punish," "smite," or "destroy" a sinner or a sinning nation. In the Hosea passage God is no longer using the idiomatic expressions He often uses based on the Hebrew language in which He is said to personally bring about what He merely allowed or permitted. In Hosea 4 we get it plain and clear that He will not *personally* or *directly* punish Israel. He will let them fall by the consequences of their own rebellion.

We should not mistake this for God becoming exasperated and throwing in the towel. He is not like us where after one or two tries of convincing a wayward person we lose our patience, become angry, and tell the person, "well, you made your own bed, so lie in it." On the contrary, God will continually try to convince wayward sinners to turn from their destructive wicked ways until they have passed the point of no return to which He is unable to do anything else without violating His covenant of free-will.

In Hosea 4:17 the deal is sealed with this statement, *"Ephraim is joined to idols: let him alone."* Once this has happened then God is left with no choice but to let go of the restraints and allow the people to fall by their own foolish choices. When they have become joined to their idols He has no choice but to "let them alone" and allow them to fall. Yet, He wants to make sure that it is understood that their fall will not come about by His direct involvement.

God is absolved from all evil, even the evil that comes as a result of punishment. He punishes but He doesn't. In other words, He punishes by removing all protective restraints and allowing the sinner to destroy himself.

November 11

Does God Lay Sickness on His Enemies?

*And the LORD will take away from thee all sickness, and
will put none of the evil diseases of Egypt, which thou
knowest, upon thee; but will **lay** them upon all them that
hate thee* (Deut. 7:15)

Reading this passage gives us the impression that God will
personally inflict Israel's enemies with sickness. For some, this is not a
concern since it is the enemies of God's people that sickness would be
inflicted upon. Yet, the fact that God would inflict sickness on anyone
makes God the author and engineer of sickness and death.

The word "lay" in Deut. 7:15 is the Hebrew word *"nathan."*
Nearly every Bible dictionary tells us that the word means to *allow, permit,
give over to,* or *deliver up.* Based on all what we understand about God's
character we believe that this word should be translated either as "permit"
or "give them over to" in this passage. At least two translations come close
to accuracy in this regard:

*The Lord will remove all sickness from you; he will not
afflict you with any of the malignant diseases that you
know from Egypt, but **will leave them** with all those who
hate you* (New American Bible (Revised Edition)).

*The Lord shall do away from thee all ache (The Lord shall
take away all thy aches and pains); and he shall not bring
to thee the full evil sicknesses of Egypt, that thou hast
known, **but to all thine enemies these sicknesses shall
come*** (Wycliffe Bible)

Both translations eliminate God from being the direct inflictor of
the evil diseases that will come upon Israel's enemies. These translations
imply more of a lack of protection or a lack of prevention rather than a
direct causation. This is consistent with the teaching of Scripture in which
God simply gave the Egyptians over to pestilence (Ex. 12:23; Psalm 78:50-
51). God is not the inflictor of sickness but He is able to protect and heal
from sickness those who obey Him. Those who refuse to obey Him He
simply removes any restraint He held against evil diseases and allows His
enemies to be inflicted (Psalm 91:1-4).

November 12

God Takes Sickness from Obedient Servants

*Thou shalt not bow down to their gods, nor serve them, nor do after their works: but thou shalt utterly overthrow them, and quite break down their images. And ye shall serve the Lord your God, and he shall bless thy bread, and thy water; and **I will take sickness away from the midst of thee*** (Ex. 23:24-25)

When we study the language carefully we can see that God is vindicated from the idea that He is the inflictor of sickness and disease. Notice the words, *"I will take sickness away from the midst of thee."* God cannot take away something that is not already there.

The sad reality is that when man fell, the earth became cursed. Many of the microbes and pathogens that were created for the good of man were corrupted by sin and Satan. The corrupted microbes and pathogens produce the germs that often cause sickness among people. These things are all around us in the air and in our foods.

Satan, and not God, is the author of death (Heb. 2:14). The curse is the absence of God's life-protection in a certain area. However, God promised the Israelites that when they obey Him that He would take away sickness from their midst. That means that God would supernaturally and miraculously deal with any distorted and corrupted microbes that brought illness.

This helps us to further understand such passages as Deut. 7:15 which tell us that God, *"will not afflict you with any of the malignant diseases that you know from Egypt, but **will leave them** with all those who hate you"* (New American Bible (Revised Edition)).

God will take away sickness from those who worship and serve Him but He will leave His enemies with the diseases that are already in their midst. God does not have to create and engineer sickness since it is already present through germ cells.

Once again we see that God is not an inflictor but a protector. It is sin that destroys lives by pushing God away, thus losing His protective presence, and leaving people open to the destructive forces all around them. These destructive forces include sickness and disease. When we server the true God then we can trust Him for His protection from the sicknesses and diseases that surround us. His enemies, on the other hand, are left with sicknesses. But they cannot blame Him for them.

November 13

Did God Cause the Flood of Noah?

*The earth also was corrupt before God, and the earth was filled with violence. And God looked upon the earth, and, behold, it was corrupt; for all flesh had corrupted his way upon the earth. And God said unto Noah, The end of all flesh is come before me; for the earth is filled with violence through them; and, behold, **I will destroy them with the earth**.... And, behold, I, even I, do bring a flood of waters upon the earth, to destroy all flesh, wherein is the breath of life, from under heaven; and every thing that is in the earth shall die* (Gen. 6:11-13, 17)

Sometimes when we teach the Biblical truth that God is not necessarily responsible for the often violent and destructive things that He occasionally takes credit for, some understandably ask questions like, "What about the flood of Noah, Sodom and Gomorrah, the plagues of Egypt and other natural disasters attributed to God in Scripture?"

In today's devotion we will briefly look at the flood that occurred in Noah's time. Keeping with our Biblical understanding that because God had given man dominion over the earth and the actions of man not only affect him but all that he was given dominion over, we can see how His violence negatively affected the earth itself. The earth was corrupt because *it was filled with violence*. The Bible plainly teaches that our sinful acts have a negative impact upon the earth (Gen. 3:17-18; 4:10-12; Lev. 18:24-28; 20:22; Isa. 24:4-5; Hose 4:2-3; Zech. 12:12; Rom. 8:18-22).

There is a moral order in the world that works like the law of gravity (Rom. 8:2; Gal. 6:5-7). When the moral order is violated, there are consequences. The Hebrews often credited God with the consequences though God was not actively bringing them about (for example, compare 1 Chron. 10:3-6 with 10:13-14 and 1 Sam. 15:23).

In ancient Near Eastern literature, there are fictional accounts of the flood in which the gods become frustrated with all the noise that humans are making and selfishly destroy them with a flood. This is not the true God of the Bible. As one scholar has noted, "Genesis, however, emphasizes the moral dimension and claims that human beings through their wickedness and violence are destroying the earth."[57] Tomorrow, we will see that it was men pushing God away that brought them this destructive flood.

---

[57] McKeowen, James **Genesis: The Two Horizons Old Testament Commentary** (Grand Rapids, MI: William B. Eerdmans, 2008), P. 53, 54

November 14

Did God have a Choice Concerning the Flood of Noah?

And the Lord said, **My spirit shall not always strive with man***, for that he also is flesh: yet his days shall be an hundred and twenty years* (Gen. 6:3)

Some have mistakenly understood the above passage to teach that God lowered man's lifespan. Since men were living for hundreds of years around this time, some believe that God decreed a decrease concerning this. However, this is not what the passage is teaching. The passage is saying that the Spirit of God would continue to convict men and draw them to repentance for 120 years.

The Living Bible paraphrases this passage best: *"Then Jehovah said, 'My Spirit must not forever be disgraced in man, wholly evil as he is.* ***I will give him 120 years to mend his ways.'"*** This is a lot of time to repent. What a merciful God. However, after a constant rejection of God's drawing mercy, the Spirit would depart, taking along with Him His protective presence and allow men to receive the destructive consequences of their rebellion.

Like Nineveh, if the antediluvians had repented, the flood would not have come (Jonah 3:4-10). God *waited* and suffered long, desiring the people to repent so that He would not have to bring judgment (1 Pet. 1:20). Like Jonah, Noah preached to the people of his time but they refused to listen (2 Pet. 2:5). Instead, they asked God to leave them alone:

Hast thou marked the old way which wicked men have trodden? Which were cut down out of time, whose foundation was overflown with a flood: ***Which said unto God, Depart from us: and what can the Almighty do for them?*** *Yet he filled their houses with good things: but the counsel of the wicked is far from me.* (Job 21:15-18)

Notice that they asked, "What can the Almighty do for them?" Fallen angels had produced children through women and these were giants of ancient fame (Gen. 6). The people had their "gods" (fallen angels and giant Nephilim) and their hearts became more wicked because these "gods" allowed them to indulge their fleshly passions. There was no need for Yahweh. Therefore, when God is asked to leave a situation, He is a gentleman. But He does so very reluctantly. But when God leaves, *"....woe also to them when I depart from them!"* (Hosea 9:12b).

November 15

How Did God bring the Flood of Noah?

*And it came to pass after seven days, that the waters of the flood were upon the earth. In the six hundredth year of Noah's life, in the second month, the seventeenth day of the month, **the same day were all the fountains of the great deep broken up**, and the windows of heaven were opened* (Gen. 7:10-11)

In Genesis 6 God says, *"And, behold, I, even I, do bring a flood of waters upon the earth, to destroy all flesh,"* Yet, God often says that He will do that which He merely allowed or permitted by the removal of His restraining protection.

Genesis 7 tells us that *"all the fountains of the great deep broken up."* It was by God's power that the waters were kept from overflowing and destroying (Genesis 1:6-10; Hebrews 1:3; 2 Pet. 3:5-7). Man would not repent so God "destroyed" by removing His protection. He abandoned them (except for Noah and his family) and allowed the *consequences* of their sin and corruption of the earth to bring the inevitable destruction:

*For a small moment **have I forsaken thee**; but with great mercies will I gather thee. **In a little <u>wrath</u> I hid my face from thee** for a moment; but with everlasting kindness will I have mercy on thee, saith the LORD thy Redeemer. **For this is as the waters of Noah unto me**: for as I have sworn that the waters of Noah should no more go over the earth; so have I sworn that I would not be wroth with thee, nor rebuke thee.* (Isa. 54:7-9)

The Living Bible paraphrases it, *"Just as in the time of Noah I swore that **I would never again <u>permit</u> the waters of a flood to cover the earth and destroy its life**, so now I swear that I will never again pour out my anger on you."*

Notice that God did not actively bring about the consequences of Israel's sin but He abandoned them, hid His face, and withdrew His protection. *Abandonment* and *hiding His face* is the normal way that God exercises His wrath (Deut. 31:16-18; 1 Kings 14:15-16; 2 Kings 17:17-20; 2 Chron. 29:6-8; Psalm 27:9; 89:46; Isa. 57:17; Jer. 33:5; Hos. 11:7-9; Matt. 18:34; Rom. 1:18, 24-28). The same is true concerning the people of Noah's time who told God to *depart from them*. Therefore, His Spirit stopped striving with them, thus removing His protection, and allowing the consequences of their corruption of the earth to take place.

November 16

The Healing of the Land

*If my people, which are called by my name, shall humble themselves, and pray, and seek my face, and turn from their wicked ways; then will I hear from heaven, and will forgive their sin, and will **heal their land*** (2 Chron. 7:14)

I have heard this passage quoted and preached numerous times. I have used it in my own preaching and teaching throughout the years. Yet, it is only in recent times that I have come to understand what is meant by the healing of the land.

My Charismatic/Pentecostal mindset (one which I still hold to) focused my ideas about healing only on the physical body. I have always been and continue to be an advocate for the miraculous power of God to heal our bodies. I have always recognized the fact that sin (be it personal or general) is the reason for sickness in the body. Jesus' redemptive work to deliver us from our sin also included the healing from the results of sin, which is our body.

However, it is only in recent years that I have begun to understand that sin makes *everything* it touches sick. God warned the Israelites not to engage in the sinful practices of the Canaanites so *"that the land vomit not you out also, when ye defile it, as it vomited out the nation that was before you"* (Lev. 18:28; American Standard Version).

It is this sickness and vomiting of the land that brings famine, drought, bad crops, physical sickness, and natural disasters. Many of the things that people claim are "Acts of God" and are "under God's control" are actually the results of sin affecting the land in a negative way and causing it to become sick.

Therefore, the repentance of a nation not only comes with a spiritual revival where people come back into relationship with God and begin to uphold His standards of morality, but the physical land itself needs a supernatural healing from God in order to relieve it from all of the sickness that sin has put upon it.

The United States of America is becoming sicker due to sin not only being practiced but legislated as law within the government. Morality and righteousness is nearly looked upon as being criminal. Certain sinful practices such as abortion and homosexuality are placing its practitioners into protected classes. Is there any wonder why our economy is in such shambles? We need national repentance. When we repent, God is willing to not only forgive our sins, but He will heal the land and make it a great place to live.

November 17

Saving Health of the Nations

God be merciful unto us, and bless us; and cause his face to shine upon us; Selah. That thy way may be known upon earth, thy saving health among all nations (Psalm 67:1-2)

Contrary to unpopular belief, God's goal is not to be an arbitrary dictator over the nations. God certainly has the physical omnipotent power to do it but the fact that He has not tells us something wonderful about His character. God is full of love and respects the freedom of men and nations.

It is Satan who desires to be dictator supreme and has usurped the authority of man in order to bring this about. Yet, even he is limited by what he can do. While Satan is not even close to having God's power, he still has a certain amount of power that was given to him when God created him. He did not lose this power when he rebelled. But Satan cannot use his physical power to bring his desires to pass. Therefore, his primary weapon is deception.

Sadly, men have fallen for Satan's deceptions for centuries. Men who remain under satanic deception, and this includes many of our world leaders and the elected officials in the USA, do not realize the long term effects of satanic influence upon the land. Due to the desire for temporal gratification, most do not even seem to care. Satan's only objective is to steal, kill, and destroy. Since he is the author of sickness and death, his agenda is to destroy the earth by this method.

God is waiting for men and nations to cry out to Him for mercy. He wants men to repent and walk in His ways because His way is the saving health of the nations. His way is the way of deliverance from the devastating effects of Satan and sin upon the land and within our nations. Note the wonderful result of God's saving health:

O let the nations be glad and sing for joy: for thou shalt judge the people righteously, and govern the nations upon earth. Selah. Let the people praise thee, O God; let all the people praise thee. ***Then shall the earth yield her increase;*** *and God, even our own God, shall bless us* (Psalm 67:4-6)

In Genesis 4:12 God told the murderous Cain, *"When thou tillest the ground, it shall not henceforth yield unto thee her strength."* When God rules and righteousness is in the nations, the earth yields her increase. This is better than the curse brought by sin in which the earth refuses to yield it. We need God's saving health for the nations. Let's pray for it.

November 18

The Healing of the Waters

*And he went forth unto the spring of the waters, and cast the salt in there, and said, **Thus saith the Lord, I have healed these waters**; there shall not be from thence any more death or barren land. So the waters were healed unto this day, according to the saying of Elisha which he spake.* (2 Kings 2:21-22)

God's healing is not only for bodies and lands, but His desire to heal extends to the very things in which our life depends on, which is water. Water is the most important life sustaining substance that we have on this earth. I have been told that the body can go 90 days without food but can only go seven days without water.

This could be why God announced His nature as healer, not when He healed someone's physical body, but when He did a miraculous healing of the waters in the desert:

*And he cried unto the Lord; and the Lord shewed him a tree, which when he had cast into the waters, **the waters were made sweet**: there he made for them a statute and an ordinance, and there he proved them* (Ex. 15:25)

It was right after this that God announced, *"I am the Lord that healeth thee"* (v. 26). This comes from the compound name, "Jehovah-Rophe" which means that God is in covenant to heal. He revealed this truth while bringing healing and health to bitter waters so that His people would be sustained in their wilderness journey.

Several books have been written about the healing effects of drinking water. In our day and age people are drinking a lot of sugar filled, carbonated, and artificially colored drinks. Yet, we wonder why there is so much cancer, diabetes, and asthma among us. We are not only eating unhealthy but we are drinking unhealthy.

Drug companies keep inventing drugs that are supposed to help deal with things that could be prevented and healed if we would drink more water and less (or no) other drinks. These man-made drugs come with a list of possible side effects with lawyers standing by ready to bring lawsuits. Yet, if we drink more water, we would have less of a need for these drugs. God announced Himself a healer when He healed water, thus emphasizing the importance of it.

November 19

The Mental Illness of Nebuchadnezzar (Part 1)

The same hour was the thing fulfilled upon Nebuchadnezzar: and he was driven from men, and did eat grass as oxen, and his body was wet with the dew of heaven, till his hairs were grown like eagles' feathers, and his nails like birds' claws (Dan. 4:33)

Nebuchadnezzar had become arrogant and prideful. He boasted of how he had built the great nation of Babylon with his great power and for the honor of his majesty (v. 30). God then spoke to him from heaven and told him what was about to happen. Later, Nebuchadnezzar lost his mind, became mentally ill, and began to act like an animal.

All of this could have been avoided. God warned Nebuchadnezzar in a dream and gave the interpretation to Daniel and then Daniel told the king, *"Wherefore, O king, let my counsel be acceptable unto thee, and **break off thy sins by righteousness**, and thine iniquities by shewing mercy to the poor; **if it may be a lengthening of thy tranquility**"* (Dan. 4:27).

Breaking off from his sins could have lengthened this king's sanity but he remained in pride (v. 29). Therefore, this mental illness was brought upon him. The question we have continued to wrestle with in these devotions is whether or not God would personally inflict Nebuchadnezzar with such a malady. In verse 23 we read:

*And whereas the king saw a watcher and an holy one coming down from heaven, and saying, Hew the tree down, and destroy it; yet leave the stump of the roots thereof in the earth, even with a band of iron and brass, in the tender grass of the field; and **let** it be wet with the dew of heaven, and **let** his portion be with the beasts of the field, till seven times pass over him.*

The work of the angel (watcher) is no different than the four angels in Revelation 7:1-3 who hold back the winds from destroying the earth. They are commanded by another angel "not to hurt the earth" until God's people are sealed. The only way that these angels would "hurt the earth" is by removing their restraint from the winds.

In Daniel 4:23, the angel commands another to remove the restraint that has kept Nebuchadnezzar from going mad. When this protection is removed then they will *let* the king be wet and *let* him be with the beasts. This is *permission* and not *causation*.

November 20

The Mental Illness of Nebuchadnezzar (Part 2)

The same hour was the thing fulfilled upon Nebuchadnezzar: and he was driven from men, and did eat grass as oxen, and his body was wet with the dew of heaven, till his hairs were grown like eagles' feathers, and his nails like birds' claws (Dan. 4:33)

As we saw in yesterday's devotion Nebuchadnezzar had become arrogant and prideful. God had warned him about what would happen to him through a dream if he did not repent. God even gave Daniel the interpretation of the dream and told the king how to prevent what was about to come. Instead, Nebuchadnezzar remained arrogant. Therefore, God sent an angel to, *"**let** it be wet with the dew of heaven, and **let** his portion be with the beasts of the field"* (v. 23). God removed His protection from the king and he suffered a serious mental illness.

While God protects and restrains, He is not the ultimate source of the mental illness that inflicted the king of Babylon. In Luke 8:27-35 Jesus healed a man who had the same type of illness as Nebuchadnezzar. The text tells us that the source of this illness was *demonic*. Once the man was healed, he was mentally stable:

*Then they went out to see what was done; and came to Jesus, and found the man, out of whom **the devils were departed**, sitting at the feet of Jesus, clothed, and **in his right mind**: and they were afraid* (Luke 8:35)

The same type of healing would later come to Nebuchadnezzar: *"And at the end of the days I Nebuchadnezzar lifted up mine eyes unto heaven, and **mine understanding returned unto me**, and I blessed the most High"* (Dan. 4:34a). When we compare Scripture with Scripture then we can see that Nebuchadnezzar's mental illness was the result of demon possession. God was only involved in removing the restraints of these evil forces and allowing them to have their way.

What a difference it would make if God's people recognized the true source of mental illness and would rise against it using the weapons of prayer and our authority in Christ. Instead, we have attempted to treat it with drugs, mental hospitals, secular psychiatry, and twelve step programs. Just as with Nebuchadnezzar and with the man at the tombs, the only true deliverance from mental illness is to recognize Satan as its source and the power of God as its only remedy.

November 21

Does the Bible teach that Miracles are NOT for Today?

*Charity never faileth: but whether there be prophecies, they shall fail; whether there be **tongues, they shall cease;** whether there be knowledge, it shall vanish away. For we know in part, and we prophesy in part. But when that which is perfect is come, then that which is in part shall be done away. When I was a child, I spake as a child, I understood as a child, I thought as a child: but when I became a man, I put away childish things* (1 Cor. 13:8-11)

There are a group of theologians who believe that the miracles that we read about in Scripture are no longer for us today. They are referred to as "cessationists" (meaning miracles have ceased.). These theologians read where Paul says that "tongues shall cease" and "the perfect is come," and claim that the word "perfect" in verse 10 is in reference to the completion of the Scriptures.

Yet Paul told the Corinthians, *"So that ye come behind in no **gift;** waiting for **the coming of our Lord Jesus Christ.**"* (1 Cor. 1:7) The word "gift" is the Greek word "charisma" which refers to the miraculous faculties mentioned in 1 Cor. 12. If Paul was intending to teach the Corinthians that these gifts would end at the completion of the New Testament, then why would he, in the very same epistle, commend them for possessing the gifts while *waiting for the Lord Jesus to come*?

When we add 1 Cor. 13:12 to the rest of the verses, we are left with little doubt that the "perfect" is that which is to come at the second coming of the Lord Jesus Christ: *"For now we see through a glass, darkly; but then face to face: now I know in part; but then shall I know even as also I am known."* There is no doubt that "face to face" is referring to the time in which we will see Jesus.

The Apostle John, regarding the Lord's second coming, writes, *"Beloved, now are we the sons of God, and it doth not yet appear what we shall be: but we know that, when he shall appear, we shall be like him; for we shall see him as he is"* (1 John 3:2). Jesus is the perfect One who we will see face to face, and it is when we see Him face to face that we will know even as we are known.

Taking 1 Cor. 13:12 along with 1 John 3:2, it is fallacious to insinuate that 1 Cor. 13 is teaching that miracles were no longer necessary with the completion of the New Testament. It simply stands to reason that Paul was not teaching cessation of the Charismata at the completion of the Bible but rather at the coming of our Lord Jesus Christ.

November 22

Confronting the Powerless Gospel (Part 1)

*For our gospel came not unto you in word only, **but also in power**, and in the Holy Ghost, and in much assurance; as ye know what manner of men we were among you for your sake* (1 Thess. 1:5)

The Greek word for power in this passage is *"dunamis"* which means "miracle or supernatural power". The Gospel is not in word only but in POWER!! Paul taught that the gospel is to be accompanied with POWER.

Not only is God's power lacking in most of our Western churches, but some "ministers" hold conferences and write books promoting a powerless gospel. Their books often attack ministers and movements in which God is sought to manifest His power.

This powerless gospel has its primary roots in the teaching of John Calvin, a "protestant reformer" in the 16th century. In his "Institutes," Calvin advocates for a gospel *without* power:

> But the gift of healing disappeared with the other miraculous powers which the Lord was pleased to give for a time, that it might render **the new preaching of the gospel for ever wonderful**. Therefore, even were we to grant that anointing was a sacrament of those powers which were then administered by the hands of the apostles, it pertains not to us, to whom **no such powers have been committed**" (Calvin, Institutes IV, 19, 18).

Calvin admits to preaching a "new" gospel. Paul says that if anyone preached any other gospel than what he preached then that man is accursed (Gal. 1:6-9). Paul said that his gospel came with miraculous power. Calvin claims that his new gospel needs no such power.

Furthermore, Calvin contradicts Scripture when he claims that his new preaching makes the gospel "wonderful". Scripture, contrary to Calvin, defines "wonderful" as being in line with miracles: *"And the blind and the lame came to him in the temple; and **he healed them**. And when the chief priests and scribes saw **the wonderful things** that he did...."* (Matt. 21:14-15a). The testimony of divine Scripture runs in direct contrast to the teaching of John Calvin.

Men have followed the teaching of John Calvin rather than the teaching of the Bible. Our world needs a true manifestation of God's power if we will defeat the forces of darkness that holds sway over the minds of sinners. We must reject the powerless gospel of men and stay with the miracle-power gospel of the Bible.

November 23

Confronting the Powerless Gospel (Part 2)

*So, as much as in me is, I am ready to preach the gospel to you that are at Rome also. For I am not ashamed of **the gospel of Christ: for it is the power of God unto salvation** to every one that believeth; to the Jew first, and also to the Greek* (Rom. 1:15-16)

The word "power" in Romans 1:16 is the same Greek word for "miracle" in Mark 9:39 in which Jesus said, *"....for there is no man which shall do a **miracle** in my name, that can lightly speak evil of me."* It is also the same Greek word which is translated as "Power" in Acts 10:38 which says, *"How God anointed Jesus of Nazareth with the Holy Ghost and with **power**: who went about doing good, and healing all that were oppressed of the devil; for God was with him."* All three are *"dunamis".*

The powerless gospel is an intellectual substitute for the true gospel of Jesus Christ and is devoid of miraculous power. It depends on educational scholasticism for proclaiming its gospel rather than the power of God. This so-called manner of proclaiming the gospel has become the test of orthodoxy in many parts of the church.

What is the driving force behind this powerless gospel? This gospel does not have its foundation in Scripture but in John Calvin's teaching. Calvinistic theology with its teachings of an all-controlling despot is the foundation of the powerless gospel. Theologian Benjamin B. Warfield, whose popular arguments for cessationism are still used in our day, wrote:

> Therefore it is that the miraculous working which is but the sign of God's revealing power, cannot be expected to continue, and in point of fact does not continue, after the revelation of which it is the accompaniment has been completed. **It is unreasonable to ask miracles, says John Calvin—or to find them—where there is no new gospel**. (Benjamin B. Warfield, Counterfeit Miracles, pp. 26, 27)

Notice that Warfield's belief in this powerless gospel is not founded upon Scripture. You will find no Biblical support for Warfield's gospel without miraculous power. He relies primarily on Calvinist theologians, John Calvin himself being the most prominent. Many of the present day cessationists have heavily relied upon Warfield's teaching to promote their own version of this false teaching. Do not embrace a "gospel" without power and without a foundation in Scripture.

The Bible is the Word of God

*Knowing this first, that **no prophecy of the scripture is of any private interpretation**. For the prophecy came not in old time by the will of man: **but holy men of God spake as they were moved by the Holy Ghost*** (2 Pet. 1:20-21)

There are way too many foundational truths being questioned in today's so-called "evangelical" churches. One of them is whether or not the Bible is truly God's Word. Some churches have bought into the age-old liberal theological lie that claims that the Bible is not itself the inspired Word of God but that it *contains* the Word of God. This is nothing more than another satanic deception to destroy faith and get one to lose confidence in the Bible's message.

To claim that the Bible is not the Word of God and to question its veracity is to charge the character of God with extreme unkindness. Why would a loving God not leave men with a reliable document concerning His requirements for them and how they may fulfill them? Why would a loving God, knowing that men needed salvation, not ensure that they had accurate information about how to obtain it?

Even worse, why would a God of love allow men to present a document which only *contains* His Word and leave it at the mercy of men to guess (or decide) which parts of it are actually His Word? If that was true then that means Scripture would have to be of "private interpretation" because men can decide which portion of it is really God's Word and which portions of it are not.

Many unbelievers and liberal theologians are quick to say, "The Bible is a book written by a number of fallible men". Perhaps they were fallible but we have it on good record that these men were "holy men of God." That means that they were set apart by God and committed to Him. We are also told that these writers of Scripture *"spake as they were moved by the Holy Ghost."* This means that, though God may have used their unique personalities, it was He who spoke through them and they recorded what He said.

This understanding should also enable us to throw away the ridiculous arguments about the type of inspiration given by God to the Scriptures (mechanical, verbal, etc.). The record of Scripture itself says that holy men spoke as they were moved by the Holy Spirit. Therefore, the Bible is reliable and trustworthy and is indeed, without question, the Word of God. Its promises and commands can be trusted. Reject all ideas that cast doubts on the truth that the Bible is the divine inspired Word of God.

November 25

The Bible is the Infallible Word of God

*For this cause also thank we God without ceasing, because,
when ye received the word of God which ye heard of us, ye
**received it not as the word of men, but as it is in truth, the
word of God**, which effectually worketh also in you that
believe* (1 Thess. 2:13)

For centuries Satan has inspired skeptics to cast doubt on the fact
that the Bible is a divine document that has come from the mind and mouth
of God. Every attack imaginable has been launched against it. The devil
has used persecution, intellectualism, so-called science, so-called
theologians, and other devices in his ongoing war against this book.

Satan has attempted to make the Bible nothing more than classic
literature or just another religious book equal to the Koran or other non-
Christian literature. Therefore, it has been necessary for valiant Christian
scholars and researchers to provide us with the essential proof that validates
the accuracy of the Bible.

One researcher, *Stephen Caesar,* has been very helpful in this
regard. Based on his presentation of irrefutable historical, archeological,
and scientific evidence, Caesar writes, "….that over the past two hundred
years, there have been hundreds upon hundreds of archeological discoveries
which have proven the Bible true and accurate, and none which have
proven it wrong."[58] Caesar concludes:

> The evidence is overwhelming, the verdict is clear: God's Word
> is not some unreliable work of fiction produced by mere men
> who peppered and polluted it with their own biases, opinions,
> and interpretations. The Bible is not the error-filled word of man
> but the error-free Word of God. Its truths have withstood the test
> of time, and it has overcome all attempts to eradicate it from the
> face of the earth and remove it from the human heart.[59]

God has made His faith building truth accessible to anyone and everyone
who desires knowledge of it. It is called *the Bible*. If God is truth and has
no ability to lie, and if the Bible is His Word, then the Bible is a completely
reliable document concerning God's will for His creatures. However, it is
necessary for *you* to believe this.

---

[58] Caesar, Stephen **Many Infallible Proofs** (Nashua, NH: Bible Proof Ministries,
1994), p. 12

[59] 3. Ibid., p. 361

November 26

The Bible is a Revelation directly from God

But I certify you, brethren, that the gospel which was preached of me is not after man. For I neither received it of man, neither was I taught it, but by the revelation of Jesus Christ (Gal. 1:11-12)

The liberal lie that the Bible is nothing more than a collection of writings written by man is refuted by Paul when He says that his gospel did not come from man but was a revelation of Jesus Christ. If Paul lied about this then no part of the Bible can be trusted since it is possible that other contributors to Scripture lied about writing what God inspired them to write.

Did Moses imagine having been given commandments directly by God on the mountain? If he did then we cannot trust any portion of the first five books of the Bible. Since most of the other books and the teachings of Jesus makes reference to Moses teaching as if it were the Word of God then these writings cannot be trusted. Therefore the ridiculous idea espoused by Liberal theologians that "the Bible is *not* the Word of God but only *contains* the Word of God" is self-defeating.

Everyone must make a choice and decide who and what they will believe. Will you believe the witness of the Bible writers themselves who claim that they received their revelation directly from God, or will you accept the erroneous teachings of the liberal theologians and emergent church proponents who question the authenticity of this sacred book?

Personally, I have chosen to believe Paul and the other contributors to the Scriptures. I firmly believe that this book we have called the Bible is God's holy and written Word as He revealed it to men. The apostle Peter, who was with Jesus almost from the beginning of His ministry on earth, agreed that Paul's epistles were inspired Scripture (2 Pet. 3:15-16).

Our affirmation or rejection of the Bible as a revelation from God affects our salvation. Paul wrote, *"For I am not ashamed of the gospel of Christ: for it is the power of God unto salvation to every one that believeth"* (Rom. 1:16). If we believe that Paul's words were the mere words of a fallible man then we do not believe that it is the gospel of Jesus Christ. If we do not believe that the Bible comes from God then we cannot be saved.

There really is no way around this. It is important to affirm that the Bible is a revelation from God and live according to it, or look at it as a document from man and live a life that is contrary to it. We have been given a choice. Choose wisely.

The Deity of Christ

In the beginning was the Word, and the Word was with God, and the Word was God. The same was in the beginning with God. All things were made by him; and without him was not any thing made that was made (John 1:1-3)

A close friend of mine was attending classes at a well-known theological institute in order to finish his doctorates in theology. During a discussion session with some of his classmates one of the female students said, "I just don't believe that Jesus is God. Am I the odd-ball here?" He told me that the other students began to make attempts to comfort her in this false belief with words like, "Aw, it's okay, etc." He told me that he was shocked at this.

Sadly, these are the "pastors" that are being placed into our denominational churches. These are the "Christian leaders" that are currently feeding people. It is no wonder that so many people are dying and going to hell. If we deny the deity of Christ then we deny the sinless purity of His blood and it is only by His pure, sinless, shed blood that He is able to save us.

A multitude of pseudo-Christian cults such as the Jehovah's Witnesses, The Way International, and a number of other demonic substitutes for the truth have at the forefront of their doctrines the denial of Christ's deity and the denial of the personhood of the Holy Spirit (one denial often leads to the other). It would be easy to deal with this lie if it were limited to these cultic groups, but when these lies begin creeping into the "Evangelical" churches then more people are susceptible to deception.

To deny Christ's deity is to malign the loving character of God. If Jesus is God then that means God Himself was willing to sacrifice Himself for the sake of men. God Himself was willing to suffer at the hands of His own creatures in order to save them. God Himself was willing to become just like one of His own creatures with all of our weaknesses so that He can legally redeem us from the kingdom of darkness without being accused of unfair use of omnipotent power.

The deity of Christ is important to the truth about God's character. To affirm it is to affirm the self-sacrificing love of God. To deny this truth is to cast aspersions on God's love and integrity.

November 28

What Christ Gave Up for Us

Let this mind be in you, which was also in Christ Jesus:
*Who, **being in the form of God, thought it not robbery to***
***be equal with God:** But made himself of no reputation, and*
took upon him the form of a servant, and was made in the
likeness of men: And being found in fashion as a man, he
humbled himself, and became obedient unto death, even the
death of the cross (Phil. 2:5-8)

Years ago I visited a young man who stopped coming to church. I enquired of him as to why we had not seen him in several weeks. He replied, "Because you guys worship Jesus. I cannot worship him because I read the holy book and it tells me that Jesus is not God." I kept asking him what is this "holy book" that he was referring to but he never did divulge that information (though I suspect that it was the Koran).

There are people who would like to deny that Christ ever existed. Those who cannot deny His *existence* are doing all that they can to deny His *deity*. It is understandable for a world under the government of Satan to do such a thing but when so-called theologians and so-called "holy religions" do this then undiscerning followers are susceptible to deception.

Denying Christ's deity is denying a very important aspect of God's nature, which is His self-sacrificing love. Religions such as Islam do not have a deity who is willing to become like one of his creatures in order to save them. Instead, their deity requires that they torture, dismember, and murder Christians and Jews and others who refuse to conform to their beliefs. Their religion brings oppression upon women and children and treats them as lower class citizens. Their religion promotes selfish indulgent prophets and an angry deity who cares little to nothing for his followers.

Is it any wonder that these religions must deny the deity of Christ? Is it any wonder that they relegate Him to being nothing more than a mere prophet? You see, Christ taught and demonstrated a different perspective about God than what is taught among these religions. He taught about a God who wanted so much to rescue His creatures from the consequences of their own rebellion that He was willing to become one of them.

Paul tells us in Philippians that Christ gave up a whole lot for us. He was God and equal with the Father. Yet He humbled Himself, became like us and suffered all that we suffer. Only Heaven can tell the large extent to which He sacrificed for us. However, if He was never God then He really did not give up anything much. Thankfully, we know for a fact that Jesus is truly God. Because He is God, He sacrificed much to save us.

November 29

The Virgin Birth of Christ

And in the sixth month the angel Gabriel was sent from God unto a city of Galilee, named Nazareth, To a virgin espoused to a man whose name was Joseph, of the house of David; and the virgin's name was Mary. ... And the angel said unto her, Fear not, Mary: for thou hast found favour with God. And, behold, thou shalt conceive in thy womb, and bring forth a son, and shalt call his name JESUS (Luke 1:26-27, 30-31)

Another truth that is often under severe attack is the virgin birth of Christ. Some cannot understand how a virgin can have a child apart from sexual intimacy. They make the claim that Jesus is the result of a sexual union between Mary and Joseph. Many of these teachings are propagated across some church pulpits in the United States and other parts of the world.

When I asked some advocates of this teaching as to how Christ could be God apart from a virgin birth the answer was, "God can still infuse Himself in a man without a virgin birth." A virgin birth makes much more sense than this mythological idea and is more scientifically accurate.

Some secular scientists have shown that the DNA make up of children has more of the father's genetic code than the mother's. In an article on a science magazine's website titled, "Genetically Speaking, You're More Like Your Dad" we are told that after a number of tests on mice, the genetic makeup more strongly resembles the paternal parent than the maternal one:

> Overall, they found that most genes showed parent-of-origin effects in their levels of expression, and that paternal genes consistently won out. For up to 60 percent of the mouse's genes, the copy from dad was more active than the copy from mom. This imbalance resulted in mice babies whose brains were significantly more like dad's, genetically speaking.[60]

The scientific research helps us to see that if Jesus was the result of a sexual union He would have been born a sinner. He could never have redeemed us. It would take a much greater miracle to make Him "God" than a virgin birth. Being born of a virgin is much more Biblical—and scientifically believable.

---

[60] http://blogs.discovermagazine.com/d-brief/2015/03/03/genetically-more-like-dad/ (Last accessed: April 11, 2015)

338

November 30

The Virgin Birth Essential to the Deity of Christ

Now all this was done, that it might be fulfilled which was spoken of the Lord by the prophet, saying, Behold, a virgin shall be with child, and shall bring forth a son, and they shall call his name Emmanuel, which being interpreted is, **God with us** (Matt. 1:22-23)

There are some religions and cults that affirm the virgin birth of Christ but they deny His deity. Other false teachers somewhat affirm that Christ was God but deny His virgin birth. Both doctrines question the integrity of God, malign His character, and go directly against the plain teaching of Scripture.

We are told in John 1:1 that *"....the Word was God."* Several verses later we are told, *"And the Word was made flesh, and dwelt among us"* (John 1:14). Some who affirm the deity of Christ while denying His virgin birth believe that God was able to infuse deity into Jesus *after* He came about as a result of the sexual union between Mary and Joseph.

If this were true then John's words in John 1:14 would have to be worded much differently. It would have to say, "And **flesh was made the Word**, and dwelt among us." However, since John tells us that "the Word was made flesh" then there can be no other logical way of understanding this than what the Scriptures themselves affirm, which is the fact that Christ was born of a virgin. Hence, that is why we can rightly say that Jesus is Emmanuel—God with us.

Those who claim the virgin birth but deny the deity of Christ do not understand how they mischaracterize God and pervert His Word. We are told that the virgin birth results in "God with us". Again John tells us that the Word, who was affirmed to be God, *"....was made flesh, and dwelt among us."* If Jesus was indeed born of a virgin then He has to be God.

Christ did not begin His existence when He was born as a man. He is not a created being. He has always been just as the Father and the Holy Spirit. Christ is the Creator of all things, including man. Man was created in His image. This is not something that is ever said about angels.

Christ became like one of the creatures created in His image. No angel could ever die to save us. Only God could do that and He can only do it as a sinless man with whom Satan had no charges against or no rights to control. Therefore, He had to be born of a virgin and He had to be God. The two truths—the deity of Christ and His virgin birth—are the two that Satan vehemently attacks because they are contributors to his defeat and the loss of his hold over mankind.

December 1

God Created the Waster to Destroy

*Behold, I have created the smith that bloweth the coals in
the fire, and that bringeth forth an instrument for his work;
and **I have created the waster to destroy*** (Isa. 54:16)

Many believe that the "waster" in this passage is the devil. Others
believe that it is in reference to the enemy armies that might possibly come
against Israel and destroy it. Both understandings are valid since any army
that comes against Israel would have been moved by Satan to do so.

However, some use this passage to teach that God created Satan in
the beginning as the evil being that he presently is. They gleefully present
their proof that God created Satan from the beginning with the express
purpose of destroying men. One person even claims that God purposefully
created this enemy because Christians needed someone to fight in order for
them to grow. I am not sure if they take into account how unsuccessful this
"purpose" has been (Mark 4:14-17).

This passage is using the exact same idiomatic language found in
Isaiah 45:7: *"I form the light, and create darkness: I make peace, and
create evil: I the Lord do all these things"* (Isa. 45:7). God "creates evil" by
permitting the evil that men bring upon themselves as a result of their own
rebellion (Deut. 30:15, 19; 31:16-18; Jer. 8:3). In actuality, God is not the
source of evil or its results. It is evil that produces evil (Matt. 7:15-20 (Ps.
25:8; 34:4-10; 85:12; 86:5; 105; 106:1; 107:1; 118:1, 29; 135:3; 136:1).

The same is true concerning "the waster" or Satan. The being
currently known as Satan was an anointed cherub (angel) who was perfect
until iniquity was found in him (Eze. 28:14-16). God did not put the
iniquity in him. Jesus says that everything that Satan does, he does it of his
own initiative (John 8:44). Jesus said that Satan's desire to destroy is
opposed to God's desire to protect and give life (John 10:10). God is only
said to have *created* the waster in the sense that He takes responsibility for
its actions when He removes His protection and allows the waster to
destroy (Job 1:8-12; 2:1-7; 42:10-11).

Those who use this passage to claim that God made Satan as he
presently is miss the context of Isa. 54:16. God said that He created the
smith. Does this mean that the one who became a smith left the mother's
womb with the equipment and skills needed to perform this task apart from
training? Smiths then and now had to be trained for these tasks. Therefore,
the passage is not saying that God created the person as a smith but He
created the person who would someday become a smith. The same is true
concerning Satan. God created a good angel but the devil later decided to
become a waster who destroyed.

340

December 2

No Weapon against You Can Succeed

No weapon that is formed against thee shall prosper; and every tongue that shall rise against thee in judgment thou shalt condemn. This is the heritage of the servants of the Lord, and their righteousness is of me, saith the Lord (Isa. 54:17)

Yesterday we saw that verse 16 of this same chapter says that God, "created the waster to destroy." We learned that God is only said to have *created* the waster in the sense that He takes responsibility for its actions when He removes His protection and allows the waster to destroy (Job 1:8-12; 2:1-7; 42:10-11).

Here in verse 17 we learn that even though the waster may use weapons formed by the blacksmith (who was also created by God), that, as long as we remain under God's protective presence, none of these weapons that have been formed against us shall succeed.

When we understand the background of verse 16 it will help us to appreciate the promise in verse 17. God will allow the waster to destroy those who choose to live in rebellion but no weapon that Satan can produce can prosper against those who God protects (1 John 5:18-19). This is the heritage—the divine right—of God's faithful servants. The waster cannot destroy those under God's protection.

In verse 15 God says, *"Behold, they shall surely gather together, but not by me."* God says that even when an enemy does attack His people He will not be the blame for it. God's protection over us does not mean that we will never come under attack. On the contrary, we are to expect opposition from the enemy. Christians often fall under defeat by failing to recognize that the enemy is attacking of his own initiative and God has nothing whatsoever to do with it.

When the enemy does attack we, and he will, we are not to wallow in despair or passivity. We are to take this promise from God and stand on it. We are promised that every tongue, including the ones that attempt to curse us are to be condemned. This is our heritage (our divine right) as a servant of Christ. We have authority over all of the demonic forces that attempt to rise up against us physically, spiritually, and emotionally. They cannot hurt a child of God who is living obediently for his or her Master.

.

December 3

Is God a Promise Breaker?

*Therefore, God in his desire to make it abundantly clear to those to whom he made his promise, that his purpose was unalterable, **bound Himself with an oath**, so that by these two unalterable things, which make it **impossible for God to break his promise**, we who have taken refuge with him may be greatly encouraged to seize the hope that is offered to us.* (Heb. 6:17-20; An American Translation by Edgar J. Goodspeed).

God not only makes promises, but binds and obligates Himself to their fulfillment. We never have to doubt the Word of God or be powerless in prayer when we have His very oath that He will do the very things that he promised.

Sadly, men in their extreme teachings on God's sovereignty have taught contrary to this faith-building truth. In an old magazine article one man wrote, "....God is no further bound by his general promise to hear the prayers of His people, than to give such things as in his wisdom he shall judge most suitable in the case."[61] This author further writes:

.....they have no certainty, nor can they arrive at it by any process whatever. God is not bound, nor can they certainly tell what he will do until the event shall declare it, unless you suppose a special revelation.[62]

This author believes that God can make promises to answer prayer but one cannot be absolutely sure that He will fulfill them because, according to this author, God is not bound by them. This type of teaching on God's sovereignty maligns His character and puts His integrity at stake.

Even worse, it goes directly against the teaching of God's Word. Hebrews tells us that God went out of His way to guarantee that He will fulfill His promises. God did all that He could to give us faith-building assurance. It takes satanically influenced "ministers" to destroy it. Stay with God's Word and reject the teachings of men and your faith will grow strong (Rom. 4:20-21; 10:17).

---

[61] M'Laren, John F. (Editor) **The Christian magazine, Volume 1** (Geneva: Associate Reformed Presbyterian Church, 1832), p. 277

[62] Ibid, p. 280

December 4

Does God have a Set Time for Everyone to Die?

And as it is appointed unto men once to die, but after this the judgment: So Christ was once offered to bear the sins of many; and unto them that look for him shall he appear the second time without sin unto salvation (Heb. 9:27-28)

I have found it strange that some theologians use this passage as proof that God has an appointed time for everyone to die. We sometimes hear of people who have died, and in many cases, tragic deaths, and even worse, without having known Christ. Someone will remark concerning their death, "Well I guess his number was up. God took him." When challenged concerning this statement we are quoted this passage and told that God has set a date and time for everyone's death.

First, this could not be true concerning unbelievers since, if they died apart from Christ, they would be eternally lost, suffering in hell until the white throne judgment to which they would then be cast into the lake of fire (Rev. 20:11-15). God is not willing for that to happen (2 Tim. 2:4-6; 2 Pet. 3:9). For that very reason He takes no pleasure in the death of the wicked (Eze. 18:23, 32; 33:11).

For the Christian, God has promised to satisfy him with long life (Psalm 21:4; 91:16). We are taught things that we can personally do to lengthen or shorten our lives (Deut. 4:40; 5:16; 22:6-7; Prov. 3:1-2, 16; Eph. 6:1-3). Therefore, how long we live on the earth in many cases has a lot to do with our personal decisions.

What is it then that is being taught in Heb. 9:27? When we read chapters 7, 8 and 9 we learn that the writer of Hebrews is making a comparison between the work that Christ has done in bringing about our redemption with that of the Levitical High Priest of the Mosaic covenant. Every high priest that was appointed according to Mosaic law had to die sooner or later just as all men do due to the fall of Adam (Heb. 7:23). However, we are told that the priesthood of Jesus Christ "continueth ever" (Heb. 7:24-28). When read in context, this is the primary teaching of the passage.

Certainly the passage teaches us that all men will eventually die apart from the rapture of Christians still alive when Jesus comes to meet us in the air (1 Thess. 4:17). Adam's sin and our own has assured us of that. But Heb. 9:27 is not teaching us that God has a set appointed time of death for each individual. So trust God for health and a long life.

December 5

Is there a Predestined Date for Your Death?

*To every thing there is a season, and a time to every purpose under the heaven: **A time to be born, and a time to die**; a time to plant, and a time to pluck up that which is planted. A time to kill, and a time to heal; a time to break down, and a time to build up; A time to weep, and a time to laugh; a time to mourn, and a time to dance* (Eccl. 3:1-4)

Fatalistic theologians have used Hebrew 9:27 and the passage here in Ecclesiastes 3 to teach the false idea that God has a predestined appointed date for the death of each individual on the earth. Sadly, this idea makes God appear very unkind since He is reluctant to tell us the exact date that He has appointed for us to die. Furthermore, under this idea God will never tell us the *means* by which we will die. Therefore, many sit around, afraid of not knowing exactly when their "number will be up". This leads to the "fear of death" that Jesus rescued us from (Heb. 2:14-15).

There are children who have been killed by drunk drivers. Fathers who were the sole providers for their families have died tragic deaths while their children were very young and needed him. Others have died after being raped, molested, and tortured. Some even die in satanic rituals. Masses of people have been killed in what some call, "natural disasters," and others call "acts of God."

Some of the most horrible deaths have been placed on God's shoulders since He is said to have set a date for each individual's death. That is how Solomon's phrase, "a time to die" has been erroneously interpreted. One author claims that these are statements concerning "God's sovereign purposes for everyone."

Solomon is not teaching that God has a set appointed time for each one to be born or die no more than He is the One who determines when a person will laugh or cry. There is a time in which, under certain circumstances, one can laugh but under a different set of circumstances one should not laugh (death of a loved one for example). Under those different set of circumstances crying is more appropriate.

People have free-will and could unwisely choose to laugh at a side event or cry at an event in which there should be rejoicing. In this passage, Solomon is telling us some things are inevitable in this life and other things must be done at the appropriate times. Solomon is *not* saying that God has ordained that all of these events happen to each person, especially the "time to die". There is no preselected day for our death. Our decisions, faith, and circumstances are often the factors that determine our length of life.

December 6

Did God Shorten Man's Lifespan?

And all the days that Adam lived were nine hundred and thirty years: and he died. And Seth lived an hundred and five years, and begat Enos: And Seth lived after he begat Enos eight hundred and seven years, and begat sons and daughters: And all the days of Seth were nine hundred and twelve years: and he died (Gen. 5:5-8)

In the beginning men did not just live for many *years*, they live for several *centuries*. Some believe that God reduced man's life in Gen. 6:3. However, Gen. 6:3 is a reference to how long the Holy Spirit would attempt to change men's hearts before releasing the flood of Noah. It was actually sin that reduced man's life.

In the beginning God created a dome over the earth (Gen. 1:7). This dome was meant to protect the earth and its residents from the dangerous radiation of the sun:

God made the stars and two great lights: the larger light to rule over the day and the smaller light to rule over the night. **God put them in the dome of the sky to shine on the earth, to rule over the day** *and over the night, and to separate the light from the darkness. God saw how good it was* (Gen. 1:16-18; Common English Bible)

Man's wickedness began to bring corruption upon the earth itself (Gen. 6:5-12). Basically this resulted in "uncreation." After 120 years of attempting to bring man to repentance, God loosed His restraints on the waters (Gen. 8:2) *"....and the windows of heaven were opened"* (Gen. 7:11b).

There was a break in the dome that God created to protect the earth from both the waters above it and the harmful radiation of the sun. A number of scholars believe that once this protective shield around the earth was gone, man's longevity was gradually reduced. It was not a divine decree made by God that reduced man's previous long-lasting lifespan, but it was sin.

God warned Adam that sin would culminate in death (Gen. 2:15-17). Today we are told that sin itself brings forth death (Rom. 6:23; James 1:12-14). Sin destroyed God's protective dome over the earth, bringing forth dangerous cosmic radiation and reduced man's lifespan. This is not God's doing but ours. God does all that He can to protect us. We do much to forfeit that protection and bring destruction upon ourselves.

December 7

The Danger of NOT Listening to the Spirit

And said unto them, Sirs, I perceive that this voyage will be with hurt and much damage, not only of the lading and ship, but also of our lives. Nevertheless the centurion believed the master and the owner of the ship, more than those things which were spoken by Paul (Acts 27:10-11)

Years ago I read the testimony of a Christian woman who had been raped. She would jog along the same trail every day. One day she heard a still small voice tell her not to run down that trail on this particular day. Ignoring the voice she continued down the trail and was accosted by a man who began to rape her. However, her life was spared and she lived to tell about it.

While such a violation of her body is horrific, she still survived this incident with her life and health. Many others have ignored the still small voice to their own demise. All of us can attest to times when an alarm seemed to be going off inside of us and something inside of us was telling us to move in a different direction. Our obedience to this voice saved our lives and saved us from a loss of limb as well.

Every person who has received Christ as their Lord and Savior and who has been born again has the precious Holy Spirit dwelling on the inside of them. We are told in Scripture, *"For as many as are led by the Spirit of God, they are the sons of God"* (Rom. 8:14). God's leading helps us to discern what is sinful and detrimental to our spiritual health. However, He also alerts us to physical dangers that we can avoid if we obey Him.

Quite often God gets the blame for the bad things that happen to us when He had nothing to do with them. On the contrary He often attempts to get our attention and lead us away from danger. Sadly, many of us have not trained our spirits to listen to the Lord and we suffer as a result. Yet, so often, in His mercy, God has minimized the consequences of missing His leading as He did for the lady mentioned above.

The same is true concerning Paul's voyage to Crete. Paul perceived that the trip would be a dangerous one and he warned them concerning it. Paul was a man who had trained his spirit and knew how to follow those promptings of the Spirit. Sadly, he was ignored and this nearly got everyone on the ship killed. It was only Paul's fasting and praying that kept the people on the ship alive despite the loss of everything else.

Let us learn to be led by God Spirit. When we perceive danger ahead, obey the voice. It will save your life.

December 8

The Price for Disobeying God's Voice

And when the prophet that brought him back from the way heard thereof, he said, It is the man of God, who was disobedient unto the word of the Lord: **therefore the Lord hath delivered him unto the lion**, *which hath torn him, and slain him, according to the word of the Lord, which he spake unto him* (1 Kings 13:26)

The prophet had a successful ministry in Judah in which he prophesied and it came to pass. When Jeroboam attempted to attack the prophet he suffered as a result. The prophet prayed and King Jeroboam was healed. When the king wanted to reward him for this the prophet was insistent that he would not eat in this city, *"For so was it charged me by the word of the Lord, saying, Eat no bread, nor drink water, nor turn again by the same way that thou camest"* (1 Kings 13:9).

Sadly, the prophet believed the lie of another prophet, thus disobeying God. He began to eat and drink in the city. The very prophet that lied to him would then pronounce the judgment upon him that he would not make it alive to his destination (1 King 13:15-22). The prophet had forfeited God's protection through disobedience.

Notice that, "the Lord hath delivered him unto the lion." The Lord did not "send" the lion. The Lord knew the danger the prophet would be in if he did not do exactly as he was told. However, he failed to obey. Furthermore, we do not see any repentance on his part for his disobedience. These factors caused him to forfeit the protection God would have provided from the lion:

> **Because thou hast said, The Lord is my protection**, *the Most High hast thou made thy refuge.... Upon* **the fierce lion and asp** *shalt thou tread: thou shalt trample under foot the* **young lion and serpent** (Psalm 91:9, 13; Leeser Old Testament)

This is why we must not only train our spirits to hear God's voice, but we must go with His personal guidance to us against any other "word" that comes from someone else. If what someone else gives us contradicts what God has told us personally then we must reject it. Failure to do so could cost us our lives. However, God cannot be blamed for our demise.

December 9

Who was Eternal Damnation Prepared For?

*Then shall he say also unto them on the left hand, Depart from me, ye cursed, **into everlasting fire, prepared for the devil and his angels**: For I was an hungred, and ye gave me no meat: I was thirsty, and ye gave me no drink: I was a stranger, and ye took me not in: naked, and ye clothed me not: sick, and in prison, and ye visited me not* (Matt. 25:41-43)

God did not prepare hell and the lake of fire for mankind. This was prepared for Satan and his angels. So why do men and women go there? Because they have taken on Satan's nature and have decided to follow him (Eph. 2:1-5). Those who take on Satan's nature and follow his ways must share his eternal destiny.

Notice that Jesus says to those who are condemned to the everlasting fire that they did not feed the hungry, give drink to the thirsty, give shelter to strangers, clothe the naked, or visit those in prison. This is a lack of compassion for those in need and this is satanic in nature. While criminals and sexually immoral people will go to the lake of fire, so will those who neglect to exhibit God's love for those who are deprived. God's nature is one of selfless, others-focused love. Anyone lacking this essential characteristic is not serving Christ.

Keep in mind that God never prepared this place for man because it was never His intentions for man to take on Satan's attributes. It was never God's desire that any human being go to that place (Tim. 2:4; 2 Pet. 3:9) and He derives no pleasure from the fact that people die and separate themselves from Him (Ezekiel 18:23-32; 33:11). God cries over those who make choices to live in such ways that leaves Him no choice but to allow them the eternal consequences of their choice (Matt. 23:37; Luke 7:30; John 5:40; Hosea 11:5-7).

So why is there a hell in the first place? Hell and, later, the lake of fire is for Satan because he and his followers hated God intensely. They chose to separate themselves from Him. Therefore, God prepared a place by which they can have the separation that they wanted so badly (Isa. 14:12-15). Any place where God's presence is lacking is a place of misery.

Jesus, in His deep and intense love for us was willing to pay the full price to redeem us from this place. God does not want any man to go there and there is no reason for anyone to. Make Christ your Savior and obey His Lordship and you will never have to go to a place that was not prepared for you in the first place.

December 10

Death and Hell are God's Enemies

Whom God hath raised up, having loosed the pains of death: because it was not possible that he should be holden of it.... He seeing this before spake of the resurrection of Christ, that his soul was not left in hell, neither his flesh did see corruption (Acts 2:24, 31)

One should not embrace or take comfort in the false teaching that a literal hell does not exist. We can see that part of the redemption price that Jesus paid was to enter into hell. This proves that the doctrines of soul sleep and annihilation are utterly false and have no bearing in Scripture. Otherwise Jesus would have had to suffer both.

However, another false doctrine taught in the majority of Christianity is the idea that God personally imprisons sinners in hell upon their death. On the contrary it is the sinner himself who chooses hell because he or she refuses to repent. If men and women will choose to serve God's enemies while alive on the earth then He will give them over to these same enemies upon their death.

The fact that hell is an enemy of God is seen in how it attempted to hold Jesus in its grip upon His sacrificial death on our behalf. The word "death" in verse 24 is "Hades" which is translated "hell" in other parts of the New testament. Furthermore, in the original languages, hell takes on a living personality. One scholar says, "....it should be rendered snares of death; the figure being that of escape from the **snare of a huntsman**" (Marvin Vincent's Word Studies; emphasis mine). Another scholar notes:

> "....but the Hebrew original means 'snares' or 'traps' or 'cords' of death where sheol and death are personified as hunters laying snares for prey ....'Loosing' (lusas) suits better the notion of 'snares' held a prisoner by death" (A.T. Robertson's Word Pictures In the New Testament)

Hell attempted to hold on to Jesus. Hell was not the friend of Jesus. Jesus went to war and defeated hell on our behalf. We are told, *"God raised him up! God freed him from death's dreadful grip, since it was impossible for death to hang on to him"* (Common English Bible) and *Then God released him from the horrors of death and brought him back to life again, for death could not keep this man within its grip* (The Living Bible). Jesus defeated hell on our behalf so that those who appropriate this truth won't go there.

December 11

Man's Covenant with Hell

Because ye have said, **We have made a covenant with death, and with hell** *are we at agreement; when the overflowing scourge shall pass through, it shall not come unto us: for we have made lies our refuge, and under falsehood have we hid ourselves* (Isa. 28:15)

God cannot arbitrarily deliver people from hell apart from their acceptance of Christ as Lord and Savior because they have made a covenant with it. God has to honor those covenants that are made of our own free will. Some have become "children of hell" before they ever get there (Matt. 23:15).

Due to this covenant, Hell pulls the unrepentant sinner down like a gravitational force upon death (Psalm 116:3; Isa. 5:14; Luke 16:22-23). As S. D. Gordon wrote, "They who prefer to leave God out will gather together at some time *by a natural moral affinity, or gravitation*. The name used for such meeting-place in this old Book is that hurting word hell." (S. D. Gordon, *Quiet Talks on Personal Problems*, pp. 28-29. Emphasis is mine).

Therefore, God is not throwing people into hell upon their death as some traditions assert. Hell itself knows who belongs to it and pulls them in when they die. Hell knows who has kept a covenant with it.

The only way to keep from going to that horrible place upon death is to break one's covenant with hell. God told the Israelites, *"And your covenant with death shall be disannulled, and your agreement with hell shall not stand"* (Isa. 28:15). Through the redemptive work of Christ on our behalf we can break the covenant that we once made with death and hell and enter into the new covenant with Christ.

God has made every provision available to keep us from having to go to hell (John 3:16-21). God does not condemn anyone to hell. We were destined to go there because we chose to follow Satan. However, Jesus came to give us another choice. We choose Him and our destiny changes. We choose against Him and we will continue on the course that we have chosen (Matt. 7:13-14).

Dear reader, if you have not yet chose Christ as your Lord and Savior, why don't you choose to enter into a new covenant today by accepting His provision on your behalf. You will be eternally grateful that you did.

December 12

Did God know that Billions would go to Hell?

*And they built the high places of Baal, which are in the valley of the son of Hinnom, to cause their sons and their daughters to pass through the fire unto Molech; which I commanded them not, **neither came it into my mind**, that they should do this abomination, to cause Judah to sin* (Jer. 32:35)

Did God know before He created man that the majority of them would end up in hell? Most of the church believes that God knew this. Some even go as far as to believe that God predestined this to happen. While the latter thought makes God into a wicked tormentor, the first one unintentionally makes Him negligent (Gen. 6:5-7; Jer. 7:31; 19:5; 32:35). After all, if God saw the future eternal torment of billions of His creatures before He created them but created them anyway, does that make Him any better than if He had intentionally predestined them to this fate?

God Himself holds people responsible for knowing what would happen but not doing something about it. Concerning the parable of the wicked servant Jesus said, *"And that servant, **which knew his lord's will, and prepared not himself,** neither did according to his will, shall be beaten with many stripes"* (Luke 12:47). In this parable and other passages of Scripture we see that God holds people accountable for doing something or failing to do something based on the knowledge that they had (Matt. 25:24-30; 1 Sam. 3:11-13; 2:30). Does God hold a double standard?

If God created with full foreknowledge of the evil that would infiltrate man and eternally damn the majority of them then this makes Him reckless, negligent, and fully culpable for the evil. To have perfect knowledge that an action taken, regardless of how noble it may be, would lead to the death and eternal damnation of millions of people, as well as provide the opportunity for horrendous evil to take place, makes the actor just as responsible for the evil as if he or she is the one that committed the actual evil.

If a father leaves his loaded gun sitting on a table where his five and six year old children has access to it, and he knows the very harm of doing so, and one of the children grabs the gun and kills his sibling, is the father not fully responsible? Scriptures tell us that God was not fully aware of man's fall into sin. It never entered His mind. Therefore He is not culpable. The fact that billions are suffering eternal torment is due to the choices they made and not a predestined plan or a negligent use of divine exhaustive foreknowledge.

December 13

Do all Religions Lead to God?

Neither is there salvation in any other: for there is none other name under heaven given among men, whereby we must be saved (Acts 4:12)

Liberal theologians have deceived millions of people into believing that Islam, Buddhism, Hinduism, and other religions are all roads leading to the one true God. This strange desire for an ecumenical unity among the various religions is said to promote "compassion". However, there is nothing compassionate about giving false information that could lead to eternal damnation.

First thing we must understand is that God does not save anyone based on sincerity or a system of works. This may sound harsh but we must see this from God's perspective. Man, apart from Christ, is under the reign of Satan's government. Within his wicked government, Satan has set up multiple ways to receive worship from man. All of these religions have their origins in demonism because they reject Christ as Savior.

Furthermore, not one of the human founders of any of these religions were willing to give their lives for the salvation of their followers. Even if they did die for their followers it would have done no good since these founders were sinners themselves. Jesus not only died for His followers but for the whole world. He was our substitute who suffered the penalty for the sin we committed. Since Jesus was sinless, His death paid for our sin.

Since other religions don't have a sinless Savior, they have a system of things one must do to reach "nirvana" or "paradise" or to ensure that one's "reincarnation" gets them to a better life. None of this can lead to the true God because this is not what He is asking from anyone. The true God, the One taught in the Bible, bases salvation strictly on a loving relationship with Him. That relationship can only come through recognizing all that Christ has done on our behalf to make relationship with God possible.

Therefore, do not be deceived by Satan's tactics. All religions do not lead to the true God. All of them are based on lies (though they might have a little bit of truth in them to draw people in). God cannot partner with a lie in order to bring people to Him: *"Jesus saith unto him, I am the way, the truth, and the life: no man cometh unto the Father, but by me"* (John 14:6). Jesus is the only way to God. To look for any other way will get a person lost eternally.

December 14

Cause and Effect: Key to Understanding God's Ways in the Old Testament

The shew of their countenance doth witness against them; and they declare their sin as Sodom, they hide it not. Woe unto their soul! **for they have rewarded evil unto themselves.** *Say ye to the righteous, that it shall be well with him: for they shall eat the fruit of their doings. Woe unto the wicked! it shall be ill with him: for the reward of his hands shall be given him* (Isa. 3:9-11)

People are often perplexed by some of the things that God says that He will personally do to rebellious people. Many would rather not read the Old Testament because they believe that it portrays a totally different God than the One in the New Testament. Yet, these same people would also have to give up many portions of the New Testament.

Remember that Jesus is the God of both testaments. But how do we deal with the type of punitive vengeful language that we read in which God is said to make people sin, bring natural disasters, inflict with pestilence, kill using wild animals, attack using enemy armies and other methods by which God is said to smite, destroy, slay, take vengeance, etc.?

God created the universe with a moral orderliness. The universe has been established upon the principles of cause and effect, action and reaction, sowing and reaping. This is why Isaiah could say that the wicked have rewarded evil unto themselves and that things would go well for the righteous because they would eat the fruit of their own doings.

God often takes credit for the self-inflicted punishment of the wicked and the reward given to the righteous because of the fact that He established the laws by which each receives these things based on their actions. God's presence and protection remains over the righteous and as we pray, He ensures that we are rewarded. Since the wicked have forsaken the Lord, He *allows* them to receive the results of their wickedness and takes credit for inflicting it upon them.

This is the common principle by which the Old Testament can be interpreted. This does not mean that God is passive since He is often using His omnipotent power to protect the repentant from the results of previous sins, protecting the righteous from the sins of others, and pleading with the wicked to turn from his or her evil ways. He is certainly involved. However, He also allows His established laws to take their course when wickedness prevails. In that sense, God is said to be the doer of what He permitted. This is the true understanding of God's ways in the Old Testament.

December 15

Why do the Wicked Prosper?

Righteous art thou, O LORD, when I plead with thee: yet let me talk with thee of thy judgments: **Wherefore doth the way of the wicked prosper?** *wherefore are all they happy that deal very treacherously?* (Jer. 12:1)

In our devotions we have emphasized the truth of God's moral order and the fact that God often punishes by removing His protective presence and allowing the wicked to reap that which they have sown. We have also emphasized the fact that God keeps His hand of protection over the righteous. Yet, we cannot deny the fact that we see so much injustice in this life and the wicked seem to be very successful at their evil. They appear to get away with it.

As Jeremiah's complaint shows us, this is not something new and was even an issue in Biblical times. But why is this so? Sadly, Satan has the current governorship of this world so the moral order does not always work the way that God intended in this present life. Some righteous people do not always get the rewards of righteousness in this life nor do the wicked always suffer the consequences of their sin in this life. However, all will receive the rewards of the righteousness or wickedness whether it is here on earth or in eternity. God will make sure of it:

> *For I was envious at the foolish, when I saw the prosperity of the wicked. For there are no bands in their death: but their strength is firm. They are not in trouble as other men; neither are they plagued like other men. Therefore pride compasseth them about as a chain; violence covereth them as a garment.... Behold, these are the ungodly, who prosper in the world; they increase in riches.... When I thought to know this, it was too painful for me; Until I went into the sanctuary of God;* ***then understood I their end. Surely thou didst set them in slippery places: thou castedst them down into destruction.*** *How are they brought into desolation, as in a moment! they are utterly consumed with terrors* (Psalm 73:3-6, 12, 16-19)

The wicked often do appear to get away with evil in this life, but a day of reckoning is coming. Therefore do not fear or envy them (Psalm 37:1-2; Prov. 23:17-18). God's moral principles will take effect sooner or later.

December 16

Praying God's Will to be Done on Earth

After this manner therefore pray ye: Our Father which art in heaven, Hallowed be thy name. Thy kingdom come. Thy will be done in earth, as it is in heaven. (Matthew 6:9, 10; see also Luke 11:2)

There are a number of views concerning this passage. One view teaches that whatever happens on earth is God's sovereign will (be it sickness, tragedy, etc.). Those who advocate this view tell us that Jesus was teaching us to pray in submission to His will. Another view is the *eschatological* view in which we are to pray for the millennial reign of Christ to come on the earth. I believe that both views are a distorted understanding of the Lord's teaching here.

While we long for Christ's millennial reign, this could not be the primary purpose of this prayer. Nor could Jesus have been teaching the "whatever will be will be" attitude when He taught us to pray "thy will be done," Such resignation actually defeats the purpose of prayer. The purpose of prayer is to request God's aid and intervention in bringing a change to negative circumstances. Prayer is inviting God to do that which He otherwise would not have done had we not prayed. The Methodist founder, John Wesley, said:

> **God does nothing but in answer to prayer**; and even they who have been converted to God without praying for it themselves, (which is exceeding rare,) were not without the prayers of others. Every new victory which a soul gains is the effect of a new prayer. (emphasis are mine)[63]

Therefore the "passive submission" view promotes doubt and confusion concerning God's will. Quite often it is the foundation for many putting a doubtful "if" in their prayers and praying with a lack of assurance. There is no indication that Jesus was teaching a lack of assurance concerning the will of God when he taught us this manner of praying. On the contrary, this statement is a statement of *faith*.

Negative circumstances are usually not the will of God for the obedient child of God. Therefore we pray in order to invite God to prevail upon the situation and cause it to line up with His perfect will as revealed in His Word and by His Spirit.

---

63 Wesley, John *A Plain Account of Christian Perfection*, from **The Works of the Rev. John Wesley Vol. XI** (London: Thomas Cordeux, 1812), p. 241

December 17

What Happens when we Don't Pray?

And Asa in the thirty and ninth year of his reign was diseased in his feet, until his disease was exceeding great: yet in his disease he sought not to the LORD, but to the physicians. And Asa slept with his fathers, and died in the one and fortieth year of his reign. (2 Chron. 16:12, 13)

While we are thankful for doctors and modern medicine, these are limited in what they can accomplish. Quite often the mistakes made by doctors and the side effects of medicine prescribed by many of them do more harm than good. Sadly, more people, including Christians, put more trust in the fallible medical profession than in God. They will visit a physician before ever bothering to seek God.

Regardless of our reasons for this, failing to pray demonstrates a lack of trust in God, and it can cost one his or her life. No example in the Bible presents this better than King Asa's. Early in his reign, King Asa was promised that if he sought God that God would be found by him (2 Chron. 15:1-2). Asa believed the Word of God and commanded that all of Israel seek the Lord under the penalty of death if they refused (2 Chron. 15:9-15). Their seeking was rewarded, just as God had promised.

One would think that with a promise of this nature and the visible reward that was received for obeying it that Asa would have gone to his grave obeying this Word. Sadly, Asa began to depart from his simple faith and failed to seek the Lord at the most crucial times in his life. God was no longer able to bless Asa.

Like Asa, when we fail to meet God's conditions, we tie His hands concerning that which he desires to do in our lives and for others. It is impossible for God to lie (Num. 23:19; Psalm 89:33-35; Titus 1:2; Heb. 6:18) and He must stick to the conditions that He has given to obtain the promise as well as fulfill the promise itself when conditions are met.

If God were to solve our crisis apart from our meeting His stated conditions this would make God a liar and a violator of His own Word. This He cannot do (Psalm 138:2). Therefore, God's inability to *fulfill the promises of prayer apart from our praying* has nothing to do with a lack of power, but it has everything to do with His integrity. He is unable to do that which would violate His holiness. Contrary to the teaching of some, God does not have a standard of holiness for men and a totally different one for Himself, just because He is sovereign (Mat. 5:48; 1 Pet. 1:15, 16). Therefore, if we want the blessing that comes with prayer, we must pray.

December 18

Satan's Accusations do not come from God

*And I heard a loud voice saying in heaven, Now is come salvation, and strength, and the kingdom of our God, and the power of his Christ: for **the accuser of our brethren is cast down**, which accused them before our God day and night. And they overcame him by the blood of the Lamb, and by the word of their testimony; and they loved not their lives unto the death* (Rev. 12:10-11)

We sin and then we confess our sins before God. On this basis He has promised to forgive us (1 John 1:9). Yet, many of us still have feelings of condemnation. If we have confessed our sins, repented of them and received cleansing through the blood of Jesus then God has promised to have mercy. Therefore God is not the source of any condemnation. This is the work of Satan, the accuser.

Satan's work as an accuser is to continually point out a person's faults and sins in order to prove that the person being accused is deserving of nothing but punishment and eternal damnation. He did this to both God and Job (see Job 1-2), to Peter (Luke 22:31-32), to Joshua the high priest (Zech. 3:1-4), and to Jesus (John 14:30). However, the accuser has been *cast down* – he is a *defeated enemy*. The blood of Jesus has cleansed us from all our past sins and removed any legal access by which Satan had to accuse us and condemn us.

When you and I received Christ as our personal Lord and Savior and were born again by the precious Spirit of God we became new creations in Christ Jesus. We are told that old things passed away and all things *have become new* (2 Cor. 5:17). In other words, God is not keeping any records of past sins. On the contrary God wipes away *all* record of our sins when He forgives (Isa. 43:25; 44:22; Jer. 31:34; 50:20; Micah 7:19; Heb. 8:12; 10:15-18).

If there is no record of our sins then Satan will not be able to accuse us before God. Furthermore, we can have a clear conscience before God and man and will have confidence in God to answer our prayers (Rom. 8:1-2; 1 John 3:19-22). If we sin after we have been born again, God has made provision for that as well through the blood of Jesus. When we confess and forsake our sins we receive His cleansing (1 John 1:7-9).

God promised that He will not remember our sins. If He forgets them and we are still being reminded and condemned by them then it is the accuser of the brethren that is bringing up our past. We are to reject and refuse his taunts and remind him that Jesus has defeated him. We must remind him that we are now connected to Jesus.

December 19

Your Father REBUKES the Accuser

*And he shewed me Joshua the high priest standing before the angel of the Lord, and Satan standing at his right hand to resist him. And **the Lord said unto Satan, The Lord rebuke thee, O Satan**; even the Lord that hath chosen Jerusalem rebuke thee: is not this a brand plucked out of the fire?* (Zech. 3:1-2)

The Old Testament saints were given very few glimpses into the spirit realm to see what was actually taking place. For some reason, God decided to reveal to Zechariah the enemy spirit that was actually standing against God's plans for Jerusalem. Satan wanted Jerusalem destroyed but believed that his only chance of seeing this happen would be to point out their sin to God. Therefore, when God rescued Israel from Babylon Satan was standing by ready to oppose this plan with his usual accusations.

This is exactly how the accuser works against us today. Sadly, we give Satan plenty of ground through our sins by which he is able to accuse us before God and claim his right to destroy God's people. Yet, our Lord Jesus Christ has provided a way, through His own redemptive sacrifice, to cleanse us from our sin, remove the shame of it, and take away Satan's rights to accuse us. This is wonderfully illustrated in Zechariah 3:3-4:

*Now Joshua was clothed with filthy garments, and stood before the angel. And he answered and spake unto those that stood before him, saying, Take away the filthy garments from him. And unto him he said, **Behold, I have caused thine iniquity to pass from thee**, and I will clothe thee with change of raiment.*

God Himself removes our filth and provides us with a robe of righteousness. Because Christ is our righteousness, the Lord can now rebuke Satan when he attempts to accuse us before God. Hence God is totally on our side. He is not looking to destroy us when we sin. The work of destruction for sin is totally Satan's. God is constantly looking for ways to rescue us from the destruction that Satan desires to bring as a result of our sin.

Reach out to God in repentance for your sins. Receive His forgiveness and imputed righteousness. Begin to walk in His power over sin. When you do that He will rebuke Satan who will no longer be able to accuse or touch you.

December 20

God's Ways and Thoughts

For my thoughts are not your thoughts, neither are your ways my ways, saith the LORD. For as the heavens are higher than the earth, so are my ways higher than your ways, and my thoughts than your thoughts. (Isa. 55:8-9)

Quite often those who teach that God is behind the evils, tragedies and miseries in this world refer to this passage to justify their stance. When Christians who disagree with this false idea protest against their teachings this passage is quoted in order to silence them. After all, God can do these things because He does not think the way we mere mortals think. Neither are His ways ours.

Actually, the passage is being quoted *out of context* to support erroneous ideas about God that contradict His character of self-sacrificing love. When it is read in context it actually supports the truth about God's love:

*Seek ye the LORD while he may be found, call ye upon him while he is near: Let the wicked forsake his way, and the unrighteous man his thoughts: and **let him return unto the LORD, and he will have mercy upon him**; and to **our God, for he will abundantly pardon**. For my thoughts are not your thoughts, neither are your ways my ways, saith the LORD. For as the heavens are higher than the earth, so are my ways higher than your ways, and my thoughts than your thoughts.* (Isa. 55:6-9)

Far from teaching that God is hiding behind some mysterious sovereignty that brings about destructive events in the lives of people, this passage proclaims a loving God who is calling His people back into relationship with Him. His ways and thoughts are only higher than ours based on the fact that we are selfish and sinful and He is not.

Unlike us, God is loving and forgiving and gives us the opportunity to repent. While He will not force us He encourages us to seek Him. If we do then He promises that we will find Him. It is amazing that Satan has been able to twist this wonderful revelation of God's love to the extent that it makes Him appear as an evil, all-controlling tyrant. God's thoughts and ways are only different from unredeemed man in the sense that God's ways and thoughts are pure love and man's most often are not.

December 21

Correcting Distorted Views of God

*Sing, O heavens; and be joyful, O earth; and break forth
into singing, O mountains: for the LORD hath comforted
his people, and will have mercy upon his afflicted. But
Zion said,* **The LORD hath forsaken me, and my Lord
hath forgotten me.** (Isa. 49:13-14)

Notice the distorted picture of God that was being held in the minds
of the Israelites. They had a picture of a God who was uncaring and angry
because they were steeped in sin. When they began to suffer the
consequences of their rebellion they gave up hope because they felt that
God had forsaken them and will not answer their prayers.

Sin always gives us a distorted view of God's love (Gen. 3:7-12). It
is always Satan who gives us these perverted pictures of our loving
Heavenly Father (Gen. 3:1-6). Thankfully, in the case of Israel, God
immediately corrects their distorted view of Himself, showing that He is
more loving than the best of parents:

*Can a woman forget her sucking child, that she should not
have compassion on the son of her womb?* **yea, they may
forget, yet will I not forget thee.** *Behold, I have graven
thee upon the palms of my hands; thy walls are continually
before me.* (Isa. 49:15-16)

When we sin and suffer the consequences of our rebellion, we can
sense that we are forsaken and forgotten by God. Yet God compares
Himself to the best of mothers and says that, like a really good mother, H
could never forget you. Yet, realizing the selfish nature of many humans,
this comparison can only go so far. Someone could easily cite numerous
examples of mothers who have selfishly destroyed their own children and
forgotten them. Therefore, God goes further to say that even if a mother
acts in such a selfish unnatural way, He won't.

God is the prime example of what a parent should be like. Parents
often fall short of the true ideal (God) and God should not be compared to
our human parental failures which are often born out of selfish motives.
Distorted views of God are the major contributors to a lack of trust in Him.

Jesus echoes this same thought concerning God some centuries
later (Matt. 7:7-11). God is the model parent. Let us stop looking at human
parents to get our understanding of God. Let us look at God to see how
parents should begin to act. Being a good parent will begin with the right
understanding of God's character and nature.

December 22

Why has all this Befallen Us?

And Gideon said unto him, Oh my Lord, if the Lord be with us, why then is all this befallen us? and where be all his miracles which our fathers told us of, saying, Did not the Lord bring us up from Egypt? but now the Lord hath forsaken us, and delivered us into the hands of the Midianites. (Judges 6:13)

Gideon, like all of us, wonders "why" we are suffering. Some of our questions to God may be sincere requests for information. Perhaps we missed some important detail that has led to our problems so we are asking the Lord to show it to us and to give us wisdom. God promises to give us wisdom in the midst of our trials (James 1:2-7).

However, some questions are blatant accusations in which we are blaming God for our problems. This is the case with Gideon. Gideon received a visit from the angel of the Lord who called him to deliver Israel from the Midianites. The first thing Gideon does is ask the Lord why Israel was forsaken and delivered into their enemy's hand in the first place. Perhaps Gideon forgot that, *"....the children of Israel **did evil in the sight of the Lord: and the Lord delivered them** into the hand of Midian seven years"* (Judges 6:1).

The Israelites, by sinning against God, forfeited His protective presence. The Israelites began to serve and worship other gods. This is in essence telling the True God, "We don't need you" (Psalm 81:9-12). When they forsook God, God had no other choice but to leave them to the consequences of their sin and allow them to fall into the hands of their enemies. God makes many attempts to stop us from falling into these sins but when we persist, He honors our free-will and allows us to suffer the consequences, though it pains Him to do so.

Gideon failed to acknowledge this fact and complained about God's lack of help. He complained about something that was not God's fault. We too often blame God for circumstances of our own making. In our day we use phrases like "God is in control" and "all things work together for our good," thus implying that God is at fault for our suffering. Yet, though Gideon, like many of us today, complained, blamed God for Israel's misfortunes and accused Him of having forsaken the nation, the reality is that *the Israelites had forsaken God* (Judges 6:1-10).

One of the things that brings defeat in the life of God's people is when we move away from God. However, when we call upon Him He will come back and help us. What a wonderfully good and patient God we have who will help us to overcome our unbelief.

December 23

God's Protection against Foreign "Gods"

That the Lord sent a prophet unto the children of Israel, which said unto them, Thus saith the Lord God of Israel, I brought you up from Egypt, and brought you forth out of the house of bondage; And I delivered you out of the hand of the Egyptians, and out of the hand of all that oppressed you, and drave them out from before you, and gave you their land; And I said unto you, **I am the Lord your God; fear not the gods of the Amorites,** *in whose land ye dwell:* **but ye have not obeyed my voice** (Judges 6:8-10)

Yesterday we looked at Gideon's complaints against God in which he accused Him of forsaking Israel and giving them into the hands of the Midianites. We saw that Gideon was accusing God of wrong-doing. Despite that we can learn yet another wonderful lesson concerning the nature of God and the destructive power of sin.

God told His people that as long as they obeyed His voice that they had nothing to fear from the gods of the Amorites. Note that God did not say, "....fear not the Amorites." He said, *"....fear not the **gods** of the Amorites."* It was the spiritual forces behind the Amorites, Midianites and other heathen nations that God protected Israel from. By dealing with Satan and the demonic forces working through these enemies, God could protect His people from the *physical* enemy.

However, when we choose to line ourselves up with the enemy and begin to subject ourselves to the spiritual entities ruling over them then what more can we expect from God but for Him to "deliver us" into their hands? Is it not we who chose to go into their hands by worshipping them and engaging in profane activities that hurt and insult the true God? Sin opens the door for Satan and demonic forces to have access into the lives of God's people. God had no choice but to deliver them over to Satan (1 Cor. 5:5).

God's part is to protect and rescue. Nonetheless, this is upon condition of loyalty to Him and His covenant. Even after His covenant has been broken God has begged and pleaded for their return, often to no avail. Therefore, it has to come to a point when He has been constantly rejected that He comes to the place where He can no longer offer protection.

Satan's part is to incite opposition. Satan misleads us into acts that will remove us from God's protective presence so that he can have access to us. Satan is seeking someone to devour (1 Pet. 5:8-9). Let's be sure to give him no place in our lives (Eph. 4:27).

December 24

Your Christmas Gift

*What shall we then say to these things? If God be for us, who can be against us? He that **spared not his own Son, but delivered him up for us all**, how shall he not with him also freely give us all things?* (Rom. 8:31-32)

This Christmas Eve while many are doing their last minute shopping, preparing large meals for multiple relatives (or preparing to eat them), as well as putting up last minute decorations and Christmas trees, remember the main reason for this wonderful holiday is to reflect on why the Savior came into the world. Jesus is God's special and precious "Christmas gift" to all of mankind.

Concerning His life Jesus said, *"No man taketh it from me, but I lay it down of myself. I have power to lay it down, and I have power to take it again. This commandment have I received of my Father"* (John 10:18). This is important to remember. Jesus did not have to die if He did not want to. The Father did not have to allow His Son to be killed. Both the Father and Son made choices and in their choices you and I took precedence over all of the pain, suffering, heartbreak, and separation that the Father and Jesus would have to endure.

Look at the language used in these passages: God, "spared not his own Son, but delivered him up for us all." That means He could have used omnipotent power to prevent the killing of His Son. He could have easily blown away the men and demons that orchestrated the worse murder in all of history. Rather than stop it, Peter says, *"Him, **when he was given up**, by the decision and knowledge of God...."* (Acts 2:23). God *gave up* His Son. He gave Him up for us. God did not kill Him. Our sins put Him on that cross.

Jesus, who could have called upon a legion of angels to help Him instead decided to lay down His life (Matt. 26:53). This same Jesus, who created the universe and who created mankind, allowed His own creatures to kill Him in order that He may save them. This is the epitome of love. The Creator God who had power to stop the torment and torture that He underwent for us gave Himself over to it because we were on His mind during the whole torturous event.

On this day before Christmas, when some parents will lie to children and tell them about an overweight, white bearded man in a red suit who climbs down chimneys to bring them toys as gifts and as a reward for being good, let us tell the world about a Savior who gave us the gift of salvation. This gift wasn't given because we were good. He was given to make us good.

December 25

God's Benevolent Will Towards Men

And the angel said unto them, Fear not: for, behold, I bring you good tidings of great joy, which shall be to all people. ***For unto you is born this day in the city of David a Saviour, which is Christ the Lord.*** *And this shall be a sign unto you; Ye shall find the babe wrapped in swaddling clothes, lying in a manger. And suddenly there was with the angel a multitude of the heavenly host praising God, and saying, Glory to God in the highest, and* ***on earth peace, good will toward men*** (Luke 2:10-14)

If we are to remember one thing this Christmas day, it is that God's will towards men is not evil but for good. Jeremiah said it best when he recorded God as saying, *"For I know the thoughts that I think toward you, saith the LORD,* ***thoughts of peace, and not of evil****, to give you an expected end"* (Jer. 29:11).

One should never believe that the evil in this world is a representation of God's will. The angels that announced the birth of Jesus told us exactly what the will of God is towards men when they sang the song above. They had just announced the birth of the Savior into the world and expressed God's heartfelt intentions for sending Him, which was peace on earth and a *good will* towards men.

Some who adhere to a determinist theology and make God the cause of all that happens have a tendency to redefine what is meant by "good." However, there is no confusion about this when we see that the angels equate "peace on earth" with the good will and intentions that God has towards men.

There is much happening in our world today that could by no means be classified as "good". There are wars and rumors of wars. Immorality has become rampant and is even being legislated as law. Morality is looked upon as evil and the government is taking sides against businesses that attempt to hold on to Christ-like principles. Anarchy continues to reign in our inner cities and the murder of the unborn is seen as a legal right in the courts. Politicians and preachers are being exposed constantly for lies and hypocrisy and the Bible, if adhered to at all, is being twisted by both to justify immoral stances.

These do not represent God's good intentions. It is for this reason that we needed a Savior. This Christmas, reflect on the fact that God demonstrates His loving character by having sent Jesus Christ to save us from all of the destruction that the world is doing to itself. Embrace the One who was born to die for you.

The Hiding of God's Face

*And the heathen shall know that the house of Israel went into captivity for their iniquity: because they trespassed against me, **therefore hid I my face from them, and gave them into the hand of their enemies:** so fell they all by the sword. According to their uncleanness and according to their transgressions **have I done unto them, and hid my face from them*** (Eze. 39:23-24)

The study of God's character in light of sin and punishment has fascinated me for a number of years. Many of us have encountered some of the harsh views of God taught from the Old Testament. Ministers present passages in which God is alleged to have exercised His divine omnipotent power to bring punishment upon those who transgressed His covenant.

Yet many of these same ministers present God in a totally different light using the New Testament. It almost appears as if Jesus came for the express purpose of stopping Father God from continuing to use destructive measures in dealing with sinners. The presentation by some is that Jesus would die on behalf of sinners to appease God's wrathful vengeful nature and cause Him to stop killing and destroying wayward creatures.

Thankfully some Bible teachers have discovered that that the Old Testament was written in a *permissive* sense rather than in a *causative* sense. While most have done very little exposition to prove this point (only referring to the writings of a particular Hebrew scholar as proof for this), it does help us to see God as He appears in the Old Testament in a different light.

Nonetheless, the correct interpretation concerning God in the Old Testament is right there in front of us and very few people see it. When God is said to bring some destructive event upon a person or nation this is often done by God "hiding His face." In verse 24 of our devotional text God says that it was according to their sins that He had "done unto them" when the house of Israel was defeated by their enemies and led into captivity.

If we stop reading there as some people often do then we would falsely believe that God used divine power to stir up Israel's enemies against them. However, we read twice in this passage that God "hid His face" and "gave them into the hand of their enemies." From this we learn that God is not exerting divine power to stir up enemies. Instead He is removing His protection and allowing an already present enemy to have its way. This is the correct understanding of God's ways in the Old Testament.

December 27

He will See what their End Shall Be

*They sacrificed unto devils, not to God; to gods whom they knew not, to new gods that came newly up, whom your fathers feared not. Of the Rock that begat thee thou art unmindful, and hast forgotten God that formed thee. And when the LORD saw it, he abhorred them, because of the provoking of his sons, and of his daughters. And he said, **I will hide my face from them, I will see what their end shall be**: for they are a very froward generation, children in whom is no faith* (Deut. 32:17-20)

As we learned in yesterday's devotion, God did not exert divine power to destroy sinners in the Old Testament as is commonly taught. On the contrary, there are always enemy forces waiting to destroy mankind. Were it not for God exerting His divine power to keep these enemy forces at bay, most of us would have experienced certain destruction by now.

However, when we persist in sin and push God out of lives sooner or later He is left with no choice but to withdraw His protective presence. This is known as the *hiding of His face*. This is the exact opposite of God *shining His face on us*, which is symbolic of His protective presence:

*Tell Aaron and his sons: You will bless the Israelites as follows. Say to them: **The Lord bless you and protect you. The Lord make his face shine on you and be gracious to you.** The Lord lift up his face to you and grant you peace. They will place my name on the Israelites, and I will bless them* (Numbers 6:23-27; Common English Bible)

God prefers to "shine" rather than "hide" His face. Sadly, men have a strange propensity for ingratitude. Rather than seeing God's graciousness in protecting His people from the evil forces that surround them, men use it as a false security to sin, not realizing that persistent sin can cause the face of God to stop shining and start hiding.

When God hides His face He takes a step back to observe what will happen to the unrepentant sinner. This proves that God is not actively bringing about the results of their sin but simply removing His protection and allowing the forces surrounding the sinner to have their way. This truth should be the interpretive model for all of the statements in Deuteronomy 28 in which God is said to inflict the results of the curses that come from disobedience. God is only said to do that which He permits to happen when He removes His protection.

December 28

Did a Witch Really Raise up Samuel?

*And the king said unto her, Be not afraid: for what sawest thou? And the woman said unto Saul, I saw gods ascending out of the earth. And he said unto her, What form is he of? And she said, An old man cometh up; and he is covered with a mantle. And Saul **perceived** that it was Samuel, and he stooped with his face to the ground, and bowed himself* (1 Sam. 28:13-14)

God commanded that His people do not consult witches, wizards and others who possessed familiar spirits (Lev. 19:31; 20:6, 27; Deut. 18:11). Yet, I have heard a few sermons and read some teachings to which it is asserted that God violated one of His fundamental laws and permitted a witch to raise up Samuel's spirit.

We are told, *"And when Saul enquired of the LORD, the LORD answered him not, neither by dreams, nor by Urim, nor by prophets"* (1 Sam. 28:6). God refused to speak to Saul in any of the legitimate ways that He has established. So why assume that God would give in and allow His dead prophet's spirit to speak through an unholy vessel on His behalf?

Some may argue, "But the text says that *Samuel* spoke to Saul." It is true that the passage says this and it is also true that if this is the case either Satan is able to bring God's servants' spirits to speak through his unholy vessels, or God is a violator of His own commands and holiness. Neither of these can be true. Therefore, if this is truly Samuel that Saul is speaking to then this causes problems for God's own holy character.

Due to the idiomatic way in which the Scriptures are written, sometimes things are stated from the perspective of the personal subject, in this case Saul. Since *Saul perceived* that this was Samuel, then the rest of the passage is written from *his* perception. Nonetheless, God also provides enough information in His inspired Word to help us better interpret the incident and vindicate Him from the charge of working through witches.

In verse 7 Saul particularly asks for someone with a "familiar spirit" to which some of his own servants immediately knew of one in Endor. In 1 Chron. 10:13-14 we are told that he died due to having enquired of a *familiar spirit* and *not God*. It is obvious that some of these spirits are able to impersonate others and that is what the demon spirit did. The spirit consulted by Saul spoke through the witch and pretended to be Samuel. However, it was not Samuel but an evil demonic entity. Beloved, do not consult so-called "mediums" to talk to dead loved ones. You will certainly be deceived, will place yourself into satanic bondage, and cut yourself off from God's protection.

December 29

Did God ask Abraham to Kill Isaac?

And it came to pass after these things, that **God did <u>tempt</u> Abraham**, *and said unto him, Abraham: and he said, Behold, here I am. And he said, Take now thy son, thine only son Isaac, whom thou lovest, and get thee into the land of Moriah; and offer him there for a burnt offering upon one of the mountains which I will tell thee of* (Gen. 22:1, 2).

In today's text it appears that God is asking Abraham to imitate a pagan ritual that later revelation tells us He absolutely abhors (Lev. 18:21; 20:2-4; Deut. 12:31; 2 Kings 21:6; Jer. 7:31; 19:5; 32:35; Eze. 20:31). While many in the church are not troubled by these things ("God is sovereign. He can do what He wants. Who are we to question Him?"), others are understandably concerned with this apparent contradiction.

While it is easy to read into the passage the idea that God is asking Abraham to kill his son as a sacrifice, a much more careful study of the narrative might lead us to a different conclusion. When we truly study the passage we will see that God never told Abraham to *slay* his son nor did He tell him to *burn him* as a sacrifice.

"Burnt-offering" in the Hebrew (*olah*) can mean "whole burnt offering" or "ascent, stairway, steps" (studylight.org). Strong's Concordance says, "A primitive root; to ascend, intransitively (be high) or active (mount); used in a great variety of senses" Rotherham renders verse 2, "....*cause him to ascend there as an* **ascending-sacrifice**, *on one of the mountains which I shall name unto thee*" (The Emphasized Bible).

Therefore, adding the word "burnt" is not necessary in all cases and shows that God was not asking Abraham to perform a despised ritual. It is possible to ask for a human sacrifice without any slaughter or bloodshed. Paul wrote, "...*that ye present your bodies a <u>living sacrifice</u>, <u>holy</u>, acceptable unto God*" (Rom. 12:1.) It is against God's nature to test anyone in a way that is not "holy." Offering Isaac to God in a pagan ritual would have been unholy. As we read further in the narrative, we see that God did not intend to have Isaac slain and burned (see Gen. 22:12).

God stopped Abraham before he killed Isaac. God is testing Abraham, but not in the sense of enticing him to sin. Actually, God tests people to keep them *from* sinning: "*And Moses said unto the people, Fear not: for God is come to prove you, and that his fear may be before your faces, **that ye sin not**"* (Ex. 20:20). Therefore, God was not demanding a pagan ritual from Abraham nor would He require one from you.

December 30

God's Guarantee to Supply our Needs

*But I have all, and abound: I am full, having received of Epaphroditus the things <u>which were sent from you</u>, an odour of a sweet smell, a sacrifice acceptable, wellpleasing to God. But my <u>**God shall**</u> supply all your need according to his riches in glory by Christ Jesus* (Phil. 4:18, 19).

The Random House Unabridged Dictionary defines the word *shall* as "will have to, is determined to, or definitely will." The American Heritage Dictionary defines it as "Something that is inevitable" and also "To have to; must." When we fully meet God's conditions He has obligated Himself to meet our needs out of His own abundant supply. This is exactly what the Philippians did and why God spoke to Paul to give them this sure and concrete promise.

Many people do not see the goodness of God and His commitment to keep His Word. This is due to some traditional theological teachings that emphasize a 'sovereignty of God" doctrine that counters the teaching of Scripture. Some time ago on an internet message board I read a plea for help from a victim of this teaching:

> I am down to my last $1000 dollars. I have been working 45-50 hours a week trying to sell insurance. I have a wife and three kids to support. Every effort I make to improve our condition, God frustrates. I say he does it because he is sovereign. I have fought against despair for weeks as my bank account has dwindled. Objective truth about God proclaiming his own goodness make me sick to my stomach. I am ashamed of that.

This poor fellow makes no reference to God's promises, but blames God for his predicament "because he is sovereign." This perversion of God's sovereignty says that God does not keep His promises nor will He supply our needs. Yet Jesus says, *"And if God so clothes the wild herbage which to-day flourishes and to-morrow is thrown into the oven, is it not much more <u>certain</u> that <u>He will</u> clothe you, you men of little faith?"* (Mat. 6:30; Weymouth's New Testament).

God has promised to supply our needs as we meet His conditions. He *must* do it and He is obligated to do it for covenant reasons lest He would be a covenant breaker. It offends God When He is made out to be a promise breaker. So let's take His promises and claim them.

December 31

Satan's War against the Word and Prayer

Then said he unto me, fear not, Daniel: for from the first day that thou didst set thine heart to understand, and to chasten thyself before thy God, thy words were heard, and I am come for thy words. But the prince of the king of Persia withstood me one and twenty days: but lo, Michael, one of the chief princes, came to help me; and I remained there with the kings of Persia (Dan. 10:12-13)

It is obvious that this demon prince was attempting to keep this angel from bringing God's answer to Daniel's prayer. Daniel sought God to receive further understanding of the Scripture of Truth. Satan is at war against the Word of God and wants to be sure that we do not understand it (Mat. 13:19). Not only do we see Satan waging all-out war against God's Word, but the book of Daniel reveals to us that Satan goes to war against prayer itself. Satan makes every attempt to hinder the answers to our prayers from coming forth.

God hears our prayers the moment we pray. John tells us, *"and if we know that hear us, whatsoever we ask, we know that we have the petitions that we desired of him"* (1 John 5:15). God delights in answering prayer. When we pray and get answers, it glorifies God (John 15:7-8)

Some people are under the delusion that when they don't get their prayers answered that God either did not hear them, He's too busy running the universe to help them, or that it just wasn't His will for them to have the thing that they asked for. These people never take into account that there is another being that does not want God's glory to be manifested in the earth.

It is not God who attempts to deny us answers to prayer. Concerning Daniel's prayer, the answer was heard and sent the first day. But Satan knew the impact that the answer would bring. He knew the damage that this would do to his plans. Therefore he sent one of his ruling spirits to fight against the angel that was delivering the answer.

Thank God that Daniel was not like most Christians. He did not give up. He stayed in faith and received the manifestation of the answer to his prayer. Despite this truth many Christians would rather blame God when they have not received the answer they crave from Him. However, ***God wants to answer prayer and Satan wants to hinder it.*** Once you begin to realize this then perhaps you will do what it takes to get the answer. Your answered prayer brings glory to God and puts the devil to shame. So persevere in prayer.

370

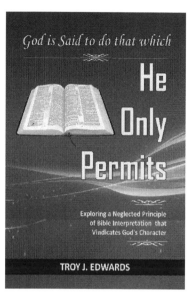
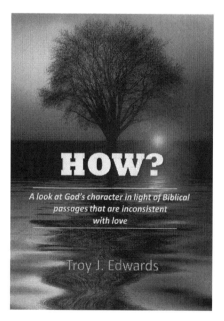

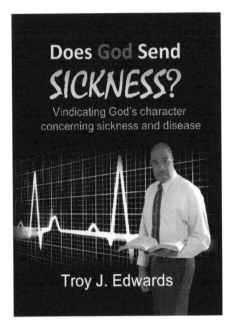
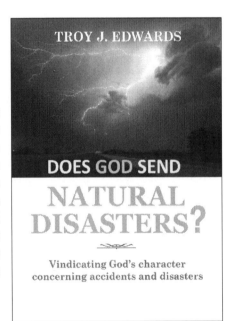
372

Other books from
Vindicating God Ministries!

Does God Engage in DESTRUCTIVE Behavior?
A study guide for understanding and vindicating God's character

What we believe about God will affect our lives. It will determine how we raise our children, treat our spouses, deal with strangers, interact with fellow employees, and how we conduct our ministry to the Lord and others. Therefore, this study is vitally important. We believe that after this study you will love God and your Bible even more and you will no longer be *afraid* of Him because you will see Him as the loving God who is just like Jesus.

Untying God's "NOTS!"
Or, How Much Control Does God Really Have?

Many Christians love to use the phrase, "God is in Control." Some take it to mean that all circumstances, good and evil, come from God. Others take it to mean that God is sovereign and omnipotent and will work in your situation if you let Him. This book examines the "God is in Control" idea in light of Scripture to understand exactly what type of control, if any, God has chosen to exercise.

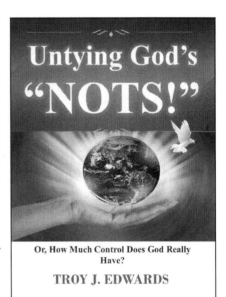

Or, How Much Control Does God Really Have?

TROY J. EDWARDS

Visit www.vindicatinggod.org